WATER

NO LONGER
TAKEN FOR GRANTED

ISSN 1536-5212

WATER

NO LONGER
TAKEN FOR GRANTED

INFORMATION PLUS® REFERENCE SERIES
Formerly published by Information Plus, Wylie, Texas

GALE®

THOMSON
━━━━★━━━━ ™
GALE

Detroit • New York • San Diego • San Francisco • Cleveland • New Haven, Conn. • Waterville, Maine • London • Munich

Water: No Longer Taken For Granted

Helen S. Fisher

Project Editor
Ellice Engdahl

Editorial
Andrew Claps, Paula Cutcher-Jackson, Kathleen J. Edgar, Dana Ferguson, Debra Kirby, Prindle LaBarge, Elizabeth Manar, Sharon McGilvray, Charles B. Montney, Heather Price

Permissions
Peg Ashlevitz

Product Design
Cynthia Baldwin

Composition and Electronic Prepress
Evi Seoud

Manufacturing
Keith Helmling

LIBRARY OF CONGRESS CATALOGING-IN-PUBLICATION DATA

ISBN 0-7876-5103-6 (set)
ISBN 0-7876-7346-3
ISSN 1536-5212

Printed in the United States of America
10 9 8 7 6 5 4 3 2 1

TABLE OF CONTENTS

PREFACE

Water: No Longer Taken for Granted is one of the latest volumes in the Information Plus Reference Series. The purpose of each volume of the series is to present the latest facts on a topic of pressing concern in modern American life. These topics include today's most controversial and most studied social issues: abortion, capital punishment, care for the elderly, crime, health care, the environment, immigration, minorities, social welfare, women, youth, and many more. Although written especially for the high school and undergraduate student, this series is an excellent resource for anyone in need of factual information on current affairs.

By presenting the facts, it is Gale's intention to provide its readers with everything they need to reach an informed opinion on current issues. To that end, there is a particular emphasis in this series on the presentation of scientific studies, surveys, and statistics. These data are generally presented in the form of tables, charts, and other graphics placed within the text of each book. Every graphic is directly referred to and carefully explained in the text. The source of each graphic is presented within the graphic itself. The data used in these graphics are drawn from the most reputable and reliable sources, in particular from the various branches of the U.S. government and from major independent polling organizations. Every effort has been made to secure the most recent information available. The reader should bear in mind that many major studies take years to conduct, and that additional years often pass before the data from these studies are made available to the public. Therefore, in many cases the most recent information available in 2003 dated from 2000 or 2001. Older statistics are sometimes presented as well if they are of particular interest and no more recent information exists.

Although statistics are a major focus of the Information Plus Reference Series, they are by no means its only content. Each book also presents the widely held positions and important ideas that shape how the book's subject is discussed in the United States. These positions are explained in detail and, where possible, in the words of their proponents. Some of the other material to be found in these books includes: historical background; descriptions of major events related to the subject; relevant laws and court cases; and examples of how these issues play out in American life. Some books also feature primary documents or have pro and con debate sections giving the words and opinions of prominent Americans on both sides of a controversial topic. All material is presented in an even-handed and unbiased manner; the reader will never be encouraged to accept one view of an issue over another.

HOW TO USE THIS BOOK

Water is one of the most vital resources on Earth. Most of the human body consists of water, and any person who is deprived of water for a significant period will die. The same can be said of all the animals and plants that people rely on for food. Only the air we breathe is more essential to human life, but while there is no shortage of air around the world, there are many regions where drinkable water is in short supply, such as the Western United States. Furthermore, even where water is available, human activities may have contaminated it with diseases and chemicals, with serious consequences for the people and wildlife that use or live in it. As a consequence of these facts, the use and care of what water is available is a controversial topic in the United States and around the world. This book explores all of the major issues surrounding water in America, from water usage rights to pollution control to safe drinking water.

Water: No Longer Taken for Granted consists of nine chapters and three appendices. Each of the chapters is devoted to a particular aspect of water in the United States. For a summary of the information covered in each chapter, please see the synopses provided in the Table of Contents at the front of the book. Chapters generally begin with an overview of the basic facts and background information on the chapter's topic, then proceed to examine subtopics of particular interest. For example, Chapter 5, Drinking Water—Safety on Tap, begins with a description of the water supply system in the United States, both public and private, as well as the uses the typical American household puts tap water to. This is followed by a detailed discussion of the contaminants most often found in drinking water, including both chemicals like arsenic and microbes such as coliform bacteria. The emphasis is on their possible sources and effects. The chapter then moves on to describe the modern water treatment system, and how it removes these contaminants and otherwise makes water fit to drink. The fluoridation of water is also discussed. Next, the chapter describes the many laws that regulate the safety of drinking water, as well as the cost of safe water. Another major section is devoted to analyses of just how safe U.S. tap water is. The chapter concludes with a number of sections on issues of special interest or concern, such as protecting drinking water supplies, bottled water use in the United States, and drinking water in other countries. Readers can find their way through a chapter by looking for the section and sub-section headings, which are clearly set off from the text. They can also refer to the book's extensive index if they already know what they are looking for.

Statistical Information

The tables and figures featured throughout *Water: No Longer Taken for Granted* will be of particular use to the reader in learning about this issue. These tables and figures represent an extensive collection of the most recent and important statistics on water and related issues—for example, graphics in the book cover water use and availability by state; leading pollutants in ground water, rivers, lakes, and other bodies of water; the number of disease outbreaks associated with drinking water, by year; prevalence and types of wetlands in the United States; and the effects of acid rain on different environments. Gale believes that making this information available to the reader is the most important way in which we fulfill the goal of this book: to help readers to understand the issues and controversies surrounding water in the United States and to reach their own conclusions.

Each table or figure has a unique identifier appearing above it for ease of identification and reference. Titles for the tables and figures explain their purpose. At the end of each table or figure, the original source of the data is provided.

In order to help readers understand these often complicated statistics, all tables and figures are explained in the text. References in the text direct the reader to the relevant statistics. Furthermore, the contents of all tables and figures are fully indexed. Please see the opening section of the index at the back of this volume for a description of how to find tables and figures within it.

Appendices

In addition to the main body text and images, *Water: No Longer Taken for Granted* has three appendices. The first is the Important Names and Addresses directory. Here the reader will find contact information for a number of government and private organizations that can provide further information on water. The second appendix is the Resources section, which can also assist the reader in conducting his or her own research. In this section, the author and editors of *Water: No Longer Taken for Granted* describe some of the sources that were most useful during the compilation of this book. The final appendix is the detailed Index, which facilitates reader access to specific topics in this book.

ADVISORY BOARD CONTRIBUTIONS

The staff of Information Plus would like to extend their heartfelt appreciation to the Information Plus Advisory Board. This dedicated group of media professionals provides feedback on the series on an ongoing basis. Their comments allow the editorial staff who work on the project to make the series better and more user-friendly. Our top priorities are to produce the highest-quality and most useful books possible, and the Advisory Board's contributions to this process are invaluable.

The members of the Information Plus Advisory Board are:

- Kathleen R. Bonn, Librarian, Newbury Park High School, Newbury Park, California

- Madelyn Garner, Librarian, San Jacinto College—North Campus, Houston, Texas

- Anne Oxenrider, Media Specialist, Dundee High School, Dundee, Michigan

- Charles R. Rodgers, Director of Libraries, Pasco-Hernando Community College, Dade City, Florida

- James N. Zitzelsberger, Library Media Department Chairman, Oshkosh West High School, Oshkosh, Wisconsin

COMMENTS AND SUGGESTIONS

The editors of the Information Plus Reference Series welcome your feedback on *Water: No Longer Taken for Granted*. Please direct all correspondence to:

Editors

Information Plus Reference Series

27500 Drake Rd.

Farmington Hills, MI 48331-3535

ACKNOWLEDGMENTS

The editors wish to thank the copyright holders of material included in this volume and the permissions managers of many book and magazine publishing companies for assisting us in securing reproduction rights. We are also grateful to the staffs of the Detroit Public Library, the Library of Congress, the University of Detroit Mercy Library, Wayne State University Purdy/ Kresge Library Complex, and the University of Michigan Libraries for making their resources available to us.

Following is a list of the copyright holders who have granted us permission to reproduce material in Information Plus: Water. *Every effort has been made to trace copyright, but if omissions have been made, please let us know.*

For more detailed source citations, please see the sources listed under each individual table and figure.

Air Quality Trends Analysis Group: Figure 9.3, Figure 9.4, Figure 9.5, Figure 9.6, Figure 9.17

Bureau of Reclamation: Table 8.2

Morbidity and Mortality Weekly Report: Figure 3.20, Table 5.5, Figure 5.12, Figure 5.13, Figure 5.14

National Center for Environmental Economics: Figure 5.2

National Oceanic and Atmospheric Administration: Table 6.1, Table 6.2, Table 6.4

Natural Resources Conservation Service: Figure 7.11

Office of Air and Radiation: Figure 9.15, Figure 9.16

Office of Ground Water and Drinking Water: Figure 5.10

Office of Technology Assessment: Figure 6.12, Table 6.5, Table 6.6, Table 7.2, Figure 7.3, Figure 9.1, Figure 9.7

U.S. Army Corp of Engineers: Figure 3.9

U.S. Bureau of the Census: Figure 2.15, Figure 8.2, Figure 8.4

U.S. Department of Agriculture: Table 2.2, Figure 2.14, Figure 3.2, Table 8.1

U.S. Department of the Interior: Figure 4.3

U.S. Environmental Protection Agency: Figure 1.2, Figure 1.3, Table 1.1, Figure 1.7, Figure 2.2, Figure 3.1, Figure 3.3, Figure 3.6, Figure 3.7, Figure 3.8, Figure 3.10, Figure 3.11, Figure 3.12, Table 3.2, Figure 3.13, Figure 3.14, Figure 3.15, Figure 3.16, Figure 3.17, Figure 3.18, Figure 3.19, Figure 4.1, Figure 4.4, Figure 4.6, Figure 4.7, Figure 4.8, Figure 4.9, Figure 4.10, Figure 4.11, Table 4.1, Figure 4.12, Figure 4.13, Figure 4.14, Table 4.2, Table 4.3, Table 5.1, Figure 5.1, Figure 5.3, Figure 5.5, Figure 5.6, Figure 5.7, Figure 5.8, Table 5.3, Figure 5.9, Figure 5.11, Figure 6.3, Figure 6.4, Figure 6.5, Figure 6.6, Figure 6.7, Figure 6.8, Figure 6.9, Figure 6.10, Figure 6.11, Figure 7.4, Figure 7.5, Table 7.4, Figure 7.7, Figure 7.8, Figure 7.9, Figure 9.2, Table 9.2, Figure 9.10, Figure 9.11, Figure 9.12, Figure 9.13

U.S. Fish and Wildlife Service: Table 7.1, Figure 7.2, Table 7.3, Figure 7.6, Figure 7.10

U.S. General Accounting Office: Figure 1.6, Figure 3.4, Figure 3.5, Figure 4.15, Figure 4.16, Figure 4.17, Figure 5.4, Table 5.4, Figure 7.12, Figure 7.13, Table 9.1, Figure 9.8, Figure 9.9, Figure 9.14, Table 9.3

U.S. Geological Survey: Figure 1.4, Figure 1.5, Figure 2.3, Table 2.1, Figure 2.4, Figure 2.5, Figure 2.6, Figure 2.7, Figure 2.8, Figure 2.9, Figure 2.10, Figure 2.11, Figure 2.12, Table 2.3, Table 2.4, Figure 2.13, Table 2.5, Table 2.6, Table 2.7, Table 3.1, Figure 4.2, Figure 4.5, Table 5.2, Figure 6.1, Table 6.3, Figure 6.2, Figure 6.13, Figure 6.14, Figure 7.1

U.S. Global Change Research Program: Figure 8.1, Figure 8.3

U.S. Water Resources Council: Figure 2.1

CHAPTER 1
WHAT IS WATER?

Water is the most common substance on Earth. It covers three-fourths of Earth's surface and makes up 65 percent of the adult human body, including 90 percent of its blood, and, according to the Environmental Protection Agency (EPA), 75 percent of its brain. Water is the main ingredient in most of the fruits, vegetables, and meats that people eat. For example, the EPA estimates that water comprises 75 percent of a chicken, 80 percent of a pineapple, 80 percent of an ear of corn, and 95 percent of a tomato. To grow an adequate diet for a human being for one year requires about 300 tons of water—nearly a ton (2,000 pounds) a day.

Water is vital to human beings. Although people can survive for about a month without food, without water they would die in about a week. Water quenches thirst and nourishes crops. Yet water is much more than a necessity; it adds pleasure to our lives. For the surfer, it is an afternoon of fun. For the fisherman, it provides the fish and floats the boat. Water, sun, and sand make the beach a favorite vacation spot. Honeymooners have always been drawn to the majestic sight and sound of Niagara Falls. Water cleans our bodies and our entire environment.

While essential to human existence, water is not always a friend. It is terror to the swimmer caught up in a current. It rusts cars and leaks through the roof. Water is hailstones that destroy crops and ice that coats the road. Too much water becomes a flood that destroys homes and people. Too little water is a drought that causes living things to wither and, eventually, die. Water can carry disease—waterborne diseases account for over three-fourths of all diseases and many deaths in developing countries.

CHEMICAL COMPOSITION

Water is a molecule made up of two hydrogen atoms and one oxygen atom: H_2O. (See Figure 1.1.) (Its composition is actually more complex, but this description serves for this discussion.) Atoms in a molecule of any substance are joined together by a process known as chemical bonding, where two or more atoms mutually share one or more electrons. This bonding is particularly strong in water. Water is also both a weak acid and a weak base—chemical properties that allow it to function as a universal solvent capable of dissolving many substances.

THREE STATES OF WATER

Water exists naturally in three states: a liquid (its most common form), a solid (ice), and a gas (water vapor). It is the only substance on Earth in which all three of its natural states occur within the normal range of climatic conditions, sometimes at the same time. Familiar examples of water in its three natural states are rain, snow or hail, and steam.

FIGURE 1.1

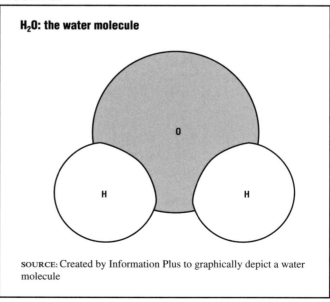

H₂O: the water molecule

SOURCE: Created by Information Plus to graphically depict a water molecule

FIGURE 1.2

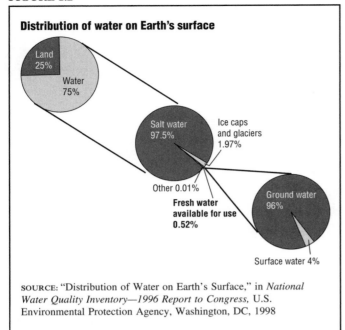

Distribution of water on Earth's surface

Land 25%

Water 75%

Salt water 97.5%

Ice caps and glaciers 1.97%

Other 0.01%

Fresh water available for use 0.52%

Ground water 96%

Surface water 4%

SOURCE: "Distribution of Water on Earth's Surface," in *National Water Quality Inventory—1996 Report to Congress*, U.S. Environmental Protection Agency, Washington, DC, 1998

Compared to other liquids, water has some unusual properties. For example, most liquids contract as they freeze. Water contracts only until it reaches 4 degrees Celsius. Then it expands until it reaches its freezing point of 0 degrees Celsius (32 degrees Fahrenheit). This expansion can exert a tremendous force on surrounding objects, enough to crack an unprotected automobile engine in winter or shatter a boulder. Expansion makes ice lighter than water, which is why ice floats. This phenomenon causes rivers and lakes to freeze from the top down, a necessity for the survival of aquatic life. If freezing occurred from the bottom up, bodies of water might freeze solid in winter, killing aquatic plant and animal life, and never thaw completely, even in summer.

When ice is warmed to 0 degrees Celsius, the freezing/melting point, it becomes liquid. As a liquid, its molecules are more loosely bound together and can move around each other rather freely. The molecules' ability to slip and slide around gives water and other liquids their fluid properties.

In the gaseous or vapor state, water molecules move rapidly about and have very little attraction for each other, creating the diffuse appearance of steam or mist, or the haze of a humid day (humidity is the measure of the amount of water vapor in the air). Evaporation is the general term used to describe the process by which water in its liquid form is changed to its gaseous state. Evaporation can occur under a wide variety of conditions. Examples include water vaporizing off of wet pavement following rainfall, boiling water to produce steam, or the heating of materials under a wide range of temperatures to dry them.

EARTH MOVER

Scientists believe planet Earth was formed about 4 billion years ago. Within its primitive atmosphere were the basic elements needed to form water. As Earth cooled from a mass of molten rock, water formed in the atmosphere and then fell to Earth in a rain that lasted for many years, forming the oceans.

Ever since the formation of the oceans, water has been wearing the earth into a smooth surface with its flowing and rubbing actions. If other forces on the planet were not counteracting these actions by constantly raising up new hills and mountains, the planet would eventually become one vast, shallow ocean.

The flow of water flattens mountains and cuts canyons deep into the surface of Earth. It hollows out underground caverns and leaves behind attractive formations. Water creates soil by breaking down rocks and organic material and depositing it elsewhere. Water in the form of ice redesigned the face of Earth as glaciers advanced and receded many thousands of years ago. The slow, relentless processes of water freezing, melting, flowing, and evaporating will likely make Earth's appearance as different a million years from today as it was a million years ago.

HYDROLOGIC CYCLE

Earth is a vast reservoir, containing an estimated 861 million cubic miles of water. (A cubic mile of water equals 1.1 trillion gallons.) It is all around us: in the atmosphere, on Earth's surface, and in the ground. The relative distribution of the world's water supply is shown in Figure 1.2. Only a very tiny amount of the water is found in the atmosphere, mainly in the form of invisible water vapor. Oceans account for over 97 percent of Earth's water, with less than 3 percent in ice caps, glaciers, lakes, rivers, streams, and groundwater.

All water on Earth is in continual motion. It is constantly being exchanged between the earth and the air. This exchange is caused by the heat of the Sun and the force of gravity. Water evaporates from moist ground, from the leaves of vegetation, and from water bodies such as lakes, streams, and reservoirs. It is then carried into the atmosphere as water vapor, a gas. When the water vapor condenses, it is transformed from a gas to a liquid and falls as precipitation, in the form of rain, mist, sleet, hail, or snow.

The precipitation, in turn, replenishes Earth's surface and underground waters, which eventually join the oceans and seas. Evaporation from both the land and the ocean puts the water (as vapor) back into the air, in a constant exchange, leaving impurities behind. In this way, water travels from the ground to the atmosphere and back to the ground continuously. The exchange of water between the earth and the air is called the hydrologic cycle or water

FIGURE 1.3

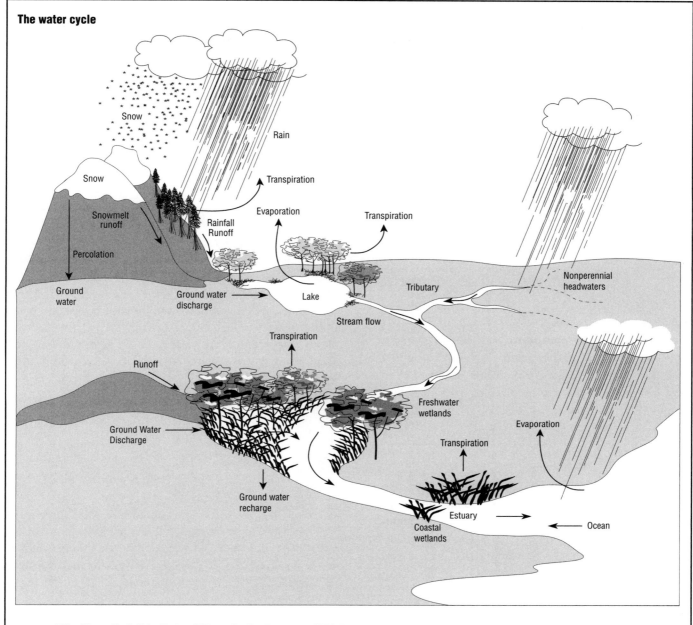

The water cycle

SOURCE: "The Water Cycle," in *National Water Quality Inventory: 1998 Report to Congress*, EPA 841-F-00-006, U.S. Environmental Protection Agency, Washington, DC, June 2000

cycle. (See Figure 1.3.) The term "hydrologic" is derived from two Greek words: hydro, which means having to do with water, and loge, an ancient Greek word meaning "knowledge of."

The hydrologic cycle is a natural, constantly running distillation and pumping system. As a cycle, this flow has no beginning and no end. Within the hydrologic cycle water is neither lost nor gained, it simply changes form as it progresses through the cycle. The molecules of water in the world's oceans, lakes, rivers, ponds, streams and atmosphere today are the same molecules that were formed 4 billion years ago.

Although constantly in motion, water is transferred between phases of the hydrologic cycle at different rates depending on where it is located. For instance, a molecule of water exists as water vapor in the atmosphere an average of eight days, but when it enters the ocean, it may reside there for the next 2,500 years.

The hydrologic cycle has shaped and sustained life on Earth in its present form. It is largely responsible for determining climate and types of vegetation. Because it is a "closed system," actions that affect any phase of the cycle may have consequences not only today and tomorrow but for centuries to come.

FIGURE 1.4

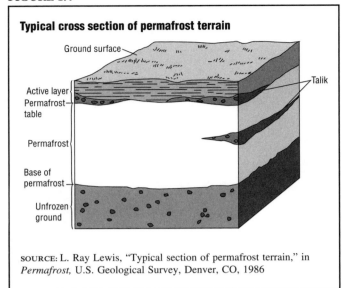

Typical cross section of permafrost terrain

- Ground surface
- Active layer
- Permafrost table
- Permafrost
- Base of permafrost
- Unfrozen ground
- Talik

SOURCE: L. Ray Lewis, "Typical section of permafrost terrain," in *Permafrost*, U.S. Geological Survey, Denver, CO, 1986

Soil Moisture

Although it represents only a very small percentage of Earth's water supply, soil moisture is extremely significant. It supplies water to plants, a vital link in the food chain. Some plants grow directly in water or in marshy ground, but most live on "dry" land. This is possible because the land is really dry in just a few places, and often only temporarily.

Dust is generally considered dry, but the dust kicked up by a car on a "dry" dirt road may contain up to 15 percent water by weight. Vegetation, however, could not grow and flourish on that road because soils hold small percentages of moisture so strongly that plant roots cannot get it out. Other than desert plants, which store water in their own tissues during infrequent wet periods, most plants can grow only where there is extractable water in the soil. Since Earth's vegetation continually withdraws moisture from the ground in large amounts, frequent renewals of soil moisture, either by precipitation or irrigation, are needed.

Atmospheric Moisture

Rain, snow, sleet, and hail are all known as precipitation. This moisture in the air comes from the evaporation of water from the ground and from bodies of water such as lakes, rivers, and, especially, the oceans. Plants also give up moisture into the air through their leaves. This process is called transpiration. For example, an acre of corn gives off 3,000 to 4,000 gallons of water to the atmosphere every day. A large tree may release 50 gallons per day. The plant moisture is first taken up by the roots from the soil, moves up the plant in the sap, and then emerges from the plant through thousands of tiny holes on the underside of each leaf.

Transpiration from plants is one of the important sources of water vapor in the air, and usually produces more moisture than evaporation from the ground, lakes, and streams. The most important source of water vapor in the air, however, is evaporation from the oceans, especially those parts of the ocean that are located in the warmest parts of the planet. Heat is required to change water from a liquid to a vapor. Thus, the higher the temperature, the faster the water evaporates from oceans. The winds in the upper air carry this moisture long distances from the oceans. Someone who lives in the central part of the United States may receive rain that is composed of water particles evaporated from the ocean near the equator or the Gulf of Mexico.

Ice Caps and Glaciers

About three-fourths of all freshwater in the world is stored as ice. After the oceans, the single greatest body of water is the Antarctic ice sheet. It covers about 6 million square miles with a total volume of between 6 and 7 million cubic miles—90 percent of all existing ice and about 70 percent of all freshwater. To get an idea of how much water covers Antarctica, if the ice sheet were to melt, it could:

- Supply the Mississippi River for more than 50,000 years, or all the rivers in the United States for about 17,000 years

- Supply the Amazon River for approximately 5,000 years, or all the rivers in the world for about 750 years

The Greenland ice cap is about 667,000 square miles in area and is, on average, 5,000 feet thick; its total volume is 630,000 cubic miles. If melted, it would produce enough water to keep the Mississippi River flowing for over 4,700 years.

A glacier is any large mass of snow or ice that persists on land for many years. Glaciers are formed in locations where, over a number of years, more snow falls than melts. As this snow accumulates, it is compressed and changed into dense, solid ice. Glacial masses tend to flow due to their own weight—downhill if on a slope or in all directions from the center if on a flat surface.

Although most people associate glaciers with remote, frozen regions such as Antarctica, there are over 1,650 glaciers in the lower 48 states, most of them quite small. They cover about 227 square miles in parts of Washington, Wyoming, Montana, Oregon, California, Colorado, Idaho, and Nevada. Alaska has uncounted numbers of glaciers that cover many thousands of square miles.

Because the study of glaciers is a relatively new science, there is considerable debate over the significance of the expansion or shrinkage of glaciers or ice caps over

FIGURE 1.5

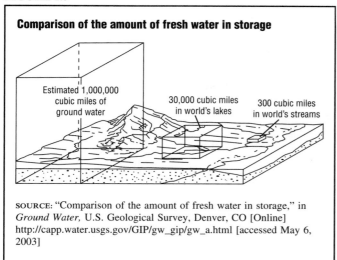

Comparison of the amount of fresh water in storage

Estimated 1,000,000 cubic miles of ground water

30,000 cubic miles in world's lakes

300 cubic miles in world's streams

SOURCE: "Comparison of the amount of fresh water in storage," in *Ground Water*, U.S. Geological Survey, Denver, CO [Online] http://capp.water.usgs.gov/GIP/gw_gip/gw_a.html [accessed May 6, 2003]

5- to 20-year time frames. Some studies suggest that many glaciers are melting and shrinking in size. Other scientists argue that these are short-term changes that occur routinely in geologic time, and should not be given too much significance. Extensive studies are underway in Antarctica, Greenland, and other areas of the world to investigate the formation, duration, and melting of glaciers and ice caps, but it will be many years before these phenomena are well understood.

Permafrost

Permafrost is permanently frozen ground, which underlies approximately one-fifth of Earth's entire land surface. It exists in Antarctica, but is more extensive in the Northern Hemisphere. In the land surrounding the Arctic Ocean, its maximum thickness has been measured in thousands of feet, about 5,000 feet in Siberia and 2,000 feet in Alaska. Even though the surface areas of permafrost (termed the active layers) thaw quickly in the summer and refreeze in winter, it would take thousands of years of thawing conditions to melt the thickest permafrost. The deepest layers were formed during the ancient cold temperatures of the Great Ice Age, which occurred about 3 million years ago. Figure 1.4 is an illustration of the permafrost layer.

In North America, the discovery of gold in the early 1900s in Alaska and the Yukon sparked an increased interest in the nature of the vast areas of permafrost. After World War II (1939–45), more and more nonnative people migrated to areas of frozen ground, and the construction of roads, railroads, and buildings, and the clearing of land, led to the disruption and thawing of previously undisturbed permafrost. This caused unstable ground, landslides, mudflows, and, consequently, dangerous living conditions. Some scientists believe that the total area of permafrost is declining. Like glaciers and ice caps, permafrost regions are areas of scientific scrutiny and intense debate.

Snowmelt

Except for the disruption of day-to-day life caused by winter snowstorms in certain areas of the United States, most people are largely unaware of the importance of snow. Unlike many other countries (Italy or Ireland, for example), the United States is economically dependent on snow. Almost all the water in the arid West that can be tapped on a large-volume basis comes directly from spring snowmelt. The amount of water in a given year's snowpack varies greatly from one year to another. The snowpack volume is of crucial importance to regional economics. Too much snow can cause flooding and extensive damage to crops, livestock, businesses, and homes. Too little snow can mean water shortages for drinking water, irrigation, and hydroelectric power, affecting their availability and cost.

The importance of snow was highlighted in a May 2003 article in the *Denver Post* ("San Luis Valley Still in the Grip of Record Drought. Snowpack Goes into Ground, Not Streams"). Mark H. Hunter described drought conditions in Northern Colorado, caused in part by a significant decrease in snowpack in the upper Rio Grande basin. According to the article, in 2003 snowpack in the upper Rio Grande basin was only 71 percent of average, with a snow-water content of 13 inches. Drought conditions have affected the region for three consecutive years, diminishing the San Luis Valley's underground aquifer. The aquifer sustains thousands of acres of natural wetlands and one-half million acres of farm land and ranch land.

FRESHWATER

Despite the enormous amount of water that surrounds us, only about 3 percent of it is freshwater and, therefore, suitable for use by land-based animals, plants, and humans. Almost four-fifths of freshwater is frozen in ice caps and glaciers, and not accessible. The availability of freshwater depends on many factors: climate, location, rainfall, and local activity. The world's freshwater lakes contain about 30,000 cubic miles of water, and about 300 cubic miles of freshwater are found in the world's rivers and streams. Together, lakes, rivers, and streams make up about .009 percent of total water. Groundwater (subsurface water) totals about 1 million cubic miles or .52 percent of the total water supply. Figure 1.5 shows the comparative volumes of these freshwater sources.

SOMETIMES IT RAINS, SOMETIMES IT DOESN'T

The amount of precipitation that falls around the world can range from less than one-tenth of one inch per year in the deserts to hundreds of inches per year in the tropics. In 2000 the National Climatic Data Center reported that the lowest average annual precipitation occurs in Arica, Chile, with 0.03 inches. The world's wettest spot is Mawsynram,

FIGURE 1.6

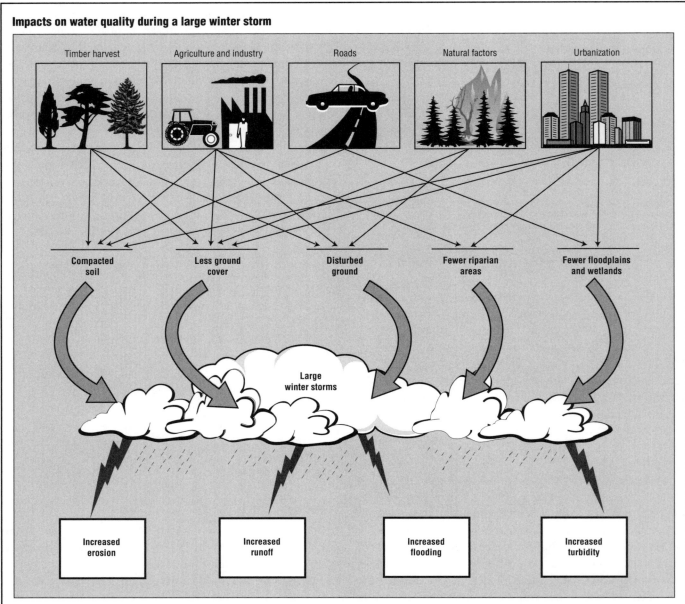

Impacts on water quality during a large winter storm

Timber harvest | Agriculture and industry | Roads | Natural factors | Urbanization

Compacted soil | Less ground cover | Disturbed ground | Fewer riparian areas | Fewer floodplains and wetlands

Large winter storms

Increased erosion | Increased runoff | Increased flooding | Increased turbidity

SOURCE: "Figure 2, Impacts on water quality during a large winter storm," in *Many Activities Contribute to Turbidity During Large Storms*, GAO/RCED-98-220, U.S. General Accounting Office, Washington DC, July 1998

India, with an average annual rainfall of 467.4 inches. The single wettest year recorded was in Cherrapunjii, India, with 905 inches in 1861. By contrast, the Central Valley in California, which produces a large percentage of the U.S. vegetable crops, averages only 15 inches of rainfall per year. Without supplemental water from irrigation, this area would not be productive. The lower 48 states receive enough rain in an average year that, were it to fall all at one time, it would cover the entire country to a depth of about 30 inches of water, weighing 6.6 billion tons.

What happens to rainwater after it reaches the ground depends upon such factors as the rate of rainfall, topography, soil conditions, density of vegetation, temperatures,

and the extent of urbanization. For example, the direct runoff in a highly urbanized area is relatively great, not only because of impermeable roofs and pavements, but also because storm-sewer systems carry water directly to streams and lakes. Figure 1.6 illustrates this point. Urbanization leads to fewer floodplains and wetlands, fewer riparian areas (for example, riverbanks), less ground cover, and compacted soil. A large winter storm could lead to increased turbidity (cloudiness or discoloration of the water), flooding, runoff, and erosion.

Variations in precipitation occur not only seasonally but also annually. For example, southern Florida has a rainy season (May to October) followed by a dry season

(November to April). Most of the 45–60 inches of annual rainfall (normal conditions) in this area occur in the rainy season. In exceptionally dry years, droughts occur because the area receives little or no precipitation in the rainy season; in exceptionally wet years, flooding may occur.

Natural phenomena known as El Niño and La Niña influence weather and precipitation. El Niño is a naturally occurring disruption of the ocean-atmosphere system in the tropical Pacific Ocean, which has important consequences for weather around the globe. It is characterized by an unusually warm current of water that appears every three to five years in the eastern Pacific Ocean. Unusually warm sea surface temperature results in a decline in primary productivity (microscopic plants and animals), which in turn brings sharp declines in commercial fisheries and bird populations that are also dependent on fish. Unusual weather conditions occur around the globe as jet streams, storm tracks, and monsoons are shifted. Some other consequences are increased rainfall across the southern tier of the United States and Peru, which historically has caused destructive flooding, and drought in Australia and Indonesia. El Niño brings warmer than normal temperatures to the north-central states and cooler than normal temperatures to the southeastern and southwestern United States.

La Niña global climate impacts tend to be the opposite of El Niño since La Niña is characterized by unusually cold ocean temperatures in the Equatorial Pacific. In the United States, winter temperatures are warmer than normal in the Southeast and cooler than normal in the Northwest. La Niña events occur after some, but not all, El Niño events. Generally, La Niña occurs half as frequently as El Niño.

POPULATION PRESSURE ON WATER RESOURCES: WHAT ARE HUMANS DOING TO THE WATER?

As populations continually modify the environment to suit their needs and desires, the natural processes, including the hydrologic cycle, are significantly disrupted. People are finding out that Earth, even with its remarkable recuperative powers, has limits beyond which it cannot sustain a livable environment.

There are two ways by which humanity can change the basic quality and natural distribution of water: by introducing materials and organisms into a body of water (including the atmosphere), commonly known as pollution, and by intervening in any phase of the hydrologic cycle in such a way that the cycle is altered. Dams, irrigation, and hydroelectric plants are examples of alterations.

Pollutants That Degrade Water Quality

For centuries, lakes, rivers, and oceans have been dumping sites for many of the undesirable by-products of civilization. People have dumped indiscriminately, believing the waters had the inexhaustible capacity to disperse and neutralize any amount of wastes thrown into them. What was not dissolved or dispersed settled to the bottom, where it could not be seen.

Dumping wastes into the oceans and waterways led to few apparent problems as long as wastes were few and consisted mainly of naturally occurring materials. As the world's population grew and technology began introducing huge numbers of new products and processes, however, this natural disposal system began breaking down under an overload of natural and synthetic contaminants. Fish and marine animals died; "dead zones," where no life could survive, developed in harbors and oceans; drinking water became contaminated; and beaches became littered with garbage.

According to an article in the EPA's *WaterNews for April 1, 2003,* G. Tracy Meehan III, Assistant Administrator for EPA's Office of Water, announced approximately $10 million in grants for eligible states and territories to improve their water testing and notify the public of health risks during the coming summer season. Data from the National Health Protection Survey of Beaches for the 2001 swimming season showed that more than a quarter (27 percent) of beaches surveyed (about 672) had issued at least one swimming advisory or closure during the summer of 2001. Most of the advisories and closures were due to elevated bacteria levels caused by sewage overflows or storm water runoff. The May 2002 EPA press release detailing highlights of the beach survey reported that 87 percent of beaches that issued advisories or had closed during the summer of 2001 did so because of elevated bacteria levels.

Concern over water pollution launched the environmental movement of the 1970s. The 1972 Federal Water Pollution Control Act (Public Law 92-500), commonly known as the Clean Water Act, was the first major piece of environmental legislation enacted by Congress. Since then, many laws and regulations designed to protect, preserve, and clean up the national waters have been passed. Although substantial progress has been made, many problems remain to be solved.

There are many sources and types of water pollution. Every day, industrial by-products and household wastes, such as nutrients, toxic chemicals, metals, plastics, medical refuse, radioactive waste, and sludge (the solid material left after water is extracted from raw sewage) are deposited into the nation's rivers, lakes, harbors, and oceans. Septic tanks, landfills, and mining operations often produce hazardous contaminants that seep into the soil and then into underground aquifers (aggregates of water that flow through rocks and soil, and eventually into surface rivers or oceans). Table 1.1 lists the most common sources of

TABLE 1.1

Pollution source categories

Category	Examples
Industrial	Pulp and paper mills, chemical manufacturers, steel plants, metal process and product manufacturers, textile manufacturers, food processing plants
Municipal	Publicly owned sewage treatment plants that may receive indirect discharges from industrial facilities or businesses
Combined sewer overflows	Single facilities that treat both storm water and sanitary sewage, which may become overloaded during storm events and discharge untreated wastes into surface waters
Storm sewers/ Urban runoff	Runoff from impervious surfaces including streets, parking lots, buildings, and other paved areas
Agricultural	Crop production, pastures, rangeland, feedlots, animal operations
Silvicultural	Forest management, tree harvesting, logging road construction
Construction	Land development, road construction
Resource extraction	Mining, petroleum drilling, runoff from mine tailing sites
Land disposal	Leachate or discharge from septic tanks, landfills, and hazardous waste sites
Hydrologic modification	Channelization, dredging, dam construction, flow regulation
Habitat modification	Removal of riparian vegetation, streambank modification, drainage/filling of wetlands

SOURCE: "Table 1-1. Pollution Source Categories Used in This Report," in *National Water Quality Inventory: 1998 Report to Congress*, EPA 841-F-00-006, U.S. Environmental Protection Agency, Washington, DC, June 2000

pollution. Figure 1.7 shows how bacteria, viruses, and other microorganisms can be introduced into water.

Reducing Water Pollution

The term "water pollution" is very broad. Water is often classified into different categories: drinking water, wastewater, coastal waters, surface water, groundwater, freshwater, estuarine, and salt water. In nature, however, all water is part of the hydrologic cycle. When it rains, a pesticide applied to a cornfield may run off into a nearby stream and from there into the ocean. It can seep into the earth and contaminate underlying groundwater, which, in turn, feeds into a lake or reservoir. While a heavy buildup of contaminants in any one area is a local concern, increased sources and types of pollutants have also made water pollution a global problem.

Reducing water pollution is a complex issue as all substances have the potential to be contaminants and to cause harmful effects, thereby demonstrating "toxicity." The mere presence of a substance does not mean a threat exists either to humans or other species. Not all contaminants are harmful, or the contaminant may be harmful only at certain levels, or in certain waters. For example, salt is not a problem in ocean and estuarine environments but can be highly toxic to aquatic life in freshwater rivers and streams. Whether or not a substance exerts toxicity depends on the characteristics of the particular environment, its concentration in the environment, its particular chemical composition, the dose experienced by humans or other species, and the duration of exposure. Reducing water pollution is further complicated by the many pathways by which contaminants reach water, and the limits on our ability to identify and minimize or eliminate these pathways.

The issues of water pollution and waste disposal are interrelated. Because there are only three options for disposing of waste (placement in land, water, or air), water will continue to be used as a depository for waste for the foreseeable future. While the concept of "zero discharge" of pollutants is a laudable goal, it is terribly expensive and, in most cases, not technologically achievable. Zero discharge means that the wastewater is treated to remove all traces of any substance present in the water. In many cases, low levels of the pollutants would either occur naturally in the water, or their presence would do no harm.

Several approaches are used to minimize, or in some cases, eliminate the effects of contaminants on water. These include introducing new processes or techniques that require use of fewer contaminants, thereby reducing the amount of contaminant that reaches water; treating the wastewater to remove contaminants; water reuse; and land disposal of waterborne wastes. The effectiveness of these approaches varies in each situation depending on the amount and complexity of the waste, the cost of waste treatment or the alternate method of disposal, and the effects of the alternate disposal method on land and air environments. In some cases, the public refuses to accept alternative methods because of cost, fear, or cultural bias. For example, some communities object to having highly treated wastewater used to water their golf courses, while several large cities, such as San Diego, California,

FIGURE 1.7

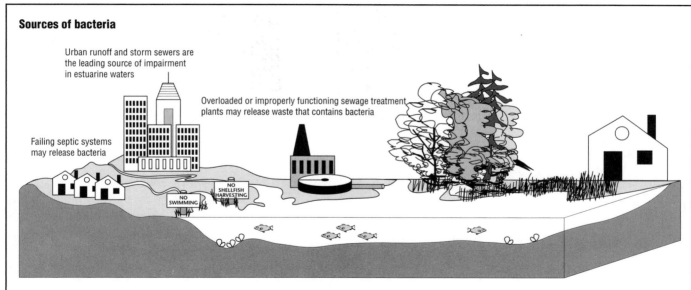

Sources of bacteria

Urban runoff and storm sewers are the leading source of impairment in estuarine waters

Overloaded or improperly functioning sewage treatment plants may release waste that contains bacteria

Failing septic systems may release bacteria

NO SHELLFISH HARVESTING

NO SWIMMING

SOURCE: "Figure 5-5. Sources of Bacteria," *National Water Quality Inventory: 1998 Report to Congress,* EPA 841-F-00-006, U.S. Environmental Protection Agency, Washington, DC, June 2000

routinely use treated wastewater to water lawns and landscaping.

Recognizing that there is a continued need to discharge wastes to water, the Federal Water Pollution Control Act and its amendments, such as the Clean Water Act, established the National Pollutant Discharge Elimination System, which uses water quality standards and discharge permits to regulate contaminant discharge. Water quality standards establish the upper limit for the amount of contaminant that will not cause an adverse effect on humans or other species. Cities, companies, and other entities that want to discharge into water apply for permission, and if approved, receive a permit. The permit specifies the amount and type of contaminants that may be discharged and not cause a violation of the water quality standard. Dischargers are required to monitor their discharges and report the results. When limits are exceeded, fines and other penalties are imposed, including requirements for additional treatment and cleanup.

Human Intervention Processes That Degrade Water Quality

People alter the environment by directly or indirectly intervening in the hydrologic cycle. The purpose of this intervention is to increase or divert water from surface water or groundwater supplies for household use (including drinking), irrigation, industrial uses, flood control, hydroelectric power generation, and other uses. Sometimes the environment absorbs the modification with little or no perceptible change. In other cases, the intervention may be disruptive on a local scale. In extreme cases, the intervention may completely change the environment in a large area.

Modern technological developments allow massive quantities of water to be pumped out of the ground, for use as drinking water and in irrigation of crops. When large amounts of water are removed from the ground, underground aquifers can become depleted much more quickly than they can naturally replenish themselves. In some areas, this has led to the subsidence, or sinking, of the ground above major aquifers. Removing too much water from an aquifer in coastal areas can result in saltwater intrusion into aquifer, rendering the water too brackish to drink. The natural filtering process that occurs as water travels through rocks and sand is also impaired when aquifer levels become depleted, leaving the aquifer more vulnerable to contamination.

Building dams has also changed the hydrologic cycle. The huge dams built in the United States just before and after World War II have substantially changed the natural flow of rivers. By reducing the amount of water available downstream and slowing stream flow, a dam not only affects a river but also the river's entire ecological system. For example, wetlands have the ability to clean water by trapping and filtering pollutants. This water cleansing process can be stopped or reduced if dams cause wetlands to dry up.

Deforestation and overgrazing worldwide have destroyed thousands of acres of vegetation that play a vital role in controlling erosion. Erosion is the process in which a material is worn away by a stream of water or air, usually because of the abrasive particles in the water or air. Erosion results in soil runoff into rivers and streams, causing turbidity (cloudiness or discoloration), siltation, and disruption of stream flow. Removal of vegetation reduces the amount of water released into the atmosphere by transpiration. In some areas, less water in the atmosphere can mean less rainfall, causing fertile regions to become deserts.

WORLDWIDE WATER CRISIS

Despite conservation and reclamation efforts, the world still faces a severe scarcity of sanitary water. According to a January 26, 2003, article in *USA Today* (Dan Vergano, "Water Shortages Could Leave World in Dire Straits"), the United Nations (UN) predicted that within 50 years, more than half of the world's population will be living with water shortages, depleted fisheries, and polluted coastlines. The UN study, *World Water Development,* based on data provided by the National Aeronautics and Space Administration (NASA), the World Health Organization (WHO) and other organizations, found that the severe water shortages faced by at least 400 million people today will affect 4 billion people by 2050. The study also concluded that waste and inadequate management of water, especially in poverty-stricken areas, were the main causes of the problems.

A March 6, 2003, article from the Associated Press ("Tackling World's Water Crises Would Cost Up to US$100 Billion a Year, Says U.N. Official") reported that, according to Gordon Young, coordinator of the UN World Water Assessment Program, most of the world's water problems can be resolved, but solving them would require political will and would cost from $50 billion to $100 billion per year. Mr. Young also stated that in order to reach the UN goal of cutting by half the number of people without access to clean water by 2015, every day 270,000 people would have to have clean drinking water and 340,000 people would have to see improvements in sanitation.

The scarcity of clean water throughout the world also has significant implications for public health. According to a March 5, 2003 article in the *Washington Post,* the UN *World Water Development* study found that water contaminated with bacteria, parasites, and other microbes causes about 6,000 deaths every day, including those of 1.4 million children under the age of 5.

Water shortages also affect the world's political situation. The *Washington Post* article states that more than 260 of the world's river basins are shared by at least two countries. Conflicts arise when one country tries to dam up, siphon off, or pollute the shared water. A March 23, 2003, press release from the United Nations Environment Programme (UNEP) reports that since 1820 there have been more than 400 agreements related to water as a limited and consumable resource. Aaron T. Wolf of Oregon State University, compiler of the *Atlas of International Freshwater Agreements,* said that while cooperation about water resources between and among countries over the past 50 years has outnumbered conflicts by more than two-to-one, problems still can occur. Professor Wolf also stated that since 1948 only 37 incidents of violent conflict have occurred over water, 30 of which were between Israel and one or another of its neighbors.

CHAPTER 2
WATER USE

Water must be considered as a finite resource that has limits and boundaries to its availability and suitability for use.

— Wayne B. Solley, et al., *Estimated Use of Water in the United States in 1995,* U.S. Geological Survey, 1998

Water is a fundamental need in every society. Individuals use water for drinking, cooking, cleaning, and recreation. Industry needs it to make chemicals, manufacture goods, and clean factories and equipment. Cities use water to fight fires, clean streets, and fill public swimming pools and fountains. Farmers use water for their livestock, to clean barns, and to irrigate crops. Hydroelectric power stations use water to drive generators, while thermonuclear power stations use it for cooling. Very few human activities do not require the use of water.

FRESHWATER AVAILABILITY

Most human and land-based animal and plant activities that use water require freshwater. In the vast majority of cases, saline or salt water cannot be used without treatment. Of the estimated 861 million cubic miles of water on the planet, barely 3 percent (26 million cubic miles) is freshwater. If this water were distributed over the planet relative to population density and animal and plant needs, it would be more than enough to sustain all life forms on Earth.

Water, however, is randomly distributed. Freshwater supplies vary not only from region to region but from year to year within regions. Within the continental United States, some parts of the country do not have adequate supplies at the same time that other areas may be experiencing floods. For example, in 2001, while rains flooded the Mississippi Valley for weeks, severe drought threatened Florida. Figure 2.1 shows the water supply available to the United States through the hydrologic cycle and how it is used, while Figure 2.2 illustrates the abundant water resources available in the United States.

The first human settlements were based on the availability of water. Where water was plentiful, large numbers of people flourished; where water was scarce, small groups eked out a living. Villages and cities thrived in areas of constant water supply. In more arid regions, nomads wandered in search of water. Great nations grew up along the Nile River in Egypt, the Tigris and the Euphrates Rivers in western Asia, the Indus River in India, and the Yellow River in China. Modern societies have more control over the water supply. They have developed technologies to bring water to arid regions and divert water from areas likely to flood. Elaborate irrigation systems have made it possible for cities to exist today in places where one hundred years ago only the hardiest plants and animals could survive. For example, without these water systems, Los Angeles would be a semiarid desert.

HOW WATER IS SUPPLIED

Freshwater that is potable (suitable for human consumption) is the most crucial resource for the maintenance of human societies. Freshwater, however, is limited in total supply, unevenly distributed, and often of unacceptable quality, particularly in areas where the supply is limited.

Most water users in the United States obtain water through a water utility company. These companies are called public water suppliers because they supply water to the public, although the company may be owned by a city, a town, or a private entity. Water utility companies withdraw water from either surface or groundwater sources to supply their customers. The customers pay the utility companies for the water they use. Water may also be self-supplied, that is, withdrawn directly from wells, lakes, or rivers by those users who have the equipment, technology, and water rights necessary to withdraw and process water for their individual use.

FIGURE 2.1

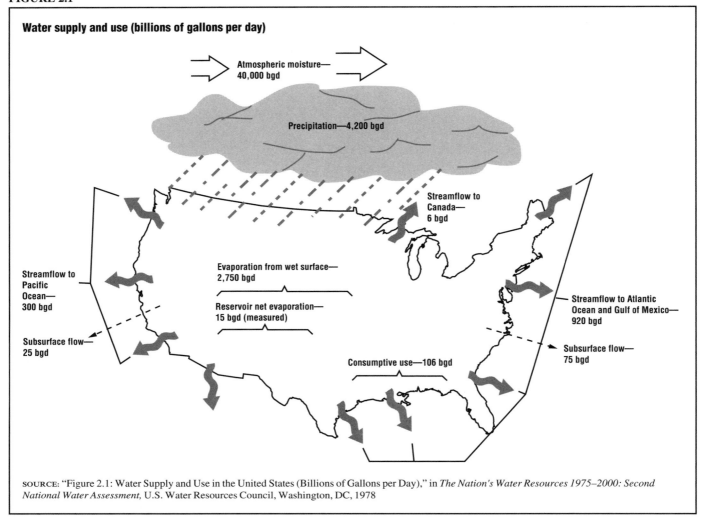

Water supply and use (billions of gallons per day)

Atmospheric moisture—
40,000 bgd

Precipitation—4,200 bgd

Streamflow to
Canada—
6 bgd

Evaporation from wet surface—
2,750 bgd

Reservoir net evaporation—
15 bgd (measured)

Streamflow to
Pacific
Ocean—
300 bgd

Streamflow to Atlantic
Ocean and Gulf of Mexico—
920 bgd

Subsurface flow—
25 bgd

Consumptive use—106 bgd

Subsurface flow—
75 bgd

SOURCE: "Figure 2.1: Water Supply and Use in the United States (Billions of Gallons per Day)," in *The Nation's Water Resources 1975–2000: Second National Water Assessment,* U.S. Water Resources Council, Washington, DC, 1978

Water for a particular use (such as domestic, commercial, or industrial) may come entirely from public supplies or be entirely self-supplied, but most often it comes from a combination of both. For example, city homes get water from the local water utility companies (public supply), while homes in rural areas may have private wells (self-supplied).

Eventually, of course, all water returns to the hydrologic cycle in some form or another, but sometimes it is returned in a condition different from that in which it was withdrawn. This can greatly affect the ability to reuse it. Agricultural runoff may contain pesticides and fertilizers, making it unfit for other uses, such as drinking water. Water that runs down the drain when a person washes a bunch of carrots is in basically the same condition as when it came from the tap, but it will likely enter a sewage line where it mixes with raw sewage.

Figure 2.3 shows a model of the different ways in which off-stream water might be withdrawn, delivered to the user, and returned to its source. The water user, in the middle of the picture, receives water from three sources:

a public-supply system, which itself has withdrawn water from a surface source (the river) and a groundwater source (a well); and two self-supplied sources, a well and the river. Water that is not consumed is returned directly to the river or to a wastewater treatment plant where, after treatment, it is discharged into the river.

TYPES OF WATER USE IN THE UNITED STATES

For reporting purposes, water use in the United States is classified as in stream or off stream. In in-stream use, the water is used at its source, usually a river or stream, and the vast majority of the water is returned immediately to the source. The water user consumes little or no water but uses it only for a process, after which it is all returned to its source. Examples are hydroelectric plants where water flows through the generators and goes right back into the river it came from ("return flow"), or water-powered mills used to grind corn.

In off-stream use, the water is diverted from a surface source or withdrawn from a groundwater source and conveyed to the place where it is actually used. Table 2.1

FIGURE 2.2

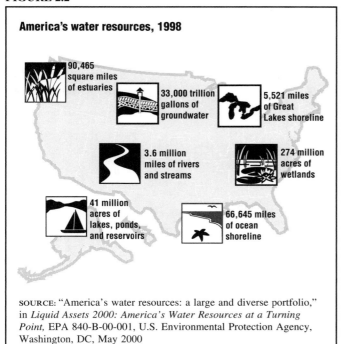

America's water resources, 1998

SOURCE: "America's water resources: a large and diverse portfolio," in *Liquid Assets 2000: America's Water Resources at a Turning Point,* EPA 840-B-00-001, U.S. Environmental Protection Agency, Washington, DC, May 2000

FIGURE 2.3

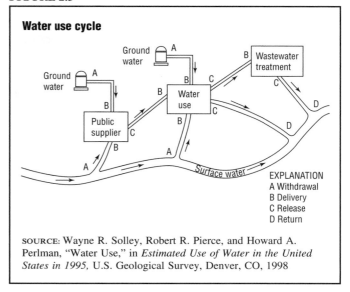

Water use cycle

EXPLANATION
A Withdrawal
B Delivery
C Release
D Return

SOURCE: Wayne R. Solley, Robert R. Pierce, and Howard A. Perlman, "Water Use," in *Estimated Use of Water in the United States in 1995,* U.S. Geological Survey, Denver, CO, 1998

shows 1995 total off-stream water use in each state by population served, per capita use, and source and type; and the amounts of water reclaimed for reuse, lost in transport, or consumed (the latest data available). Figure 2.4 shows the total water withdrawals in 1995 by the water-resources regions established by the U.S. Geological Survey. The Mid-Atlantic, South Atlantic-Gulf, Missouri, and California regions used the greatest volumes of water. These regions withdrew between 36,000 to 47,000 million gallons of water per day.

In many cases, off-stream use results in substantial consumptive use of water. Consumptive use may be quantitative or qualitative. Quantitative consumption occurs when part of the water withdrawn is evaporated, transpired by plants, incorporated into products or crops, consumed by humans or livestock, or otherwise removed from the immediate water environment, so that the quantity returned to the source is substantially less than the quantity of water withdrawn. An example of consumptive use is spray irrigation where less than 60 percent of the water used to irrigate crops is returned to the source. Qualitative consumption occurs when the quality of the water is substantially altered so that it is no longer acceptable for use by downstream users, but the quantity remains substantially unchanged. An example would be discharge of industrial wastes to a water body that renders the water unfit for drinking water. Many water withdrawals result in both quantitative and qualitative consumption.

Off-Stream Use

Water use in the United States is monitored and reported by the U.S. Geological Survey (USGS) in its *Estimated Use of Water in the United States,* published at five-year intervals since 1950. The 1995 report (the latest data available, published in 1998) found that an estimated 402 billion gallons of water per day (freshwater and saline water) were withdrawn from surface or groundwater sources for off-stream use in the United States. This was slightly less than the 408 billion gallons withdrawn in 1990. Of the water involved in off-stream use, 85 percent is freshwater. Per capita use for all off-stream uses in 1995 was 1,500 gallons per day of fresh and saline water combined (1,280 gallons per day of freshwater). Figure 2.5 diagrams the source, use, and disposition of freshwater in the United States. (See the footnote in Figure 2.5 for an example of how to read this diagram.)

Off-stream use is further divided into eight categories:

- Public supply
- Domestic
- Commercial
- Irrigation
- Livestock
- Industrial
- Mining
- Thermoelectric power

PUBLIC SUPPLY. Public supply refers to water withdrawn by public and private water suppliers (utility companies) and delivered to users for domestic, commercial, industrial, and thermoelectric power uses. The latest data available show that public suppliers serviced

TABLE 2.1

Total offstream water use, by state, 1995

(Figures may not add to totals because of independent rounding. Mgal/d = million gallons per day; gal/d = gallons per day)

State	Popula-tion, in thou-sands	Per capita use, fresh-water, in gal/d	Withdrawals, in Mgal/d (includes irrigation conveyance losses)									Reclaimed waste-water, in Mgal/d	Convey-ance losses, in Mgal/d	Consump-tive use, fresh-water, in Mgal/d
			By source and type						Total					
			Groundwater			Surface water								
			Fresh	Saline	Total	Fresh	Saline	Total	Fresh	Saline	Total			
Alabama	4,253	1,670	436	9.1	445	6,650	0	6,650	7,090	9.1	7,100	0.1	0	532
Alaska	604	350	58	75	132	154	43	196	211	117	329	0.	1	25
Arizona	4,218	1,620	2,830	12	2,840	3,980	2.3	3,990	6,820	14	6,830	180	1,030	830
Arkansas	2,484	3,530	5,460	0	5,460	3,310	0	3,310	8,770	0	8,770	0	416	760
California	32,063	1,130	14,500	185	14,700	21,800	9,450	31,300	36,300	9,640	45,900	334	1,670	500
Colorado	3,747	3,690	2,260	17	2,270	11,600	0	11,600	13,800	17	13,800	11	3,770	230
Connecticut	3,275	389	166	0	166	1,110	3,180	4,290	1,280	3,180	4,450	0	0	97
Delaware	717	1,050	110	0	110	642	743	1,390	752	743	1,500	0	0	71
D.C.	554	18	.5	0	.5	9.7	0	9.7	10	0	10	0	0	15
Florida	14,166	509	4,340	4.6	4,340	2,880	11,000	13,800	7,210	11,000	18,200	236	32	2,780
Georgia	7,201	799	1,190	0	1,190	4,560	64	4,630	5,750	64	5,820	.6	0	1,170
Hawaii	1,187	853	515	16	531	497	906	1,400	1,010	922	1,930	6.2	98	542
Idaho	1,163	13,000	2,830	0	2,830	12,300	0	12,300	15,100	0	15,100	0	5,480	4,340
Illinois	11,830	1,680	928	25	953	19,000	0	19,000	19,900	25	19,900	2.0	0	857
Indiana	5,803	1,570	709	0	709	8,430	0	8,430	9,140	0	9,140	0	0	505
Iowa	2,842	1,070	528	0	528	2,510	0	2,510	3,030	0	3,030	0	0	290
Kansas	2,565	2,040	3,510	0	3,510	1,720	0	1,720	5,240	0	5,240	6.8	143	3,620
Kentucky	3,860	1,150	226	0	226	4,190	0	4,190	4,420	0	4,420	0	.5	318
Louisiana	4,342	2,270	1,350	0	1,350	8,500	0	8,500	9,850	0	9,850	0	166	1,930
Maine	1,241	178	80	0	80	141	105	246	221	105	326	0	0	48
Maryland	5,042	289	246	0	246	1,210	6,270	7,480	1,460	6,270	7,730	70	0	150
Massachusetts	6,074	189	351	0	351	795	4,370	5,160	1,150	4,370	5,510	0	0	180
Michigan	9,549	1,260	858	4.4	862	11,200	0	11,200	12,100	4.4	12,100	0	0	667
Minnesota	4,610	736	714	0	714	2,680	0	2,680	3,390	0	3,390	0	0	417
Mississippi	2,697	1,140	2,590	0	2,590	502	112	614	3,090	112	3,200	0	17	1,570
Missouri	5,324	1,320	891	0	891	6,140	0	6,140	7,030	0	7,030	11	0	692
Montana	870	10,200	204	13	217	8,640	0	8,640	8,850	13	8,860	0	4,410	1,960
Nebraska	1,637	6,440	6,200	4.7	6,200	4,350	0	4,350	10,500	4.7	10,500	2.0	906	7,020
Nevada	1,530	1,480	855	42	896	1,400	0	1,400	2,260	42	2,300	24	473	1,340
New Hampshire	1,148	388	81	0	81	364	877	1,240	446	877	1,320	0	0	35
New Jersey	7,945	269	580	0	580	1,560	3,980	5,530	2,140	3,980	6,110	1.1	0	210
New Mexico	1,686	2,080	1,700	0	1,700	1,800	0	1,800	3,510	0	3,510	0	628	1,980
New York	18,136	567	1,010	1.5	1,010	9,270	6,500	15,800	10,300	6,500	16,800	0	0	469
North Carolina	7,195	1,070	535	2.1	535	7,200	1,550	8,750	7,730	1,560	9,290	1.0	0	713
North Dakota	641	1,750	122	0	122	1,000	0	1,000	1,120	0	1,120	0	5.1	181
Ohio	11,151	944	905	0	905	9,620	0	9,620	10,500	0	10,500	0	.2	791
Oklahoma	3,278	543	959	259	1,220	822	0	822	1,780	259	2,040	0	4.9	716
Oregon	3,140	2,520	1,050	0	1,050	6,860	0	6,860	7,910	0	7,910	0	1,300	3,210
Pennsylvania	12,072	802	860	0	860	8,820	0	8,820	9,680	0	9,680	1.1	0	565
Rhode Island	990	138	27	0	27	109	275	383	136	275	411	0	0	19
South Carolina	3,673	1,690	322	0	322	5,880	0	5,880	6,200	0	6,200	0	0	321
South Dakota	729	631	187	0	187	273	0	273	460	0	460	0	54	249
Tennessee	5,256	1,920	435	0	435	9,640	0	9,640	10,100	0	10,100	.5	0	233
Texas	18,724	1,300	8,370	411	8,780	16,000	4,860	20,800	24,300	5,280	29,600	109	540	10,500
Utah	1,951	2,200	776	14	790	3,530	143	3,670	4,300	157	4,460	14	612	2,200
Vermont	585	967	50	0	50	515	0	515	565	0	565	0	0	24
Virginia	6,618	826	358	0	358	5,110	2,800	7,900	5,470	2,800	8,260	0	2.9	218
Washington	5,431	1,620	1,760	0	1,760	7,060	38	7,100	8,820	38	8,860	0	1,090	3,080
West Virginia	1,828	2,530	146	.5	146	4,470	0	4,470	4,620	.5	4,620	0	0	35
Wisconsin	5,102	1,420	759	0	759	6,490	0	6,490	7,250	0	7,250	0	0	44
Wyoming	480	14,700	317	18	335	6,720	0	6,720	7,040	18	7,060	9.1	2,470	2,80
Puerto Rico	3,755	154	155	0	155	422	2,260	2,680	576	2,260	2,840	0	15	18
Virgin Islands	103	113	.5	.2	.7	11	190	201	12	190	202	0	0	1.9
Total	267,068	1,280	76,400	1,110	77,500	264,000	59,700	324,000	341,000	60,800	402,000	1,020	25,300	100,000

SOURCE: Wayne R. Solley, Robert R. Pierce, and Howard A. Perlman, "Table 2. Total offstream water use by State, 1995," in *Estimated Use of Water in the United States in 1995*, U.S. Geological Survey, Denver, CO, 1998

about 225 million people in 1995 (about 84 percent of the total population of the United States at that time). This represented a 7 percent increase over the number of people supplied with water by public suppliers in 1990, just 5 years earlier. Of the 40.2 billion gallons per day supplied for public use, over half (56 percent) was for domestic use. The remaining uses were commercial (17 percent), public (fire fighting, street washing, municipal

FIGURE 2.4

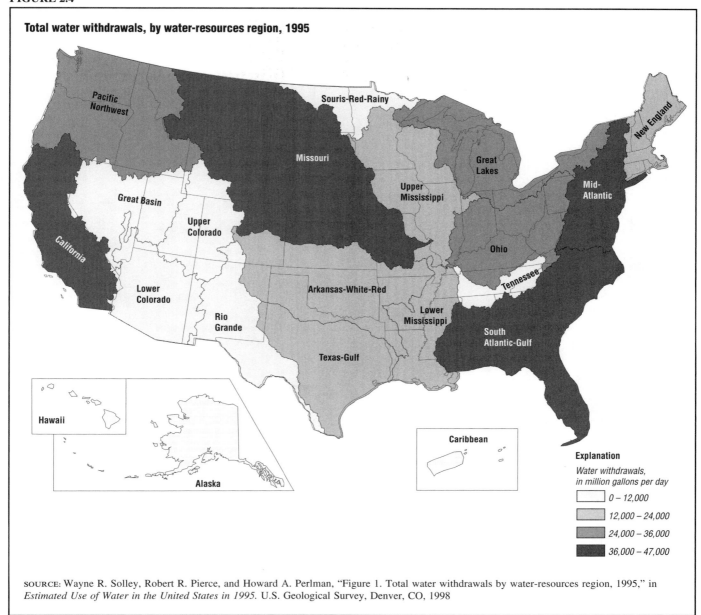

Total water withdrawals, by water-resources region, 1995

Explanation

Water withdrawals, in million gallons per day

☐ 0 – 12,000

▨ 12,000 – 24,000

▨ 24,000 – 36,000

■ 36,000 – 47,000

SOURCE: Wayne R. Solley, Robert R. Pierce, and Howard A. Perlman, "Figure 1. Total water withdrawals by water-resources region, 1995," in *Estimated Use of Water in the United States in 1995.* U.S. Geological Survey, Denver, CO, 1998

office buildings, parks, and swimming pools; 15 percent), industrial (12 percent), and thermoelectric power production (.3 percent). (See Figure 2.6.)

Public suppliers withdrew 63 percent of their water from surface sources and 37 percent from groundwater sources. Figure 2.7 shows the latest data available on the total amount of water withdrawn for public supply in 1995 by state and the amount of surface water and groundwater withdrawn.

According to the latest data available from the U.S. Geological Survey, in its *Estimated Use of Water in the United States in 1995,* the public water systems of the nation provided, on average, 179 gallons of water per person per day in 1995, down from 184 gallons per

person per day reported for 1990. This was the first time public supply per capita use had declined since 1950. The five most populous states—California, Florida, Illinois, New York, and Texas—accounted for 39 percent of U.S. public-supply withdrawals.

DOMESTIC USE. Domestic water use includes water for typical household purposes, such as drinking; food preparation; bathing; washing clothes, dishes, and cars; flushing toilets; and watering lawns and gardens. Although a person needs less than two quarts a day (from liquid and solid foods) to survive, actual daily household use (indoor and outdoor) is much higher. The latest data available, from the 1995 USGS report, show that in 1995 the daily water consumption per person for domestic use was 121

FIGURE 2.5

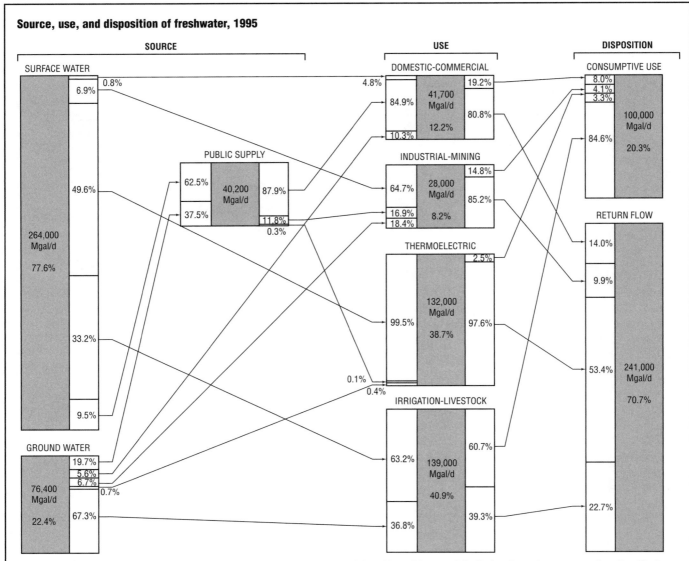

Source, use, and disposition of freshwater, 1995

For each water-use category, this diagram shows the relative proportion of water source and disposition and the general distribution of water from source to disposition. The lines and arrows indicate the distribution of water from source to disposition for each category; for example, surface water was 77.6 percent of total freshwater withdrawn, and going from "Source" to "Use" columns, the line from the surface-water block to the domestic and commercial block indicates that 0.8 percent of all surface water withdrawn was the source for 4.8 percent of total water (self-supplied withdrawals, public-supply deliveries) for domestic and commercial purposes. In addition, going from the "Use" to "Disposition" columns, the line from the domestic and commercial block to the consumptive use block indicates that 19.2 percent of the water for domestic and commercial purposes was consumptive use; this represents 8.0 percent of total consumptive use by all water-use categories.

SOURCE: Wayne R. Solley, Robert R. Pierce, and Howard A. Perlman, "Figure 7. Source, use, and disposition of freshwater in the United States, 1995," in *Estimated Use of Water in the United States in 1995*, U.S. Geological Survey, Denver, CO, 1998

gallons. By 2000 this figure was estimated to have risen to 122 gallons, still shy of the high reached in 1990 (123 gallons). (See Table 2.2.) The estimated 2000 figure appears in a 1999 U.S. Forest Service report written by Thomas C. Brown and entitled *Past and Future Freshwater Use in the United States.*

In 1995 public suppliers provided 87 percent of the 26,100 million gallons per day (mgd or Mgal/d) withdrawn and delivered for home use. The remainder was self-supplied from groundwater and surface water. (See

Figure 2.8.) Sixteen percent of all Americans (42.4 million people) had their own (self-supplied) water systems. Figure 2.9 shows total freshwater withdrawals for domestic use by state. In 1995 California (3,830 mgd), Texas (2,580 mgd), New York (1,960 mgd), Florida (1,560 mgd), and Illinois (1,060 mgd) led the nation in domestic water use.

The American Water Works Association Research Foundation (AWWARF) studied residential end-uses of water in 14 North American cities from 1996–99. Their report, *Residential End Uses of Water Study* concluded

FIGURE 2.6

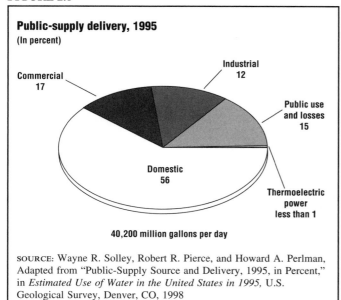

Public-supply delivery, 1995
(In percent)

Commercial 17

Industrial 12

Public use and losses 15

Domestic 56

Thermoelectric power less than 1

40,200 million gallons per day

SOURCE: Wayne R. Solley, Robert R. Pierce, and Howard A. Perlman, Adapted from "Public-Supply Source and Delivery, 1995, in Percent," in *Estimated Use of Water in the United States in 1995,* U.S. Geological Survey, Denver, CO, 1998

that flushing the toilet used the most water (20.1 gallons per person per day) of all indoor household water uses in homes not equipped with water-efficient fixtures. Laundering clothes ranked second in water use (15 gallons per person per day), and taking showers (13.3 gallons per person per day) ranked third. Outdoor household water use, for activities such as filling swimming pools, watering lawns, and washing cars accounts for 50–70 percent of total household water usage, according to a 1999 Environmental Protection Agency (EPA) fact sheet, *Water Facts.*

In 1992 Congress passed the Water Efficiency Act. This legislation established uniform national standards for manufacture of water-efficient plumbing fixtures, such as low-flow toilets and showers. The purpose was to promote water conservation by residential and commercial users. Since that time, many water suppliers have sponsored programs offering rebates on water bills and other incentives to encourage the use of these devices to reduce water use. The experience of New York City with these devices is one example of the many efforts nationwide.

COMMERCIAL USE. Commercial water users include restaurants, hotels and motels, office buildings, government buildings and institutions, military institutions, golf courses, and museums. Slightly more than 9,590 mgd of water were withdrawn and supplied for commercial use in 1995 (the latest data available), up 16 percent from 1990. Only 14 percent of that was consumed; the remainder was return flow. (See Figure 2.10.) Seventy percent of the water for commercial use came from public supplies, accounting for 17 percent of the total public-supply deliveries.

Total freshwater withdrawals in 1995 for commercial use nationwide, by state, are shown in Figure 2.11 (the latest data available). Withdrawals and deliveries were greatest in California (1,380 mgd), Oregon (835 mgd), New York (609 mgd), and Illinois (544 mgd).

IRRIGATION. The word "irrigation" usually brings to mind arid or semiarid deserts transformed into lush green fields of crops by the turn of a handle, bringing life and prosperity where before there had been only sagebrush and cactus. To some extent this is true. Many parts of the midwestern and western United States do not average enough yearly rainfall to sustain the crops that are grown there; the cultivation of those crops is made possible only with the water supplied by irrigation. Irrigation is also used to supplement rainfall in areas with adequate water supplies in order to increase the number of plantings per year, improve yield, and reduce the risk of crop failure during drought years.

According to the 1995 USGS report, irrigation accounted for 39 percent (134,000 mgd) of freshwater withdrawals for all off-stream categories in 1995. Approximately 63 percent of withdrawals that year were from surface water sources, and the other 37 percent from groundwater sources. In 2000, according to Thomas C. Brown, estimated withdrawals of freshwater for irrigation purposes dropped to 491 gallons per day per capita, compared with the 1995 per day per capita figure of 553 gallons. (See Table 2.2.)

The quantity of freshwater used for irrigation varies greatly from region to region. Irrigation is by far the largest water use category in the West. California alone used 21 percent of all irrigation water in 1995. Total withdrawals for irrigation by state are shown in Figure 2.12. Table 2.3 provides data on the number of acres irrigated in each of the twelve states with the highest rates of water usage for irrigation in 1995.

Irrigation has the highest consumptive use of any of the eight categories of off-stream water use. In many irrigated areas, about 75 to 85 percent of the irrigation water is lost to evaporation, transpiration, or retained in the crops. The remaining 15 to 25 percent either infiltrates through the soil to recharge groundwater or is returned to nearby surface water through the drainage system. Average quantities of water applied range from several inches to more than 20 inches per year, depending on local conditions.

Significant changes in water quality can be caused by irrigation. The water lost in evapotranspiration is relatively pure because chemicals are left behind to precipitate as salts and to accumulate in the soil. The salts continue to accumulate as irrigation continues. In many areas, this causes the dissolved solids concentration in the irrigation return flows to be higher than in the original irrigation

FIGURE 2.7

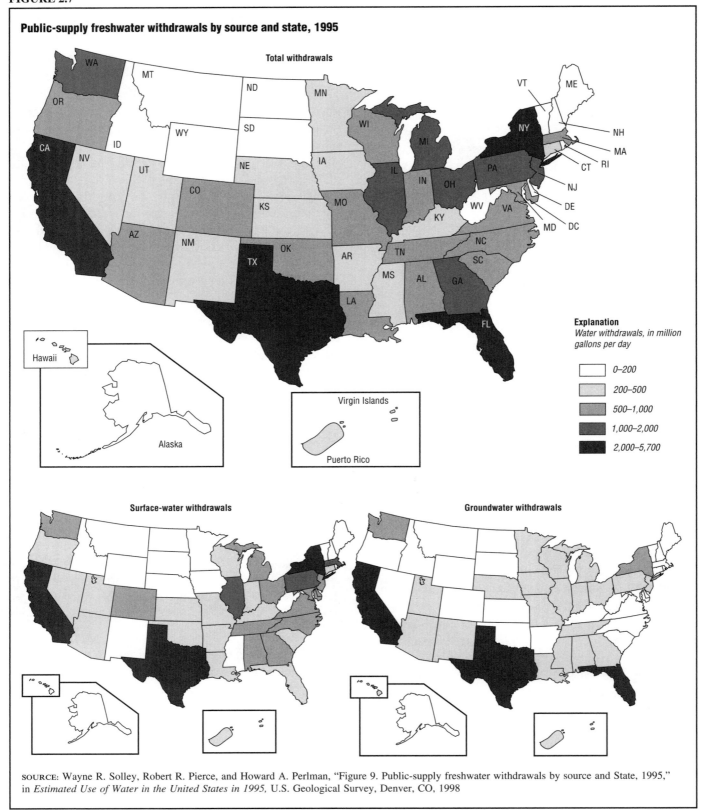

Public-supply freshwater withdrawals by source and state, 1995

Total withdrawals

Explanation
Water withdrawals, in million gallons per day

- 0–200
- 200–500
- 500–1,000
- 1,000–2,000
- 2,000–5,700

Surface-water withdrawals

Groundwater withdrawals

SOURCE: Wayne R. Solley, Robert R. Pierce, and Howard A. Perlman, "Figure 9. Public-supply freshwater withdrawals by source and State, 1995," in *Estimated Use of Water in the United States in 1995,* U.S. Geological Survey, Denver, CO, 1998

water. Excessive salts can interfere with crop growth because plants are not able to filter out the salt from the water that they take up and need. In some cases, excessive salt from salt laden water has rendered the soils unable to grow crops. To stop excessive buildup of the salts in the soil, extra irrigation water is required to flush out the salts and transport them into the groundwater. In locations where these dissolved solids reach high concentrations, the artificial

TABLE 2.2

Freshwater withdrawals by end use category, selected years, 1960–2000

(Gallons per day per-capita)

	Live-stock	Domestic & public	Industrial	Thermo-electric	Irrigation	Total
1960	9	90	224	417	478	1,217
1970	9	104	237	597	631	1,579
1980	9	114	225	625	675	1,649
1990	18	123	147	529	553	1,370
2000	21	122	134	486	491	1,254

SOURCE: Adapted from Thomas C. Brown, "Table A1.7 U.S. per-capita withdrawals (gallons per day)," in *Past and Future Freshwater Use in the United States,* RMRS-GTS-39, U.S. Department of Agriculture, Forest Service, Rocky Mountain Research Station, Fort Collins, CO, December 1999

FIGURE 2.8

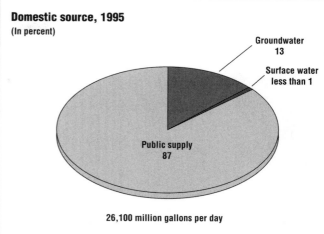

Domestic source, 1995
(In percent)

Groundwater 13

Surface water less than 1

Public supply 87

26,100 million gallons per day

SOURCE: Wayne R. Solley, Robert R. Pierce, and Howard A. Perlman, Adapted from "Domestic Source and Disposition, 1995, In Percent," in *Estimated Use of Water in the United States in 1995,* U.S. Geological Survey, Denver, CO, 1998

recharge from irrigation return flow can result in degradation of the quality of groundwater, and the surface water to which the groundwater discharges.

LIVESTOCK. Livestock water use includes fish farming, along with four-legged stock watering, dairy and feedlot operations, and other on-farm needs. According to the 1995 USGS report, 5,490 mgd of water were used for livestock in 1995, 22 percent more than in 1990. Of that water, 58 percent was consumed. The Pacific Northwest and lower Mississippi regions had the most water withdrawn for livestock in 1995, and accounted for almost half the U.S. total livestock use. Idaho accounted for the largest use of water for livestock (1,460 mgd), followed by California (459 mgd), Mississippi (396 mgd), Arkansas (354 mgd), Louisiana (325 mgd), and Texas (315 mgd).

On a per capita basis, freshwater used for livestock was consumed at a rate of 21 gallons per day in 1995. According to Thomas C. Brown, withdrawals of freshwater for livestock usage were estimated to have remained unchanged between 1995 and 2000. (See Table 2.2.)

INDUSTRIAL. Even those industries that do not use water directly in their products may use substantial quantities of water during operations. Water for industrial use is commonly divided into four categories: (1) cooling water, (2) process water, (3) boiler feed water, and (4) sanitary and service water (for personal use by employees, for cleaning plants and equipment, and for the operation of valves and other equipment). Major water-using industries include steel, chemical and allied products, paper and related products, and petroleum refining.

Water supplied for industrial use in 1995 totaled 27,100 mgd, 2 percent less than in 1990. Most of that water was self-supplied, and 60 percent was withdrawn from surface water. Of water used for industry, 85 percent was returned; only 15 percent was consumed. Withdrawals by

state are shown in Table 2.4. The Great Lakes and Ohio regions withdrew the largest amount of water for industry. By state, Louisiana (2,620 mgd), Indiana (2,400 mgd), Michigan (2,120 mgd), Pennsylvania (1,870 mgd), and Texas (1,570 mgd) led the nation in industrial water use.

On a per capita basis, withdrawals of freshwater for industrial and commercial use equaled 140 gallons per day in 1995. This figure was projected to decline by 2000 to a rate of 134 gallons per day, according to Thomas C. Brown. (See Table 2.2.)

By far, the biggest users of cooling water are power plants. Oil refineries and chemical plants use cooling water to condense products and protect equipment from the excessive heat that often builds up during industrial processes. A blast furnace in a steel plant may use as much as 30,000 gallons of cooling water for each ton of crude iron produced and may require as much as 35 million gallons of water every day the plant is in operation.

Most manufacturers use processed water at some point in the course of making a product. Water is the solvent in many chemical processes. In some plants, the item being manufactured is in contact with water at almost every step in its conversion from raw materials to finished product. For example, in the production of pulp and paper, water is used for removing bark from pulpwood, moving the ground wood and pulp from one process to another, cooking the wood chips for removal of lignin (the woody pulp of plant cells), and washing the pulp. Another example is the food industry, which uses huge quantities of water for cleaning and cooking vegetables and meat, canning and cooling canned products, and cleaning equipment and facilities.

FIGURE 2.9

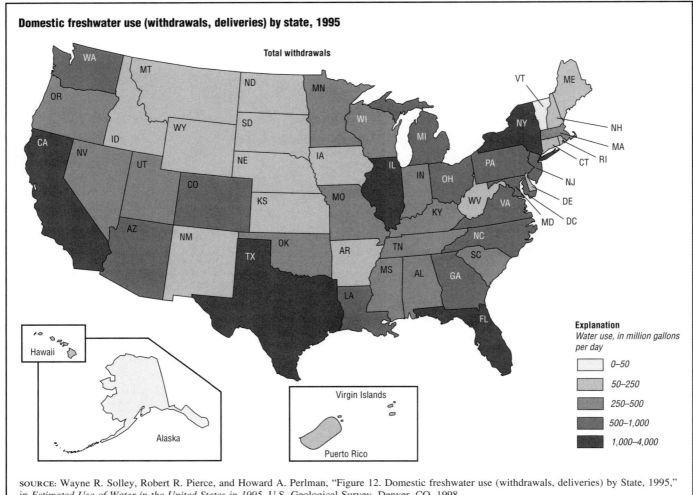

Domestic freshwater use (withdrawals, deliveries) by state, 1995

Total withdrawals

Explanation
Water use, in million gallons per day

0–50

50–250

250–500

500–1,000

1,000–4,000

SOURCE: Wayne R. Solley, Robert R. Pierce, and Howard A. Perlman, "Figure 12. Domestic freshwater use (withdrawals, deliveries) by State, 1995," in *Estimated Use of Water in the United States in 1995,* U.S. Geological Survey, Denver, CO, 1998

The need for large quantities of easily accessible water has led to industrial development around or near coastlines, rivers, and lakes. The Great Lakes region and the Ohio River Valley are examples. This development has often caused serious deterioration of water quality in the area, since after it is used, water may be returned to its source carrying contaminants.

MINING. Mining can be defined as the extraction of naturally occurring materials, including petroleum, from Earth's crust. Water is used for washing and milling. Some withdrawals are actually the by-product of mineral extraction and are considered an operational problem, since the water has to be removed from the mines. All water for mining operations is self-supplied, and may come from a freshwater or saline source. The USGS classifies water as saline if it has more than 1,000 parts per million of dissolved solids (salts).

The USGS estimated that 3,770 mgd of water were withdrawn for mining in 1995 (the latest data available),

and 27 percent of that was consumed. Most water withdrawn for mining purposes was in the Texas Gulf area, followed by the Great Lakes region. Texas (621 mgd), Minnesota (298 mgd), and Florida (296 mgd) were the leading states in withdrawal of water for mining.

Acid mine drainage is a by-product of mining activity. It is the drainage that results from the activity of removing and processing large amounts of natural strata to recover desired ores of heavy metals, minerals, and coal. Thousands of stream miles are severely affected by drainage and runoff from abandoned coal mines, which are the single-largest source of adverse water-quality impacts to surface water and groundwater in the United States.

THERMOELECTRIC POWER. Thermoelectric power generation is the largest user of withdrawal water. Water from both freshwater and saline sources is used in the generation of electric power with fossil fuel, nuclear, or geothermal energy. Most withdrawals are used for cooling condensers or reactors. As water flows through condensers or reactors, it absorbs and removes heat. There are several

FIGURE 2.10

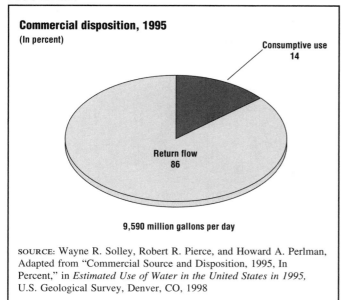

Commercial disposition, 1995
(In percent)

Consumptive use
14

Return flow
86

9,590 million gallons per day

SOURCE: Wayne R. Solley, Robert R. Pierce, and Howard A. Perlman, Adapted from "Commercial Source and Disposition, 1995, In Percent," in *Estimated Use of Water in the United States in 1995*, U.S. Geological Survey, Denver, CO, 1998

ways of disposing of the heated water. One method is to channel it to a cooling tower or pond and reuse it. Over 60 percent of the water may be lost through evaporation during recycling, although new cooling tower recycling methods are much more efficient. Another method is to return the water directly to the source, resulting in an evaporation rate that is usually less than 2 percent. When water is returned to a lake or river at a significantly higher temperature than when it was withdrawn, however, it can damage aquatic life. For this reason, these plants are strictly regulated to assure that return water is properly cooled before discharge.

Water used for thermoelectric power generation accounted for almost half (47 percent) of all withdrawals for off-stream use in 1995 (the latest data available). Nearly all (98 percent) withdrawals were return flow. States in the eastern third of the country accounted for five times the amount of water used for thermoelectric power than in the western United States. (See Figure 2.13.) Illinois (17,100 mgd) led the nation in use of water for thermoelectric power generation, nearly double Texas's second-place 9,620 mgd.

If measured on a per capita basis, the water used for thermoelectric power generation in 1995 was 504 gallons per day. By 2000, according to estimates by Thomas C. Brown, that figure was expected to have dropped to 486 gallons per day. (See Table 2.2.)

In-Stream Use

HYDROELECTRIC POWER. In 1995, according to the USGS report of that year, 3,160 billion gallons of water per day were used for hydroelectric power generation,

where falling water drives the plant's turbine generators. All water withdrawals come from surface sources, which include reservoirs. No water is consumed directly during the cooling process, but return flow (water that is supplied but not consumed) may be less than 100 percent due to indirect factors such as evaporation from reservoirs that supply the power plant.

The Pacific Northwest, however, used the most water for hydroelectric power in 1995 (the latest data available). Three states with many natural waterfalls—Oregon, Washington, and New York—used about 46 percent of the water used to generate hydroelectric power in the United States. (See Table 2.5.) In the flatter terrain of the United States, dams create artificial waterfalls, allowing hydroelectric power generation. Building dams for hydroelectric power generation has had severe environmental impacts on river and stream systems, however.

WASTE DISPOSAL—A LEGITIMATE WATER USE. Although not traditionally recognized as a beneficial use, water has been used to dilute and disperse wastes since man's earliest settlements. If the wastewater is properly treated, the water environment can dilute, disperse, and assimilate wastes without harm to water quality or aquatic communities. The first step in the process is to identify the total maximum daily load (TMDL) of contaminant that a water body can receive. The next step is to design, construct, and operate wastewater treatment facilities that provide the necessary level of treatment before discharging wastewater.

For the first time in 1995 (the latest data available), the USGS reported wastewater releases and return flow. This category includes facilities that collect, treat, and dispose of water through sewer systems and wastewater treatment plants, generally to surface waters. About 16,400 publicly owned treatment facilities released some 41,000 mgd of treated wastewater nationwide in 1995. (See Table 2.6.) The annual average is one to two million gallons of treated water per facility per day. The largest wastewater return flows occurred in regions with large populations. Illinois (4,850 mgd) and Ohio (4,690 mgd) reported the largest releases of treated wastewater.

Not all treated wastewater is return flow. Because of the increasing demand for water and the cost of treating drinking water, more emphasis is being placed on water conservation and water reclamation (water reuse). Reclaimed water is wastewater that has been treated for uses such as irrigation of golf courses or public parks instead of being discharged back to source waters. Florida (271 mgd), California (216 mgd), and Arizona (209 mgd) reported large uses of reclaimed wastewater in 1995 (the latest data available). (See Table 2.6.)

In November 2000 Congress gave impetus to water reuse practices in the Alternative Water Sources Act of

FIGURE 2.11

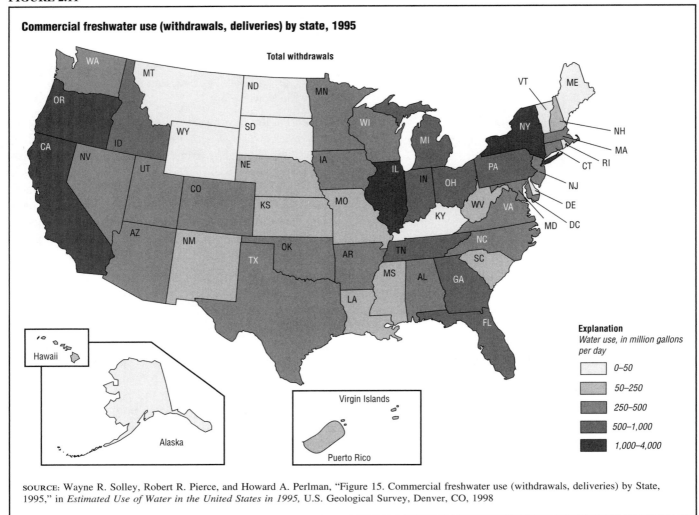

Commercial freshwater use (withdrawals, deliveries) by state, 1995

SOURCE: Wayne R. Solley, Robert R. Pierce, and Howard A. Perlman, "Figure 15. Commercial freshwater use (withdrawals, deliveries) by State, 1995," in *Estimated Use of Water in the United States in 1995,* U.S. Geological Survey, Denver, CO, 1998

2000. These amendments to Title II of the Clean Water Act provide for "alternative water source projects" designed to provide municipal, industrial, and agricultural water supplies in an environmentally sustainable manner by conserving, managing, reclaiming, or reusing water or wastewater or by treating wastewater in areas where existing or reasonably anticipated future water supply needs cannot be met. A total of $75 million was authorized for 2003 to 2005 to implement this section, but the federal contribution to each project was limited to no more than 50 percent.

RIGHT TO WATER USE

Water is a precious commodity that has many uses that are important to people. The eight off-stream water-use categories described above are generally recognized as capturing those uses. Sometimes there is not enough water available at a given location to meet all the demands for water. In those situations, whose water is it?

State laws, regulations, and procedures establish how an individual, company, or other organization obtains and protects water rights. When water rights are disputed, the question is usually resolved through adjudication. Adjudication is an administrative or judicial determination of all rights to use water in a particular water body or watershed to establish the priority, point of diversion, place and nature of use, and the quantity of water used among the various claimants. When the water involved crosses state boundaries, states enter into various agreements for water sharing. When agreement cannot be reached between states, the matter is usually settled in federal courts, or in some cases by an act of Congress.

Riparian Rights

In most eastern states, some midwestern and southern states, and California (which also uses the appropriation doctrine), the riparian doctrine is in effect. The fundamental principles of this doctrine are:

• Ownership of land along a water body (riparian ownership) is essential to the existence of a right to that water

FIGURE 2.12

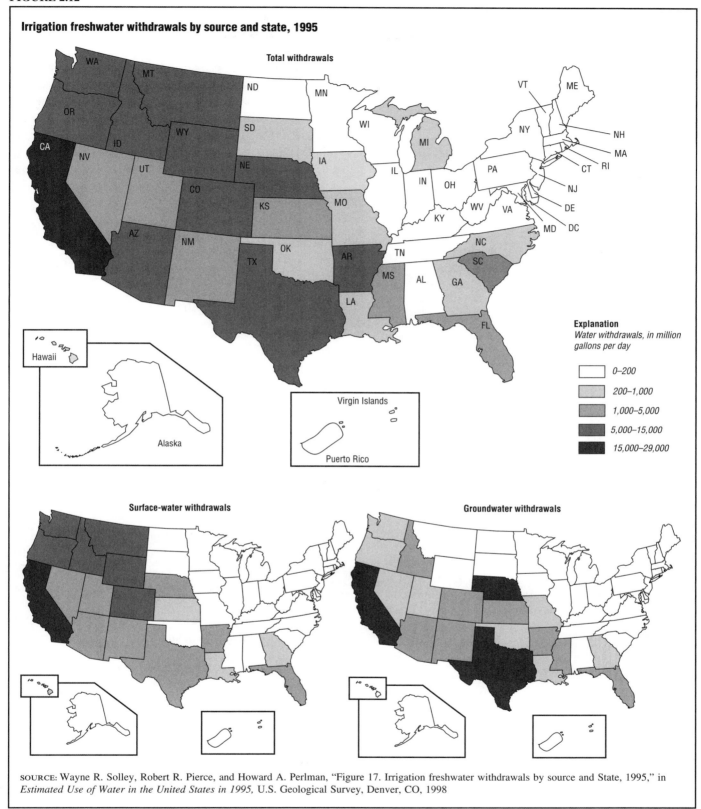

Irrigation freshwater withdrawals by source and state, 1995

Total withdrawals

Explanation
Water withdrawals, in million gallons per day

- 0–200
- 200–1,000
- 1,000–5,000
- 5,000–15,000
- 15,000–29,000

Hawaii

Alaska

Virgin Islands

Puerto Rico

Surface-water withdrawals

Groundwater withdrawals

SOURCE: Wayne R. Solley, Robert R. Pierce, and Howard A. Perlman, "Figure 17. Irrigation freshwater withdrawals by source and State, 1995," in *Estimated Use of Water in the United States in 1995,* U.S. Geological Survey, Denver, CO, 1998

- Each riparian owner has equal right to make use of the water in its natural state (no storage), no matter when use of the water was initiated; therefore, water shortages are shared

In almost all jurisdictions this doctrine has been modified to fit local conditions. It applies to all bodies of water including streams, lakes, ponds, and marshes, and grants to all riparian owners the right to make reasonable use of the

TABLE 2.3

Number of acres of agricultural land being irrigated by state in the states with the greatest number of acres irrigated, 1995

State	Acres irrigated (000)	Method used to irrigate		
		Flooded (percent)	Sprayed (percent)	Dripped (percent)
California	9,480	74.0	19.0	7.0
Nebraska	7,450	47.0	53.0	0.0
Texas	6,310	56.0	43.0	1.0
Arkansas	4,520	85.0	15.0	0.0
Colorado	3,310	76.0	24.0	0.0
Kansas	3,090	32.0	68.0	<1.0
Idaho	3,010	33.0	67.0	0.0
Washington	2,120	24.0	71.0	5.0
Florida	2,130	49.0	23.0	28.0
Wyoming	1,990	85.0	15.0	<1.0
Oregon	1,840	42.0	58.0	<1.0
Montana	1,810	71.0	29.0	0.0
United States	59,250	55.0	42.0	3.0

SOURCE: Adapted from *Water Science for Schools*, U.S. Geological Survey, Washington, DC, June 2001, [Online] http://wwwga.usgs.gov/edu/qausage.html [accessed May 12, 2003]

water as long as that use does not interfere with the reasonable use of water by the other riparian users. Disputes over what constitutes reasonable use are generally resolved by the courts.

"Rule of Capture"

Water laws in the arid western states, where water supplies are limited and often inadequate, were developed under the Appropriation Doctrine. This doctrine is essentially a rule of capture, and awards a water right to the person actually using the water, and applies to both surface water and groundwater. It has two fundamental principles:

- First in time of use is first in right (that is, the earliest appropriation on a surface water or groundwater has the first right to use the water)

- Application of the water to a beneficial use is the basis and measure of the right

Beneficial use has two components: the nature or purpose of the use and the efficient or nonwasteful use of water. State constitutions, statutes, or case law may define the beneficial uses of water. The uses may be different in each state, and the definitions of what uses are beneficial may change over time. The right to use water established under state law may be lost if the beneficial use is discontinued for a prescribed time. Abandonment requires an intent to permanently give up the right. Forfeiture results from the failure to use the water in the manner described in state statutes. Either requires a finding by the state resource agency that a water right has been abandoned or forfeited.

Priority determines the order of rank of the rights to use the water in a system. Under the Appropriation

Doctrine, priority means that the person first using the water for a beneficial purpose has a right superior to those who begin to use the water at a later date. Priority becomes important when the quantity of available water is insufficient to meet the needs of all those having rights to use water from a common source. Under the priority system, water shortages are not shared. Some western state statutes contain priority or preference categories of water use, under which higher priority uses (such as domestic water supply) have first right to water in times of shortage, regardless of the priority date. There may also be constraints against changes or transfers involving these priority uses.

When an individual, company, or other organization has completed all the necessary steps to secure a state water appropriation right, a perfected right is secured. At that time, a water license or certificate is usually issued. This document is evidence of a water right and is considered real property. Western water rights are zealously guarded and are frequently litigated.

Sometimes conflicts over water rights arise between the states and the federal government. Since the 1990s, the U.S. Forest Service has been involved in water rights problems with several states. According to a 1997 report of the Federal Water Rights Task Force, in the early 1990s, the Arapaho-Roosevelt National Forest informed the owners of a number of existing water facilities along the Colorado Front Range that they would have to renew the federal land use authorizations for those facilities. Furthermore, the Forest Service asserted that the renewal of these authorizations would include conditions for requiring that certain minimum amounts of water be left in the stream (bypass flows). The Forest Service defended the imposed conditions as being required to achieve the numerical standards for aquatic habitat protection adopted in the 1984 Arapaho and Roosevelt Forest Plan. The Forest Service asserted that its legal authority for the imposition of bypass flow requirements was based in the Property Clause of the United States Constitution, and was delegated to it by Congress in the 1897 Organic Administration Act, Multiple Use and Sustained Yield Act (1960), Federal Land Policy and Management Act (1976), and the National Forest Management Act (1976).

Although the controversy originated in Colorado, several other states (Alaska, Arizona, Idaho, Nevada, New Mexico, and Wyoming) objected to the policy of the Forest Service, contending that the Forest Service has no authority to impose bypass flows on existing water users. They also argued that the policy goes against the longstanding deference Congress has shown the states in regard to water rights. A legal challenge to bypass flow policies, *Trout Unlimited v. United States Department of Agriculture* has been filed in Colorado District Court and was still in litigation as of May 2003.

TABLE 2.4

Industrial water use by state, 1995

(In million gallons per day)

State	Self-supplied withdrawals — Groundwater Fresh	Groundwater Saline	Surface water Fresh	Surface water Saline	Total Fresh	Total Saline	Total	Reclaimed waste water	Public-supply deliveries Fresh	Total Use — Withdrawals and deliveries Fresh	Consumptive use Fresh	Consumptive use Saline
Alabama	34	0	699	0	733	0	733	0	213	946	116	0
Alaska	3.8	0	51	1.8	55	1.8	57	0	12	66	9.9	.3
Arizona	39	0	0	0	39	0	39	2.3	66	106	98	0
Arkansas	108	0	80	0	187	0	187	0	57	245	14	0
California	522	10	16	26	538	36	575	3.6	283	821	239	9.1
Colorado	37	0	86	0	123	0	123	0	19	143	42	0
Connecticut	3.5	0	6.2	0	9.6	0	9.6	0	42	51	1.1	0
Delaware	17	0	43	3.2	61	3.2	64	0	16	76	11	0
D.C.	.5	0	0	0	.5	0	.5	0	.7	1.2	.1	0
Florida	240	0	106	8.0	345	8.0	353	.7	103	449	46	0
Georgia	295	0	337	32	633	32	664	.6	194	827	85	2.2
Hawaii	19	.9	0	0	19	.9	20	0	5.6	25	2.5	.1
Idaho	39	0	7.9	0	47	0	47	0	6.7	54	3.1	0
Illinois	162	0	290	0	452	0	452	0	118	570	63	0
Indiana	119	0	2,160	0	2,270	0	2,270	0	125	2,400	144	0
Iowa	74	0	184	0	258	0	258	0	78	335	44	0
Kansas	50	0	3.2	0	53	0	53	.2	37	90	45	0
Kentucky	92	0	255	0	347	0	347	0	197	543	22	0
Louisiana	356	0	2,230	0	2,580	0	2,580	0	35	2,620	266	0
Maine	4.6	0	5.9	0	11	0	11	0	14	25	2.5	0
Maryland	19	0	45	261	65	261	326	70	44	109	16	26
Massachusetts	38	0	47	0	85	0	85	0	86	171	10	0
Michigan	177	3.6	1,670	0	1,850	3.6	1,850	0	270	2,120	160	.4
Minnesota	58	0	83	0	140	0	140	0	41	181	26	0
Mississippi	166	0	124	0	290	0	290	0	20	310	49	0
Missouri	21	0	18	0	39	0	39	0	140	179	27	0
Montana	31	0	29	0	60	0	60	0	1.0	61	9.3	0
Nebraska	26	0	4.4	0	30	0	30	0	26	57	16	0
Nevada	7.4	0	7.5	0	15	0	15	0	2.2	17	4.9	0
New Hampshire	5.6	0	38	0	43	0	43	0	13	56	6.6	0
New Jersey	43	0	158	195	201	195	396	0	91	292	22	15
New Mexico	6.3	0	2.0	0	8.3	0	8.3	0	15	23	12	0
New York	127	0	132	0	259	0	259	0	356	615	62	0
North Carolina	61	0	308	0	369	0	369	0	193	562	112	0
North Dakota	3.6	0	7.9	0	11	0	11	0	2.5	14	9.4	0
Ohio	158	0	399	0	557	0	557	0	355	912	190	0
Oklahoma	3.8	0	17	0	21	0	21	0	122	142	8.9	0
Oregon	13	0	365	0	378	0	378	0	71	448	18	0
Pennsylvania	147	0	1,530	0	1,680	0	1,680	1.1	193	1,870	158	0
Rhode Island	1.1	0	0	0	1.1	0	1.1	0	12	13	1.3	0
South Carolina	60	0	640	0	700	0	700	0	44	744	112	0
South Dakota	4.1	0	1.0	0	5.1	0	5.1	0	7.9	13	1.9	0
Tennessee	68	0	795	0	863	0	863	0	130	993	109	0
Texas	226	.5	1,070	996	1,300	996	2,300	32	268	1,570	430	599
Utah	55	.1	31	0	86	.1	86	0	17	103	45	0
Vermont	1.9	0	7.4	0	9.4	0	9.4	0	7.7	17	1.7	0
Virginia	107	0	410	67	516	67	583	0	88	605	72	8.0
Washington	133	0	478	38	611	38	649	0	331	942	120	4.2
West Virginia	13	0	1,300	0	1,320	0	1,320	0	14	1,330	200	0
Wisconsin	78	0	363	0	441	0	441	0	151	592	95	0
Wyoming	1.6	0	1.2	0	2.8	0	2.8	0	2.4	5.1	.8	0
Puerto Rico	10	0	1.1	0	11	0	11	0	15	26	7.6	0
Virgin Islands	.1	.2	2.9	17	3.0	17	20	0	0	3.0	.4	.3
Total	4,090	15	16,700	1,640	20,700	1,660	22,400	110	4,750	25,500	3,370	665

Note: Figures may not add to totals because of independent rounding.

SOURCE: Wayne R. Solley, Robert R. Pierce, and Howard A. Perlman, "Table 20. Industrial water use by State, 1995," in *Estimated Use of Water in the United States in 1995*, U.S. Geological Survey, Denver, CO, 1998

FIGURE 2.13

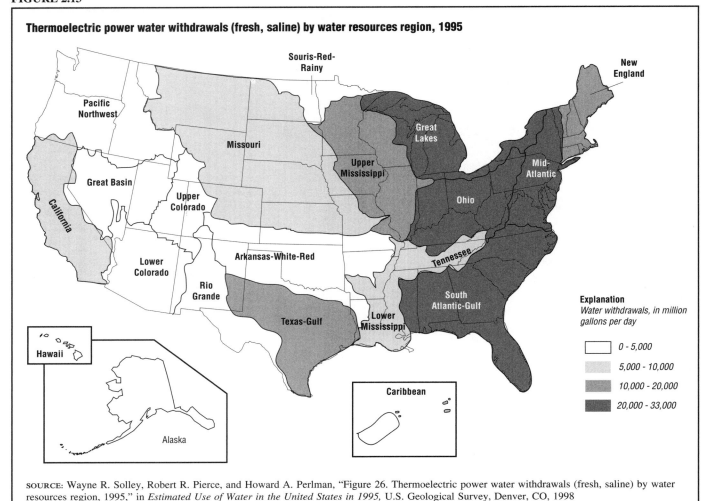

Thermoelectric power water withdrawals (fresh, saline) by water resources region, 1995

Explanation
Water withdrawals, in million gallons per day

- 0 - 5,000
- 5,000 - 10,000
- 10,000 - 20,000
- 20,000 - 33,000

SOURCE: Wayne R. Solley, Robert R. Pierce, and Howard A. Perlman, "Figure 26. Thermoelectric power water withdrawals (fresh, saline) by water resources region, 1995," in *Estimated Use of Water in the United States in 1995,* U.S. Geological Survey, Denver, CO, 1998

Some additional measures are being undertaken to assert states' rights over water. The State Water Sovereignty Protection Act of 2003 was introduced by Senator Mike Crapo of Idaho on March 6, 2003, and cosponsored by Senator Pete Domenici of New Mexico. The purpose of the legislation is to reaffirm the dominance of state water laws in cases where the federal government is attempting to acquire water. Provisions of the Act:

- Whenever the United States seeks to appropriate water or acquire a water right, it will be subject to state procedural and substantive water law.

- States control the water within their boundaries. The federal government may exercise management or control over water only in compliance with state law.

- In any administrative or judicial proceeding in which the United States participates pursuant to the McCarran Amendment, the United States is subject to all costs and fees to the same extent as costs and fees may be imposed on a private party.

The Act was introduced in response to fears that the federal government, in its efforts to enforce the Clean Water Act, the Endangered Species Act, the Federal Land Policy Management Act, and other laws is encroaching on the states' water laws.

Public Trust Doctrine

The Public Trust Doctrine refers to the responsibility of a state to hold property rights in trust for the benefit of the citizens of the state. Historically, the doctrine applied to the beds of navigable rivers. This doctrine, however, has since been extended to include beaches and parks, and to apply generically to all natural resources. The doctrine has been employed to assure stream access to the public in Montana. In California, it was successfully used to challenge water rights held by the City of Los Angeles when it was discovered that the city's diversions from Mono Lake tributaries were causing the lake's unique habitat to be destroyed.

TABLE 2.5

Hydroelectric power use by state, 1995

State	Water use Mgal/d	Thousand acre-feet per year	Power generated in million kWh
Alabama	157,000	177,000	9,510
Alaska	2,090	2,340	1,440
Arizona	21,200	23,700	7,960
Arkansas	42,700	47,900	2,630
California	146,000	164,000	47,100
Colorado	6,810	7,630	2,140
Connecticut	3,610	4,050	317
Delaware	0	0	0
D.C.	0	0	0
Florida	16,900	19,000	443
Georgia	50,900	57,100	4,850
Hawaii	229	256	148
Idaho	115,000	129,000	11,300
Illinois	55,800	62,500	1,010
Indiana	12,300	13,800	467
Iowa	2,350	2,630	21
Kansas	1,250	1,410	11
Kentucky	83,000	93,100	2,880
Louisiana	76,100	85,400	1,110
Maine	85,200	95,500	3,440
Maryland	14,400	16,100	1,450
Massachusetts	24,200	27,100	992
Michigan	39,800	44,600	1,410
Minnesota	19,800	22,200	1,030
Mississippi	0	0	0
Missouri	17,100	19,200	1,920
Montana	66,200	74,200	10,400
Nebraska	15,000	16,800	1,040
Nevada	6,080	6,810	6,320
New Hampshire	33,000	37,000	1,460
New Jersey	309	346	241
New Mexico	2,750	3,090	353
New York	356,000	399,000	24,600
North Carolina	56,400	63,200	5,810
North Dakota	13,900	15,600	2,480
Ohio	14,200	15,900	227
Oklahoma	49,100	55,100	3,300
Oregon	456,000	511,000	40,400
Pennsylvania	55,900	62,600	352
Rhode Island	339	380	6.1
South Carolina	42,200	47,300	3,070
South Dakota	62,400	69,900	6,420
Tennessee	122,000	137,000	9,430
Texas	18,600	20,900	1,520
Utah	3,720	4,170	931
Vermont	17,500	19,600	983
Virginia	14,800	16,600	922
Washington	653,000	733,000	82,300
West Virginia	51,500	57,700	1,210
Wisconsin	50,800	57,000	1,600
Wyoming	5,150	5,770	793
Puerto Rico	349	391	101
Virgin Islands	0	0	0
Total	**3,160,000**	**3,540,000**	**310,000**

Notes: Figures may not add to totals because of independent rounding. Mgal/d = million gallons per day; kWh = kilowatthour.

SOURCE: Wayne R. Solley, Robert R. Pierce, and Howard A. Perlman, "Table 28. Hydroelectric power use by State, 1995," in *Estimated Use of Water in the United States in 1995*, U.S. Geological Survey, Denver, CO, 1998

TABLE 2.6

Wastewater treatment water releases by state, 1995

State	Number of facilities Public	Other	Public releases Return flow, in Mgal/d	Reclaimed waste water, in Mgal/d
Alabama	255	0	474	0
Alaska	126	107	61	0
Arizona	150	300	359	209
Arkansas	313	442	241	0
California	1,049	857	3,250	216
Colorado	393	179	422	11
Connecticut	94	47	411	0
Delaware	15	48	103	0
D.C.	1	6	309	0
Florida	387	228	1,540	271
Georgia	501	370	777	4.0
Hawaii	32	171	137	6.2
Idaho	76	6	99	0
Illinois	532	610	4,850	0
Indiana	407	422	762	0
Iowa	754	475	522	0
Kansas	442	343	217	7.4
Kentucky	223	1,465	341	0
Louisiana	153	159	1,450	0
Maine	71	0	115	0
Maryland	161	870	422	70
Massachusetts	86	443	867	0
Michigan	295	698	2,540	0
Minnesota	436	0	516	0
Mississippi	307	1,575	307	0
Missouri	1,164	1,284	1,030	0
Montana	228	118	202	0
Nebraska	290	285	181	1.0
Nevada	68	67	179	24
New Hampshire	79	0	89	0
New Jersey	209	467	915	0
New Mexico	46	59	99	5.6
New York	596	0	2,760	0
North Carolina	307	1,348	1,330	1.5
North Dakota	277	99	45	0
Ohio	1,236	2,510	4,690	0
Oklahoma	332	159	312	0
Oregon	189	23	483	0
Pennsylvania	289	140	1,340	.6
Rhode Island	115	0	182	0
South Carolina	274	481	404	22
South Dakota	207	0	64	0
Tennessee	251	0	739	.1
Texas	1,308	3,113	2,180	96
Utah	50	10	236	39
Vermont	95	0	42	0
Virginia	67	1	561	0
Washington	329	1,791	736	0
West Virginia	594	1,342	199	0
Wisconsin	411	231	653	0
Wyoming	79	203	50	0
Puerto Rico	70	0	185	0
Virgin Islands	8	0	4.1	0
Total	**16,428**	**23,700**	**41,000**	**983**

Notes: Figures may not add to totals because of independent rounding. Mgal/d = million gallons per day.

SOURCE: Wayne R. Solley, Robert R. Pierce, and Howard A. Perlman, "Table 30. Wastewater treatment water releases by State, 1995," in *Estimated Use of Water in the United States in 1995*, U.S. Geological Survey, Denver, CO, 1998

AQUATIC LIFE—AN OLD AND NEW USER

Since the enactment of the 1972 Federal Water Pollution Control Act, with its emphasis on maintaining the physical, chemical, and biological characteristics of the nation's waters, there has been an increasing awareness of the need to protect and maintain the insects, plants, and animals that make up the ecosystem of surface water bodies. Since life on Earth first began in the ancient seas, aquatic life has been an integral part of overall water resources. This fact has frequently been ignored as man and his civilizations evolved, resulting in widespread change in and annihilation of aquatic systems.

Until the last two decades of the 20th century in the United States, allocating water to maintain aquatic systems was rarely recognized as a legitimate use. As a result, dam construction frequently disrupted whole ecological systems by reducing the water available to aquatic life in large stretches of rivers and streams below dams, interfering with the life cycles of migrating fish and other organisms, and flooding habitats. In some river systems, such as the Colorado River, the entire flow was allocated and appropriated, resulting in drastic changes to the lush waterscape observed decades before at the delta of the Sea of Cortez, where the Colorado River deposited its rich silt. Rivers and streams have been lined with impermeable surfaces such as concrete or channelized to conserve water, control flooding, or provide passage for boats.

These practices are slowly changing. Permits issued for dam construction or reissued for dam operation are beginning to contain a provision for maintenance of minimum flow below the dam at a level sufficient to protect the natural system. In several cases, this has required reduction in the water allocated to other users. Many states have programs to restore natural systems by removing abandoned or obsolete dams, and other waterway obstructions, and to construct fish ladders to facilitate fish passage, recognizing this as a legitimate water use. Water allocation decisions in areas where water is a scarce resource are increasingly allocating a portion for aquatic life protection. Proposals to divert or use water are more closely scrutinized to avoid adverse impacts to aquatic life. Recognizing aquatic life protection as a legitimate water use will have a profound effect on future water allocation decisions.

Except for a few rare instances, water is owned by the states, not the federal government. Therefore, the U.S. Fish and Wildlife Service (USFWS) has adopted a policy of obtaining water rights. The objective is to obtain water supplies of adequate quantity and quality, and the legal rights to use that water from the states, for development, use, and management of USFWS lands and facilities, and for other congressionally authorized objectives, such as protection of endangered species and maintenance of in-stream flows.

Here are some examples of the evolving recognition of aquatic life protection as a legitimate water use:

- A February 26, 2003, news report issued by the National Marine Fisheries Service (NMFS) states that for the second consecutive year, federal agencies have made substantial progress in implementing the National Marine Fisheries Service's 2000 Biological Opinion (BiOp) for the Federal Columbia River Power System. Hundreds of millions of electric ratepayer and taxpayer dollars each year have been used on a performance-based approach aimed at achieving the highest biological results at the lowest cost. These efforts have resulted in the protection of hundreds of miles of habitat, and a 2002 record return of adult fish to the Columbia River.

- A 2002 EPA Region 9 Progress Report discusses the success of the salmon recovery project in Northern California's Butte Creek. The project, undertaken by CALFED Bay-Delta Program, has resulted in an average spring salmon spawning of about 6,000 fish—up from about 1,000 fish per spring from the 1960s through the 1990s. The removal of four small dams that had blocked salmon passage was funded by the local Western Canal Water District and Southern California's Metropolitan Water District.

- In March 2000 Thurston County Superior Court Judge Richard Hicks ruled that the Washington Department of Ecology had to implement a 1993 statute requiring metering of water use throughout the state. The implementation had to include both surface water and groundwater. The water metering statute was adopted as part of a larger salmon recovery package and was seen as an essential element in the wise management of the state's water resources for both people and salmon. Metering is viewed as the way to get the basic information about who is using the water and how much.

- In 1999 the Oregon Water Trust completed 51 water rights acquisitions throughout Oregon to improve fish habitat, water quality, and recreation by enhancing flow.

- A March 5, 2002, press release from the Environmental Protection Agency (EPA) announced that on February 28, 2002, EPA administrator Christie Whitman signed a proposed regulation that would reduce the number of fish, shellfish, and other aquatic life harmed by the effects of the withdrawal of cooling water from rivers, streams, lakes, reservoirs, estuaries, and oceans. The regulation would apply to already existing power-producing facilities that use large amounts of water to cool machinery, and would establish requirements based on the best available technology. Under the proposed regulation, waterbodies that

TABLE 2.7

Estimated water use trends, 1950–95

(The water-use data are in thousands of million gallons per day and are rounded to two significant figures for 1950-80, and to three significant figures for 1985-95; percentage change is calculated from unrounded numbers)

	Year										Percentage change
	1950[1]	1955[1]	1960[2]	1965[2]	1970[3]	1975[4]	1980[4]	1985[4]	1990[4]	1995[4]	1990-95
Population, in millions	150.7	164.0	179.3	193.8	205.9	216.4	229.6	242.4	252.3	267.1	+6
Offstream use:											
Total withdrawals	180	240	270	310	370	420	440[5]	399	408	402	-2
Public supply	14	17	21	24	27	29	34	36.5	38.5	40.2	+4
Rural domestic and livestock	3.6	3.6	3.6	4.0	4.5	4.9	5.6	7.79	7.89	8.89	+13
Irrigation	89	110	110	120	130	140	150	137	137	134	-2
Industrial:											
Thermoelectric power use	40	72	100	130	170	200	210	187	195	190	-3
Other industrial use	37	39	38	46	47	45	45	30.5	29.9	29.1	-3
Source of water:											
Ground:											
Fresh	34	47	50	60	68	82	83[5]	73.2	79.4	76.4	-4
Saline	([6])	.6	.4	.5	1	1	.9	.652	1.22	1.11	-9
Surface:											
Fresh	140	180	190	210	250	260	290	265	259	264	+2
Saline	10	18	31	43	53	69	71	59.6	68.2	59.7	-12
Reclaimed wastewater	([6])	.2	.6	.7	.5	.5	.5	.579	.750	1.02	+36
Consumptive use	([6])	([6])	61	77	87[7]	96[7]	100[7]	92.3[7]	94.0[7]	100[7]	+6
Instream use:											
Hydroelectric power	1,100	1,500	2,000	2,300	2,800	3,300	3,300	3,050	3,290	3,160	-4

[1] 48 States and District of Columbia.
[2] 50 States and District of Columbia.
[3] 50 States and District of Columbia, and Puerto Rico.
[4] 50 States and District of Columbia, Puerto Rico, and Virgin Islands.
[5] Revised.
[6] Data not available.
[7] Freshwater only.

SOURCE: Wayne R. Solley, Robert R. Pierce, and Howard A. Perlman, "Table 31. Trends of estimated water use in the United States, 1950-95," in *Estimated Use of Water in the United States in 1995*, U.S. Geological Survey, Denver, CO, 1998

are more sensitive or that have more extensive aquatic resources will receive increased protection. The regulation also would allow facilities to use restoration measures in addition to, or in lieu of, direct controls on the cooling water intake to protect aquatic life. Because several options are available in the proposal, the public is afforded the opportunity to comment on a range of potential scenarios for protection of fish, shellfish, and other aquatic life. The proposed regulation also partially fulfills EPA's obligation to comply with the terms of a court order brought against the EPA by a coalition of environmental groups and individuals.

- According to the July 16, 2002 Environmental Bulletin of the New Hampshire Department of Environmental Services, removal of the Winchester Dam on the Ashuelot River was slated to begin on July 22. The dam's removal was expected to restore approximately 15 miles of the Ashuelot River to free-flowing for the first time in 100 years. The project is a large part of a river restoration plan that would help bring back thousands of American shad, blueback herring, and

Atlantic salmon to the river. One of New Hampshire's major tributaries to the Connecticut River, the Ashuelot is historically important for migratory fish. David Deen of the Connecticut River Watershed Council (one of the project's financial backers), cites the Ashuelot River restoration project as a model of public-private partnerships that can benefit the Connecticut River and the communities located within its four-state watershed.

TRENDS IN WATER USE SINCE 1995

After continual increases in U.S. total water withdrawals since the USGS began reporting in 1950, water use peaked in 1980, then declined and has remained generally constant since. From 1990 to 1995 (the latest data available), a period that experienced a 6 percent increase in population, total off-stream water use declined 2 percent. Consumptive use, however, increased by 6 percent. While use in most categories declined, water use for public supply (4 percent) and livestock (13 percent) increased. In-stream use (hydroelectric power) also peaked in 1980

FIGURE 2.14

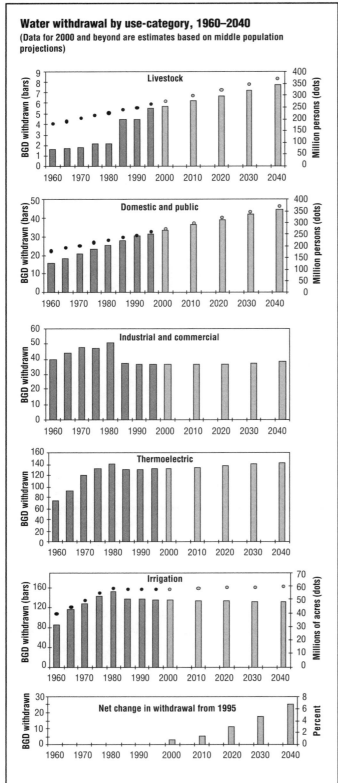

Water withdrawal by use-category, 1960–2040
(Data for 2000 and beyond are estimates based on middle population projections)

SOURCE: Adapted from Thomas C. Brown, "Figure 16.1. Withdrawal projections for the U.S. using middle population projections," in *Past and Future Freshwater Use in the United States,* RMRS-GTS-39, U.S. Department of Agriculture, Forest Service, Rocky Mountain Research Station, Fort Collins, CO, December 1999

and declined 4 percent between 1990 and 1995. Use of reclaimed water increased 36 percent from 1990 to 1995. (See Table 2.7.)

Experts believed the general increase in water use from 1950 to 1980 and the decrease from 1980 to 1995 could be attributed to several factors, including:

- Expansion of irrigation systems and increases in energy development from 1950 to 1980

- The development and increasing use of two irrigation methods that are more efficient in delivering water to crops than the traditional sprayer arms that project the water into the air, where much is lost to wind and evaporation: center-pivot irrigation systems and drip irrigation (the application of water directly to the roots of plants)

- Higher energy prices in the 1970s and a decrease in groundwater levels in some areas increased the cost of irrigation water

- A downturn in the farm economy in the 1980s, which reduced demands for irrigation water

- New industrial technologies requiring less water, improved efficiency, increased water recycling, higher energy prices, and changes in the law to reduce pollution

- Increased awareness by the general public of the need to conserve water and active conservation programs

WATER USE—THE FUTURE

Although water itself can neither be created nor destroyed, its usefulness and availability can. Both the quality and quantity of water resources need to be protected for the nation's present and future generations. Although present water use can be determined, total water needs for most uses are changing. Water use is dependent on prices, technology, customs, and regulations. Even though water-use data are good indicators of where and how the nation consumes water today, they are not necessarily good predictors of future water-use trends.

For much of the country, the era of free and easily developed water supplies has ended; in some areas, water use is approaching or has exceeded the available supply. In most areas, however, the nation is not running out of water.

Projections of freshwater usage by use-category are presented in a Forest Service publication, *Past and Future Freshwater Use in the United States* (Thomas C. Brown, December 1999). According to this publication, by the year 2040 freshwater usage in the United States will reach 364.1 billion gallons per day. That figure represents a 7 percent increase over the 1995 usage rate of 340.3 billion gallons per day.

By use-category the Forest Service projections anticipated increased freshwater usage for livestock, thermoelectric power generation, and domestic and public water services. (See Figure 2.14.) The quantity of water used by industry and for commercial applications and irrigation was anticipated to decline slightly over the period. Because water usage is closely linked to population size, one might assume that the population was expected to grow at a similar rate (7 percent) between 2000 and 2040. However, population growth was anticipated to be much higher (41 percent) over this period.

As a result, although the estimate for freshwater usage was for an increase of 7 percent, on a per-capita basis, projections of freshwater usage actually declined, from 1,254 gallons per day per person in 2000 to 992 in 2040.

Several factors are expected to contribute to the lower per capita freshwater usage rates. According to Thomas C. Brown, the two most prominent factors are:

1. Improved efficiencies projected for the municipal, industrial, and thermoelectric generating sectors

2. Reduced irrigation withdrawals

Increasing awareness among the traditional users of water and the general public of the finite nature of clean water supplies, particularly freshwater, has resulted in growing conservation efforts, and innovative approaches to water conservation and reclamation. Competition for use of this resource has increased in some areas, particularly between urban and rural users, especially in the western United States. More and more off-stream users are abandoning the traditional pattern of using water once and then discarding it. Increased emphasis on more efficient delivery systems, recapturing water after use and treating it for reuse if necessary, recharging of aquifers, and the need to maintain base flows in streams and rivers will affect future use.

Water Conservation

In an article titled "How We Can Do It" (*Scientific American,* February 2001), Diane Martindale and Peter H. Gleick described a massive water conservation project undertaken in New York. To prevent a pending water crisis in the early 1990s, New York City needed an extra 90 million gallons of water per day, about 7 percent of the city's total daily use. Faced with the need to raise $1 billion for a new pump station to bring additional water from the Hudson River, the city came up with a cheaper alternative: reduce the demand on the current supply. Using a three-year toilet rebate program, budgeted at $295 million for up to 1.5 million rebates, the city sought to replace about one-third of the existing toilets that used five gallons per flush with the water-saving models that did the same job with less than two gallons. By the end of the program in

1997, 1.33 million inefficient toilets in 110,000 buildings had been replaced with low-flow toilets. The result was about a 29 percent reduction in water use per building per year. The low-flow toilets were estimated to save about 70 million to 90 million gallons per day.

New York City saved 30 to 50 mgd (million gallons a day) of water from its leak detection program, 200 mgd from meter installation, and 4 mgd from home inspections.

Concurrently, New York City had a water audit program under which property owners who wanted to reduce water use to keep water bills down could request a free water efficiency survey from the company that oversaw the city's audit program. Inspectors checked for leaky plumbing, offered advice on retrofitting with water-efficient fixtures, and distributed low-flow showerheads and water-efficient faucet aerators. Low-flow showerheads use about one-half the water of the old units. Faucet aerators, which replace the screen in the faucet head and add air to the spray, can reduce the flow from four gallons per minute to one gallon per minute. The company made several hundred thousand of these inspections, saving an estimated 11 million gallons of water.

Overall, the program has shown that water conservation works. Per person water use in New York City dropped from 195 to 169 gallons per person per day between 1991 and 1999, although the city's population continued to grow.

A 2002 Environmental Protection Agency (EPA) report, *Cases in Water Conservation: How Efficiency Programs Help Water Utilities Save Water and Avoid Costs* discusses conservation methods and incentives adopted by New York City and 16 other North American locations. Each location was beset by problems such as a strain on the water supply, unaccounted-for water loss, and water shortages. One of the more significant conservation efforts took place in Gallitzin, Pennsylvania. In the mid-1990s, the Gallitzin Water Authority reported water losses exceeding 70 percent. After identifying the major problems (high water loss, recurring leaks, high overall operational costs, low pressure complaints, and unstable water entering the distribution system), the water authority developed accurate water production and distribution records using 7-day meter readings at its water plant and pump systems. Then it developed a system map to locate leaks. A leak detector located 95 percent of leaks in the water system. After repairs were made there was an 87 percent drop in unaccounted-for water, and savings of $5,000 on total chemical costs and $20,000 on total annual power costs from 1994 to 1998.

FIGURE 2.15

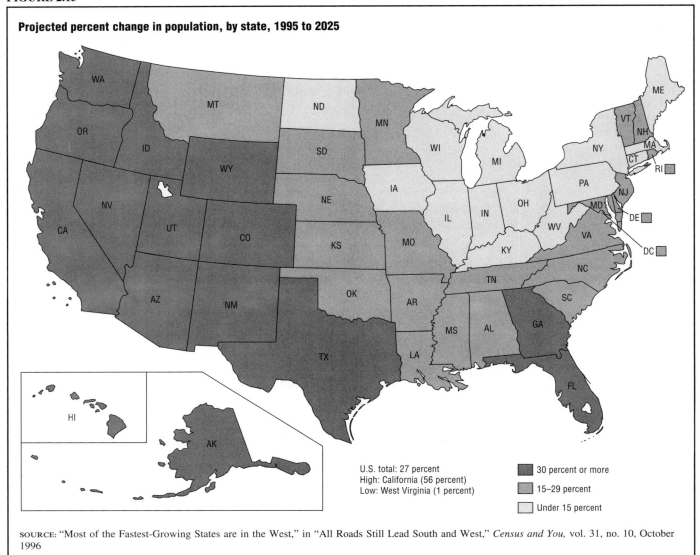

Projected percent change in population, by state, 1995 to 2025

U.S. total: 27 percent
High: California (56 percent)
Low: West Virginia (1 percent)

■ 30 percent or more
▨ 15–29 percent
□ Under 15 percent

SOURCE: "Most of the Fastest-Growing States are in the West," in "All Roads Still Lead South and West," *Census and You*, vol. 31, no. 10, October 1996

Water Reclamation

The Water Department in Tampa, Florida, has been working to maximize the yield from its water supply. The South Tampa Area Reclaimed (STAR) water project featured the use of high-quality reclaimed water from the Howard F. Curran Wastewater Treatment Facility to satisfy the demands of high volume irrigation users in South Tampa. Water would be made available through a water system that would be separate from the drinking water supply to prevent any possibility of cross contamination. The project began as a grassroots effort by Westshore residents concerned about future water supplies. Important conditions of the project were:

- Voluntary participation

- Only citizens who wanted reclaimed water would have to participate in the project

- User fees would make the project self-supporting

In the first four months of the project sign-up, 4,500 homeowners and businesses enrolled. Construction of Phase I was scheduled to begin in early 2002, and to be operational early in 2003, at a cost of $40 million. Recommended uses for reclaimed water are crop irrigation, lawn and landscape watering, washing cars, and general cleaning. The Water Department estimated that the 4,500 residents enrolled would save 1.7 million gallons of water a day.

The City of San Diego in California operates the San Pasqual water reclamation plant, located in the San Pasqual Valley near Escondido, California. The purpose of the plant, which can treat up to one million gallons of water per day, is to supply reclaimed water to the community. The wastewater received at the treatment facility is treated to the primary level when solids are removed. The screened primary effluent is then fed into as many as 24 aquatic treatment ponds where the wastewater is biologically stabilized. The ponds are stocked with water hyacinth, mosquito fish, crayfish, and other organisms to create an aquatic ecosystem that removes pollutants from wastewater. Water hyacinths grow quickly in the ponds. About 50 percent of the plants are harvested weekly from the ponds, dried for composting and sold for reuse as a soil amendment. After the water passes through the aquatic treatment ponds, it is clarified, filtered, and disinfected for use in irrigation and research.

Water Crisis Looming in the West?

Most of the fastest-growing states are in the West. (See Figure 2.15.) Census projections show that population growth in the United States for the first 25 years of the 21st century will be concentrated in states in the West and the South, especially in California, Texas, Florida, Georgia, Washington, Arizona, and North Carolina, which were expected to gain more than two million people each by 2025. California alone was expected to leap by 18 million over that period—by far the nation's biggest gain, which would boost that state from 12 to 15 percent of the nation's population. With the casino building boom in Las Vegas and the surrounding areas, Nevada became the fastest-growing state in the 1990s and Las Vegas the fastest-growing metropolitan area. This population growth was expected to put enormous pressure on natural resources, including water, and to force huge changes in water consumption practices and prices.

WHERE WATER IS POWER—INTERNATIONAL WATER WARS?

As usable water becomes rarer because of increasing population and the pollution of water supplies, it is expected to become a commodity like iron or oil. Some experts have predicted that at some point, water will be more expensive than oil. Of the 200 largest river systems in the world, 120 flow through two or more countries. All are potential objects of world political power struggles over this critical resource.

Three areas of the world are particularly short of water—Africa, the Middle East, and South Asia. Other dry areas include the southwest of North America, limited areas in South America, and large parts of Australia.

The Middle East countries, where rivers are the lifeblood of the arid region, are especially threatened as growing nations compete for a shrinking water supply. Freshwater has never come easily to the area. Rainfall occurs only in winter and drains quickly through the parched land. Most Middle East countries are joined by common aquifers—underground layers of porous rock that contain water. The United Nations has cautioned that future wars in the Middle East could be fought over water.

Since April 2001 tensions between Israel and Lebanon and Syria have been escalating over the Lebanese construction of a pumping station along the Hasbani River. The Hasbani accounts for 14 percent of the flow into the Sea of Galilee, which is Israel's primary freshwater reservoir. In 2001 Israel was undergoing a water crisis, and the sea was at its lowest level ever. Periodically tensions arise as droughts tighten supply in the area but as of the summer of 2003 the tensions between Israel, Syria, and Lebanon regarding Lebanon's pumping of water from the Hasbani River have always been handled diplomatically.

The oil-rich Middle Eastern nation of Kuwait has little water, but it has the money to secure it. To use seawater, Kuwait has constructed six large-scale, oil-powered desalination plants. Saudi Arabia, farther down the Arabian Peninsula, leads the world in desalination. As of August 2000, its 27 plants were producing 30 percent of all the desalinated water in the world. It is also a leader in the pumping of fossil water—water accumulated in an earlier geologic age. Mining nonrenewable water is like extracting oil—someday it will run out.

In April 2001 the Australian National Land and Water Resources Audit reported that one-third of the nation's groundwater reserves and 25 percent of its surface waters were being overused. With 14 million acres of farmland already affected by salinity, another 44 million acres were expected to be salt-affected by the middle of the 21st century. As fields are irrigated and trees are cleared along rivers, water tables rise, bringing salt naturally present in the soil to the surface. The salt contaminates the agricultural land. Australia's Murray-Darling River Basin, which produces most of the country's food and export crops, was and remains at great risk.

Water quality and water shortages are just two of the problems facing the world in the years to come. After the terrorist attacks in the United States on September 11, 2001, concerns about bioterrorism increased. On June 12, 2002, Congress passed the Public Health Security and Bioterrorism Act of 2002. Title IV of the Act (Drinking Water Security and Safety) mandates that every community water system that serves a population of more than 3,300 persons must

- Conduct a vulnerability assessment.

- Certify and submit a copy of the assessment to the EPA Administrator.

- Prepare or revise an emergency response plan that incorporates the results of the vulnerability assessment.

- Certify to the EPA Administrator, within six months of completing the vulnerability assessment, that the system has completed or updated their emergency response plan.

CHAPTER 3
SURFACE WATER—RIVERS AND LAKES

At any one time, over 97 percent of all the water in the hydrologic cycle is contained in Earth's oceans. By comparison, the world's rivers contain only 0.0001 percent of its water at any one time and its lakes 0.007 percent. Nonetheless, this tiny fraction of the total water supply has shaped the course of human development. Throughout human history, societies have depended on these water resources for food, drinking water, transportation, commerce, power, and recreation.

In the United States, water from streams, rivers, and lakes accounts for 77 percent of the total freshwater consumption; the rest comes from groundwater. Of the total available supply—about 1,380 billion gallons per day (bgd)—only about 8 percent, or 117 bgd, is actually used daily. Public utilities depend on surface water for about 65 percent of their water needs; industries consume surface water for 74 percent of their requirements; and crop irrigation uses surface water for about 60 percent of its water needs.

The withdrawal of surface water varies greatly by location. In New England, for example, where rainfall is plentiful, less than 1 percent of the annual renewable water supply is used. In contrast, almost the entire annual supply is consumed in the area of the arid Colorado River Basin and the Rio Grande Valley.

CHARACTERISTICS OF RIVERS AND LAKES
Rivers and Streams

The great rivers of the world have been very influential in human history. Settlement locations on rivers have thrived since earliest recorded history, with most of the world's great civilizations growing up along rivers. Flowing rivers provided water to drink, fish and shellfish to eat, dispersion and removal of wastes, and transport for goods. The bountiful supply of freshwater in flowing rivers is one of the primary reasons for the rapid growth of settlement, industry, and agriculture in the United States during colonial and modern times.

Rivers and streams, unlike lakes, consist of flowing water. Perennial rivers and streams flow continuously, year-round, although the volume may vary with runoff conditions. Intermittent, or ephemeral, rivers and streams stop flowing for some period, usually because of dry conditions. Both large and small rivers and streams are an important part of the hydrologic cycle.

Rivers receive water from rain and snowmelt drainage, springs from underground aquifers, and lakes. A large river is usually fed by tributaries (smaller rivers and streams), and so increases in size as it travels from its source, or origin. Its final destination may be an ocean, a lake, or sometimes open land, where the water simply evaporates. This phenomenon usually happens only with small rivers or streams.

As water flows down a river, it carries with it grains of soil, sand, and, where there is a very strong current, small stones and other debris. These objects are important in two ways. First, as they are pulled along by the river's current, they grind against the bottom and sides of the riverbank and slowly cut the riverbed deeper and deeper into the earth (for example, the Grand Canyon), thereby changing the contour of the land. Second, when the river reaches its destination (an ocean or lake), the flow is slowed and then stopped where the bodies of water meet, and the soil that has been carried along is deposited as silt (sediment).

Eventually, these deposits build into substantial accumulations. Over long periods, they form deltas, which often provide a rich base for agriculture. The great civilizations of Egypt, for example, depended on the delta of the Nile River for their food supply. On the other hand, silt can also be a nuisance, filling lakes and harbors, and smothering aquatic life. Many ports and harbors in the United

TABLE 3.1

Largest rivers in the United States

River	Location at mouth	Average volume at mouth (cfs)	Length [a] (mi.)
Mississippi	LA	593,000	2,340
St. Lawrence	Canada	348,000	1,900
Ohio	IL, KY	281,000	1,310
Columbia	WA	265,000	1,240
Yukon	AK	225,000	1,980
Missouri	MO	76,200	2,540
Tennessee	KY	68,000	886
Mobile	AL	67,200	774
Kuskoswim	AK	67,000	724
Copper	AK	59,000	286
Atchafalaya	LA	58,000	140 [b]
Snake	WA	56,900	1,040
Stikine	AK	56,000	379
Red	LA	56,000	1,290
Susitna	AK	51,000	313
Tanana	AK	41,000	659
Arkansas	AR	41,000	1,460
Susquehanna	MD	38,200	447
Willamette	OR	37,400	309
Nushagak	AK	36,000	285

cfs = cubic feet per second

[a] Including headwaters and sections in Canada.

[b] Below Mississippi diversion, without headwaters.

SOURCE: "Largest rivers in the United States," in *Water Fact Sheet: Largest Rivers in the United States*, U.S. Geological Survey, Reston, VA, 1990

States must be dredged regularly to remove deposits that would otherwise obstruct navigation.

The two longest rivers in the world are the Nile (4,157 miles) and the Amazon (3,915 miles). The Mississippi-Missouri river system is the third longest in the world. The Mississippi River has a watershed of 1,150,000 square miles, or about 40 percent of the total land area of the lower 48 states. A watershed, or drainage area, is the land from which a river receives runoff water from rainfall or snowmelt. The Mississippi River discharges water into the Gulf of Mexico at an average rate of 620,000 cubic feet per second. This amounts to 133 cubic miles per year, or approximately 34 percent of the total discharge from all the rivers in the United States. (A cubic mile contains about one billion gallons of water.)

By comparison, the Columbia River discharges less than 75 cubic miles of water per year. The Colorado River, which carved the Grand Canyon, discharges only about 5 cubic miles each year. Table 3.1 shows the largest rivers in the United States.

Lakes

Unlike rivers and streams, lakes and ponds are depressions in the earth that hold water for extended periods of time. Reservoirs are man-made lakes that are generally used for recreation or to provide drinking water. Some ponds are also man-made, for purposes including livestock watering, fire control, stormwater management, duck and fish habitat, and recreation. The source of the water in lakes, reservoirs, and ponds may be rivers and streams, groundwater, rainfall, or melting-snow runoff, or any combination thereof. Any of these sources may carry contaminants. Because water exits from these water bodies at a slow rate, pollutants become trapped. For this reason, lakes, ponds, and reservoirs are particularly vulnerable to the deposit of pollutants from the air and to pollution from human activity.

Many of the world's lake beds were formed during the Ice Age, when advancing and retreating glaciers gouged holes in the soft bedrock and spread dirt and debris in uneven patterns. Some lakes fill the craters of extinct volcanoes, and others have formed in the shallow basins of ocean bottoms uplifted by geological activity to become part of Earth's solid surface.

As soon as a lake or pond is formed, it is destined to die. "Death" occurs over a long time, particularly in the case of large lakes. Soil and debris carried by in-flowing rivers and streams slowly build up the basin floor. At the same time, water is removed by out-flowing rivers and streams, whose channels become ever wider and deeper, allowing them to carry more water away. Even lakes that have no river inlets or outlets eventually fill with soil eroded from the surrounding land.

FRESHWATER VERSUS SALTWATER. The large freshwater lakes of the world contain nearly 30,000 cubic miles of water and cover a combined surface area of about 330,000 square miles. About 26 percent of the world's freshwater stored in lakes is found in North America. By surface area, Lake Superior, located on the U.S.–Canada border, is the largest freshwater lake in the world. Lake Baikal, however, in Asiatic Russia, is so deep that it could hold all the water in Lake Superior and the other four Great Lakes, and an additional 300 cubic miles of water. Lake Superior has over two-and-a-half times the surface area (26,418 square miles) of Lake Baikal, but at maximum depth Lake Baikal is over four times deeper (5,715 feet).

The large lakes of Africa contain nearly 29 percent of the water of all freshwater lakes in the world, followed by North America, with 26 percent, and Asia, with 21 percent (almost all of which is in Lake Baikal). Large lakes in Europe, South America, and Australia account for only 2 percent of the world's freshwater.

The saline (saltwater) lakes of the world contain almost as much water as freshwater lakes (25,000 cubic miles) and cover almost as many square miles (270,000). Of that water, however, 75 percent is in the Caspian Sea, which borders Russia and Iran (19,240 cubic miles), and most of the remainder is in lakes in Asia. North America's

FIGURE 3.1

	Levels of summary use support		
Symbol	Use support level	Water quality condition	Definition
[fish symbol]	Fully supporting all uses	Good	Water quality meets designated use criteria.
[plant symbol]	Threatened for one or more uses	Good	Water quality supports beneficial uses now but may not in the future unless action is taken.
[organism symbol]	Impaired for one or more uses	Impaired	Water quality fails to meet designated use criteria at times.
[dead fish symbol]	Not attainable	—	The state, tribe, or other jurisdiction has performed a use-attainability analysis and demonstrated that use support is not attainable due to one of six biological, chemical, physical, or economic/social conditions specified in the *Code of Federal Regulations*.

SOURCE: "Levels of summary use support," in *National Water Quality Inventory: 1996 Report to Congress*, EPA-841-F-00-006, U.S. Environmental Protection Agency, Washington, DC, 1998

shallow Great Salt Lake is comparatively insignificant, with 7 cubic miles of water.

THE NEED FOR POLLUTION CONTROL

People have always congregated on the shores of lakes and rivers. They established permanent homes, then towns, cities, and industries, benefiting from the many advantages of nearby water sources. One of these advantages has been that lakes or rivers were convenient places to dispose of wastes. As technological societies developed, the amount of wastes became enormous. Frequently, the wastes contained synthetic and toxic materials that could not be assimilated by the waters' ecosystems. Millions of tons of sewage, pesticides, chemicals, and garbage were dumped into waterways worldwide until there were few that were not contaminated to some extent. Some were—and some still are—contaminated to the point of ecological "death," unable to sustain a balanced aquatic-life system.

Clean Water Act

On October 18, 2002, President George W. Bush proclaimed the beginning of the Year of Clean Water in commemoration of the 30th anniversary of the signing of the Clean Water Act. The Federal Water Pollution Control Act (PL 92-500) is the full name of the environmental law that has come to be known more commonly as the Clean Water Act (CWA).

The CWA was enacted by Congress in 1972 in response to growing public concern over the nation's polluted waters. The problem of environmental pollution was thrust into the public consciousness when the Cuyahoga River in Cleveland, Ohio, burst into flames on June 22, 1969, the result of oil and debris that had accumulated on the river's surface.

The objective of the CWA was to "restore and maintain the chemical, physical, and biological integrity of the Nation's waters." The law is jointly enforced by the Environmental Protection Agency (EPA) and the U.S. Army Corps of Engineers.

The act requires that, where attainable, water quality be such that it "provides for the protection and propagation of fish, shellfish, and wildlife and provides for recreation in and on the water." This requirement is referred to as the act's "fishable/swimmable" goal. Many people credit the Clean Water Act with reversing, in a single generation, what had been a decline in the health of the nation's water since the mid-19th century.

Water-quality standards are the driving force of the CWA. A water-quality standard has three components:

- Designated uses—the CWA envisions that all waters, at a minimum, be able to be used for recreation and the protection and propagation of aquatic life (fish and shellfish, and the plants, insects, and other organisms that are required to support them). Examples of additional uses are drinking water and water where the fish are safe to eat. Water bodies frequently have more than one designated use.

- Criteria—the numerical or narrative limits assigned to protect each use. Examples are chemical-specific levels (numerical) that protect humans or fish from exposure to levels that may cause harm, or descriptions (narrative) of the best-possible biological condition of aquatic communities.

- Antidegradation policy—a statement of intent to prevent waters that meet their standards from deteriorating from their current condition.

Each state is required under the CWA to adopt water-quality standards for each of its water bodies. The EPA is required to approve each state's standards. Each state must specifically designate a use for every surface-water body in the state. The state then establishes water-quality numeric and narrative criteria to protect each use. More than one designated use is frequently assigned to a water body. Most water bodies are designated for recreation, drinking-water use, and protection of aquatic life. For water bodies with more than one designated use, the states consolidate the individual use support information into a summary use. Figure 3.1 shows the summary uses.

FIGURE 3.2

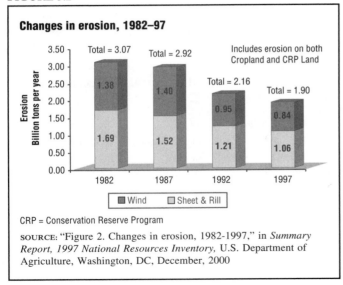

Changes in erosion, 1982–97

CRP = Conservation Reserve Program

SOURCE: "Figure 2. Changes in erosion, 1982-1997," in *Summary Report, 1997 National Resources Inventory,* U.S. Department of Agriculture, Washington, DC, December, 2000

The states collect data and other information that allow them to assess whether the quality of their water meets the designated uses expressed in the water-quality standards that each state sets. Under section 305(b) of the CWA, the states are required to submit their assessments of their water quality to the EPA every two years. The EPA is required to summarize this information in a biennial report. As of the summer of 2003, the most recent EPA report to have been published was the *2000 National Water Quality Inventory.*

The CWA also established the National Pollutant Discharge Elimination System (NPDES). This program requires anyone who discharges pollutants to get a permit. Congress intended that, after the EPA had established regulations for obtaining a NPDES permit, each state would be granted "primacy." Primacy means that the states would have the primary responsibility for issuing permits and enforcing the requirements of the NPDES program. To be given primacy by the EPA, a state must adopt NPDES regulations and conduct monitoring and enforcement programs at least as stringent as those established by the EPA.

Agriculture Takes Up the Challenge

According to the U.S. Census Bureau's most recent report on the subject *1997 Census of Agriculture,* 41 percent of the continental United States (about 9 million acres) is used for agricultural production. Cropland accounts for 46 percent of the acreage, while pasture and rangeland make up another 43 percent. Agricultural land use is recognized in many jurisdictions and localities throughout the United States as the most desirable land use for economic, environmental, and social reasons. At the same time, the public and the agricultural community recognize that agricultural practices are a source of nonpoint pollution nationwide.

This situation presents a challenge to water-quality management efforts.

The growing national concern over water-quality degradation has also permeated the agricultural community. There has been a steady increase in the use of best management practices and implementation of farm water-quality plans to protect wetlands and water bodies. The success of this effort can be seen in the decrease since 1982 in soil erosion reported in the U.S. Department of Agriculture's (USDA) *National Resources Inventory—2001 Annual NRI.* (See Figure 3.2.) (Note that the amount of soil erosion remained at a steady level from 1997 to 2001.) The USDA, together with state and local agencies, is providing technical assistance and financial incentives through numerous programs to help farmers balance good stewardship of natural resources with market demands. Technical assistance through these programs has had success in getting farmers to voluntarily adopt more environmentally sensitive practices.

SECTION 319 GRANTS. Grant money for use in supporting environmental projects is made available under the Clean Water Act. These funds have been instrumental in the development of many programs that have been successful in restoring and repairing impaired watersheds across the nation. In 1994 the EPA published the first in a series of reports highlighting successful programs developed under section 319 of the CWA. The most recent report is *Section 319 Success Stories Volume III: The Successful Implementation of the Clean Water Act's Section 319 Nonpoint Source Pollution Program,* which was published in February 2002. One of the many stories highlighted in the publication reports on the Little Rabbit River Watershed Project.

This project was designed to improve the water quality in the Little Rabbit River Watershed, located in southwest Michigan. The dominant land use in the watershed is agriculture. The primary means identified for accomplishing the goal were to reduce the amount of sediment and nutrients entering the surface water. A section 319 CWA watershed grant in the amount of $380,936 was awarded to the Allegan Conservation District for use in implementing the Little Rabbit River Watershed Project.

As reported in the EPA's *Section 319 Success Stories Volume III,* the success of this project was measurable within the first three years. A total of 19,852 tons of sediment were prevented from entering the Little Rabbit River during the first three years of the project. Nutrients entering the system were also reduced. A total of 19,706 pounds of phosphorus and 39,321 pounds of nitrogen were kept from entering the watershed due to the project.

The implementation of best management practices (BMPs) by landowners in the area was credited for the

FIGURE 3.3

Percentage of waters assessed for the 2000 National Water Quality Inventory, by type of water

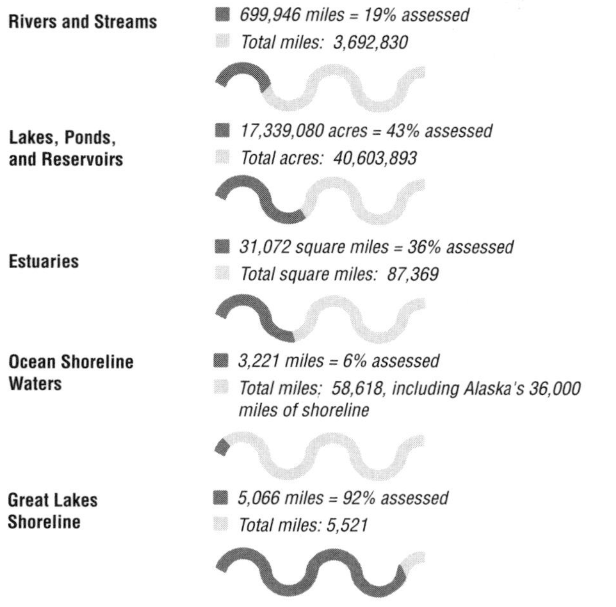

Rivers and Streams

■ 699,946 miles = 19% assessed
▨ Total miles: 3,692,830

Lakes, Ponds, and Reservoirs

■ 17,339,080 acres = 43% assessed
▨ Total acres: 40,603,893

Estuaries

■ 31,072 square miles = 36% assessed
▨ Total square miles: 87,369

Ocean Shoreline Waters

■ 3,221 miles = 6% assessed
▨ Total miles: 58,618, including Alaska's 36,000 miles of shoreline

Great Lakes Shoreline

■ 5,066 miles = 92% assessed
▨ Total miles: 5,521

SOURCE: Adapted from "Figure 1-2. Percentage of Water Assessed for the 1998 Report," in *National Water Quality Inventory: 1998 Report to Congress,* EPA-841-F-00-006, and updated material in *2000 National Water Quality Inventory,* EPA-841-R-02-001, U.S. Environmental Protection Agency, Washington, DC, August 2002

pollution abatement success. The project required a partnership between government agencies, local governing bodies, and landowners in the area. Together these stakeholders took the following actions, among others, that lead to the success of the Little Rabbit River Watershed Project.

- Installed 18 acres of filter strips

- Restored more than 9 acres of wetlands

- Installed four stream crossings and a watering facility

- Stabilized 190 linear feet of streambank

- Built 5 animal waste storage facilities

- Implemented mulch-till and no-till practices on 3,000 acres

Although the section 319 portion of the project was completed in 2000, water quality improvements and protection efforts continue in the area. Awareness of water quality issues in the community increased during the project and the BMPs put into place during the project itself continue to reduce the entry of silt and nutrients into the watershed.

ASSESSING WATER QUALITY

Defining water quality is a little like trying to determine "how clean is clean?" Currently, the best measure is the degree to which a water body is capable of supporting its designated uses.

State 305(b) Reports

Because of funding limitations, most states assess only a portion of their total water resources during each CWA-required two-year reporting cycle. The goal is to rotate the sites that are assessed in each cycle so that over a five-year period all waters are assessed. In the most recent EPA water quality inventory, *2000 National Water Quality Inventory,* the states evaluated about 19 percent of the nation's river and stream miles and about 43 percent of lake, pond, and reservoir acres. (See Figure 3.3.)

The states use chemical and biological monitoring results and other types of data, such as water-quality models, surveys of fisheries, and information from citizens, to evaluate their water quality. The data are compared with the water-quality criteria adopted to protect each use designated for a particular water body, and water bodies are rated as to how they meet their uses. Every two years, the results of these evaluations are reported to the EPA in each state's 305(b) report.

Because of sparse reporting by the states and differences in criteria and measurement techniques between states, a completely accurate assessment of the quality of the nation's surface waters is not yet possible. The reports, however, are valuable as a measure of estimated overall water quality and as a means of identifying the major sources and causes of pollution.

States use two categories of data to assess water quality. The first and best category is monitored data. Monitored data are field measurements of biological, habitat, toxicity, physical, and chemical conditions in water, sediment, and fish tissue. These data are gathered at least every five years. The second category, used to fill information gaps, is evaluated data. Evaluated data include field measurements more than five years old and estimates that are generated using land-use and pollution-source information, predictive models, and surveys of fish and game. These data can provide an indicator of water quality, but because they vary in quality and confidence, their use is limited.

Index of Watershed Indicators

Reporting the health of the nation's aquatic resources is more difficult than reporting water quality. To meet this challenge, the EPA, the states, and their many public and private partners have developed the Index of Watershed Indicators (IWI). IWI looks at a variety of "indicators" that point to whether rivers, lakes, streams, wetlands, and coastal areas are "well" or "ailing," and whether the

FIGURE 3.4

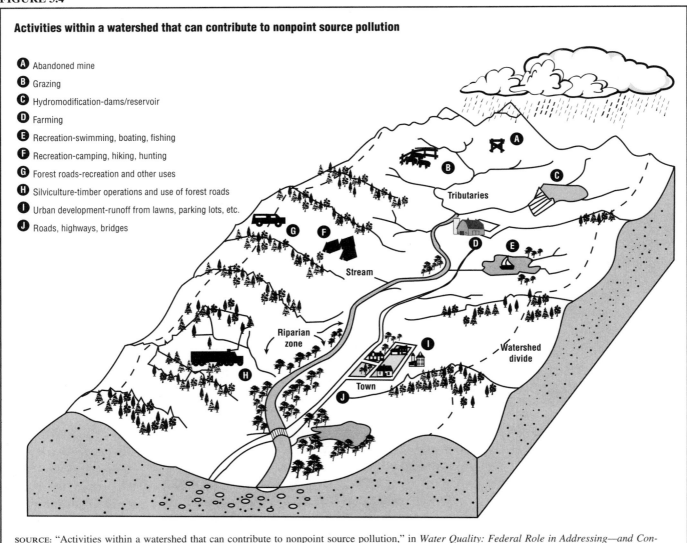

Activities within a watershed that can contribute to nonpoint source pollution

- **A** Abandoned mine
- **B** Grazing
- **C** Hydromodification-dams/reservoir
- **D** Farming
- **E** Recreation-swimming, boating, fishing
- **F** Recreation-camping, hiking, hunting
- **G** Forest roads-recreation and other uses
- **H** Silviculture-timber operations and use of forest roads
- **I** Urban development-runoff from lawns, parking lots, etc.
- **J** Roads, highways, bridges

Tributaries

Stream

Riparian zone

Watershed divide

Town

SOURCE: "Activities within a watershed that can contribute to nonpoint source pollution," in *Water Quality: Federal Role in Addressing—and Contributing to—Nonpoint Source Pollution,* U.S. General Accounting Office, Washington, DC, 1999

activities taking place on surrounding lands are placing them at risk. The objective is to establish a national baseline on the condition and vulnerability of aquatic resources—a baseline that can be used, over time, to help measure progress toward the goal that all watersheds be healthy and productive places. In a 2002 report by the EPA, called *Index of Watershed Indicators: An Overview,* the following watershed conditions were reported:

- 15 percent of the nation's watersheds had relatively good water quality.

- 36 percent had moderate problems.

- 22 percent of the watersheds had more serious water-quality problems.

- 27 percent did not have enough information to be characterized.

The report also states that 1 in 15 watersheds nationally was highly vulnerable to further degradation.

Point and Nonpoint Sources of Pollution

The designated use of a water body is "impaired" when the amount of pollutant in that water body reaches the level where the water cannot meet the water-quality criteria for its designated use or uses. This does not necessarily mean that the water body is badly degraded. For example, a stream may exceed the water-quality criteria for temperature established to protect a cold-water fish such as trout and still support an active trout fishery. The "impairment" may be only slightly in excess of water-quality criteria. A water body can be impaired for one designated use and still fully support other designated uses. For example, a lake may have a thriving recreational fishery but be unsafe for swimming because of high bacteria levels in the

FIGURE 3.5

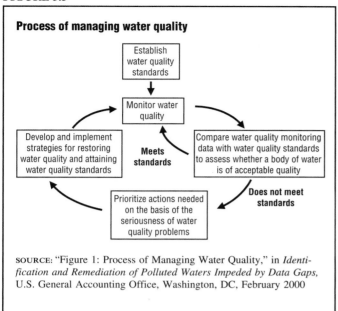

Process of managing water quality

Establish water quality standards

Monitor water quality

Develop and implement strategies for restoring water quality and attaining water quality standards

Meets standards

Compare water quality monitoring data with water quality standards to assess whether a body of water is of acceptable quality

Does not meet standards

Prioritize actions needed on the basis of the seriousness of water quality problems

SOURCE: "Figure 1: Process of Managing Water Quality," in *Identification and Remediation of Polluted Waters Impeded by Data Gaps*, U.S. General Accounting Office, Washington, DC, February 2000

water, thereby meeting the "fishable" designation but not the "swimmable" designation. In other cases, impairment may be so bad that one or more uses are lost. An example would be a lake that has been choked by noxious weeds from excessive nutrients, resulting in fishkills and severely reduced fish populations, leading to the loss of an active recreational fishery.

Where impaired conditions are deemed irreversible, the water quality is determined to be unattainable. To reach this determination, the states perform what is called a use-attainability analysis to show that one or more designated uses cannot be supported because of biological, physical, chemical, or economic/social conditions. Examples of conditions that might result in a determination that a use is not attainable include low flow, naturally occurring high levels of pollutants, or the presence of dams or other hydrologic modifications that permanently alter water body characteristics.

Pollutants enter a body of water in any number of ways. Pollutant sources can be divided into two major types: point and nonpoint. Point sources are those that disperse pollutants from a specific source or area, such as a wastewater treatment plant discharge. Pollutants that are commonly discharged from point sources include bacteria, toxic and nontoxic chemicals, nutrients, and heavy metals from industrial plants.

Nonpoint sources are those that are spread out over a large area and have no specific outlet or discharge point (for example, agricultural and urban runoff; runoff from mining and construction sites; and accidental spills, as when a train or truck carrying toxic chemicals derails or overturns, releasing its contents). Nonpoint source

pollutants can include bacteria from cat and dog wastes, pesticides, fertilizers, toxic chemicals, and salts from road construction. (Figure 3.4 shows activities that can contribute to nonpoint pollution.)

Managing Water Quality

Once states have determined that a specific water body does not meet the water-quality criteria needed to protect its designated uses, they begin the process of determining what actions are necessary to restore water quality. (See Figure 3.5.) The first step is to identify the total maximum daily load (TMDL) for each pollutant. The TMDL is the maximum amount of a pollutant that a water body can receive on a periodic basis and still support its intended uses. TMDLs are generally developed by identifying the pollutants and the source of the pollutants causing a water-quality problem, and determining how much the pollutants need to be reduced in order to enable the water body to meet the water-quality standards. Reductions in pollutants are then achieved through limits in discharge permits, requirements for best management practices, and other regulatory or voluntary practices.

WATER QUALITY OF THE NATION'S RIVERS AND STREAMS

The EPA's *2000 National Water Quality Inventory* showed that 61 percent of the rivers and streams evaluated by the states were found to be fully supporting their designated uses. However, an estimated 8 percent of those same waters were identified as threatened waters that might become impaired if pollution control action was not taken. Of the rivers and streams that were assessed, 39 percent were impaired for one or more uses.

Causes of Pollution in Rivers and Streams

The states reported that pathogens (bacteria), siltation (the smothering of river and stream beds by sediment, usually from soil erosion), habitat alterations, and oxygen-depleting substances were the four most common causes of pollution in our nation's rivers and streams. (See Figure 3.6.) In 2000 pathogens from point and nonpoint sources affected about 34 percent of the all polluted river miles. Silt was the second-most common cause of pollution in the assessed rivers and streams, affecting 31 percent of impaired rivers and streams. Habitat alterations were listed as the cause for impairment to 8 percent of the assessed river and stream miles, or 22 percent of the impaired miles. Oxygen-depleting substances were responsible for approximately 20 percent of the polluted miles. (Note that these percentages total more than 100 percent, as pollution in some areas came from more than one source.)

PATHOGENS. In the *2000 National Water Quality Inventory,* pathogens (bacteria) were identified as the leading cause of water-quality impairment, responsible for

FIGURE 3.6

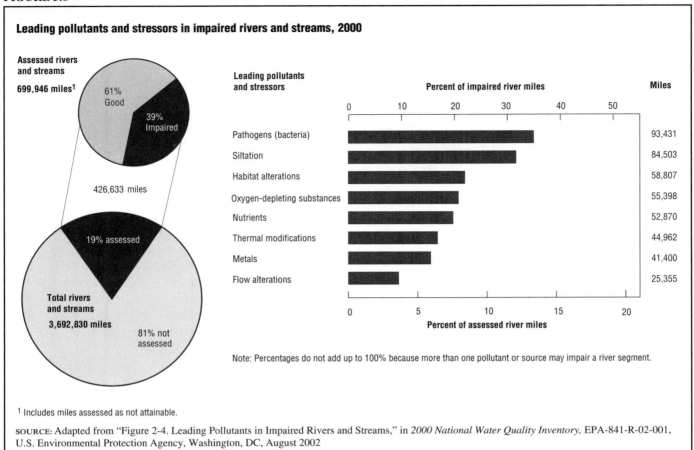

Leading pollutants and stressors in impaired rivers and streams, 2000

Note: Percentages do not add up to 100% because more than one pollutant or source may impair a river segment.

[1] Includes miles assessed as not attainable.

SOURCE: Adapted from "Figure 2-4. Leading Pollutants in Impaired Rivers and Streams," in *2000 National Water Quality Inventory,* EPA-841-R-02-001, U.S. Environmental Protection Agency, Washington, DC, August 2002

polluting 93,431 river and stream miles. Bacteria provide evidence of possible fecal contamination that may cause illness. States use bacterial indicators to determine if rivers are safe for drinking or swimming. The most common sources of bacteria are urban runoff, inadequately treated human sewage, and runoff from pastures and feedlots. Figure 1.7 in Chapter 1 shows the pathways of bacteria to surface waters.

SILTATION. Silt was the second most important source of pollutants to rivers and streams. In an earlier report (*National Water Quality Inventory—1998 Report to Congress*), silt had ranked as the top cause of pollution entering the waterways of the nation. In the more recent report, siltation had dropped to second place. Silt, composed of tiny soil particles, impaired 12 percent of the assessed rivers and streams, which is 31 percent of the impaired river and stream miles reported in the 2000 EPA *Inventory.* (See Figure 3.6.)

Silt alters aquatic habitats, suffocates bottom-dwelling organisms and fish eggs, interferes with light transmission to underwater plants, and clogs the gills of fish. The habitat of aquatic insects that live in the spaces between pebbles and rocks is destroyed when these spaces are filled with

silt. Loss of aquatic organisms can radically affect the health of certain fish species and other wildlife that eat them. (See Figure 3.7.) Excessive silt can also interfere with recreational use and drinking-water treatment. The primary sources of silt are agriculture, urban runoff, forestry, logging, and construction.

OXYGEN-DEPLETING SUBSTANCES. Oxygen is vital for the animal life in waterways. Lack of oxygen occurs as a result of the oxygen-consuming processes by which organic matter decays. The risk of oxygen depletion is therefore greatest in waters affected by high discharge of organic matter, and also where substantial production of algae and other plants occur.

Oxygen-depleting substances were the third leading pollutant type listed in the *2000 National Water Quality Inventory* affecting 55,398 impaired river miles. The third item listed in Figure 3.6 is "habitat alterations"; however this is a stressor to the system and not a pollutant as are the three listed above. Modifications or alterations to the habitat are discussed in the next section.

Sources of Pollution in Rivers and Streams

The EPA's *2000 National Water Quality Inventory* listed pathogens, siltation, and oxygen-depleting substances

FIGURE 3.7

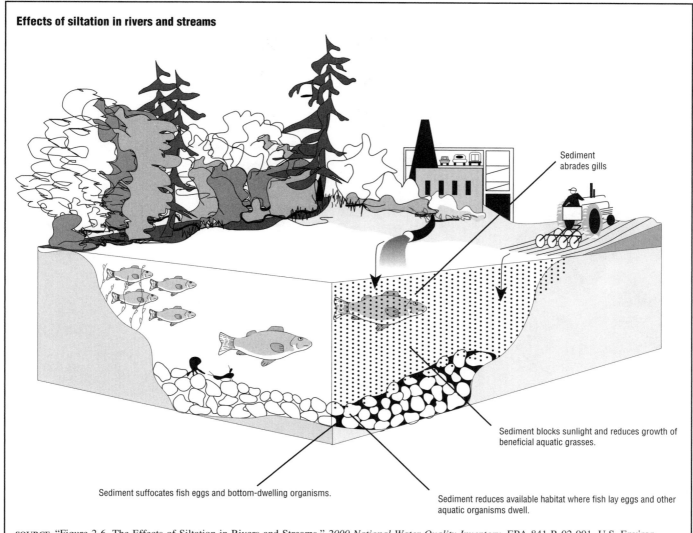

Effects of siltation in rivers and streams

Sediment abrades gills

Sediment blocks sunlight and reduces growth of beneficial aquatic grasses.

Sediment suffocates fish eggs and bottom-dwelling organisms.

Sediment reduces available habitat where fish lay eggs and other aquatic organisms dwell.

SOURCE: "Figure 2-6. The Effects of Siltation in Rivers and Streams," *2000 National Water Quality Inventory,* EPA-841-R-02-001, U.S. Environmental Protection Agency, Washington, DC, August 2002

as the leading pollutants impairing the nation's waterways; the three leading sources of these pollutants were agriculture, hydrologic modifications, and habitat modifications. (See Figure 3.8.)

AGRICULTURE. Agriculture was the leading source of pollution, responsible for about 48 percent of the reported water-quality problems in impaired rivers and streams. (See Figure 3.8.) The term "agriculture" captures a number of activities, from large-scale farming to egg production, landscape plant nurseries, and fish farming. The agricultural uses that are most frequently responsible for contributing pollutants to water were:

• Nonirrigated crop production (rain is the sole water source).

• Irrigated crop production.

• Range grazing.

• Pasture grazing (land where a specific crop is grown to feed animals either by grazing animals among the crops or harvesting the crops).

• Animal-feeding operations.

The EPA's 2000 report shows that the three agricultural activities that had the most degrading impact on rivers and streams together were responsible for 53.7 percent of the impaired river and stream miles reported; nonirrigated crop production (26,830 miles); animal feeding operations (24,616 miles), and irrigated crop production (17,667 miles).

HYDROLOGIC MODIFICATIONS. Hydrologic modifications were responsible for 20 percent of the impaired miles of rivers and streams (53,850 miles). These modifications include such things as flow regulation, channelization, dredging, and the construction of dams. Modifications

FIGURE 3.8

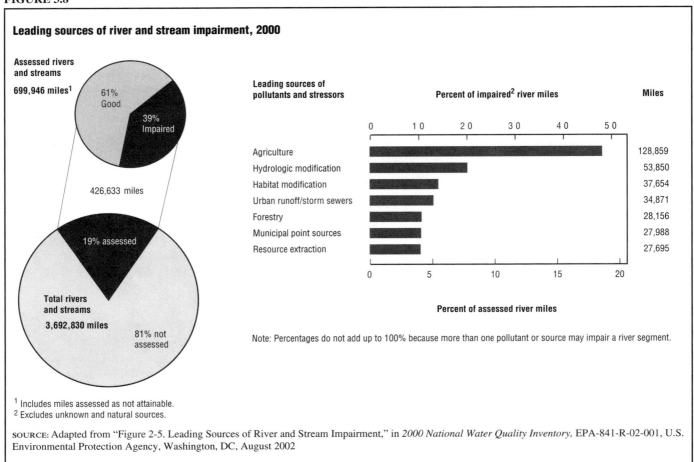

Leading sources of river and stream impairment, 2000

Assessed rivers and streams

699,946 miles[1]

61% Good

39% Impaired

426,633 miles

19% assessed

Total rivers and streams

3,692,830 miles

81% not assessed

Leading sources of pollutants and stressors — Percent of impaired[2] river miles — Miles

Source	Miles
Agriculture	128,859
Hydrologic modification	53,850
Habitat modification	37,654
Urban runoff/storm sewers	34,871
Forestry	28,156
Municipal point sources	27,988
Resource extraction	27,695

Percent of assessed river miles

Note: Percentages do not add up to 100% because more than one pollutant or source may impair a river segment.

[1] Includes miles assessed as not attainable.
[2] Excludes unknown and natural sources.

SOURCE: Adapted from "Figure 2-5. Leading Sources of River and Stream Impairment," in *2000 National Water Quality Inventory,* EPA-841-R-02-001, U.S. Environmental Protection Agency, Washington, DC, August 2002

of these kinds alter the river's habitat and in so doing can cause them to become far less suitable for aquatic life.

HABITAT MODIFICATIONS. The modification of river and stream habitats can have a similar and equally destabilizing impact on aquatic life. The EPA report defines habitat modifications as all those changes to habitat that do not directly affect water flow. That would include such things as the removal of woody debris, logging activities, and/or land-clearing practices. Habitat modifications were ranked third in terms of sources of pollutants impairing rivers and streams in the *2000 National Water Quality Inventory.* A reported 37,654 river and stream miles were degraded due to habitat modifications, accounting for 14 percent of the impaired river and stream miles.

Municipal Sewerage Systems

Large cities, suburban areas, and many small towns are served by municipal sewerage systems. Wastewater treatment facilities vary in capacity from treating as little as 10,000 gallons per day (gpd) to 400 million gpd. The degree of treatment provided to the sewage also varies and may be primary, secondary, or tertiary treatment. Primary sewage treatment uses screens to remove debris, a grit chamber to settle out grit and sand, and solids settling. Following this process, the liquid waste is generally disinfected with chlorine and discharged to a water body. The settled solids are transported to a sludge digester for microbial digestion and conversion to biosolids. Primary treatment achieves a 40–60 percent reduction in bacteria and total solids (nutrients and oxygen-demanding substances).

Secondary sewage treatment uses primary treatment, adds another settling step, and aerates the effluent to accelerate microbial digestion, resulting in a 70–90 percent reduction in bacteria and suspended solids. The liquid waste is disinfected before discharge. Tertiary treatment removes nutrients and additional suspended solids by adding chemical or microbial treatments, or filtration to remove additional suspended solids and reduce nutrients. Sometimes wetlands are also used to provide additional treatment. The effluents are generally disinfected before discharge. Tertiary treatment is generally used in nutrient reduction strategies to reduce algae blooms, trophic levels, and hypoxia (oxygen deficiency). The success of each category of wastewater treatment is directly dependent on whether the treatment plant is properly sized for the volume of wastes handled, and the treatment method selected. If the plant is overloaded, treatment success declines. Since 1974 much progress has been made in upgrading sewage treatment plants, but much remains to be done.

Sewage sludge is the solid, semisolid, or liquid untreated residue generated during the treatment of domestic sewage in a treatment facility. The method of biosolids disposal depends on the level of treatment the sludge receives, and its contaminants. The most common methods are land application as fertilizer or soil conditioner, transport to landfills, incineration, and composting for sale as a lawn and garden additive. Overboard disposal of sludge in oceans and estuaries is no longer permitted. When properly treated and processed, sewage sludge becomes biosolids, a nutrient-rich material that can be safely recycled and applied as fertilizer. Biosolids production is strictly controlled by federal and state regulations.

Many older towns and cities have combined sewer systems; that is, sewer systems that transport sewage in dry weather and sewage and rainwater in wet weather. Combined sewers during heavy rainfall events can quickly overload a wastewater treatment plant, resulting in the need to "bypass" or divert portions of the combined flow overboard. Bypass releases a mixture of rainwater, raw sewage, oil, and gasoline from runoff, and fertilizers and pesticides from lawns and gardens, into waterways.

Combined sewer overflows are one of the major sources of bacteria, nutrients, and silt in waterways. The solution to combined sewer overflow is separation of the sewer and stormwater system. This is prohibitively expensive, as it frequently requires tearing up urban streets and, in some cases, buildings to replace the existing combined sewer with separate lines for sewage and stormwater runoff. Alternatives include expanding the wastewater treatment plant treatment capacity, building separate treatment facilities for the stormwater flow, capturing and storing stormwater flow and feeding it into the treatment plant during periods of low sewage flow, and constructing special wetlands to treat the effluent. Each of these alternatives is land-intensive and costly. One estimate has placed the cost of correcting the combined sewer problem as greater than the annual gross national product of the United States.

DAMS—UNEXPECTED CONSEQUENCES

The United States is second only to the Republic of China in the use of dams. Some 100,000 dams regulate America's rivers and creeks; 5,550 are more than 50 feet high. Nationwide, reservoirs created by dams encompass an area equivalent to New Hampshire and Vermont combined. Of all the rivers more than 600 miles in length in the lower 48 states, only the Yellowstone River still flows freely.

Being a world leader in dams was a point of pride during the golden age of dam building, a 50-year flurry of construction ending in approximately 1980. Dam construction

was also a way to employ many people out of work during the Great Depression of the 1930s and to foster national pride. Dams epitomized progress, Yankee ingenuity, and humanity's mastery of nature. After 1980, dam construction fell into disfavor. Three factors accounted for most of the decline: public resistance to the enormous costs, a growing belief that politicians were foolishly spending taxpayers' monies on "pork barrel" (local) projects such as dams, and a developing public awareness of the environmental degradation that dams can cause.

Where Have All the Rivers Gone?

Dams provide a source of energy generation; flood control; drinking water; irrigation; recreation for pleasure boaters, skiers, and anglers; and locks for the passage of barges and commercial shipping vessels. But dams also alter rivers and streams, the land abutting them, the water bodies they join, and the aquatic life throughout, resulting in significant changes in the river system.

Recognizing the need to protect and maintain the aquatic environment and the biological diversity of river systems, more dam operators are now required to maintain a minimum flow in the river below the dam. In addition, many dams are being retrofitted with fish ladders and other means of access to permit fish to reach spawning areas above the dam. These fish ladders are also helpful in allowing juvenile fish to reach the river below the dam. Some states have programs that remove abandoned or obsolete dams, such as those that once served to power flour mills, or remove other obstructions to fish passage, such as road culverts.

Snake River Dams

Correcting the environmental damage done by dams can be a costly and time consuming undertaking. One example of a project designed to remedy damage caused by dams is the U.S. Army Corps of Engineers' project on the Snake River. As of the summer of 2003, the project was into its ninth year of planning. The goal for this ongoing project is to improve salmon and steelhead migration cycles through the dams on the Lower Snake River. Wild salmon and steelhead use the waters of the Columbia River Basin as their spawning grounds. The 1,040-mile Snake River is a major tributary of the Columbia River, running from Yellowstone National Park in Wyoming through southern Idaho to join the Columbia River in Washington State. Its watershed drains 10,900 square miles.

The U.S. Army Corps of Engineers (often referred to simply as the corps) operates 9 of 10 major federal projects in the Columbia and Snake River Basin. Of these, four are hydroelectric power generating dams on the Lower Snake River. These Snake River dams are used (1) to generate 5 percent of the hydroelectric power for the Pacific Northwest, (2) for irrigation in the region, and (3) to enable

FIGURE 3.9

The Lower Granite Dam, on the Snake River in Idaho. *(Source: U.S. Army Corps of Engineers.)*

navigation on the Snake River. Each of the dams is about 100 feet high and 2,655–3,791 feet wide. (See Figure 3.9.)

Salmon stocks have declined in the Pacific Northwest during the 20th century. In 1991 the National Marine Fisheries Service officially declared Snake River sockeye salmon an endangered species. The following year Snake River chinook salmon were designated as a threatened species. These declarations triggered a series of actions required by law under the federal Endangered Species Act of 1973. One of the actions required was the development of a recovery plan. The Columbia River Fish Migration program grew out of this recovery plan.

According to a report by the Pacific Salmon Coordination Office of the U.S. Army Corps of Engineers (*Columbia River Basin — Dams and Salmon* [Online] http://www.nwd.usace.army.mil/ps/colrvbsn.htm [accessed June 6, 2003]), there are many factors that account for the sharp decline of salmon stock in the Columbia and Snake River Basin. Among those factors are dams.

> Dams clearly have had a significant impact, particularly those that eliminated access to fresh water habitat (preventing adult fish from returning to spawn), and those

through which fish passage is provided but at reduced levels from natural conditions. The dams impede juvenile and adult migrations to and from the ocean by their physical presence and by creating reservoirs. The reservoirs behind the dams slow water velocities, alter river temperatures, and increase predation potential.

Studies have been going on for many years to determine how best to alter the Snake River dams so as to reduce their negative impact on salmon and steelhead populations. All four of the dams on the Snake River have fish ladders for upriver migration of salmon returning to spawn, and a bypass system for the downriver migration of juvenile salmon. As part of its Columbia River Fish Mitigation program, the corps is focusing on improving the passage of adult and juvenile salmon around these dams.

The corps has been evaluating four fish passage alternatives, the most controversial of which is breaching the dams; that is, removing the earthen portions of the dams and allowing the river to course around the remaining concrete structure. Breaching the dams would help the salmon but it would eliminate a source of hydroelectric power, water for irrigation, and a waterway for barge transport to ports 140 miles upstream. The other alternatives are to:

FIGURE 3.10

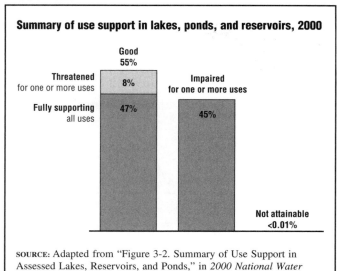

Summary of use support in lakes, ponds, and reservoirs, 2000

Good
55%

Threatened
for one or more uses 8%

Impaired
for one or more uses

Fully supporting
all uses 47% 45%

Not attainable
<0.01%

SOURCE: Adapted from "Figure 3-2. Summary of Use Support in Assessed Lakes, Reservoirs, and Ponds," in *2000 National Water Quality Inventory,* EPA-841-R-02-001, U.S. Environmental Protection Agency, Washington, DC, August 2002

- Maintain current operations.

- Increase the transportation of juvenile salmon around the dams.

- Make improvements to the dams' systems for collecting the juvenile salmon and barging or trucking them past the dams.

Because changing the dams' operation can have significant environmental consequences, the corps prepared a draft environmental impact statement (EIS), which was published in February 2002. The corps' recommendation in the EIS was to move forward with the last alternative mentioned—improving the dams for the collection of juvenile salmon. However, no direct action on this plan had been taken as of summer 2003. Furthermore, a legal ruling in a related case rendered in May 2003 makes it likely that the dam breaching alternative of the corps plan will have to be reconsidered.

On May 7, 2003, U.S. District Judge James A. Redden ruled in a case brought against the National Marine Fisheries Service (NMFS) by 17 conservation and fishing organizations (*Ruling Against NMFS BiOp Revives Dam Breaching Debate,* Columbia River Inter-Tribal Fish Commission, [Online] http://www.critfc.org/text/press/20030513.html [accessed] June 6, 2003). The ruling found that the NMFS' 2000 biological opinion, upon which the corps' Columbia River Fish Mitigation program was based, fell far short of the requirements of the Endangered Species Act. As a result, the corps may be required to prepare a revised EIS based on a more stringent NMFS biological opinion, yet to be rendered as of summer 2003.

WATER QUALITY OF THE NATION'S LAKES

In the *2000 National Water Quality Inventory* report, which assessed 43 percent of the nation's 40.6 million acres of lakes, ponds, and reservoirs, 47 percent were fully supporting their designated uses. However, about 8 percent of the lake acres were threatened. Of the lakes assessed, 45 percent could only partially support their designated uses. (See Figure 3.10.)

Leading Pollutants in Lakes, Ponds, and Reservoirs

A lake's water quality reflects the condition and management of the lake's watershed, that is, the land area that drains to the lake. Elevated levels of nutrients were identified as the most common pollutants, contributing to 50 percent of the impaired water quality in lakes. Figure 3.11 shows the top pollutants and the percent of impaired lake acres affected by each type.

NUTRIENTS. The leading pollutant of lakes, ponds, and reservoirs was an excess of nutrients. Excess nutrients were reported in 22 percent of the assessed lake acres and 50 percent of the impaired lake acres. Nutrients in small quantities are found in healthy lake ecosystems. The presence of excess nutrients disrupts the balance of a lake's ecosystem by creating an environment in which algae and aquatic weeds become too abundant. As these plants die off they sink to the bottom of the lake, pond, or reservoir and decompose. In the process of decomposing, dissolved oxygen is used, leaving oxygen levels lower than they would be in a more balanced environment. Two things that typically occur when a lake environment is low on dissolved oxygen is that fish die off and the lake emits foul odors.

METALS. Metals were the second-most prevalent pollutant, affecting 42 percent of the impaired lake acres. This finding was caused mostly by the widespread detection of mercury in fish tissue. Because it is difficult to measure mercury in water, and because mercury readily accumulates in tissue (bioaccumulates), most states measure mercury contamination using fish tissue samples. Evaluating the extent of the mercury problem is complex because it involves atmospheric transport from power-generating facilities, waste incinerators, and other sources.

SILTATION. The third most common pollutant of lakes reported in the EPA's 2000 inventory was siltation or sedimentation. Nine percent of the lakes accessed in the report were shown to have been impaired by siltation, making this pollutant responsible for 21 percent of the lake acres designated as impaired.

Sources of Pollutants in Lakes

AGRICULTURE. As in the case of rivers and streams, agricultural runoff was the most extensive source of pollution for lakes, affecting 41 percent of impaired lake acres.

FIGURE 3.11

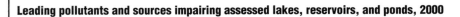

Leading pollutants and sources impairing assessed lakes, reservoirs, and ponds, 2000

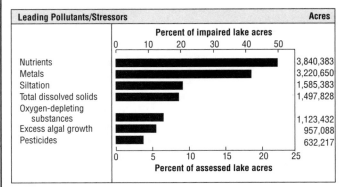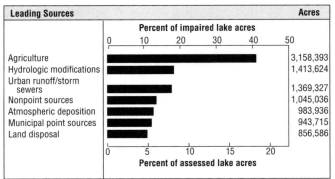

SOURCE: Adapted from "Figure 3-4. Leading Pollutants in Impaired Lakes," and "Figure 3-5. Leading Sources of Lake Impairment," in *2000 National Water Quality Inventory,* EPA-841-R-02-001, U.S. Environmental Protection Agency, Washington, DC, August 2002

(See Figure 3.11.) Pasture grazing and both irrigated and nonirrigated crop production were the leading sources of agricultural impairments to lake water quality.

HYDROLOGIC MODIFICATIONS. The second most commonly found cause of lake impairment was hydrologic modifications. These modifications, resulting from flow regulation, dredging, and construction of dams, degraded 8 percent of the assessed lake, pond, and reservoir acres and 18 percent of the impaired acres.

URBAN RUNOFF AND STORM SEWERS. A nearly equal percentage of lake acres were degraded by urban runoff and storm sewers as were degraded by hydrologic modifications.

Trophic Status of U.S. Lakes

Lakes naturally change over the years, filling with silt and organic material that alter many of the basic characteristics, such as lake depth, biological life, oxygen levels, and the inherent clearness of the water. This natural aging process is called eutrophication. Human activities often speed up eutrophication by increasing nutrient levels. Excessive nutrients cause explosive growth of undesirable algae and aquatic weeds. The algae drop to the lake bottom after they die, where bacteria break them down. The bacteria consume dissolved oxygen in the water while decomposing the algae. This process deprives fish and other organisms of oxygen. Fishkills and bad odors can result when the dissolved oxygen in water is depleted. Figure 3.12 compares a healthy lake system with a system impaired by excessive nutrients.

Naturally occurring eutrophication progression includes several stages. Oligotrophic lakes are clear waters with little organic matter or silt; mesotrophic waters contain more organic material, and the oxygen level is being depleted; eutrophic waters are extremely high in nutrients, and the water is murky and shallow with lots of algae and a depleted oxygen level. (See Table 3.2.) Under natural conditions, eutrophication of a large lake can take thousands of years. Human activity can speed up this process, reducing the time to a few decades.

THE GREAT LAKES

The 2000 EPA Inventory of the Great Lakes

The Great Lakes basin, which is shared with Canada, is home to more than 33 million people, 30 million of whom rely on it for drinking water. The five lakes are the largest system of fresh surface water in the world, containing about 20 percent of the world's freshwater. The water in the Great Lakes accounts for 95 percent of all the freshwater in the United States. The total shoreline in the United States and Canada, a "fourth seacoast," is more than 10,000 miles long and equal to about one-quarter of Earth's circumference. The region generates more than 50 percent of the total U.S. manufacturing output. The eight Great Lake states (Illinois, Indiana, Michigan, Minnesota, New York, Ohio, Pennsylvania, and Wisconsin) account for 30 percent of U.S. agricultural sales. International shipping annually transports 50 million tons of cargo while sport and commercial fishing contribute $4.5 billion to the economy.

This prosperity has taxed the ecological health of the Great Lakes system. Urban and industrial discharges, agricultural and forestry activity, development of recreation facilities, poor waste disposal practices, invasive species, and habitat degradation have all contributed to ecosystem decline. Despite these problems, however, the watershed still contains many ecologically rich areas. Over 30 of the basin's biological communities, and over 100 species, are found only in the Great Lakes basin or are globally rare.

FIGURE 3.12

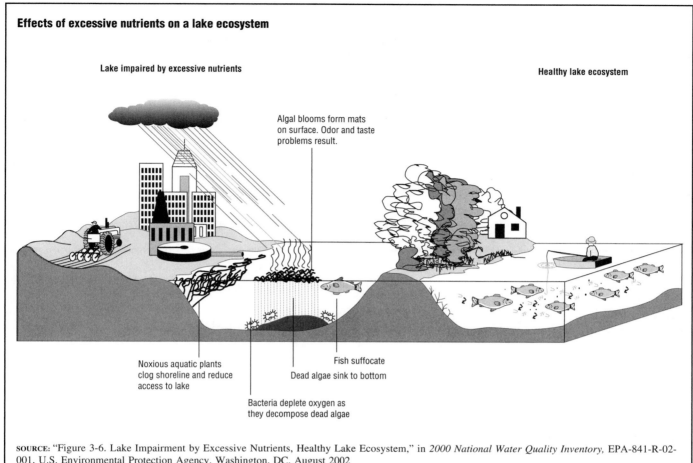

Effects of excessive nutrients on a lake ecosystem

Lake impaired by excessive nutrients

Healthy lake ecosystem

Algal blooms form mats on surface. Odor and taste problems result.

Noxious aquatic plants clog shoreline and reduce access to lake

Fish suffocate

Dead algae sink to bottom

Bacteria deplete oxygen as they decompose dead algae

SOURCE: "Figure 3-6. Lake Impairment by Excessive Nutrients, Healthy Lake Ecosystem," in *2000 National Water Quality Inventory,* EPA-841-R-02-001, U.S. Environmental Protection Agency, Washington, DC, August 2002

In 2000 the states assessed 92 percent of the 5,521 miles of Great Lakes shoreline. The states reported that 22 percent of the assessed shoreline supported designated uses and 78 percent was impaired. (See Figure 3.13.) Only four of the eight Great Lake states reported specific pollutants and sources of those pollutants for use in the EPA's 2000 report. As the report states, "limited conclusions can be drawn from this fraction of the nation's Great Lakes shoreline miles."

The data presented in Figure 3.14 show the percentage of Great Lakes shoreline miles that either fully support or only partially support (or fail to support) each of six use categories. In all but one case, the percentage of assessed miles that support their use category well exceed the percentage that only partially support or fail to support a use category. The one use category in which partial failure to support or total failure to support was reported for all shoreline miles was fish consumption. Not being able to eat fish was the greatest use impairment. All of the states bordering the Great Lakes have issued advisories to restrict the eating of fish caught in the lakes.

Great Lakes Water Quality Agreement

Since the 1960s and 1970s, when Lake Erie was so degraded that it was considered by many to be "dead," much time and effort has been invested in trying to restore the Great Lakes system. In 1972 the United States and Canada entered into the Great Lakes Water Quality Agreement (GLWQA), which is a worldwide model for cooperative environmental protection and natural resource management.

There have been many successes and the ecosystem is in recovery. For example, excess phosphorous and nitrogen loads that smothered the Great Lakes with nuisance algae have been successfully stabilized, and in some cases reduced, through strict nutrient goals. Figure 3.15 illustrates the trends in the concentrations of phosphorous loads in the open waters of the Great Lakes. The trend has been mostly downward and stable on all lakes other than Lake Erie where readings from 2001 and 2002 show an upward spike. The endangered double-crested cormorant, a large fish-eating bird that was near extinction in the 1970s, is now more numerous on Lake Ontario than at any time in its previous recorded history.

TABLE 3.2

Trophic states

Oligotrophic	Clear waters with little organic matter or sediment and minimum biological activity.
Mesotrophic	Waters with more nutrients and, therefore, more biological productivity.
Eutrophic	Waters extremely rich in nutrients, with high biological productivity. Some species may be choked out.
Hypereutrophic	Murky, highly productive waters, closest to the wetlands status. Many clear water species cannot survive.
Dystrophic	Low in nutrients, highly colored with dissolved humic organic matter. (Not necessarily a part of the natural trophic progression.)

The eutrophication process

Eutrophication is a natural process, but human activities can accelerate eutrophication by increasing the rate at which nutrients and organic substances enter lakes from their surrounding watersheds. Agricultural runoff, urban runoff, leaking septic systems, sewage discharges, eroded streambanks, and similar sources can enhance the flow of nutrients and organic substances into lakes. These substances can overstimulate the growth of algae and aquatic plants, creating conditions that interfere with the recreational use of lakes and the health and diversity of native fish, plant, and animal populations. Enhanced eutrophication from nutrient enrichment due to human activities is one of the leading problems facing our nation's lakes and reservoirs.

SOURCE: Adapted from "Trophic States," in *National Water Quality Inventory: 1998 Report to Congress*, EPA-841-F-00-006, U.S. Environmental Protection Agency, Washington, DC, 2000

FIGURE 3.13

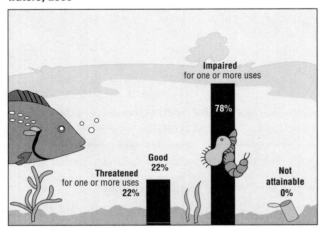

Summary of use support in assessed Great Lakes shoreline waters, 2000

Of the 5,066 miles of Great Lakes shoreline assessed, 22% fully support their designated uses but are threatened, and 78% are impaired for one or more uses.

SOURCE: Adapted from "Figure 4-5. Summary of Use Support in Assessed Great Lakes Shoreline Waters," in *2000 National Water Quality Inventory*, EPA 841-R-020-001, U.S. Environmental Protection Agency, Washington, DC, August 2002

State of the Lakes Ecosystem Conferences

The GLWQA imposes reporting requirements on both of its member countries and in an attempt to meet these requirements a conference series was established. The conferences are called the State of the Lakes Ecosystem Conference (SOLEC) and are held every two years. The first such conference convened in 1994.

The SOLEC meetings are designed as a venue for scientists and policy makers to share information about the state of the Great Lakes ecosystem. The focus is on assessing and sharing information about the results of Great Lakes programs and studies. In the year following each conference, the U.S. and Canada prepare a report that presents the findings accumulated at the SOLEC.

According to the EPA's Web site on the subject (http://www.epa.gov/grtlakes/solec/ [accessed June 23, 2003]), after the 1996 SOLEC those involved recognized a need for a standard set of basin-wide indicators. When many parties are involved in studying a subject and then comparing the results of their studies, it is helpful to work with a standard set of indicators so that progress can be measured reliably across both time and geography.

Since the 1996 SOLEC, work has been done to establish a formalized set of indicators with which to assess the state of the Great Lakes at each consecutive SOLEC. The indicators are used sort of like a doctor might use a patient's weight and blood pressure to gauge his or her general health. Over time if an adult patient's weight and blood pressure are rising it is a sign of troubled health. Similarly, a rising phosphate level in a lake is a sign that the lake's ecosystem is ailing.

The report that came out after SOLEC 2000, *State of the Great Lakes 2001,* presented the following mixed news about the chemical, physical, and biological integrity of the waters of the Great Lakes Basin ecosystem:

- Surface waters were still amongst the best sources of drinking water in the world.

- Progress had been made both in cleaning up contaminants and in rehabilitating some fish and wildlife species.

- Invasive species continued as a significant threat to Great Lakes biological communities.

FIGURE 3.14

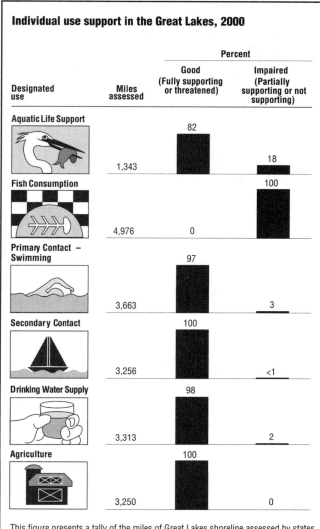

Individual use support in the Great Lakes, 2000

Designated use	Miles assessed	Percent	
		Good (Fully supporting or threatened)	Impaired (Partially supporting or not supporting)
Aquatic Life Support	1,343	82	18
Fish Consumption	4,976	0	100
Primary Contact – Swimming	3,663	97	3
Secondary Contact	3,256	100	<1
Drinking Water Supply	3,313	98	2
Agriculture	3,250	100	0

This figure presents a tally of the miles of Great Lakes shoreline assessed by states for each category of designated use. For each category, the figure summarizes the proportion of the assessed water rated according to quality.

SOURCE: "Figure 4-6. Individual Use Support in the Great Lakes," in *2000 National Water Quality Inventory*, EPA-841-R-02-001, U.S. Environmental Protection Agency, Washington, DC, August 2002

FIGURE 3.15

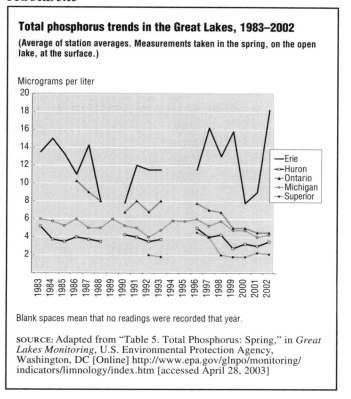

Total phosphorus trends in the Great Lakes, 1983–2002

(Average of station averages. Measurements taken in the spring, on the open lake, at the surface.)

Blank spaces mean that no readings were recorded that year.

SOURCE: Adapted from "Table 5. Total Phosphorus: Spring," in *Great Lakes Monitoring*, U.S. Environmental Protection Agency, Washington, DC [Online] http://www.epa.gov/glnpo/monitoring/indicators/limnology/index.htm [accessed April 28, 2003]

Pollutants and Sources of Pollution in the Great Lakes

The U.S. strategy for meeting the goals of the GLWQA is embodied in *Great Lakes 2001—A Plan for the New Millennium*. The draft strategy was a partnership among the eight Great Lakes states, Great Lakes tribal governments, the Great Lakes Fishery Commission, and nine federal agencies. These groups were working together to implement the actions described in the strategy by coordinating and enhancing their environmental protection and natural resource management efforts.

Priority toxic organic chemicals, nutrients, and pathogens are the three most common pollutants affecting the waters of the Great Lakes. (See Figure 3.16.) Toxic substances such as mercury, heavy metals, dichlorodiphenyltrichloroethane (DDT), and polychlorinated biphenyls (PCBs) have been responsible for many of the problems. There has been some improvement, however. The levels of DDT, a banned pesticide, have steadily decreased since the mid-1970s, and there are currently no DDT-based advisories against eating fish from the Great Lakes. Total PCB levels have shown the same decline as DDT. PCB concentrations in lake trout, walleye, and salmon are one-tenth of the concentrations reported in the mid-1970s. The PCB levels, however, are still high enough to keep advisories against eating these fish from places in all five lakes. Contaminated sediments and urban runoff are the primary sources of the pollutants impairing the Great Lakes. (See Figure 3.16.)

- Atmospheric deposition of contaminants, often referred to as acid rain, from distant sources outside the basin confounded efforts to eliminate these substances.

- Urban sprawl continued to threaten high quality natural areas, rare species, farmland, and open space.

- Development, drainage, and pollution were shrinking coastal wetlands.

These findings were based on the assessments of 33 of the 80 official indicators that are now being used to measure the health of the Great Lakes ecosystem. The SOLEC 2002 meeting reported on 43 indicators. The official paper presenting the finding of the SOLEC 2002 had yet to be published as of June 2003.

FIGURE 3.16

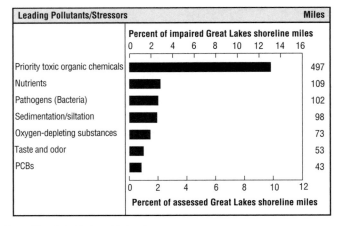
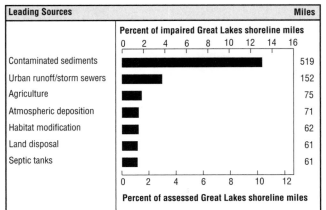

Leading pollutants and sources impairing Great Lakes shoreline, 2000

Note: PCBs = Polychlorinated biphenyls

SOURCE: Adapted from "Figure 4-7. Leading Pollutants in Impaired Great Lakes Shoreline Waters," and "Figure 4-8. Leading Sources of Great Lakes Shoreline Impairment," in *2000 National Water Quality Inventory*, EPA-841-R-02-001, U.S. Environmental Protection Agency, Washington, DC, August 2002

MIXING ZONES. A mixing zone is an area in a river or lake where pollutants are mixed with cleaner waters to dilute pollutant concentrations in the water. Inside a mixing zone, discharges are allowed to exceed water-quality criteria by a fixed amount determined on a case-by-case basis. Outside the mixing zone, pollutant levels must meet water-quality standards.

Certain organic pollutants such as DDT, PCBs, and methyl mercury, even though their concentrations are so low that they cannot be measured in surrounding waters, bioaccumulate. The EPA has identified 22 bioaccumulative chemicals of concern. In November 2000 the EPA adopted a new regulation for the Great Lakes prohibiting the use of mixing zones with new discharges of bioaccumulative chemicals. The rule also phased out over a 10-year period the use of existing Great Lakes mixing zones for these chemicals. The regulation was aimed at reducing, by up to 700,000 pounds, the annual discharge into the Great Lakes of chemicals that had the potential to accumulate in fish and wildlife. The EPA estimated that this new regulation would affect about 300 of the 600 major Great Lakes dischargers.

BIOACCUMULATION. Certain organic pollutants such as PCBs and DDT have two properties that lead to high bioaccumulation rates. These pollutants do not have an affinity to water (they are hydrophobic) and therefore readily attach to particles such as clay and small aquatic plants called phytoplankton. The pollutants have an affinity for lipids or fatty tissues (they are lipophilic) and are therefore stored readily in the fatty tissues of plants and animals. Because of these properties, these organic pollutants bioaccumulate in phytoplankton, sediment, and fat tissue at concentrations that exceed the pollutant concentrations in surrounding waters. Frequently, the concentration in surrounding waters is so low that it cannot be measured even with very sensitive instruments and methods.

Zooplankton (microscopic plant-eaters) and fish consume vast quantities of phytoplankton. As a result, any organic chemicals accumulated by the phytoplankton are further concentrated in the fish, particularly in their fatty tissues. These concentrations are increased at each level of the food chain. (See Figure 3.17.) The process of increasing pollutant concentration through the food chain is called biomagnification.

The top predators in a food chain, such as lake trout and Chinook salmon, and fish-eating gulls, hawks, and eagles, may accumulate concentrations of these organic chemicals high enough to cause serious deformities or death, or impair their ability to reproduce. DDT, for example, causes the eggs of eagles, osprey, and other fish-eating birds to easily break, and also causes deformities in chicks, impairing the birds' ability to successfully reproduce.

Biomagnification of pollutants in the food chain can also be a significant concern for human health. To protect their residents from these risks, states issue fish consumption advisories or warnings about eating certain types of fish or shellfish.

The Threat of Alien Invasive Species

The introduction of a non-native species into an ecosystem can have serious consequences. In fact, according

FIGURE 3.17

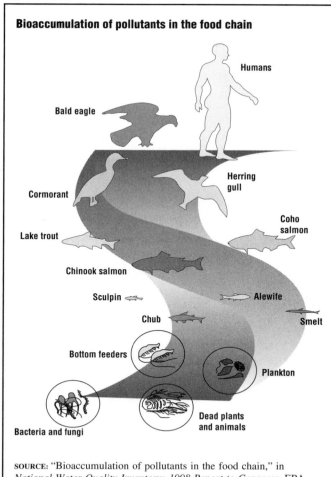

Bioaccumulation of pollutants in the food chain

Humans

Bald eagle

Herring gull

Cormorant

Coho salmon

Lake trout

Chinook salmon

Sculpin

Alewife

Chub

Smelt

Bottom feeders

Plankton

Bacteria and fungi

Dead plants and animals

SOURCE: "Bioaccumulation of pollutants in the food chain," in *National Water Quality Inventory: 1998 Report to Congress,* EPA-841-F-00-006, U.S. Environmental Protection Agency, Washington, DC, 2000

biological pollution from alien invasive species are both massive and rising. The costs to native ecosystems, natural resources, fisheries, and agriculture are estimated in one study to reach $137 billion per year in the United States alone. By comparison, the costs associated with loses from Hurricane Andrew in 1992 totaled $16 billion.

Invasive alien species are introduced into the Great Lakes in various ways, including aquaculture, canals, bait-fish disposal, recreational boating, and ship fouling. The most significant source of introduction of such species is through ballast water on ships, the water that ships take in at sea to equalize their loads. This ballast water, which may contain non-native species, is often discharged in the Great Lakes.

Guidelines for ballast water were introduced as a part of the Nonindigenous Aquatic Nuisance Prevention and Control Act of 1990 as amended by the National Invasive Species Act of 1996. Nonetheless, according to the International Joint Commission's 2002 report "despite increased awareness of the risks, the 1990s saw no discernable improvement" in the introduction of non-native species into the Great Lakes.

The Great Lakes and St. Lawrence River basin ecosystem is home to more than 160 non-native species of fish, invertebrates, plants, parasites, algae, and pathogens. According to the 2002 International Joint Commission report, governments are making progress towards addressing the threat of alien invasive species with legislation, rulemaking, and international agreements, such as those proposed by the International Maritime Organization for the year 2003.

DO THE NATION'S WATERS MEET THE "FISHABLE/SWIMMABLE" GOALS?

Fishing

Meeting the "fishable" goal of the Clean Water Act means providing a level of water quality that protects and promotes successful populations of fish, shellfish, and wildlife. The "fish consumption" use—the ability for humans to safely eat the fish—is a higher use than most states assign to their waters. When fish or shellfish in particular locations contain harmful levels of pollutants, the state issues advisories against eating the fish to recreational fishermen. Commercial fishing is usually banned.

Figure 3.18 shows the number of advisories against eating fish or wildlife reported by the states in the EPA's *America's Water Resources at a Turning Point* (May 2000 and August 2002). These advisories are specific as to location, species, and pollutant. Some advisories caution against eating any fish from a particular location; others caution against eating a particular species of fish only because it is more likely to bioaccumulate the chemical of

to the *State of the Great Lakes Ecosystem 2001,* jointly published by the U.S. Environmental Protection Agency and Environment Canada, "invasive, non-native aquatic species are the greatest biological threat to the Great Lakes aquatic ecosystem."

Within an ecosystem there exists a balance. A new non-native species brought into a system causes an imbalance and can cause great damage as native species are not capable of resisting infection, infestation, predation, or competition from the alien species. Two examples of such invasive non-native species are the zebra mussel and purple loosestrife, an aquatic plant. In a paper (*The Challenge to Restore and Protect the Largest Body of Fresh Water in the World,* September 2002) published by the International Joint Commission, a combined Canadian and United States intergovernmental agency, the challenge of alien invasive species is discussed at length.

According to the International Joint Commission's 2002 report, researchers widely believe that the costs of

FIGURE 3.18

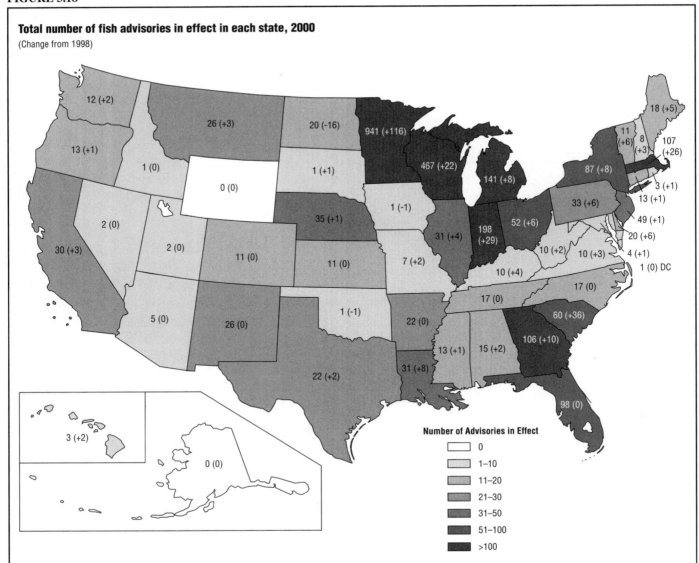

Total number of fish advisories in effect in each state, 2000
(Change from 1998)

12 (+2)
26 (+3)
20 (-16)
941 (+116)
18 (+5)
13 (+1)
1 (0)
1 (+1)
467 (+22)
11 (+6)
8 (+3)
107 (+26)
0 (0)
141 (+8)
87 (+8)
2 (0)
1 (-1)
35 (+1)
33 (+6)
3 (+1)
30 (+3)
2 (0)
11 (0)
11 (0)
31 (+4)
198 (+29)
52 (+6)
13 (+1)
7 (+2)
10 (+2)
10 (+3)
49 (+1)
5 (0)
26 (0)
1 (-1)
10 (+4)
20 (+6)
22 (0)
17 (0)
4 (+1)
1 (0) DC
17 (0)
60 (+36)
13 (+1)
15 (+2)
106 (+10)
22 (+2)
31 (+8)
98 (0)
3 (+2)
0 (0)

Number of Advisories in Effect
0
1–10
11–20
21–30
31–50
51–100
>100

Note: States that perform routine fish tissue analysis (such as the Great Lakes states) will detect more cases of fish contamination and issue more advisories than states with less rigorous fish sampling programs. In many cases, the states with the most fish advisories support the best monitoring programs for measuring toxic contamination in fish, and their water quality may be no worse than the water quality in other states.

SOURCE: Adapted from "Figure 7-1. Fish and Wildlife Consumption Advisories in the United States," in *2000 National Water Quality Inventory,* EPA-841-R-02-001, and "Total Number of Fish Advisories in each State in 1998," in *Liquid Assets 2000, America's Water Resources at a Turning Point,* U.S. Environmental Protection Agency, May 2000 and August 2002

concern. Other fish advisories may suggest that individuals limit their eating of fish from a particular water body to one or two meals per week or per month.

In 2000, 48 states reported 2,822 fish and wildlife consumption advisories. The bioaccumulative chemicals—mercury, PCBs, chlordane, dioxins, and DDT—caused almost all the advisories. (See Figure 3.19.) Air deposition is believed to be the most significant source of mercury contamination; industries and wastewater treatment plants discharge very little mercury to surface waters. The use of PCBs, chlordane, and DDT has been banned for more than

20 years, yet these compounds persist in the sediments and are taken in through the food chain and biomagnified.

Swimming

Meeting the "swimmable" goal is defined by the EPA as providing water quality that allows recreational activities both in and on the water. In the *2000 National Water Quality Inventory,* 4 states reported that they had no record of recreation restrictions reported to them by their respective health departments; 13 states and tribes identified 233 sites where recreation was restricted at least once during the reporting cycle. Local health departments closed many

FIGURE 3.19

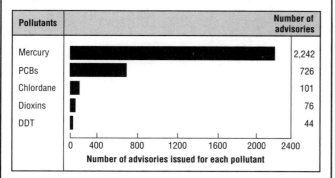

Pollutants causing fish and wildlife consumption advisories in effect in 2000

Note: PCBs = Polychlorinated biphenyls
DDT = Dichloro-diphenyl-trichloroethane

SOURCE: "Figure 7-2, Pollutants Causing Fish and Wildlife Consumption Advisories in Effect in 2000," in *2000 National Water Quality Inventory,* EPA-841-R-02-001, U.S. Environmental Protection Agency, Washington, DC, August 2002

FIGURE 3.20

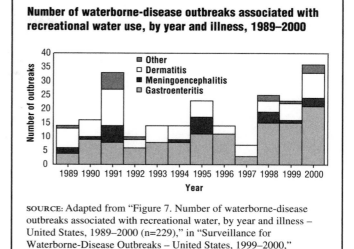

Number of waterborne-disease outbreaks associated with recreational water use, by year and illness, 1989–2000

SOURCE: Adapted from "Figure 7. Number of waterborne-disease outbreaks associated with recreational water, by year and illness – United States, 1989–2000 (n=229)," in "Surveillance for Waterborne-Disease Outbreaks – United States, 1999–2000," *Morbidity and Mortality Weekly Report,* vol. 51, no. SS-8, November 22, 2002

of those sites more than once. Pathogens (bacteria) caused most of the restrictions. State reporting on recreational restrictions, such as beach closures, is often incomplete because agencies rely on local health departments to voluntarily monitor and report beach closures.

The Centers for Disease Control and Prevention (CDC) report "Surveillance for Waterborne-Disease Outbreaks—United States, 1999–2000" (*Morbidity and Mortality Weekly Report,* November 22, 2002) showed the following incidence of disease outbreaks caused by recreational water contact. During this two-year period, 23 states reported 59 outbreaks, affecting 2,093 persons. Of the 59 recreational waterborne disease outbreaks

reported, 61 percent involved gastroenteritis. There were 15 such outbreaks in 1999 and 21 in 2000. Figure 3.20 shows the number of waterborne disease outbreaks due to recreational water use annually from 1989–2000 with a breakdown by illness. The year 2000 saw the highest number of outbreaks for the entire period.

As part of the Beaches Act of 2000, the U.S. Congress has directed the EPA to develop a new set of guidelines for recreational water based on new water-quality indicators. Beginning in 2003 the EPA will conduct a series of epidemiologic studies at recreational fresh water and marine beaches. These studies will be used to help in the development of the new guidelines for recreational water.

CHAPTER 4
GROUNDWATER

VAST HIDDEN RESOURCE

Water lies beneath almost every part of Earth's surface—mountains, plains, and deserts—but underground water is not always easy to find, and once found, it may not be readily accessible. Groundwater may lie close to the surface, as in a marsh, or it may occur many hundreds of feet below the surface, as in some dry areas of the nation's West. The amount of groundwater lying within a half mile under the U.S. land surface is approximately four times that filling the Great Lakes.

Underground water has been known to man since ancient times, but it is only recently that geologists have learned how to gauge the quantity of groundwater and have begun to estimate its vast potential for use. While an estimated one million cubic miles of Earth's groundwater is located within about one-half mile of the surface (there are about one billion gallons in a cubic mile), only a small amount of this reservoir of underground water can be tapped and made available for human use through wells and springs.

HOW GROUNDWATER OCCURS

Groundwater is not in underground lakes, nor is it water flowing in underground rivers. Groundwater is simply water that fills pores or cracks in subsurface rocks. When rain falls or snow melts on a ground surface, water may run off into lower land areas or lakes and streams. What is left is absorbed into the soil where it can be used by vegetation, seeps into deeper layers of soil and rock, or evaporates back into the atmosphere.

Below the topsoil is an area called the unsaturated zone, where, in times of adequate rainfall, the small spaces between rocks and grains of soil contain at least some water, while the larger spaces contain mostly air. After a major rain, the zone may become saturated, that is, all the open spaces fill with water. During a drought, the area may become drained and almost completely dry. In the unsaturated zone, a certain amount of water is held in the soil and rocks by molecular attraction, making the soil moist, but not wet. This is similar to having enough water in a wet towel to make it feel damp after it has stopped dripping. A well dug into the unsaturated zone will not fill with water because the water in the unsaturated zone is at atmospheric pressure.

With continued rainfall, excess water will drain through the unsaturated zone (which now has absorbed as much water as it can hold) to the saturated zone to recharge the aquifer. (See Figure 4.1.) The saturated zone is full of water—all the spaces between soil and rocks, and the rocks themselves, contain water. Water from streams, lakes, wetlands, and other water bodies may seep into the saturated zones. Streams are commonly a significant source of recharge to groundwater downstream from mountain fronts and steep hillsides in arid and semiarid areas, and in areas underlaid by limestone and other soluble rocks.

FIGURE 4.1

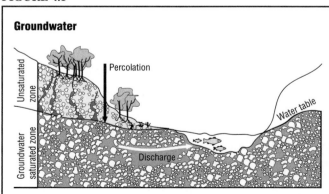

SOURCE: "Figure 1.1: Ground Water," in *National Water Quality Inventory: 1998 Report to Congress,* EPA 841-F-00-006, U.S. Environmental Protection Agency, Washington, DC, 2000

FIGURE 4.2

Direction and rate of groundwater movement

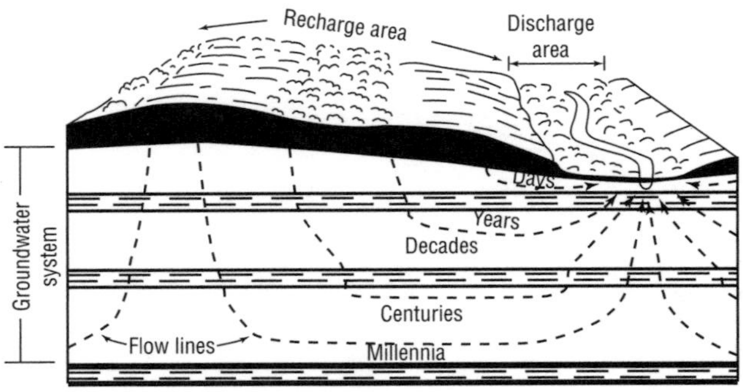

SOURCE: Roger M. Waller, "Direction and rate of ground-water movement," in *Ground Water and the Rural Homeowner*, U.S. Geological Survey, Denver, CO, 1982

FIGURE 4.3

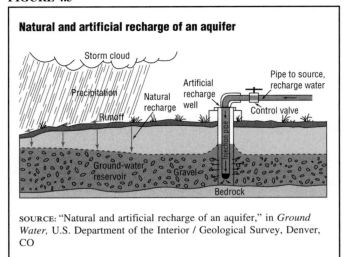

Natural and artificial recharge of an aquifer

SOURCE: "Natural and artificial recharge of an aquifer," in *Ground Water*, U.S. Department of the Interior / Geological Survey, Denver, CO

In the saturated zone, water is under pressure that is higher than atmospheric pressure. When a well is dug into the saturated zone, water flows from the area of higher pressure (in the ground) to the area of lower pressure (in the hollow well), and the well fills with water to the level of the existing groundwater. In some cases, the pressure is high enough to force the water to flow to the surface without pumping.

The water table is the level at which the unsaturated zone and the saturated zone meet. The water table is not fixed, but may rise or fall, depending on water availability. In areas where the climate is fairly consistent, the level of the water table may vary little; in areas subject to extreme flooding and drought, it may rise and fall substantially.

GROUNDWATER FLOW

Water is always in motion. Groundwater generally moves from recharge areas, where water enters the ground, to discharge areas, where it exits from the ground into a wetland, river, lake, or ocean. Transpiration by plants whose roots extend to a point near the water table is another form of discharge. The path of groundwater movement may be short and simple or incredibly complex, depending on the geology of the areas through which the water passes. The complexity of the path also determines the length of time a molecule of water remains in the ground between recharge and discharge points. (See Figure 4.2.)

The velocities of groundwater flow generally are low and are orders of magnitude less than the velocities of stream flow. Groundwater movement normally occurs as slow seepage through the spaces between particles of unconsolidated material or through networks of fractures and openings in consolidated rocks. A velocity of one foot per day or more is a high rate of movement in groundwater. Groundwater velocities can be as low as one foot per

decade or one foot per century. Stream flows on the other hand are generally measured in feet per second. A velocity of one foot per second is about 16 miles per day. The low velocities of groundwater flow can have important implications, particularly in relation to the movement of contaminants.

The age of water (time since recharge) varies in different parts of groundwater flow systems. Groundwater gets steadily older along a particular flow path from an area of recharge to an area of discharge. In shallow, local scale flow systems, groundwater age at areas of discharge can vary from less than a day to a few hundred years. (See Figure 4.2.) In deep, regional flow systems with long flow paths, groundwater age may reach thousands or tens of thousands of years.

Aquifers

An aquifer is a saturated zone that contains enough water to yield significant amounts of water when a well is sunk. The zone is actually a path of porous or permeable material through which substantial quantities of water flow relatively easily. The word "aquifer" comes from the Latin *aqua* (water) and *ferre* (to bear or carry). An aquifer can be a layer of gravel or sand, a layer of sandstone or cavernous limestone, a rubble zone between lava flows, or even a large body of massive rock, such as fractured granite. An aquifer may lie above, below, or in between confining beds that are layers of hard, nonporous material (clay or solid granite, for example).

There are two types of aquifers: unconfined and confined (artesian). In an unconfined or water table aquifer, precipitation filters down from the land's surface until it hits an impervious layer of rock or clay. The water then accumulates and forms a zone of saturation. Because runoff water can easily seep down to the water table, an unconfined aquifer is very susceptible to contamination.

FIGURE 4.4

Principal aquifers of the United States

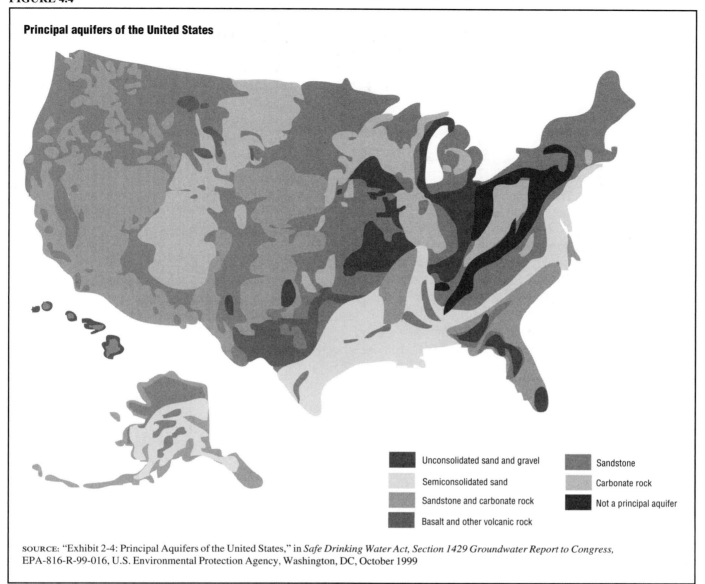

SOURCE: "Exhibit 2-4: Principal Aquifers of the United States," in *Safe Drinking Water Act, Section 1429 Groundwater Report to Congress,* EPA-816-R-99-016, U.S. Environmental Protection Agency, Washington, DC, October 1999

In a confined aquifer, the confining beds act more or less like underground boundaries, discouraging water from entering or leaving the aquifer, so that the water is forced to continue its slow movement to its discharge point. Water from precipitation enters the aquifer through a recharge area, where the soil lets the water percolate down to the level of the aquifer. The ability of an aquifer to recharge is dependent on various factors, such as the ease with which water is able to move down through the geological formations (permeability) and the size of the spaces between the rock particles (porosity). Figure 4.3 illustrates natural and artificial aquifer recharge.

Usually, the permeability and porosity of rocks decrease as their depth below the surface increases. How much water can be removed from an aquifer depends on the type of rock. A dense granite, for example, will supply almost no water to a well even though the water is near the surface. A porous sandstone, however, thousands of feet below the surface can yield hundreds of gallons of water per minute. Porous rocks that are capable of supplying freshwater have been found at depths of more than 6,000 feet below the surface. Saline (salty) water has been discovered from aquifers that lie more than 30,000 feet underground.

Aquifers vary from a few feet thick to tens or hundreds of feet thick. They can be located just below Earth's surface or thousands of feet beneath it. An aquifer can cover a few acres of land or many thousands of square miles. Any one aquifer may be a part of a large system of aquifers that feed into each other. Figure 4.4 shows the principal aquifers of the United States.

OGALLALA AQUIFER. The Ogallala or High Plains Aquifer is one of the world's largest aquifers. It is located in

FIGURE 4.5

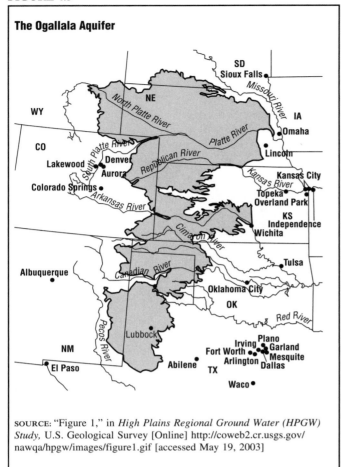

The Ogallala Aquifer

the United States and covers 156,000 square miles, stretching from southern South Dakota to the Texas panhandle. Figure 4.5 shows the aquifer's location. The Ogallala's average thickness ranges from 300 feet to more than 1,200 feet in Nebraska. For over 50 years, the Ogallala has supplied most of the water for irrigation and drinking to the Great Plains states. Approximately 200,000 wells tap into this vast aquifer and extract huge quantities of water. The Environmental Protection Agency (EPA) has designated the Ogallala Aquifer a sole source aquifer. This means that at least 50 percent of the population in the area depend on the Ogallala Aquifer for its water supply.

The U.S. Geological Survey (USGS) reported in its 1996 publication *Ground Water Atlas of the United States, Oklahoma, Texas, HA 730-E* that because the Ogallala Aquifer was being pumped far in excess of recharge, the USGS and the Texas Department of Water Resources projected an increasing shortage of Ogallala aquifer water for future irrigation needs. The projections suggested that the irrigated acreage in the High Plains of Texas (69 percent of irrigated Texas cropland) would be reduced to one-half of its present acreage by 2030 unless an effective water conservation plan was implemented.

Concerns about excessive pumping of the Ogallala Aquifer prompted Senators Sam Brownback of Kansas and Jeff Bingaman of New Mexico to introduce to Congress the Ogallala Aquifer Bill on July 23, 2002. According to Senator Brownback's press release on that date, the bill is intended to extend the life of the aquifer. Officially named the High Plains Aquifer Hydrogeologic Characterization, Mapping and Modeling Act, the bill would establish a program within the Department of the Interior to map and study the Ogallala Aquifer, which serves Colorado, Kansas, Nebraska, New Mexico, Oklahoma, South Dakota, Texas, and Wyoming. The USGS would coordinate the program and would provide grants and technical assistance to those eight states (or local agencies and educational institutions) for projects that address groundwater issues. According to a March 18, 2003 Congressional Budget Office (CBO) report, for fiscal years 2003 through 2011 the bill would authorize the appropriation of whatever amounts are necessary for federal projects, technical assistance, and state grants. The CBO estimates that implementation of the bill would cost about $1 million in fiscal year 2003 and $44 million over the 2003-08 period. For the 2003 through 2013 period, the CBO estimates the cost at $90 million.

Senator Ben Nighthorse Campbell of Colorado expressed his concerns about the proposed legislation on March 6, 2003. According to a press release from his office on that date, Campbell expressed his belief to the Senate Energy Committee that the legislation would result in unnecessary government involvement in the issue. Despite his concerns, the bill was passed by the Senate on April 7, 2003, but had not yet passed the United States House of Representatives as of June 2003.

Springs

A spring is a natural discharge of water at Earth's surface from a saturated zone that has been filled to overflowing. Springs are classified either according to the amount of water they produce or according to the temperature of the water (hot, warm, or cold). Giant Springs in Great Falls, Montana, is the largest freshwater spring in the United States and is the source of water for the Missouri and Roe Rivers. Giant Springs removes 7.9 million gallons per hour from underground reserves and maintains a constant temperature of 54 degrees Fahrenheit. Its flow accounts for approximately one-sixth of the water flowing downstream in the Missouri River, and its water has been carbon-dated to be about 3,000 years old.

Thermal springs have water that is warm or, in some places, hot. They are fed by groundwater that is heated by contact with hot rocks deep below the surface. In some areas, water can descend slowly to very deep levels, getting warmer the farther down it goes. If it rises faster than it descended, it does not have time to cool off before it emerges on the surface. Well-known thermal springs are

FIGURE 4.6

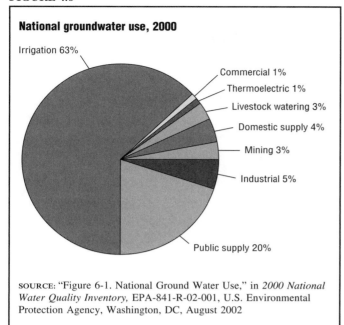

National groundwater use, 2000

Irrigation 63%

Commercial 1%

Thermoelectric 1%

Livestock watering 3%

Domestic supply 4%

Mining 3%

Industrial 5%

Public supply 20%

SOURCE: "Figure 6-1. National Ground Water Use," in *2000 National Water Quality Inventory,* EPA-841-R-02-001, U.S. Environmental Protection Agency, Washington, DC, August 2002

the Warm Springs in Georgia and the Hot Springs in Arkansas. Geysers are thermal springs that erupt periodically. Old Faithful in Yellowstone National Park is perhaps the most famous and spectacular geyser in the world. It erupts at intervals of 30 to 90 minutes.

NATURAL CHARACTERISTICS OF GROUNDWATER

As groundwater travels its course from recharge to discharge area, it undergoes chemical and physical changes as it mixes with other groundwater and reacts with the minerals in the sand or rocks through which it flows. These interactions can greatly affect water quality and its suitability or unsuitability for a particular use.

Minerals

Water is a natural solvent capable of dissolving other substances. Spring waters may contain dissolved minerals and gases that give them the subtle tastes enjoyed by many people. Without minerals and gases, water tastes flat. The most common dissolved mineral substances are calcium, magnesium, sodium, potassium, chloride, sulfate, and bicarbonate. Water is not considered desirable for drinking if it contains more than 1,000 milligrams per liter (mg/l) of dissolved minerals. However, in areas where less-mineralized water is not available, water with a few thousand mg/l of dissolved minerals is used routinely, although classified as saline.

Some well and spring waters contain such high levels of dissolved minerals that they cannot be tolerated by humans, plants, or animals. In high concentrations, certain minerals can be especially harmful. A large quantity of

sodium in drinking water is bad for people with heart disease. Boron, a mineral that is good for some plants in small amounts, is toxic to other plants in only slightly elevated concentrations. Such highly mineralized groundwater usually lies deep below the surface and has very limited uses.

Water Hardness

Water that contains a lot of calcium and magnesium is said to be hard. The hardness of water can be expressed in terms of the amount of calcium carbonate (the principal constituent of limestone) or equivalent minerals that would remain if the water were evaporated. Water is considered soft when it contains 0 to 60 mg/l of hardness constituents, moderately hard with 61 to 120 mg/l, hard with 121 to 180 mg/l, and very hard if more than 180 mg/l are present.

Very hard water is not desirable for many domestic uses, and leaves a scaly deposit on the insides of pipes, boilers, and tanks. Hard water can be made soft at a fairly reasonable cost, although it is not always desirable to remove all the minerals from drinking water since some are beneficial to health. Extremely soft water can corrode metals but is suitable for doing laundry, dishwashing, and bathing. Most communities seek a balance between hard and soft water in their municipal water systems, when possible.

CURRENT GROUNDWATER USE

The nation's use of groundwater grew dramatically in the last several decades of the 20th century. According to a report from the United States Geological Survey (USGS) (*Estimated Use of Water in the United States in 1995*), the United States withdrew about 33 billion gallons per day (gpd) in 1950, reached a high of 82 billion gpd in 1980, dropped to 76 billion gpd in 1985, rose to 81 billion gpd in 1990, and declined somewhat to 78 billion gpd in 1995 (the latest data available). Figure 4.6 shows the percentage of groundwater allocated to various uses in the United States.

Human Needs

The USGS's *Estimated Use of Water in the United States in 1995* (the latest data available) reported that approximately 51 percent of the nation's population depended on groundwater as the primary source of drinking water. Figure 4.7 shows the distribution of the population that used groundwater for its domestic needs. The percentage was much higher in rural areas, where about 95 percent of the population depended on groundwater.

Plentiful groundwater is critical to the economy of the United States. According to an October 1999 USGS report (*Safe Drinking Water Act, Section 1429 Ground Water Report to Congress*), nationally, over 40 percent of all water used for crop irrigation and livestock watering and more

FIGURE 4.7

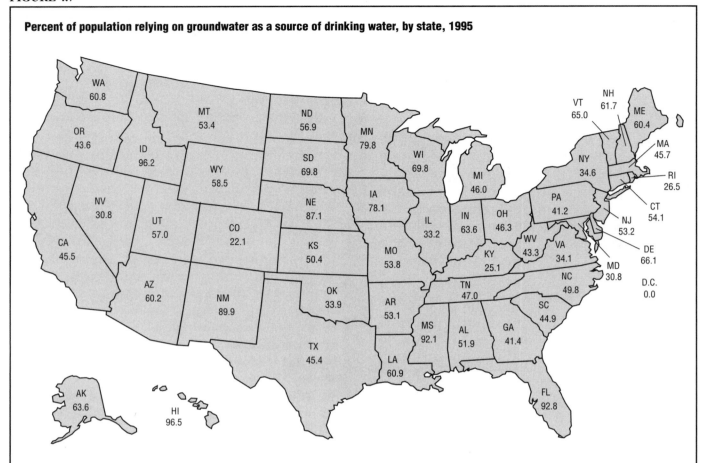

Percent of population relying on groundwater as a source of drinking water, by state, 1995

SOURCE: Adapted from "Exhibit 2-2: Percentage of Population Relying on Ground Water as a Drinking Source by State," in *Safe Drinking Water Act, Section 1429, Ground Water Report to Congress,* EPA-816-R-99-016, U.S. Environmental Protection Agency, Office of Water, Washington, DC, October 1999

than 20 percent of water used by industries comes from a groundwater source. Seventeen states obtain more than 25 percent of their overall water supply from groundwater. Another seven states depend on groundwater for more than 50 percent of their total water supply. The 13 states with the greatest groundwater withdrawals account for 69 percent of all groundwater used nationally. Of these 13 states, California, Texas, and Nebraska are the three largest users. Groundwater withdrawal is generally the highest in the western United States where the water is used to sustain important agricultural activities and to support a growing population. Figure 4.8 shows the volume of groundwater used by each state.

Ecological Needs

Historically, groundwater and surface water have been managed as separate resources. Since the 1970s, there has been a growing awareness that these two sources are inseparably linked. Groundwater seeps into rivers, streams, lakes, and other water bodies, and breaks the surface as springs. In some parts of the United States, especially arid regions, aquifers contribute a large portion of the water found in rivers and streams. Figure 4.9 shows groundwater contribution to surface water.

This source of surface water recharge is particularly important during dry periods. Reductions in surface water can have adverse effects on the ecology of a watershed, stressing fish populations and their food supply, wetlands and the plants and animals living along the banks of rivers and streams. Groundwater depletion in some areas has obliterated the aquatic and semiaquatic life that depended on groundwater flow in surface water streams.

Overpumping

Pumping groundwater from a well always causes a decline in groundwater levels at and near the well, and it always causes a diversion to the pumping well of groundwater that was moving slowly to its natural, possibly distant, area of discharge. Pumping a single well typically has a local effect on the groundwater flow system. Pumping many wells (sometimes hundreds or thousands of wells)

FIGURE 4.8

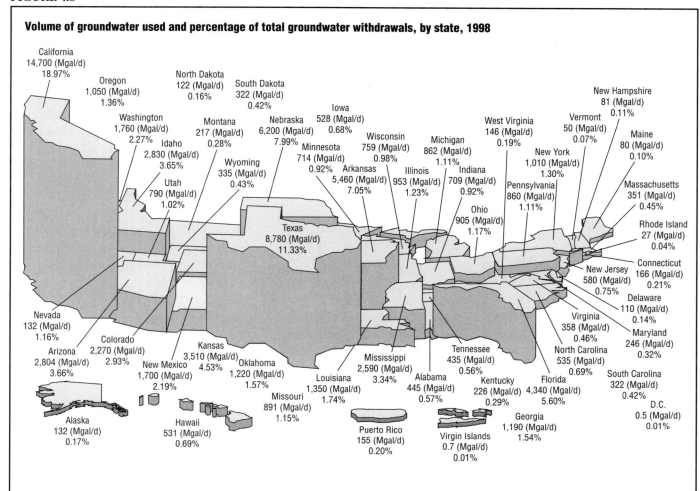

Volume of groundwater used and percentage of total groundwater withdrawals, by state, 1998

Note: Mgal/d= million gallons per day.

SOURCE: "Exhibit 2-3, Volume of groundwater used by the states (Mgal/d) and percentage of total groundwater withdrawals occurring in each state," in *Safe Drinking Water Act, Section 1429 Groundwater Report to Congress,* EPA-816-R-99-016, U.S. Environmental Protection Agency, Washington, DC, October 1999

in large areas can have regionally significant effects on groundwater systems.

If a groundwater system is not overused, the rate of groundwater recharge and discharge balances out. But in the United States, the rate has become uneven. According to a 1995 USGS report (the latest data available), every day in 1995, 78 billion gallons of groundwater were withdrawn. Figure 4.8 shows how these withdrawals are distributed across the United States.

Groundwater is pumped for a multitude of uses, including public (swimming pools, fire fighting, and street washing), domestic (drinking water and other household uses), agricultural (irrigation and livestock), industrial, mining, and other uses. When these withdrawals exceed the rate at which the groundwater source is recharged, they result in the lowering of groundwater to levels that may impair the resource.

Overpumping groundwater can have many different impacts. These include:

- Neighboring wells can dry up, requiring construction of new, deeper wells or significant changes to existing wells

- Compaction of aquifer materials causing the land above the aquifer to sink, leaving gaping holes in the land and causing damage to buildings, roads, canals, pipelines, and other infrastructure

- Permanent loss of aquifer capacity because of compaction of aquifer materials, resulting in higher pumping costs and a decrease in well yields

- Changes in the volume and direction of groundwater flow can induce flow of salty water and water of lower quality into a well.

FIGURE 4.9

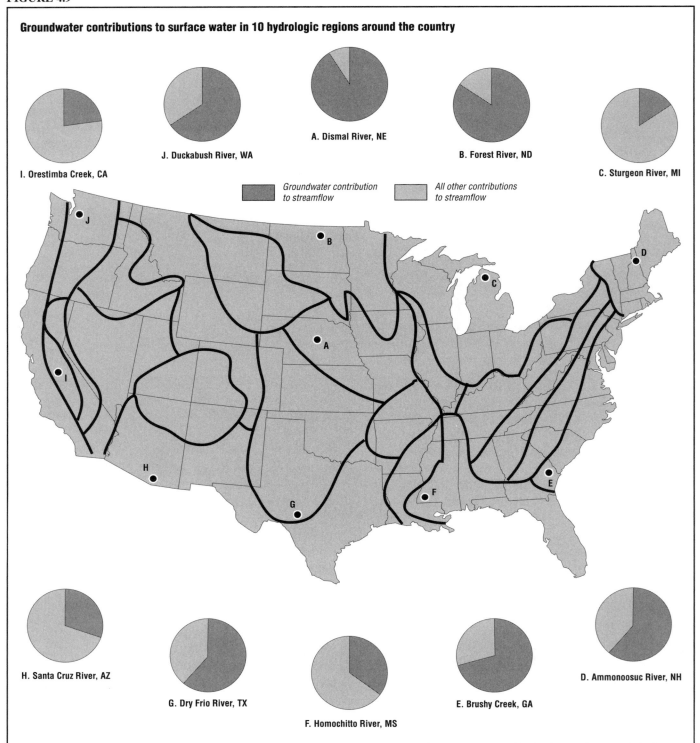

Groundwater contributions to surface water in 10 hydrologic regions around the country

I. Orestimba Creek, CA

J. Duckabush River, WA

A. Dismal River, NE

B. Forest River, ND

C. Sturgeon River, MI

Groundwater contribution to streamflow

All other contributions to streamflow

H. Santa Cruz River, AZ

G. Dry Frio River, TX

F. Homochitto River, MS

E. Brushy Creek, GA

D. Ammonoosuc River, NH

Note: In the conterminous United States, 24 regions were delineated where the interactions of groundwater and surface water are considered to have similar characteristics (i.e., groundwater accounts for a similar proportion of surface water discharge within each region). The estimated groundwater contribution to stream flow is shown for specific streams in 10 of the regions.

SOURCE: "Exhibit 2-5, Ground water contributions to surface water in 10 hydrologic regions around the country," in *Safe Drinking Water Act, Section 1429 Groundwater Report to Congress,* EPA 816-R-99-016, U.S. Environmental Protection Agency, Washington, DC, October 1999

- Lower stream baseflows can dry up wetlands and cause adverse impacts on ecological systems that are dependent on groundwater discharge

When Use Exceeds Replenishment

As early as 1940, C. V. Theis, in "The Source of Water from Wells" (*Civil Engineering,* vol. 10, no. 5, 1940), warned that pumping from wells profoundly affects aquifers. According to the USGS, large withdrawals of groundwater have altered the flow systems and geological and chemical conditions of some of the major aquifers in the United States. Declining groundwater levels can change the location and size of recharge areas and reduce discharge rates. Some aquifers in the West have suffered major losses in aquifer storage because of overpumping.

Groundwater Rights

For some Americans, droughts in the 1990s were a "wake-up call." In Texas, the 1996 drought resulted in federal disaster relief for farmers in 95 percent of the state's 254 counties and cost the Texas economy an estimated $5 billion. The disaster revived controversy surrounding the common law, "rule of capture," which permits a property owner to pump any amount of water from an aquifer beneath his or her land. Dispute over the control of groundwater prompted innumerable lawsuits, especially regarding the gradually depleted Edwards Aquifer (located in the San Antonio area).

Drought in Texas and in other states continued to be a concern in 1998. An August 5, 1998 Federal Emergency Management Administration (FEMA) press release described the strain put on underground water supplies in Texas during the week beginning August 3, 1998. Water flows from the Edwards Aquifer typically amount to 125,000 gallons per minute, but during that week, flow was reduced to 80,000 gallons.

RULE OF CAPTURE. Water laws in the arid Western states, where water supplies are limited and often inadequate, were developed under the Appropriation Doctrine. This doctrine is essentially a rule of capture, and awards a water right to the person actually using the water, and applies to both surface water and groundwater. It has two fundamental principles:

- First in time of use is first in right (that is, the earliest appropriation on a surface or groundwater has the first right to use the water)

- Application of the water to a beneficial use is the basis and measure of the right

EDWARDS AQUIFER: CITIES AND RURAL AREAS IN CONFLICT. The 160-mile-long Edwards Aquifer, one of the nation's most productive, is located in south-central Texas and conflict over its use is an example of the growing competition for water. This aquifer has supplied water to farmers for over half a century. As the only source of water for San Antonio, the nation's ninth largest city as of 2003, it has been designated a sole source aquifer by the EPA. Rain and runoff filter through the Edwards Aquifer before emerging in springs. But increased pumping for irrigation, additional water use for the rapidly growing population of San Antonio, and periodic droughts are steadily depleting the vast underground reservoir. The amount of water taken from this vital aquifer doubled over two decades. The once plentiful and seemingly infinite supply of water that was previously taken for granted is now recognized as an endangered resource.

The Edwards Aquifer has been the subject of bitter dispute between farmers and San Antonio residents as to who has rights to the water. The agricultural population is dependent on the Edwards Aquifer for the production of crops and, therefore, the farmers' livelihood. Officials in San Antonio, however, contend that the water needs of the city must be protected for present and future citizens. The rural and urban interests represent two factions involved in a modern-day version of a classic Western battle over water rights.

In 1993 Texas established the Edwards Aquifer Authority (EAA) to limit water withdrawal from this aquifer. Prior to the establishment of the EAA, the governing water-use principle was the appropriation doctrine, which simply stated was "if it's under your land, it's your water" (the rule of capture). Under the EAA, every Edwards Aquifer user, except for domestic and livestock owners using fewer than 25 gallons per day, had to have a permit with a specified annual withdrawal limit. The intent was to ensure fair distribution of water among all users.

In 1998 the Texas legislature adopted the Texas Critical Management Plan (CMP). The CMP allowed the EAA to further reduce withdrawals, despite the levels specified in permits, during low rainfall or critical periods by imposing restrictions on water-use activities and monthly limits on total water use. The purpose was to protect the aquifer's integrity and to conserve water. In addition, the CMP took water management to another level, requiring all Texas water suppliers and users to develop 50-year water management plans that address both surface and water supplies. These plans were the first step in statewide water source management and conservation.

According to the EAA Web site (www.edwards aquifer.net), conflict over pumping water from the Edwards Aquifer continues. According to the EAA, the 1993 law that created the Authority contains conflicting provisions. The law mandates that the Authority issue minimum annual pumping rights to those who could prove that they had been using the water during the previous 21 years, but it also set a pumping cap of 450,000 acre-feet per year. In

FIGURE 4.10

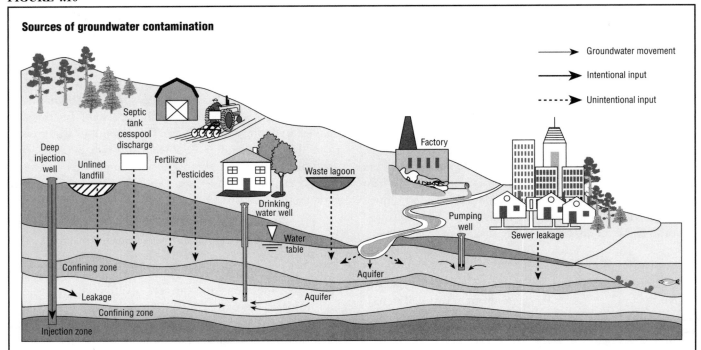

Sources of groundwater contamination

SOURCE: "Figure 6-2: Sources of ground water contamination," in *National Water Quality Inventory: 2000 Report,* EPA-841-R-02-001, U.S. Environmental Protection Agency, Washington, DC, August 2002

February 2003 the Authority had already issued pumping permits for about 482,000 acre-feet, and was considering the granting of another 82,000 acre-feet in annual pumping rights for 184 pending permit applications. In March 2003 the Authority voted to support newly proposed legislation that would raise the pumping cap to 550,000 acre-feet of water per year.

Preservation of the integrity of the Edwards Aquifer and conservation of its water also have implications for endangered species. According to the U.S. Fish & Wildlife Service (USFWS), the Edwards Aquifer is a critical habitat for nine endangered species (three beetles, one harvestman, and five spiders). A critical habitat is defined by the Endangered Species Act as a specific area deemed essential for the conservation of a threatened or endangered species, which may require special management consideration or protection. An April 8, 2003 USFWS press release reported that these endangered species are underground karst-dwelling invertebrates which are found only in karst limestone areas of Bexar County, Texas. According to Dale Hall, Director of the Southwest Region of the USFWS, "These species are particularly vulnerable to groundwater pollution and are an indicator species for the health of the Edwards Aquifer, which is the source of drinking water for more than one million people. Designating habitat that is critical to their survival is another step toward ensuring their future and the health of the aquifer itself."

VULNERABLE RESOURCE— GROUNDWATER QUALITY

Not too long ago, it was thought that soil provided a barrier or protective filter that neutralized the downward migration of contaminants from the land surface and prevented water resources from becoming contaminated. The discovery of pesticides and contaminants in groundwater, however, demonstrated that human activities do influence groundwater quality.

The potential for a contaminant to affect groundwater quality is dependent upon its ability to migrate through the overlying soils to the groundwater resource. Figure 4.10 shows the different mechanisms that can lead to groundwater contamination. Contamination can occur as a relatively well-defined localized plume coming from a specific source. It also can occur as a generalized deterioration over a large area because of diffuse nonpoint sources such as fertilizer and pesticide application.

Once it became apparent that groundwater was being contaminated, the questions of which waters were polluted, the severity of contamination, and what should be done about it had to be addressed. Many government and private organizations are working to find the answers, but it is not an easy task. As with other types of pollution control, problems include lack of accurate data, inadequate reporting and measurement techniques, the difficulty of setting acceptable standards, illegal dumping, designation of cleanup responsibilities, and funding.

FIGURE 4.11

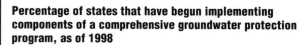

Percentage of states that have begun implementing components of a comprehensive groundwater protection program, as of 1998

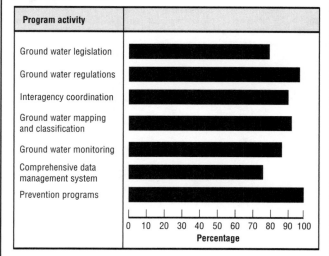

Note: Based on 30 states.

SOURCE: "Exhibit 4-1, Percentage of states that have begun implementing components of a comprehensive ground water protection program as reported by the states in the 305(b) report," in *Safe Drinking Water Act, Section 1429 Groundwater Report to Congress,* EPA-816-R-99-106, U.S. Environmental Protection Agency, Washington, DC, October 1999

The quality of most available groundwater in the United States is believed to be good according to the EPA's *Safe Drinking Water Act, Section 1429 Groundwater Report to Congress* (October 1999) and its *2000 National Water Quality Inventory.* The worst groundwater contamination is generally in the areas where use is heaviest—towns and cities, industrial complexes, and agricultural regions such as California's Central Valley.

Although very positive strides were made in assessing water quality in 2000, groundwater data collection is still too immature to provide a good national assessment. Accurate and representative assessment of groundwater quality requires a well planned and well carried out monitoring plan. The states are working to develop and implement these plans as manpower and monetary resources allow. At this time because the aquifer monitoring data reported by states represent different sources and differing monitoring purposes, care must be exercised in drawing conclusions.

Recognizing the need to protect valuable and vulnerable groundwater sources, the states have begun to implement comprehensive groundwater protection programs. (See Figure 4.11.) These programs are being integrated with surface water protection programs in recognition of the fact that baseflow in the nation's surface waters is dependent on groundwater.

FACTORS AFFECTING GROUNDWATER CONTAMINATION

All pollutants do not result in the same rate of contamination for the same amount of pollutant. Groundwater is affected by many of the following factors:

- The distance between the land surface where pollution occurs and the depth of the water table. The greater the distance, the greater the chance that the pollutant will biodegrade (be absorbed by) or react with soil minerals

- The mineral composition of the soil and rocks in the unsaturated zone. Heavy soil and organic materials lessen the potential for contamination

- The presence or absence of biodegrading microbes in the soil

- The amount of rainfall. Less rainfall results in less water entering the saturated zone and, therefore, lower quantities of contaminants

- The evapotranspiration rate. (This is the rate at which water is discharged into the atmosphere as a result of evaporation from the soil, surface water, and plants.) High rates reduce the amount of contaminated water reaching the saturated zone

POLLUTANTS

Types of Major Contaminants in Groundwater

In the EPA's *National Water Quality Inventory—1998 Report to Congress* (the latest data available for information on specific contaminants in groundwater) 31 of the 37 reporting states identified the types of contaminants they found in groundwater. The states said that nitrates, metals, volatile and semivolatile organic compounds, and pesticides were the pollutants found most often.

ARSENIC. Arsenic is a naturally occurring element in rocks and soils, and is the twentieth most common element in Earth's crust. In groundwater, arsenic is largely the result of minerals dissolving from naturally weathered rocks and soils over time. The USGS reported that the nation's groundwater typically contains less than one or two parts per billion (ppb) arsenic. A ppb is equal to about one drop in an Olympic-size swimming pool. Moderate to high arsenic levels do occur in some areas throughout the nation in a pattern related to geology, geochemistry, and climate. Elevated arsenic concentrations in groundwater are commonly found in the West, and in parts of the Midwest and the Northeast.

Arsenic research has shown that humans need arsenic as a trace element in their diet to survive. Too much arsenic, however, can be harmful. Arsenic can contribute to skin, bladder, and other cancers after prolonged exposure. In January 2001 the EPA proposed lowering the current

TABLE 4.1

Monitoring results for nitrates, 1998

Monitoring type	Number of states reporting	Number of states reporting MCL exceedances	Total number of units for which data were reported	Number of units having MCL exceedances	Total number of wells for which data were reported	Number of wells impacted by MCL exceedances	Highest number of wells that exceeded MCL within a single unit	Average number of wells that exceeded MCL within a single unit
Ambient monitoring network	16	10	95	38 (40%)	7,555	307	55 out of 114	8
Unfinished water quality data from PWS wells	8	0	20	0	538	0	0 out of 173	0
Unfinished water quality data from private or unregulated wells	4	3	4	3 (75%)	12,180	62	48 out of 3,165	21
Finished water quality data from PWS wells	17	10	57	26 (46%)	32,936	379	284 out of 3,057	14
Special studies	2	2	6	4 (67%)	424	68	33 out of 96	17

MCL = Maximum contaminant level.
PWS = Public water supply.

SOURCE: "Table 7-2. Monitoring results for nitrates," in *National Water Quality Inventory: 1998 Report to Congress,* EPA-841-F-00-006, U.S. Environmental Protection Agency, Washington, DC, 2000

maximum contaminant level (MCL) for arsenic in drinking water from 50 ppb to 10 ppb. The effective date of the new arsenic rule was February 22, 2002. Public water systems must comply with the 10 ppb level by January 23, 2006.

NITRATES. Many scientists and geologists consider nitrates to be the most widespread groundwater contaminant. Many states use its presence as an "indicator" of human impact on groundwater quality. Generally, a level of 3 ppb or more is considered indicative of human impact. Table 4.1 shows nitrate monitoring data reported by 31 states to the EPA in 1998 (the latest data available). Except for data on water quality prior to treatment from public water supply wells, the drinking water MCL of 10 ppb was exceeded in at least 40 percent of the hydrogeologic settings monitored. (A hydrogeologic setting is the geologic-related groundwater and surface water factors that affect and control groundwater movement in an area, and can be used to map areas with common characteristics for the purpose of predicting the vulnerability of similar settings to potential contaminants.) The percentage of monitored wells that were affected by nitrate levels above the MCL was less than 5 percent, and less than 1 percent for drinking water sources. The two special studies were specifically designed to monitor land-use effects with the potential to contribute nitrate to the environment, so those results may be skewed.

Nitrate contamination occurs most frequently in shallow groundwater (less than 100 feet below the surface) and in aquifers that allow the rapid movement of water. Regional differences in nitrate levels are related to soil drainage properties, other geologic characteristics, and agricultural practices. Nitrate in groundwater is generally highest in areas with well-drained soils and intensive cultivation of row crops, particularly corn, cotton, and vegetables. Low nitrate concentrations are found in areas of poorly drained soil and where pasture and woodland are intermixed with cropland. Crop fertilization is the most important agricultural practice for introducing nitrogen into groundwater. The primary source of nitrates is fertilizers used in agriculture, and in some areas, feedlot operations.

Nitrates are important because they affect both human health and ecological health. They can cause a public health risk to infants and young livestock. In surface waters, phosphorus and nitrogen were responsible for 29 percent of the impaired river miles and 44 percent of the impaired lake acres identified by the EPA in its *National Water Quality Inventory—1998 Report to Congress.* In some areas of the country, substantial amounts of nitrates in surface water are contributed by groundwater sources. For example, the USGS reported in 1997 that groundwater discharge was a significant source of nitrate loading to tidal creeks, coastal estuaries, and the Chesapeake Bay.

PESTICIDES. Pesticide concentrations in groundwater are generally low and rarely exceed EPA drinking water standards. In 1999 (the latest data available), the USGS reported that pesticide concentrations exceeded standards of guidelines in less than 1 percent of the wells sampled in the National Water Quality Assessment Program. This assessment, however, may be incomplete with respect to the overall health and environmental risks associated with pesticide presence in shallow groundwater. According to a 1999 report from the USGS (*The Quality of Our Nation's Waters: Nutrients and Pesticides. Circular 1225*) drinking water standards and guidelines exist for only 46 of

FIGURE 4.12

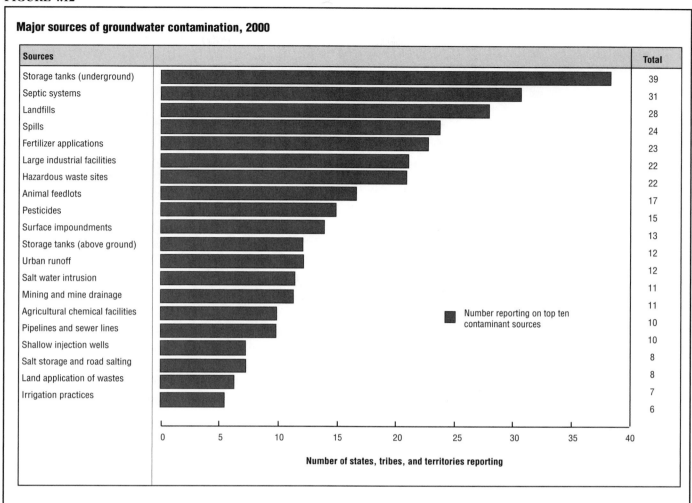

Major sources of groundwater contamination, 2000

Sources		Total
Storage tanks (underground)		39
Septic systems		31
Landfills		28
Spills		24
Fertilizer applications		23
Large industrial facilities		22
Hazardous waste sites		22
Animal feedlots		17
Pesticides		15
Surface impoundments		13
Storage tanks (above ground)		12
Urban runoff		12
Salt water intrusion		11
Mining and mine drainage		11
Agricultural chemical facilities		10
Pipelines and sewer lines		10
Shallow injection wells		8
Salt storage and road salting		8
Land application of wastes		7
Irrigation practices		6

■ Number reporting on top ten contaminant sources

Number of states, tribes, and territories reporting

SOURCE: "Major Sources of Ground Water Contamination," in *2000 National Water Quality Inventory,* EPA-841-R-02-001, U.S. Environmental Protection Agency, Washington, DC, August 2002

the 83 pesticide compounds identified. Of the sites where pesticides were detected, 73 percent had two or more compounds present. Continued research is needed to help reduce the current uncertainty in estimating risks to human health and to the environment from commonly occurring mixtures of pesticides.

METHYL TERTIARY BUTYL ETHER. Methyl tertiary butyl ether (MTBE) is a volatile organic chemical that is added to gasoline to increase octane levels and to reduce carbon monoxide and ozone levels in the air. It is more soluble in water, and less likely to be degraded than other common petroleum constituents. According to an October 2001 USGS report (*MTBE and Other Volatile Organic Compounds—New Findings and Implications on the Quality of Source Waters Used for Drinking-Water Supplies*) the EPA tentatively has classified MTBE as a potential human carcinogen. However, because of insufficient toxicity studies, the EPA has not yet instituted a drinking-water health advisory or standard.

In its National Water Quality Assessment Program (NAWQA), the USGS detected MTBE in about 5 percent of ambient groundwater samples collected across the nation. The concentrations typically were lower than the EPA's drinking-water consumer advisory concentration of 20 to 40 micrograms per liter. Less than 1 percent of the groundwater samples exceeded the EPA consumer advisory concentration of 20 micrograms per liter. MTBE was most often detected in groundwater underlying urban areas (14 percent of wells tested in urban areas had MTBE). The USGS also studied MTBE concentrations associated with drinking-water supplies from selected communities in 12 states in the Northeast and Mid-Atlantic regions. MTBE was detected in 9 percent of community water systems. These concentrations were low; less than 1 percent exceeded the EPA consumer advisory concentration.

Studies of the distribution of MTBE showed that the frequency of MTBE detection increases with its use, typically associated with urban and populated areas. MTBE

FIGURE 4.13

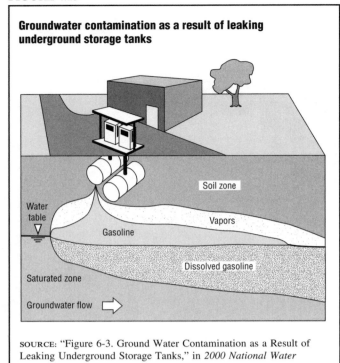

Groundwater contamination as a result of leaking underground storage tanks

SOURCE: "Figure 6-3. Ground Water Contamination as a Result of Leaking Underground Storage Tanks," in *2000 National Water Quality Inventory,* EPA-841-R-02-001, U.S. Environmental Protection Agency, Washington, DC, August 2002

as the most serious threat to their groundwater quality. Septic systems, landfills, industrial facilities, agriculture, and pesticides were also important contamination sources.

UNDERGROUND STORAGE TANKS. Leaking underground storage tanks (USTs) were identified as the leading source of groundwater contamination by the EPA in its 1996 and 1998 reports to Congress about national water quality. They were also cited as the leading source of groundwater contamination in the *2000 National Water Quality Inventory.* In general, most USTs are found at commercial and industrial facilities in the more heavily developed urban and suburban areas. USTs are used to store gasoline, hazardous and toxic chemicals, and diluted wastes. Gasoline leaking from UST systems at service stations is one of the most common causes of groundwater contamination. The primary causes of leakage in USTs are faulty installation and corrosion of tanks and pipelines.

At one time, USTs were made of steel, which eventually rusted and disintegrated, releasing their contents into the soil, leading to the discovery that a contaminant in the ground is likely to become a groundwater contaminant. One gallon of gasoline can contaminate one million gallons of water, or the amount of water needed for a community of 50,000 people. MTBE, a fuel additive, is particularly troublesome because it migrates quickly through soils into groundwater, and very small amounts can render groundwater undrinkable. Figure 4.13 shows how groundwater can be contaminated by leaking underground storage tanks.

In 1988 the EPA issued "comprehensive and stringent" rules that required devices to detect leaks, modification of tanks to prevent corrosion, regular monitoring, and immediate cleanup of leaks and spills. By December 1998 existing tanks had to be upgraded to meet those standards, replaced with new tanks, or closed. Existing tanks were to be replaced with expensive tanks made of durable, non-corrosive materials. As of February 1999, about 386,000 releases of contaminants from corroded underground storage tanks had been confirmed. Figure 4.14 shows the distribution of these releases nationwide. The EPA estimated that about half of those releases reached groundwater. In its *FY 2002 End-of-Year Activity Report* (December 23, 2002), the EPA's Office of Underground Storage Tanks reported that at the end of the 2002 fiscal year (September 30, 2002), 15,728 cleanups had been completed, bringing the total number of cleanups since the end of fiscal year 1992 to 284,602. At the end of fiscal year 2002, there were still 143,000 releases remaining to be cleaned up.

A March 5, 2003, report from the General Accounting Office (GAO) (*Environmental Protection: Recommendations for Improving the Underground Storage Tank Program*) stated that as of December 2002 at least 19 to 26 percent of states still had problems with leaking

has been detected in about 1 out of 5 wells in MTBE high-use areas. The findings also showed that some areas are more vulnerable to MTBE contamination than others. The frequency of MTBE detection increases with larger community water systems, specifically those serving more than 50,000 people. The difference in vulnerability reflects, in part, natural features, land use, and human activities such as pumping and watercraft use.

What began as an effort to reduce air pollution has become a water-quality concern that has necessitated dozens of costly studies and created a public health risk. In 1999 the EPA appointed the MTBE Blue Ribbon Panel to provide independent advice and counsel on the policy issues associated with the use of MTBE and other oxygenates in gasoline. In July 1999 the panel recommended a package of actions designed to be implemented simultaneously to maintain air quality benefits while enhancing water-quality protection and assuring a stable fuel supply at reasonable cost. The EPA was evaluating some of the recommendations, such as significantly reducing or phasing out the use of MTBE, and implementing others.

Sources of Pollution

In 2000 the EPA requested that each state identify the major sources that potentially threaten groundwater in their state. Figure 4.12 shows the results of that survey. Nearly three-fourths (39 states) rated underground storage tanks

FIGURE 4.14

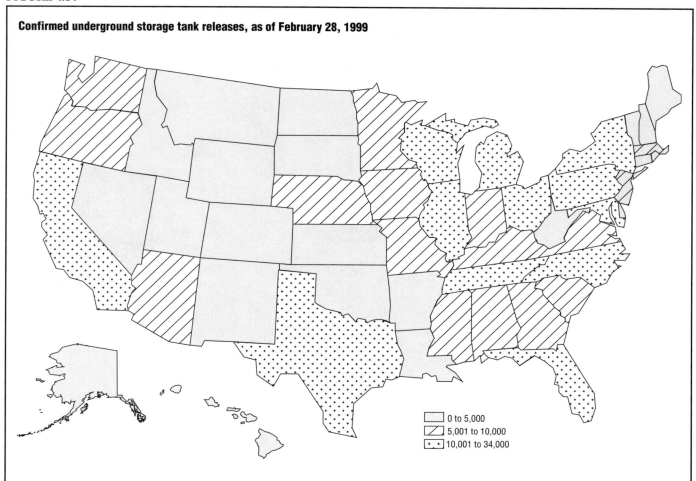

Confirmed underground storage tank releases, as of February 28, 1999

0 to 5,000
5,001 to 10,000
10,001 to 34,000

SOURCE: "Exhibit 3-2, Confirmed underground storage tank releases to soil and potentially ground water as of February 28," in *Safe Drinking Water Act, Section 1429 Groundwater Report to Congress*, EPA-816-R-99-016, U.S. Environmental Protection Agency, Washington, DC, October 1999

underground storage tanks. Although 89 percent of the 693,107 tanks subject to UST rules had leak prevention and detection equipment installed, more than 200,000 tanks were not being operated or maintained properly. The states reported that because of inadequate operation and maintenance of the leak detection equipment, even those tanks with the new equipment continued to leak. In order to address the problems, the GAO recommended that Congress provide states more funds from the UST trust fund to ensure improved training, inspections, and enforcement efforts. In addition, the GAO suggested that Congress require the states to inspect tanks at least every three years and provide the EPA and the states with additional enforcement authorities.

Underground storage tank owners and operators must also meet financial responsibility requirements that ensure they will have the resources to pay for costs associated with cleaning up releases and compensating third parties. Many states have provided financial assurance funds to help UST owners meet the financial requirements. In about 95 percent of the cases, the EPA or the states have succeeded in getting responsible parties to perform the cleanups.

In May 2001 the GAO released its report, *Environmental Protection: Improved Inspections and Enforcement Would Better Ensure the Safety of Underground Storage Tanks*. The report showed that by September 2000, approximately 1.5 million USTs had been closed permanently, leaving an estimated 693,107 tanks subject to federal regulation. To monitor this large amount of tanks, the EPA elicited the states' assistance in implementing and enforcing the UST program. Figure 4.15 shows the number of active USTs in each state that met the federal equipment requirements and the compliance rates reported. Figure 4.16 shows the states' variation in UST compliance with federal operations and maintenance requirements.

LANDFILLS AND SURFACE IMPOUNDMENTS. Septic systems and landfills were the second- and third-largest sources of groundwater contamination, respectively. (See Figure 4.12.) Landfills are areas set aside for disposal of garbage, trash, and other municipal wastes. Early

FIGURE 4.15

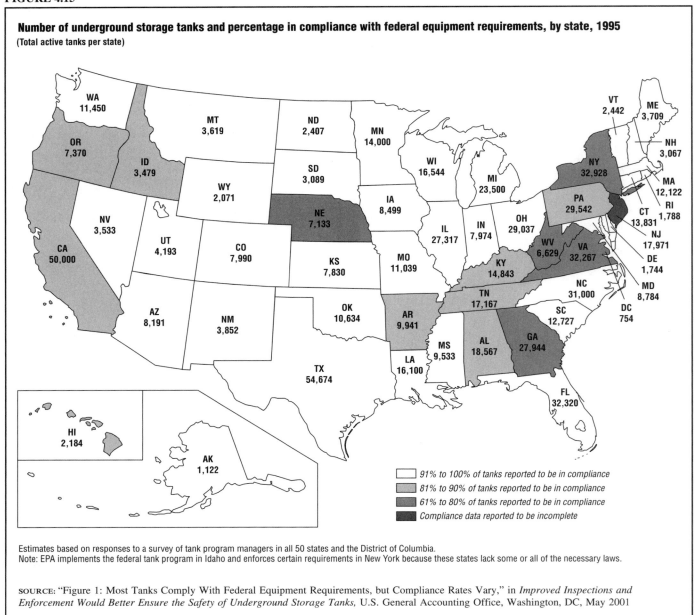

Number of underground storage tanks and percentage in compliance with federal equipment requirements, by state, 1995
(Total active tanks per state)

91% to 100% of tanks reported to be in compliance
81% to 90% of tanks reported to be in compliance
61% to 80% of tanks reported to be in compliance
Compliance data reported to be incomplete

Estimates based on responses to a survey of tank program managers in all 50 states and the District of Columbia.
Note: EPA implements the federal tank program in Idaho and enforces certain requirements in New York because these states lack some or all of the necessary laws.

SOURCE: "Figure 1: Most Tanks Comply With Federal Equipment Requirements, but Compliance Rates Vary," in *Improved Inspections and Enforcement Would Better Ensure the Safety of Underground Storage Tanks,* U.S. General Accounting Office, Washington, DC, May 2001

environmental regulation aimed at reducing air and surface water pollution called for disposing of solid wastes—including industrial wastes—underground and gave little consideration to the potential for groundwater contamination. Landfills were generally situated on land considered to have no other use. Many of the disposal sites were nothing more than large holes in the ground, abandoned gravel pits, old strip mines, marshlands, and sinkholes.

The leachate (the liquid that percolates through the waste materials) from landfills contains contaminants that can easily pollute groundwater when disposal areas are not properly lined. Landfills built and operated prior to the passage of the Resource Conservation and Recovery Act (RCRA) in 1976 are believed to represent the greatest

risk. RCRA was enacted to protect human health and the environment by establishing a regulatory framework to investigate and address past, present, and future environmental contamination of groundwater, and other media. The adoption of these new standards in 1976 forced many old landfills to close, as they could not meet the RCRA's safety standards, but in many cases the garbage dumped in them while in operation remains in place and is a threat to groundwater.

Surface impoundments are the industrial equivalent of landfills for liquids and are usually comprised of man-made pits, lagoons, and ponds that receive treated or untreated wastes directly from the discharge point. They may also be used to store chemicals for later use, to wash or treat ores,

FIGURE 4.16

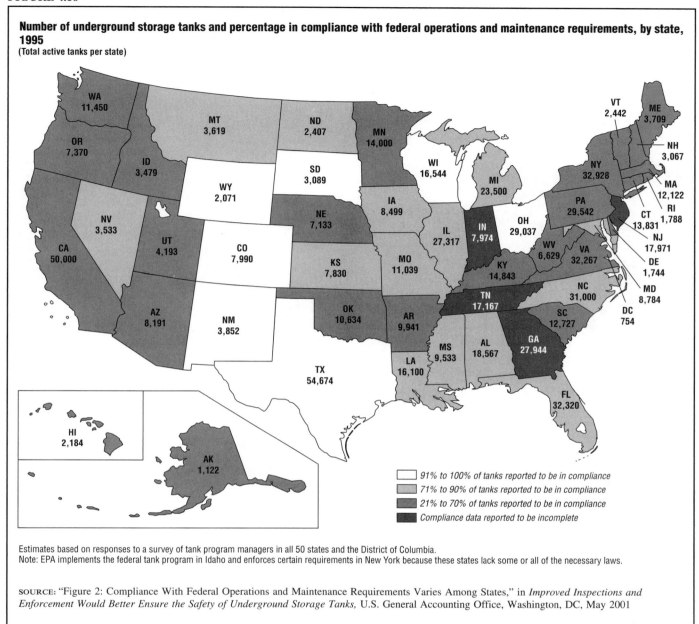

Number of underground storage tanks and percentage in compliance with federal operations and maintenance requirements, by state, 1995
(Total active tanks per state)

Legend:
- 91% to 100% of tanks reported to be in compliance
- 71% to 90% of tanks reported to be in compliance
- 21% to 70% of tanks reported to be in compliance
- Compliance data reported to be incomplete

Estimates based on responses to a survey of tank program managers in all 50 states and the District of Columbia.
Note: EPA implements the federal tank program in Idaho and enforces certain requirements in New York because these states lack some or all of the necessary laws.

SOURCE: "Figure 2: Compliance With Federal Operations and Maintenance Requirements Varies Among States," in *Improved Inspections and Enforcement Would Better Ensure the Safety of Underground Storage Tanks*, U.S. General Accounting Office, Washington, DC, May 2001

or to treat water for further use. Most are small, less than one acre, but some industrial and mining impoundments may be as large as 1,000 acres.

Prior to RCRA, most impoundments were not lined with a synthetic or impermeable natural material, such as clay, to prevent liquids from leaching into the ground. This is particularly important, since about 87 percent of impoundments were located over aquifers currently used as sources of drinking water. Aquifers located under non-lined impoundments are vulnerable to contamination. Less than 2 percent of the surface impoundments were located in areas where there is no groundwater or it is too salty for use. About 70 percent of the sites were located over thick and very permeable

aquifers that would allow any contaminant entering its waters to spread rapidly. Groundwater protection was rarely, if ever, considered during site selection.

Since the passage of RCRA, landfills and surface impoundments have been required to adhere to increasingly stringent regulations for site selection, construction, operation, and groundwater monitoring to avoid contaminating groundwater. Prevention of groundwater contamination is largely the responsibility of state and local government. Examples of the more stringent requirements are landfill liners and groundwater monitoring. (See Figure 4.17.)

HAZARDOUS WASTE SITES. Hazardous waste is an unavoidable by-product of an industrial society. Many chemicals are used to manufacture goods.

FIGURE 4.17

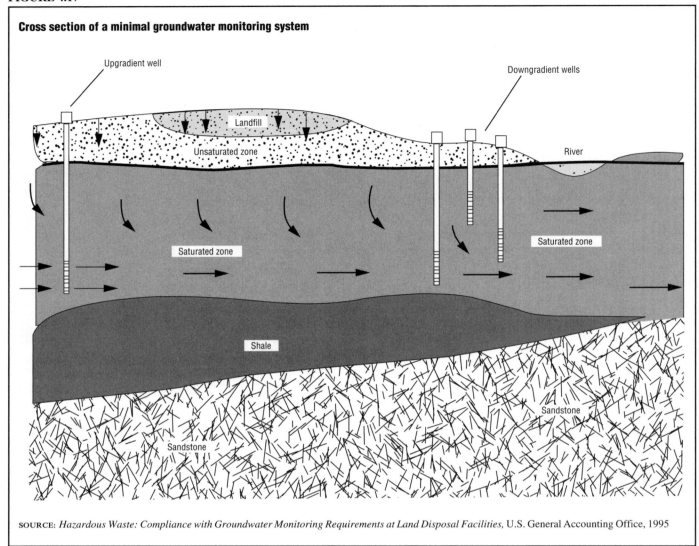

Cross section of a minimal groundwater monitoring system

Upgradient well

Downgradient wells

Landfill

Unsaturated zone

River

Saturated zone

Saturated zone

Shale

Sandstone

Sandstone

SOURCE: *Hazardous Waste: Compliance with Groundwater Monitoring Requirements at Land Disposal Facilities,* U.S. General Accounting Office, 1995

Hazardous waste generators can be large industries, such as automobile manufacturers, or small neighborhood businesses, like the local photo shop. Although the quantity of hazardous waste can be reduced through innovation and good management, it is impossible to eliminate all hazardous residue because of the demand for goods. The EPA estimated that between 2 and 4 percent of all waste was hazardous.

Contamination of groundwater with hazardous waste is frequently the result of historic indiscriminate waste disposal in landfills, impoundments, and dumps. Today, sites that handle hazardous waste or a mix of hazardous and nonhazardous waste are subject to very strict controls.

When a waste site is found to be so badly contaminated with hazardous waste that it represents a serious threat to human health (for example, contamination of groundwater used for drinking with known carcinogens), it is placed on the National Priorities List (NPL) established by the Comprehensive Environmental Response,

Compensation, and Liability Act (CERCLA, commonly known as Superfund). Sites placed on the Superfund list are eligible for federal intervention and cleanup assistance. As of April 30, 2003, 1,236 sites were listed on the NPL. Most were general sites such as industrial and municipal landfills, and military bases. About one-fifth of the listed Superfund sites were municipal landfills. The contaminants most often reported in groundwater at Superfund sites are shown in Table 4.2.

INJECTION WELLS. An injection well is any bored, drilled, driven shaft, or dug hole that is deeper than it is wide that is used for the disposal of waste underground. The EPA's underground injection control (UIC) program identifies five classes of injection wells. Class I wells are used to inject hazardous and nonhazardous waste beneath the lowest formation containing an underground source of drinking water (USDW) within one-quarter mile of the well bore. Class II wells are used to inject fluids associated with oil and natural gas recovery and storage of liquid

TABLE 4.2

Contaminants most frequently reported in ground water at Comprehensive Environmental Response, Compensation, and Liability Act (CERCLA) National Priority List sites, as of 1996

Rank	Contaminants	Number of sites
Organic compounds		
1	1,1,2-Trichloroethylene	336
2	Chloroform	167
3	Tetrachloroethene	167
4	Benzene	163
5	Toluene	160
6	1,1,1-Trichloroethane	155
7	Polychlorinated biphenyls	138
8	Trans-1,2-Dichloroethylene	107
9	1,1-Dichloroethane	103
10	1,1-Dichloroethene	94
11	Vinyl chloride	81
12	Xylene	76
13	Ethylbenzene	69
14	Carbon tetrachloride	68
15	Phenol	61
16	Methylene chloride	58
17	1,2-Dichloroethane	56
18	Pentachlorophenol	52
19	Chlorobenzene	46
20	DDT	35
Inorganic constituents		
1	Lead	306
2	Chromium ion and related species	213
3	Arsenic	149
4	Cadmium	126
5	Copper ion and related species	83
6	Mercury	81
7	Zinc ion and related species	75
8	Nickel ion and related species	45
9	Barium	41
10	Cyanides and associated salts	38

SOURCE: "Contaminants Most Frequently Reported in Ground Water at CERCLA National Priority List Sites," in *National Water Quality Inventory—1996 Report to Congress,* U.S. Environmental Protection Agency, Washington, DC, 1998

hydrocarbons. Class III wells are used in connection with the solution mining of minerals that are not conventionally mined. Class IV wells are used to inject hazardous or radioactive waste into or above a formation that is within one-quarter mile of a USDW. Class V wells are injection wells not included in Classes I through IV. Each well class has the potential to contaminate groundwater. Classes I though IV have specific regulations and are closely monitored. Class V wells are typically shallow wells used to place a variety of fluids underground.

An August 1998 EPA fact sheet (*Class V Injection Wells*) states that the EPA estimated that there were more than 1,000,000 Class V injection wells. These wells are found in every state, especially in unsewered areas. There are many types of Class V wells, including large capacity cesspools, motor vehicle waste disposal systems, storm water drainage wells, large capacity septic systems, aquifer remediation wells, and many other types. The waste

entering these wells is not treated. Certain types of these wells have great potential to have high concentrations of contaminants that might endanger groundwater.

Class V injection wells are currently regulated by the UIC program under the authority of the Safe Drinking Water Act (SDWA). Class V wells are –authorized by rule," which means that they do not require a permit if they comply with UIC program requirements and do not endanger underground sources of drinking water. In December 1999 the EPA adopted regulations addressing Class V wells that were large capacity cesspools and motor vehicle waste disposal wells. Under these regulations:

- New cesspools were prohibited as of April 2000
- Existing cesspools had to be phased out by April 2005
- New motor vehicle waste disposal wells were prohibited
- Existing wells in regulated areas were to be phased out in groundwater protection areas identified in state source water assessment programs. These requirements were scheduled to be phased in over seven years

In May 2001 the EPA announced its intent to continue to regulate Class V wells, with the exception of large capacity cesspools and motor vehicle waste disposal wells, for the foreseeable future using the "authorized by rule" approach.

AGRICULTURE. As in surface water contamination, agricultural practices play a major role in groundwater contamination. Agricultural practices that have the potential to contaminate groundwater include fertilizer and pesticide application, animal feedlots, irrigation practices, agricultural chemical facilities, and drainage wells. The contamination can result from routine applications, spillage or misuse of pesticides and fertilizers during handling and storage, manure storage and spreading, improper storage of chemicals, irrigation practices, and irrigation return drains serving as direct conduits to groundwater. Fields with overapplied or misapplied fertilizer and pesticides can introduce nitrogen, pesticides, and other contaminants into groundwater. Animal feedlots often have impoundments from which wastes (bacteria, nitrates, and total and dissolved solids) may infiltrate into groundwater.

Human-induced salinity in groundwater also occurs in agricultural regions where irrigation is used extensively. Irrigation water continually flushes nitrate-related compounds from fertilizers into the shallow aquifers along with high levels of chloride, sodium, and other metals. This increases the salinity (dissolved solids) of the underlying aquifers. Overpumping can diminish the water in aquifers to the point where salt water from nearby coastal areas will intrude into the aquifer. Salinas Valley, California, is an example of saltwater intrusion. Twelve states identified saltwater intrusion as a major source of groundwater contamination in their 2000 305(b) reports to the EPA. (See Figure 4.12.)

SEPTIC SYSTEMS. Septic systems were cited as the second most common source of groundwater contamination by 31 reporting states. Septic systems are on-site waste disposal systems that are used where public sewerage is not available. Septic tanks are used to detain domestic wastes to allow the settling and digestion of solids prior to the distribution of liquid wastes into permeable leach beds for absorption into soil. Wastewater is attacked in the leach beds by biological organisms in the soil and broken down over time. According to information collected by the National Small Flows Clearinghouse (1999), approximately 23 million Americans living mostly in rural areas use individual sewage disposal systems. Millions of commercial and industrial facilities also use these systems. American households dispose of 3.5 billion gallons of liquid waste into septic systems each day, and between 820 and 1,450 billion gallons of waste into the ground each year.

Improperly constructed and poorly maintained septic systems may cause substantial and widespread nutrient and microbial contamination to groundwater. This belief is based on some studies done in different parts of the country, which have shown nitrogen levels elevated above background nitrogen levels in areas with concentrated septic systems. There has been no systematic study done nationwide. Septic systems have also been incriminated in some bacterial and viral disease outbreaks associated with drinking groundwater.

GROUNDWATER CLEANUP

To clean up the nation's groundwater is expensive. The costs associated with alternative water supplies, water treatment, and contaminant source removal or remediation are in the millions per site. The Water Protection Council in 1996 estimated $14 billion annually is needed to remediate groundwater and soil at Superfund sites, hazardous waste sites with corrective actions, leaking UST sites, Departments of Defense and Energy waste sites, and other contaminated sites. The GAO in 1999 reported that Superfund cleanups had already cost $14 billion, and projected another $9.9 billion was needed to complete cleanup at remaining sites.

In allocating limited resources, cleanup decisions are based on a cost/benefit analysis that considers such factors as the extent of the problem, the potential health effects, and the alternatives, if any. If the pollution is localized, it may be more practical to simply shut down the contaminated wells and find water elsewhere. Cleanup options range from "capping" a section of an aquifer with a layer of clay to prevent more pollution, to more complex (and expensive) methods such as pumping out and treating the water and then returning it to the aquifer.

GROUNDWATER PROTECTION
States' Role

Prevention of groundwater contamination is largely the responsibility of state and local government. In 1991 the EPA established a national groundwater protection strategy to place greater emphasis on comprehensive state management of groundwater resources. The EPA recognized that the wide range of land-use practices that can adversely affect groundwater quality is most effectively managed at the state and local level. The states use three basic approaches to protect groundwater and address the problems of contaminants and contamination sources:

- Nondegradation policies that are designed to protect groundwater quality at its existing level

- Limited degradation policies that involve setting up water-quality standards to protect groundwater. These standards set maximum contamination levels for chemicals and bacteria and establish guidelines for taste, odor, and color of the water

- Groundwater classification systems that are similar to the classification systems for surface waters established under the Clean Water Act and its amendments

These classification systems are used by state officials to determine which aquifers should receive higher or lower priorities for protection and cleanup. High-priority areas include recharge areas, which affect large quantities of water, or public water supplies, where pollution affects drinking water. The SDWA requirements for state programs that address protection of wellheads used as drinking water sources, coupled with other federal and state source water protection programs, should lead to better, more coordinated management of potential drinking water contaminant sources within drinking water source protection areas.

Based on data provided by the states in 1996 and 1998 in their 305(b) reports, Figure 4.11 shows the percentage of states implementing key groundwater management program components. Eleven states have EPA-endorsed comprehensive groundwater protection programs in place with another 11 working toward endorsement. The most important benefit derived from comprehensive groundwater management approaches is the ability to establish coordinated priorities among the many groups involved in groundwater management. The following key components are common to successful state programs:

- Enacting legislation

- Promulgating protection regulations

TABLE 4.3

Federal laws affecting ground water administered by the Environmental Protection Agency

Clean Water Act (CWA)

Ground water protection is addressed in Section 102 of the CWA, providing for the development of federal, state, and local comprehensive programs for reducing, eliminating, and preventing ground water contamination.

Safe Drinking Water Act (SDWA)

Under the SDWA, EPA is authorized to ensure that water is safe for human consumption. To support this effort, SDWA gives EPA the authority to promulgate Maximum Contaminant Levels (MCLs) that define safe levels for some contaminants in public drinking water supplies. One of the most fundamental ways to ensure consistently safe drinking water is to protect the source of that water (i.e., ground water). Source water protection is achieved through four programs: the Wellhead Protection Program (WHP), the Sole Source Aquifer Program, the Underground Injection Control (UIC) Program, and, under the 1996 Amendments, the Source Water Assessment Program.

Resource Conservation and Recovery Act (RCRA)

The intent of RCRA is to protect human health and the environment by establishing a comprehensive regulatory framework for investigating and addressing past, present, and future environmental contamination or ground water and other environmental media. In addition, management of underground storage tanks is also addressed under RCRA.

Comprehensive Environmental, Response, Compensation, and Liability Act (CERCLA)

CERCLA provides a federal "Superfund" to clean-up soil and ground water contaminated by uncontrolled or abandoned hazardous waste sites as well as accidents, spill, and other emergency releases of pollutants and contaminants into the environment. Through the Act, EPA was given power to seek out those parties responsible for any release and assure their cooperation in the clean-up. The program is designed to recover costs, when possible, from financially viable individuals and companies when the clean-up is complete.

Federal Insecticide, Fungicide, and Rodenticide Act (FIFRA)

FIFRA protects human health and the environment from the risks of pesticide use by requiring the testing and registration of all chemicals used as active ingredients of pesticides and pesticide products. Under the Pesticide Management Program, States and Tribes wishing to continue use of chemicals of concern are required to prepare a prevention plan that targets specific areas vulnerable to ground water contamination.

SOURCE: "Federal laws administered by EPA affecting ground water" in *Safe Drinking Water Act, Section 1429 Groundwater Report to Congress*, EPA-8160R-99-016, U.S. Environmental Protection Agency, Washington, DC, October 1999

- Establishing interagency coordination with surface water and other programs

- Performing groundwater mapping and classification

- Monitoring ambient groundwater quality

- Developing comprehensive data management systems

- Adopting and implementing prevention and remediation programs

Lack of funding targeted directly to groundwater is the reason most commonly cited by states for their limited efforts in undertaking a more comprehensive approach to groundwater issues. Groundwater is not a high priority for funding. In most states the funding is directed toward state or federally mandated programs. Mandated programs are generally specific as to how and for what money can be spent, often precluding the state from using the funds to address nonmandated groundwater protection priorities even when the result would prevent groundwater pollution in the future. Funding targeted to groundwater concerns would allow the states to better address the problems of program fragmentation within the state and to provide basic program needs such as monitoring, resource characterization, and the development and implementation of protection programs.

Ultimately, surface water and groundwater protection takes place at the state and local level, where the costs and benefits are recognized initially. This financial burden is often beyond the resources of state and local governments who struggle to meet federal, state, and local mandates in many widely differing arenas with limited resources. In November 2002 a press release from the National Conference of State Legislatures ("New National Survey Reports State Budgets Fall $17.5 Billion Short") reported that states had a collective $17.5 billion budget gap to fill before fiscal year 2003 ended on June 30. The survey also found that 33 of the states (about two-thirds) reported revenue collections below forecasted levels though October 2002, 26 states had revised their revenue forecasts downward, and 29 states reported that spending was exceeding budgeted levels. Cost-containment measures adopted by the states may include cuts in programs and projects.

Federal Role

Federal laws, regulations, and programs since the 1970s have reflected the growing recognition of the need to protect the nation's groundwater and use it wisely. Table 4.3 summarizes the federal laws affecting groundwater. The Federal Water Pollution Control Act (Clean Water Act) in 1972 and the SDWA in 1974 began the federal role in groundwater protection. The passage of the RCRA in 1976 and CERCLA (or Superfund) in 1980 cemented the federal government's current focus on groundwater remediation. Since the passage of these acts, the federal government has directed billions of dollars in private and public money and resources toward cleanup of contaminated groundwater at Superfund, RCRA corrective action facilities, and leaking USTs.

Until this time, the emphasis in federal and state programs has been on cleaning up existing contamination, and not on pollution prevention. The cleanup programs have been very costly. These costs have become considerable incentives for the private, state, local, and federal sectors to investigate and implement preventive measures.

Certain federal and state programs are designed to prevent groundwater contamination. The problem is that these programs tend to focus on a narrow set of contaminants or contaminant sources. For example, the Federal Insecticide, Fungicide, and Rodenticide Act established regulations to prevent groundwater contamination resulting from pesticide use.

FUTURE GROUNDWATER MANAGEMENT

The nation's groundwater management is highly fragmented with responsibilities spread over many federal, state, and local programs. Unique legal authorities at each government level allow for controlling one or more of the groundwater threats discussed here. For groundwater management to be successful in protecting and conserving this resource, these various authorities need to complement one another to allow for comprehensive management. Programs such as the EPA's groundwater protection strategy, which places greater emphasis on comprehensive state management of groundwater resources, and the SDWA-mandated wellhead protection and the source water assessment and protection programs are a good beginning.

CHAPTER 5
DRINKING WATER—SAFETY ON TAP

SATISFYING A HUGE DEMAND

Most water is used directly or indirectly from the tap. On average, people in the United States on community water supplies use about 100 gallons of water per person per day. People with private wells use slightly less. According to the American Water Works Association report, *Residential End Uses of Water* (1999) (the latest data available), about 69 gallons per day are used indoors and the rest is used for activities done outdoors. Of this daily supply, only a small portion is actually consumed as drinking water. *American Drinking Habits,* a survey by the Yankelovich Partners for the International Bottled Water Association (2000), reported that slightly less than one gallon per person is actually drunk from the tap each day.

Residential water consumers use most water for purposes other than drinking, such as toilet flushing, bathing, cooking, and cleaning. In the United States, significant amounts of water are used for kitchen and laundry appliances, such as garbage disposals, clothes washers, and automatic dishwashers; for automobile washing; and for lawn and garden watering. Additional community use includes fire fighting, fountains, public swimming pools, and watering of public parks and landscaping.

DRINKING WATER SOURCES

The two primary sources of drinking water are fresh surface water and groundwater. In 2002 more than half (66 percent) of the population of the United States received water from sources that obtained that water from surface water like lakes, rivers, and reservoirs. The remaining population (34 percent) were supplied water that came from groundwater stored in aquifers. Aquifers are underground geologic formations that are made up of saturated layers of sand and rock fragments and store or transfer water. Aquifer water is obtained from wells and springs. In a few instances, desalinization is used to treat salt water to make it

fit to drink. Contaminants can enter water sources through a variety of pathways, but the level or amount of harmful substances in water is the main determinant as to whether the water can be treated and made safe to drink.

PUBLIC AND PRIVATE WATER SUPPLIES
Public Water Systems

According to the Environmental Protection Agency (EPA) in its April 2003 fact sheet *Public Drinking Water System Programs,* public water supply systems serve 85 to 90 percent of the U.S. population. The remainder gets its water from private water systems. Urban areas draw their supplies largely from surface water sources, while 90 percent of the drinking water in rural areas is drawn from groundwater.

A public water supply system is one that has at least 15 service connections or serves at least 25 people per day for 60 days of the year. According to the EPA report *Factoids: Drinking Water and Ground Water Statistics for 2002* (January 2003), there were 161,316 of these systems of varying size in the United States in 2002. The amount and type of treatment provided varies with source and quality. For example, some public systems using a groundwater source require no treatment, while others may need to disinfect the water or apply additional treatment.

There are three types of public water systems. Community water systems are those that supply water to the same population year-round. In 2002 there were approximately 53,437 community water systems serving 267,722,666 people in the United States or 90.3 percent of the entire population. (See Table 5.1.)

Non-transient non-community water systems are the second type. They serve the public but not the same people year-round. Examples of non-transient non-community systems are schools, factories, office buildings, hospitals which have their own water systems, and other public

TABLE 5.1

Types of public water systems by water source and population served, 2002

Community water systems

Water source	Systems	Population served	Percent of systems	Percent of population
Groundwater	41,691	84,025,121	78	31
Surface water	11,746	183,697,545	22	69
Total	53,437	267,722,666	100	100

Non-transient non-community water systems

Water source	Systems	Population served	Percent of systems	Percent of population
Groundwater	17,931	5,297,615	98	88
Surface water	756	735,174	4	12
Total	18,687	6,032,789	100	100

Transient non-community water systems

Water source	Systems	Population served	Percent of systems	Percent of population
Groundwater	87,130	12,107,193	98	53
Surface water	2,062	10,742,320	2	47
Total	89,192	22,849,513	100	100

SOURCE: Adapted from "Water Source," in *Factoids: Drinking Water and Ground Water Statistics for 2002,* EPA-816-K-03-001, U.S. Environmental Protection Agency, Washington, DC, January 2003

FIGURE 5.1

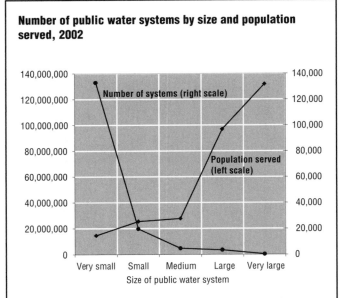

Number of public water systems by size and population served, 2002

SOURCE: Created by Information Plus from data in "Public Water System Inventory data," in *Factoids: Drinking Water and Ground Water Statistics for 2002,* EPA-816-K-03-001, U.S. Environmental Protection Agency, Washington, DC, January 2003

accommodations. There were 18,687 non-transient non-community water systems in the United States in 2002 serving just over 6 million people or 2 percent of the population. (See Table 5.1.)

Transient non-community water systems are the third type of public water system. These are systems that provide water in places such as gas stations or campgrounds where people do not remain for long periods of time. In 2002 there were 89,192 such transient non-community water systems serving 22,849,513 people or 7.7 percent of the population. (See Table 5.1.)

The EPA and state health and environment departments regulate public water supplies. Public suppliers are required to ensure that the water meets certain government-defined health standards under the Safe Drinking Water Act (SDWA; Public Law 93-523). This law mandates that all public suppliers test their water on a regular basis to check for the existence of contaminants and to treat their water supplies, if necessary, to take out or reduce certain pollutants to levels that will not harm human health.

According to the EPA report *Factoids: Drinking Water and Ground Water Statistics for 2002,* 95 percent of public water systems (152,680) are small or very small, each serving fewer than 3,300 people. (See Figure 5.1.)

The remaining 5 percent of systems are few in number (8,636) but service many more people. The medium size services each provide water to between 3,301 and 10,000 people. The large services provide to more than 10,000 people each. Together the medium and large public water services provide water for the majority of Americans, 86.5 percent of people who drink water from a public supply or 256,536,402 people.

Private Water Systems

According to the EPA, in its *Drinking Water Standards & Health Effects* (December 1999), 10 percent of Americans receive their water from private wells. System owners are solely responsible for the quality of the water provided from these sources. Individual wells serving four or fewer housing units provide the water for approximately 15 percent of homes. Only 1 percent of the nation's homes get their water directly from another source, such as creeks, rivers, lakes, springs, and cisterns.

Personal private water supplies, usually wells, are not regulated under the SDWA. Many states, however, have programs designed to help well owners protect their water supplies. Usually these state-run programs are not regulatory, but provide safety information. This type of information is vital because private wells are often shallower than those used by public suppliers. The more shallow the well, the greater the potential for contamination.

CONTAMINANTS IN DRINKING WATER

Because of its capacity to dissolve numerous substances, water is regarded as the universal solvent. Pure water rarely occurs in nature, as water dissolves minerals and other natural substances. At low levels, dissolved contaminants generally are not harmful in drinking water. Removing all contaminants would be extremely expensive and might not provide greater protection of health. The amount of harmful substances in water is the main determinant as to whether or not the water is safe to drink.

Contaminants are grouped into two broad categories: chemical and microbial. Both chemical and microbial contaminants may be naturally occurring or may be caused by human activity. Chemical contaminants include metals, pesticides, synthetic chemical compounds, suspended solids, and other chemicals. Microbial contaminants include bacteria, viruses, and microscopic parasites.

The health effects of drinking contaminated water can occur either over a short or long period. Short-term, or acute, reactions are those that occur within a few hours or days after drinking contaminated water. Acute reactions may be caused by a chemical or microbial contaminant. Long-term, or chronic, effects occur after water with relatively low doses of a pollutant has been consumed for several years or even over a lifetime. Most chronic effects are caused by chemical contaminants.

The ability to detect contaminants has improved over the past decades. Scientists can now identify specific chemical pollutants in terms of one part contaminant in one billion parts of water. In some cases, scientists can measure them in parts per trillion. One part per billion (ppb) is equal to one pound in 500,000 tons or approximately one teaspoon in five Olympic-size swimming pools. Although these measurements appear very tiny, such small amounts can be significant in terms of health effects.

Chemical Contaminants

All drinking water contains minerals dissolved from the earth. In small amounts, some of these minerals are acceptable because they often enhance the quality of the water (for example, giving it a pleasant taste). A few, such as zinc and selenium, in very small amounts, contribute to good health. Other naturally occurring minerals are not desirable because they may cause a bad taste or odor (such as excessive amounts of iron, manganese, or sulfur) or because they may be harmful to health (for example, boron).

A wide variety of contaminants may cause serious health risks in water supplies. Not all contaminants are found in all water supplies: some water supplies have no undesirable contaminants. Other supplies have no contaminants that have health significance. Contaminant presence is frequently the result of human activity, and may have long-term consequences. While harmful levels of microorganisms generally make their presence known quickly by causing illness with fairly obvious symptoms, the effects of some toxic chemicals may not be apparent for months or even years after exposure. Some chemical pollutants are known carcinogens (cancer causing), while others are suspected of causing birth defects, miscarriages, and heart disease. In many cases, the effects occur only after long-term exposure.

ARSENIC. Arsenic is a naturally occurring element in rocks and soils, and is soluble in water. Arsenic has been recognized as a poison for centuries. Recent research, however, has shown that humans need arsenic in their diet as a trace element. Too much arsenic, though, can contribute to skin, bladder, and other cancers after prolonged exposure. Because of this risk, the National Research Council recommended lowering the current maximum contaminant level (MCL) of 50 ppb for arsenic in drinking water.

In January 2001 the EPA proposed a new MCL that required public water supplies to reduce arsenic to 5 ppb by the year 2006. The EPA estimated the cost of implementation at $379 million to $445 million. The Association of State Drinking Water Administrators (ASDWA) and several organizations and states challenged the new level. Serious concerns exist about the extent of arsenic occurrence in drinking water, the health effects of arsenic at the 3 to 20 ppb level (the level found in U.S. supplies), the validity of the EPA's cost estimates (including waste disposal), and the EPA's approach to regulating non-transient non-community water supplies. The ASDWA has recommended that the EPA consider an MCL of 20 ppb, as this is the level where the EPA currently believes that the cost-benefit ratio is maximized. A maximized cost-benefit ratio is one in which the most benefit (in this case, the greatest reduction in the number of illnesses) can be achieved for the least cost per illness reduction. Money expended beyond the maximized cost-benefit ratio can result in additional illness reduction but at increasingly higher costs per illness reduced. For example, if at the maximized cost-benefit ratio an estimated 1,000 illnesses are avoided for $30 million, the avoidance of an additional 1,000 illnesses may cost an additional $75 million because of the need for additional preventive measures and treatment to achieve the additional reduction.

Most of the burden of implementing the new arsenic MCL will fall on the systems least likely to be able to afford it. According to a 2000 study by the U.S. Geological Survey (USGS), an estimated 845 public water supplies exceed 20 ppb arsenic; 88 percent of these supplies served 10,000 people or fewer. An estimated 4,635 public water systems exceed the proposed 5 ppb MCL; 95 percent of these systems served 10,000 persons or less. (See Table

TABLE 5.2

Estimated number of public water-supply systems that exceeded target arsenic concentrations in their groundwater resources, by arsenic level and size of population served, for selected counties, 1999

Arsenic (µg/L)	<100	100-500	501-1,000	1,001-3,300	3,301-10,000	10,001-50,000	50,001-100,000	100,0001-1,000,000	>1,000,000
	Population served								
	Estimated number of public water-supply systems that exceed the targeted arsenic concentration in the associated groundwater resource								
1	3,296	3,144	956	1,152	617	416	61	32	0.4
2	2,318	2,191	670	789	420	295	45	21	0.2
5	1,223	1,151	372	439	227	178	30	13	0.1
10	696	638	208	253	129	102	17	7	0.1
20	296	258	86	102	55	40	6	2	0
50	100	77	23	27	17	11	1	2	0

SOURCE: "Table 2. The estimated number of public water-supply systems in selected counties that exceeded target arsenic concentrations in the associated ground-water resource for various public water-supply system sizes categorized by population served," in *Retrospective Analysis on the Occurrence of Arsenic in Ground Water Resources of the United States and Limitations in Drinking Water Supply Characterizations*, Water Resources Investigations Report 99-4279, U.S. Geological Survey, Reston, VA, 2000

5.2.) A ppb equals a microgram per liter (µg/L), the measurement used in the table.

In April 2001 the EPA announced that it would work with the National Academy of Sciences and the National Drinking Water Advisory Council to review the science and the cost estimates supporting the proposed MCL. The effective date of the new rule was to be delayed until February 2002 to allow time to complete the full assessment and to afford the public ample opportunity to provide further input. Completed assessments and public input led to a revision of the proposed standard to 10 ppb. The new standard MCL was adopted on February 22, 2002. All public water systems are expected to comply with the new standard by January 2006.

LEAD. Lead is a toxic metal harmful to human health that can cause very serious health problems if inhaled or ingested. Children are particularly at risk because their developing bodies absorb and retain more lead than adult bodies. According to EPA reports, low-level exposures can result in lowered I.Q., impaired learning and language skills, loss of hearing, reduced attention spans, and poor school performance. High levels damage the brain and central nervous system, interfering with both learning and physical development. Pregnant women are also at risk. Lead is believed to cause miscarriages, premature births, and impaired fetal development.

The major sources of lead exposure are deteriorated paint in older houses and dust and soil that are contaminated by old paint and past emissions of leaded gasoline. Plumbing in older homes can also contribute to overall blood lead levels. Figure 5.2 shows the decline in the blood lead levels in children aged one to five from 1976 to 2000. The dramatic decline in blood lead levels between the late 1970s and the early 1990s is believed to be the result of the phaseout of leaded gasoline and the resulting decrease in lead emissions, although other exposures have also decreased. In December 2000 new data from the Centers for Disease Control and Prevention's (CDC) National Health and Nutrition Examination Survey (NHANES) III, Phase 2 and the NHANES 1999 showed that the average blood lead levels in children aged one to five declined again from the early 1990s to 2000. Some of the decline may be attributed to the continued decrease in air lead levels and lead emissions, although most of this decline occurred before 1995. The construction of new housing and the demolition or rehabilitation of old housing may be contributing to the continuing blood lead level decline. Other contributing factors, according to the EPA's *America's Children and the Environment: Measures of Contaminants, Body Burdens, and Illnesses* (February 2003), are EPA regulations reducing lead levels in drinking water; legislation banning lead from paint and restricting the content of lead in solder, faucets, pipes, and plumbing; and the elimination or reduction of lead in food and beverage containers and ceramic ware, and in products such as toys, miniblinds, and playground equipment.

Unlike many water contaminants, lead has been extensively studied for its prevalence and its effects on human health, and for ways to eliminate it from the water supply. Lead is rarely found in either surface water or groundwater sources for drinking water. Lead usually enters the water supply after it leaves the treatment plant or the well.

Lead contamination is most often a problem in older houses and other buildings. In some areas of the country until about 1930, it was common to use lead piping in interior plumbing and to use lead pipes for the service connections that tied buildings and residences into the public water supplies, and to join the pipes with lead solder. Copper pipes replaced lead pipes in many residences but the

FIGURE 5.2

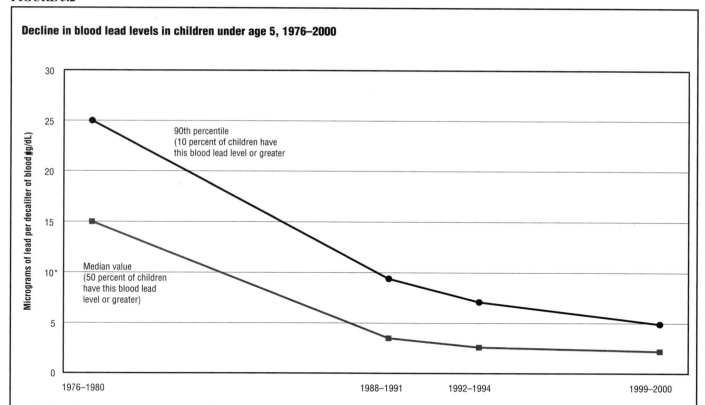

Decline in blood lead levels in children under age 5, 1976–2000

* 10 µg/dL of blood lead has been identified by CDC as elevated, which indicates need for intervention. There is no demonstrated safe concentration of lead in blood. Adverse health effects can occur at lower concentrations.

SOURCE: "Concentration of lead in blood of children ages 5 and under," in *America's Children and the Environment: Measures of Contaminants, Body Burdens, and Illnesses, Second Edition,* EPA 240-R-03-001, U.S. Environmental Protection Agency, National Center for Environmental Economics, Washington, DC, February 2003

practice of using lead solder to join the pipes continued. Lead solder is believed to be the primary cause of most lead in residential water supplies today. Corrosion, a reaction between the water and the lead pipes, solder, faucets, and fittings, is the process by which lead enters the water. Low pH (acidity), low calcium or magnesium levels in the water, and dissolved oxygen presence can all contribute to corrosion. The common practice of grounding electrical equipment to water pipes also accelerates corrosion.

No MCL had been established for lead as of June 2003. In 1991 the EPA replaced the old MCL of 5 ppb with a treatment technique (TT). The TT requires community and non-transient non-community water systems to sample tap water for lead. When more than 10 percent of these samples exceed the EPA's action level of 15 ppb, the water supplier is required to take action. Systems exceeding the action level must:

- Install corrosion control to reduce or prevent the amount of lead leaching into drinking water

- Conduct source water monitoring and install treatment if it is determined that the source level is contributing to the lead level at the tap

- Conduct public education so that citizens will learn about the dangers of lead and steps that they can take to reduce their exposure to lead

- Replace lead service lines owned by the system at the rate of 7 percent of the original number each year. This step is required only if the tap samples for lead are still above the action level after corrosion control and source water treatment are installed

NITRATES. Nitrates and nitrites are nitrogen-oxygen chemicals that combine with organic and inorganic compounds. Primary sources are fertilizer, human sewage, and livestock manure, especially from feedlots. Because they are soluble, nitrates have a high potential to migrate into groundwater.

Nitrates in drinking water can be an immediate threat to children under six months in age. In some babies, high levels of nitrate react with the red blood cells to reduce the blood's ability to transport oxygen. This can cause an anemic condition commonly known as "blue baby." The MCL for nitrates has been set at 10 parts per million (ppm). When nitrate levels exceed this limit, a water supplier must notify the public and must provide additional treatment to

FIGURE 5.3

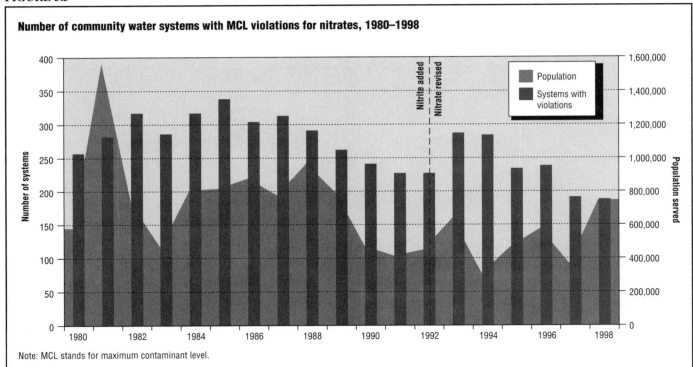

Number of community water systems with MCL violations for nitrates, 1980–1998

Note: MCL stands for maximum contaminant level.

SOURCE: "Figure 12, Number of community water systems with MCL violations for nitrates," in *25 Years of the Safe Drinking Water Act: History and Trends,* EPA 816-R-99-007, U.S. Environmental Protection Agency, Washington, DC, December 1999

reduce levels to meet the standards. Young livestock such as calves are also susceptible to blue baby. The number of community water systems with MCL violations for nitrates declined between 1980 and 1998. (See Figure 5.3.) The highest number of systems in violation was registered in 1985 with 340 community water systems.

According to the EPA's report *Factoids: Drinking Water and Ground Water Statistics for 2002,* in fiscal year 2002, nitrate violations were reported in 422 community and non-transient non-community water systems. This number is not directly comparable with the violations data presented in Figure 5.3 which reported on community water systems only and did not include violations registered for non-transient non-community water systems. The newest violation data available present a combined figure for all community water system nitrate violations and all non-transient non-community water system nitrate violations. The number of people served by suppliers cited for nitrate violations in 2002 was 296,157. In the last year presented in Figure 5.3 that figure was over 700,000 (1998). The trend towards fewer violations seen in Figure 5.3 continued through 2002.

Microbiological Organisms as Contaminants

Microorganisms (bacteria, viruses, and protozoa) are found in untreated surface water sources used for drinking water. Groundwater does not contain these microorganisms unless they have been introduced through pollution of the aquifer. Unless the treatment system fails or contaminated water is introduced accidentally into the distribution system, treated drinking water is normally free of microorganisms or they are present in very low levels. When a water source or system is contaminated with human or animal wastes, some of the microorganisms may be pathogens, that is, disease-causing microorganisms. The resulting illnesses can have symptoms that include headache, nausea, vomiting, diarrhea, abdominal pain, and dehydration. Although usually not life threatening, they can be debilitating and uncomfortable for victims. Extended illness or death may occur among individuals who are immunocompromised, that is, have weakened immune systems. Immunocompromised persons include infants, pregnant women, the elderly, human immunodeficiency virus (HIV) and acquired immunodeficiency syndrome (AIDS) patients, those receiving treatment for certain kinds of cancer, organ-transplant recipients, and people on drugs that suppress their immune system.

Historically throughout the world, pathogens have been the major cause of disease associated with drinking water. In the early 1900s in the United States, the diseases of cholera and typhoid were commonly associated with drinking water from public supplies. The practice of water treatment was begun to address this problem by reducing the number of pathogens present in water supply systems

FIGURE 5.4

Activities within a watershed that can increase turbidity

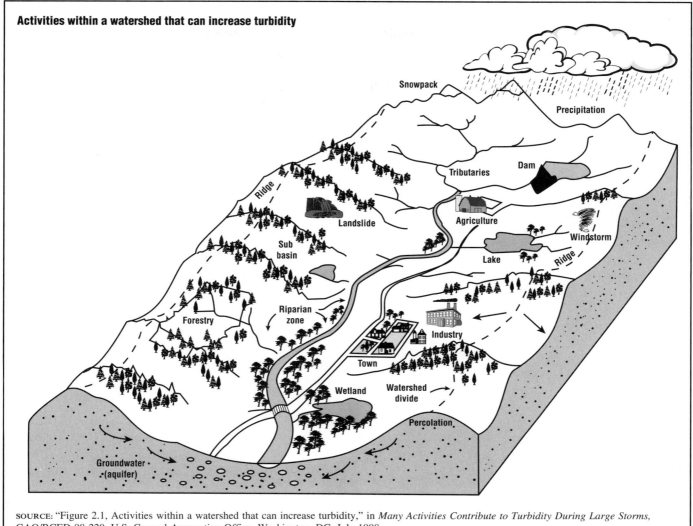

SOURCE: "Figure 2.1, Activities within a watershed that can increase turbidity," in *Many Activities Contribute to Turbidity During Large Storms,* GAO/RCED-98-220, U.S. General Accounting Office, Washington, DC, July 1998

below an infective dose. The infective dose is the number of a particular microorganism required to induce disease, and is different for different microbes. For example, one *Cryptosporidium* protozoa is believed to induce disease while the infective dose for some types of *Salmonellae* bacteria is believed to be 10,000 to 100,000 organisms.

TURBIDITY. Turbidity is a measure of the relative clarity of water. Turbidity is caused by suspended matter or impurities that make the water look cloudy. These impurities may include clay, silt, finely divided organic and inorganic matter, plankton, and other microscopic organisms. Figure 5.4 shows the types of activities in a watershed that cause turbidity in a water source.

Turbidity (i.e., excessive cloudiness in water) is unappealing, and may represent a health concern. It interferes with the effectiveness of disinfection. Disinfection is the practice of killing pathogens in water by adding certain chemicals (for example, chlorine or ozone) to water or subjecting the water to ultraviolet light. Microorganisms can find shelter in the particulate matter, reducing their exposure to attack by disinfectants. Although turbidity is not a direct indicator of health risk, numerous studies show a strong relationship between the removal of turbidity and the removal of pathogens. The EPA made control of turbidity one of its top compliance priorities for drinking water in 2000–2001.

The EPA regulates turbidity using a TT based on the cloudiness of the water. Turbidity is measured in NTUs. An NTU is a unit of measurement from a nephelometric turbidimeter, a specialized instrument that measures cloudiness by the light scattered at an angle of 90 degrees from the incident light beam. (See Figure 5.5.) Water systems that filter their water must ensure that the turbidity goes no higher than 1 NTU (.5 NTU for conventional or direct filtration) in at least 95 percent of the samples collected in any month. At no time can turbidity exceed 5 NTU. As of January 1, 2002, turbidity may never exceed 1 NTU and

FIGURE 5.5

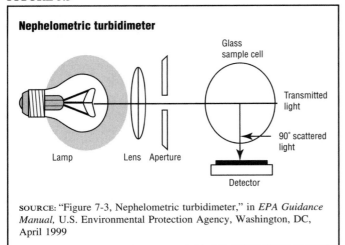

Nephelometric turbidimeter

SOURCE: "Figure 7-3, Nephelometric turbidimeter," in *EPA Guidance Manual*, U.S. Environmental Protection Agency, Washington, DC, April 1999

must not exceed .3 NTU in 95 percent of daily samples in any month.

COLIFORM BACTERIA. Coliform bacteria are a group of closely related, mostly harmless, bacteria that live in soil, water, and the gut of animals. These bacteria are generally divided into two groups: total coliform and fecal coliform. The total coliform group includes all coliform bacteria. The fecal coliform group is a subgroup found in the gut and fecal waste of warm-blooded animals. There are a few organisms in the fecal coliform group that can be harmful to humans, particularly children and persons with weakened immune systems.

The total coliform group is an indicator used to assess drinking water quality. This practice began in the early 1900s. It is based on the assumption that since coliform are always present in sewage from humans and warm-blooded animals, and pathogens may be present in this same sewage, the presence of coliform bacteria may indicate the potential presence of pathogens. The most common problem caused by pathogens is gastroenteritis, a general illness characterized by diarrhea, nausea, vomiting, and cramps. While gastroenteritis is typically not harmful to healthy adults, it can cause serious illness in children and immunocompromised individuals.

Testing the water for each of a wide variety of potential pathogens is difficult and expensive. Testing for total coliform, by comparison, is easy and inexpensive. For this reason, total coliform are used to indicate whether a water system is vulnerable to pathogens. Presence of total coliform in the water distribution system may indicate that the disinfection process was faulty, that a break or leak has occurred in the distribution piping, or that the distribution pipes need to be cleaned. No more than 5 percent of the drinking water samples collected monthly from a water supplier maybe positive for total coliform. All samples that are positive for total coliform are analyzed for the presence

of the fecal coliform group or *Escherichia coli* (*E. coli*), a specific member of the fecal coliform group, both of which are more sensitive indicators of sewage pollution.

GIARDIA LAMBLIA **AND** ***CRYPTOSPORIDIUM.*** *Giardia lamblia* and *Cryptosporidium* are microscopic protozoa that can infect humans and warm-blooded animals. They are frequently found in surface waters contaminated with animal wastes or human wastes. Both organisms have a life stage protected by an outer shell called a cyst, which allows them to exist outside a host's body for a long period. If living cysts are ingested, they can cause an intestinal illness, the symptoms of which are nausea, vomiting, fever, and severe diarrhea. The symptoms last for several days, and a healthy human can generally rid his or her body of the organisms in one or two months. These two organisms are the most frequent cause of waterborne illness in the United States today.

Since 1996 the EPA has required water suppliers using surface water or groundwater under the direct influence of surface water to disinfect their water to control *Giardia* at the 99.99 percent inactivation and removal level. Groundwater is considered to be under the direct influence of surface water when the geologic formations (usually limestone or fractured bedrock) in which the aquifer lies do not provide adequate natural filtration.

A smaller parasite than *Giardia*, *Cryptosporidium* shows more than 50-fold the resistance of *Giardia* to chlorine, the most commonly used drinking water disinfectant. Because of its high resistance to chemicals typically used to treat drinking water, it must be physically removed by filtration. As of 2002 water systems serving 10,000 or more people are required to provide filtration and achieve 99 percent removal or inactivation of *Cryptosporidium*.

Cryptosporidium was responsible for what many people view as the nation's worst drinking water disaster. In April 1993 residents of Milwaukee were infected with *Cryptosporidium* in the city water supply, which had been turbid for several days. For a week, more than 800,000 residents were without drinkable tap water. By the end of the disaster, 50 people had died and 403,000 people had been infected. In addition to the human suffering, the disease outbreak cost an estimated $37 million in lost wages and productivity. This outbreak was in large part responsible for the adoption of the EPA's Surface Water Treatment Rule.

MODERN WATER TREATMENT

Although Hippocrates is credited with emphasizing the importance of clean water to good health as early as 400 B.C. (he recommended boiling and straining rainwater), the first recorded observation of the connection between drinking water and the spread of disease came

FIGURE 5.6

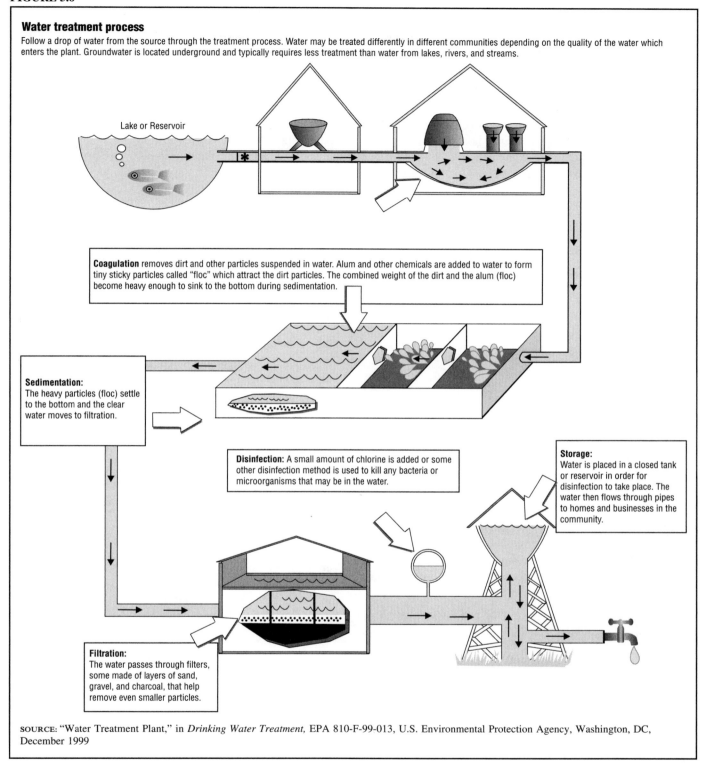

Water treatment process

Follow a drop of water from the source through the treatment process. Water may be treated differently in different communities depending on the quality of the water which enters the plant. Groundwater is located underground and typically requires less treatment than water from lakes, rivers, and streams.

Lake or Reservoir

Coagulation removes dirt and other particles suspended in water. Alum and other chemicals are added to water to form tiny sticky particles called "floc" which attract the dirt particles. The combined weight of the dirt and the alum (floc) become heavy enough to sink to the bottom during sedimentation.

Sedimentation:
The heavy particles (floc) settle to the bottom and the clear water moves to filtration.

Disinfection: A small amount of chlorine is added or some other disinfection method is used to kill any bacteria or microorganisms that may be in the water.

Storage:
Water is placed in a closed tank or reservoir in order for disinfection to take place. The water then flows through pipes to homes and businesses in the community.

Filtration:
The water passes through filters, some made of layers of sand, gravel, and charcoal, that help remove even smaller particles.

SOURCE: "Water Treatment Plant," in *Drinking Water Treatment,* EPA 810-F-99-013, U.S. Environmental Protection Agency, Washington, DC, December 1999

from Dr. John Snow, a London physician, in 1849. He noted that his patients who were getting their drinking water from one particular well were contracting cholera, while patients getting drinking water from other wells were not. His solution to the problem was to remove the handle from the contaminated well's pump so that no one could get water, thereby stopping a cholera epidemic. This event is generally credited as the beginning of modern water treatment.

The most significant water treatment event in the United States was the introduction of the use of chlorine as a disinfectant in water supplies. The introduction of chlorine in water supplies began in the early 1900s.

As towns and cities began to introduce this practice, epidemics and incidence of typhoid, cholera, and dysentery were dramatically reduced. From this humble beginning evolved the complex drinking water treatment technology available today.

The multiple barrier approach is the basis for modern water treatment. This approach recognizes that contaminants reach drinking water though many pathways. Working together, water suppliers and health professionals try to erect as many "barriers" as possible to prevent the contaminant from reaching the customer. These barriers include:

- Protecting the water source from contamination by eliminating or limiting the waste discharges to the water source through a variety of protection programs

- Improved contaminant detection methods

- New and ongoing research into contaminants and their effects

- Removing contaminants or reducing contaminant levels through various treatments

- Disinfection

- Elimination of cross-connections and breaks in the distribution lines

- Safe plumbing in residences and businesses

The water treatment process begins with choosing the highest quality groundwater or surface water source available, and ensuring its continued protection. (See Figure 5.6 for an illustration of the drinking water treatment process.) Groundwater is usually pumped directly into the treatment plant. In many cases, however, because groundwater is naturally filtered as it seeps through layers of rock and soil, disinfection is the only treatment needed before the water is distributed to consumers.

Surface water is transported to the water treatment plant through aqueducts or pipes. A screen at the intake pipe removes debris such as tree branches and trash.

Water suppliers use a variety of treatments to remove contaminants. These treatments are usually arranged in a sequential series of processes called a "treatment train." In the plant, the water is aerated to eliminate gases and add oxygen. Chemicals may be added to remove undesirable contaminants or to improve the taste. If the water is "hard," lime or soda is added to remove the calcium and magnesium. Hard water can clog pipes, stain fixtures, and interfere with soap lathering.

Coagulation or flocculation is frequently the next step. Alum, iron salts, or synthetic polymers are added to the water to combine smaller particles into larger particles (floc) to remove contaminants. In the sedimentation basins, the floc settles to the bottom and is removed. Additional treatment may be required if the raw water shows signs of high levels of toxic chemicals. The water is then sent to sand filtration beds to remove the remaining small particles and clarify the water, and to enhance the effectiveness of disinfection. Chlorine, ozone, or ultraviolet light may be used as disinfectants.

At various points in the treatment process, the water is monitored, sampled and tested using various physical, chemical, and microbial testing procedures. As the water leaves the treatment plant and enters the distribution system, chlorine is added as a disinfectant, particularly where ozone or ultraviolet light were used as disinfectants, to keep it free of microorganisms.

The water then goes to holding units where it is stored until needed. These may be water towers, which use gravity to bring the water to the consumer without extra energy expense, or ground-level containers that require pumps to move the water. The water that ultimately flows from the tap should be clear, tasteless, and safe to drink.

Chlorination

The most extensively used disinfectant in the United States is chlorine, which is used to kill infectious microorganisms and parasites in water. Disinfection with chlorine or other similar chemicals prevents waterborne disease outbreaks. The practice of chlorination first began in the early 1900s to eliminate the cholera and typhoid outbreaks that were widespread in the United States.

In the early 1970s some scientific researchers became concerned by the possible health effects of total trihalomethanes (TTHMs), a by-product of chlorination. Chlorine reacts with naturally occurring organic substances in water to form TTHMs. The level of TTHMs formed varies widely across water supplies and is dependent on the amount of organic material in drinking water and the amount of chlorine applied. TTHMs are removed by passing the water through activated carbon filters.

The health effects of TTHMs are unclear. Some studies of human populations have indicated a slightly higher incidence of bladder and colon cancer in areas where the water is chlorinated. Other studies, however, have not shown an increased cancer risk. Although animal studies have shown the carcinogenic and mutagenic potential of TTHMs, some scientists and public health officials have suggested that these studies may be unreliable because the animals had been subjected to TTHM levels 10,000 times greater than the levels experienced by humans. Currently, the available data show that the risk of getting cancer from TTHMs is extremely low.

Because the public health benefits of the practice of chlorination far outweigh the risk associated with TTHMs, an extensive research effort was conducted to better understand the potential risks of exposure to disinfection

FIGURE 5.7

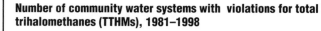

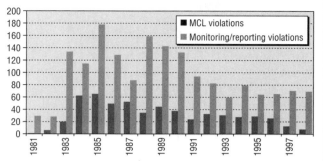

Number of community water systems with violations for total trihalomethanes (TTHMs), 1981–1998

Note: MCL stands for maximum contaminant level.

SOURCE: "Figure 11, Number of community water systems with violations for total trihalomethanes (TTHMs)," in *25 Years of the Safe Drinking Water Act: History and Trends,* EPA 816-R-99-007, U.S. Environmental Protection Agency, Washington, DC, December 1999

by-products. While this research was being completed, an agreement was reached among regulatory agencies, water suppliers, consumer groups, and environmental groups. A maximum contaminant level was established at .1 ppm until January 2002 when the level was reduced to .08 ppm.

The number of community water systems with at least one violation of the TTHM MCL declined from 65 systems violating in 1985, to fewer than 10 community systems (0.2 percent of the total systems that must comply) violating in 1998, as shown in Figure 5.7.

According to the EPA's report *Factoids: Drinking Water and Ground Water Statistics for 2002,* community water systems and non-transient non-community water systems combined accounted for 24 water systems with reported TTHM violations in fiscal year 2002. This number is not directly comparable with the violations data presented in Figure 5.7 which reported on community water systems only and did not include violations registered for non-transient non-community water systems. The number of people served by suppliers cited for TTHM violations in 2002 was 217,205.

Fluoridation

Fluoride is nature's cavity fighter, occurring naturally in combination with other minerals in rocks and soils. Water fluoridation is the process of adjusting the naturally occurring level of fluoride in most water systems to a concentration (a range of .7 to 1.2 ppm) sufficient to protect against tooth decay. The decision to add fluoride to drinking water is left to each community. If the community elects to use fluoride, the water must meet the EPA maximum concentration limit.

In 1945 Grand Rapids, Michigan, became the first city in the world to add fluoride to its drinking water to prevent tooth decay. Since that time, most community water systems in the United States have introduced water fluoridation. Fluoridation of drinking water proved so effective in reducing dental cavities that researchers also developed other methods to deliver fluoride to the public (toothpastes, rinses, dietary supplements). The widespread use of these products has assured that virtually all persons have been exposed to fluoride. The American Dental Association reported in 2000 that, thanks in large part to community fluoridation, half of all children ages 5 to 17 have never had a cavity in their permanent teeth. The CDC has recognized fluoridation as one of the 10 great public health achievements of the 20th century.

SAFE DRINKING WATER ACT OF 1974

Federal regulation of drinking water quality began in 1914 when the U.S. Public Health Service established standards for the bacteriological quality of drinking water. The standards applied only to systems that supplied water to interstate carriers such as trains, ships, and buses. The Public Health Service revised these standards in 1925, 1942, and 1962. The 1962 standards, which regulated 28 substances, were adopted by all 50 state health departments as regulations or guidance, even though they were not federally mandated. The Public Health Service continued to be the primary federal agency involved with drinking water until 1974, when the authority was transferred to the EPA.

The SDWA mandated that the EPA establish and enforce minimum national drinking water standards for any contaminant that presents a health risk and is known to, or is likely to, occur in public drinking water supplies. For each contaminant regulated, the EPA was to set a legal limit on the amount of contaminant allowed in drinking water. In addition, the EPA was directed to develop guidance for water treatment, and to establish testing, monitoring, and reporting requirements for water suppliers.

Congress intended that, after the EPA had set regulatory standards, each state would be granted primacy, that is, states would have the primary responsibility for enforcing the requirements of the SDWA. To be given primacy, a state must adopt drinking water standards and conduct monitoring and enforcement programs at least as stringent as those established by the EPA. All states, except Wyoming, and all U.S. commonwealths and territories have received primacy. The EPA implements the drinking water program in Washington, D.C., and on Native American reservations. According to an EPA fact sheet last updated April 21, 2003, the state of Wyoming had not received primacy over enforcement of the SDWA.

The EPA established the primary drinking water standards by setting MCLs for contaminants that are known to

FIGURE 5.8

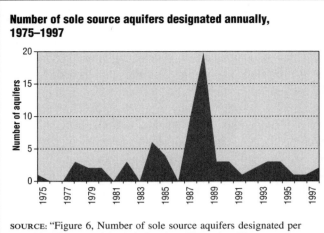

Number of sole source aquifers designated annually, 1975–1997

SOURCE: "Figure 6, Number of sole source aquifers designated per year," in *25 Years of the Safe Drinking Water Act: History and Trends*, EPA 816-R-99-007, U.S. Environmental Protection Agency, Washington, DC, December 1999

be detrimental to human health. Since 1974 the number of contaminants regulated under the SDWA has quadrupled.

All public water systems in the United States are required to meet the primary standards. Only two contaminants regulated at this time, microorganisms and nitrates, pose an immediate health problem when the standards are exceeded. All other contaminants for which standards have been established must be controlled because ingesting water that exceeds these MCLs over a long period may cause health problems such as cancer, liver or kidney disease, or other harmful effects.

Secondary standards cover aspects of drinking water that have no health risk such as odor, taste, staining properties, and color. Secondary standards are recommended but not required.

Sole Source Aquifers

Under the SDWA, the EPA has the authority to designate certain groundwater supplies as the sole source of drinking water for a community (referred to as "sole source aquifers"). This designation protects water supplies in areas with few or no alternative sources to the groundwater resource. These aquifers are characterized by having 50 percent of the population in the area depend on the aquifer for water supply so that any contamination would result in widespread public harm. If aquifer contamination occurred, using an alternative source, if available, would be extremely expensive. The EPA protects these groundwater resources by reviewing any proposed projects within the designated area that are receiving federal money, to ensure that they do not endanger the water source. The first sole source aquifer was designated in 1975, and by 1997 there were 71 designated in 25 states and territories. Figure 5.8 shows the number of sole source aquifers designated

per year from 1975 to 1997. According to the EPA as of September 2001, with the addition of the Castle Valley Aquifer System in Castle Valley, Utah, there are 72 sole source aquifers in the United States.

Underground Injection Control Program

The Underground Injection Control Program of the SDWA was created specifically to protect groundwater sources of drinking water. The program regulates wells used by various municipal, commercial, industrial, and agricultural entities to inject fluids underground. These injections are made to dispose of wastes, for hydrocarbon production and storage, or for mineral recovery. The requirements are designed to ensure that the injected fluids stay within the wells and the injection zones, and do not migrate to endanger underground sources of drinking water.

According to an EPA fact sheet, *State UIC Programs*, last updated on November 26, 2002, thirty-seven states and territories have primacy for this program. The EPA directly implements 17 programs. Together these programs regulate more than 600,000 injection wells and up to 89 percent of all hazardous waste that is land disposed in the United States.

SDWA AMENDMENTS AND REGULATIONS

The EPA is continuing its work to protect drinking water from unsafe contaminant levels, to oversee the activities of the states that enforce federal or their own stricter standards, and to solicit public input as it develops new standards or other program requirements. The SDWA has been amended to require the EPA to:

- Set a maximum contaminant level goal (MCLG). An MCLG is the maximum amount of a contaminant that is not expected to cause any health problems over a lifetime of exposure. The EPA is mandated to set the MCL as close to the MCLG as technology and economics will permit.

- Specify the "best available technology" for treating each contaminant for which the EPA sets a MCL.

- Provide states with greater flexibility to implement the SDWA to meet their specific needs while arriving at the same level of public health protection.

- Set contaminant regulation priorities based on data about adverse public health effects of the contaminant, the occurrence of the contaminant in public water supplies, and the estimated reduction in health risk that can be expected from any new regulations.

- Provide a thorough analysis of the costs to water supplies and benefits to public health.

TABLE 5.3

State wellhead protection programs, 1990–99

1990	1991	1992	1993	1994	1995	1996	1997	1998	1999
VT	VT	VT	**VT**	VT	**VT**	VT	**VT**	VT	VT
TX	TX	TX	**TX**	TX	**TX**	TX	**TX**	TX	TX
RI	RI	RI	**RI**	RI	**RI**	RI	**RI**	RI	RI
OK	OK	OK	**OK**	OK	**OK**	OK	**OK**	OK	OK
NY	NY	NY	**NY**	NY	**NY**	NY	**NY**	NY	NY
NM	NM	NM	**NM**	NM	**NM**	NM	**NM**	NM	NM
NH	NH	NH	**NH**	NH	**NH**	NH	**NH**	NH	NH
ME	ME	ME	**ME**	ME	**ME**	ME	**ME**	ME	ME
MA	MA	MA	**MA**	MA	**MA**	MA	**MA**	MA	MA
LA	LA	LA	**LA**	LA	**LA**	LA	**LA**	LA	LA
DE	DE	DE	**DE**	DE	**DE**	DE	**DE**	DE	DE
CT	CT	CT	**CT**	CT	**CT**	CT	**CT**	CT	CT
AR	AR	AR	**AR**	AR	**AR**	AR	**AR**	AR	AR
	PR	PR	**PR**	PR	**PR**	PR	**PR**	PR	PR
	NJ	NJ	**NJ**	NJ	**NJ**	NJ	**NJ**	NJ	NJ
	NE	NE	**NE**	NE	**NE**	NE	**NE**	NE	NE
	MD	MD	**MD**	MD	**MD**	MD	**MD**	MD	MD
	IL	IL	**IL**	IL	**IL**	IL	**IL**	IL	IL
		WV	**WV**	WV	**WV**	WV	**WV**	WV	WV
		UT	**UT**	UT	**UT**	UT	**UT**	UT	UT
		SD	**SD**	SD	**SD**	SD	**SD**	SD	SD
		SC	**SC**	SC	**SC**	SC	**SC**	SC	SC
		OH	**OH**	OH	**OH**	OH	**OH**	OH	OH
		ND	**ND**	ND	**ND**	ND	**ND**	ND	ND
		GA	**GA**	GA	**GA**	GA	**GA**	GA	GA
		AZ	**AZ**	AZ	**AZ**	AZ	**AZ**	AZ	AZ
		AL	**AL**	AL	**AL**	AL	**AL**	AL	AL
			WI	WI	**WI**	WI	**WI**	WI	WI
			MS	MS	**MS**	MS	**MS**	MS	MS
			KY	KY	**KY**	KY	**KY**	KY	KY
			GU	GU	**GU**	GU	**GU**	GU	GU
				WA	**WA**	WA	**WA**	WA	WA
				TN	**TN**	TN	**TN**	TN	TN
				NV	**NV**	NV	**NV**	NV	NV
				MT	**MT**	MT	**MT**	MT	MT
				MI	**MI**	MI	**MI**	MI	MI
				CO	**CO**	CO	**CO**	CO	CO
					NC	NC	**NC**	NC	NC
					MO	MO	**MO**	MO	MO
					IN	IN	**IN**	IN	IN
					HI	HI	**HI**	HI	HI
						OR	**OR**	OR	OR
						MN	**MN**	MN	MN
						KS	**KS**	KS	KS
						ID	**ID**	ID	ID
							WY	WY	WY
								FL	FL
									PA
									CA
(13)	(18)	(27)	(31)	(37)	(41)	(45)	(46)	(47)	(49)

Notes: Numbers in parentheses are total number of states and territories with federally approved wellhead protection programs. State and territory abbreviations in bold signify the states and territories that reported data in those years.
*PA - program approved in 1999 - voluntarily reported in 1995 and 1997.
*IA - unapproved/expected 1999 - no information reported.
*AK - unapproved/no expected date - no information reported.
*VA - unapproved/no expected date - information reported in 1995 and 1997.
1991–1993 - 18 states reported.
1993–1995 - 31 states reported.
1995–1997 - 42 states reported (42 plus PA - approved in 1999).

SOURCE: Adapted from "Table 2 - State WHP Program Approval Dates and Date of States Reporting Data (in bold)," in *Summary of State Biennial Reports of Wellhead Protection Program Progress: October 1995 through September 1997*, U.S. Environmental Protection Agency, Washington, DC, 1999

- Increase research to develop sound scientific data to provide a base for regulations.
- Ban the use of lead pipes and lead solder in new drinking water systems and in the repair of existing water systems.
- Establish a federal-state partnership for regulation enforcement.

Drinking Water Standards

These amendments have resulted in the following major programs within the SDWA, which serve to increase the standards for safe drinking water in the United States:

- Surface Water Treatment Rule
- Source Water Assessment
- Wellhead Protection Programs
- Drinking Water State Revolving Fund
- State Capacity Development Program
- Operator Certification Program
- Public Notice and Consumer Confidence Reports
- Health Care Provider Outreach and Education
- State Compliance Report

SURFACE WATER TREATMENT RULE. The Surface Water Treatment Rule (SWTR) is the EPA's response to Congress's mandate to require public water systems that draw water from surface sources (lakes, rivers, and reservoirs) to disinfect their water before distribution, and filter, where appropriate. The SWTR is directed against microbial contamination. All surface water systems must disinfect and filter their water to provide a minimum 99.9 percent removal and inactivation of *Giardia*, and 99.99 percent removal and inactivation of viruses. The vast majority of U.S. water suppliers filter their water. Filtration adequacy is determined by measurement of turbidity. Public water supplies that have pristine protected sources may be granted a waiver from the filtration requirement if they meet certain criteria.

SOURCE WATER ASSESSMENT. As development in the United States continues and suburban sprawl encroaches on once pristine watersheds, the potential to contaminate drinking water sources grows. By the end of 2003, states were to have examined every river, lake, and groundwater supply used as a drinking water source to identify the watershed around the source water, inventory the significant potential sources of pollution in the watershed, and determine how susceptible these water sources are to contamination. Beginning in 2001, the states also had to incorporate the results of their wellhead assessments into these reports. The results of these assessments must be made available

TABLE 5.4

Sources and amounts of states' expenditures for drinking water program implementation, 1997–99

(Dollars in millions)

Amount and percentage of total expenditures by year	Federal funds			State funds			Grand total
	Public Water System Supervision grants	Drinking Water State Revolving Fund set-asides	Total federal funds	Required matching contributions	Funding from other state sources[a]	Total state funds	
1997							
Expenditures	$82	$8	$90	$35	$89	$123	$214
Percentage of total expenditures	38.4	3.9	42.3	16.2	41.4	57.7	100.0
1998							
Expenditures	$82	$26	$108	$37	$92	$129	$237
Percentage of total expenditures	34.6	11.2	45.8	15.4	38.8	54.2	100.0
1999							
Expenditures	$84	$57	$141	$43	$91	$134	$276
Percentage of total expenditures	30.5	20.8	51.2	15.8	33.0	48.8	100.0
3-year average							
Expenditures	$83	$31	$113	$38	$91	$129	$242
Percentage of total expenditures	34.2	12.7	46.8	15.8	37.4	53.2	100.0

[a] The majority of states (57 percent) reported that less than 10 percent of their funding from other state sources, if any, was used to implement activities that are in addition to those required under federal drinking water regulations.

Note: Some totals do not add due to rounding.

SOURCE: "Table 3, Sources and amounts of states' expenditures for drinking water program implementation, fiscal years 1997 through 1999," in *Drinking Water Spending Constraints Could Affect States' Ability to Implement Increasing Program Requirements,* GAO/RCED-00-199, U.S. General Accounting Office, Washington, DC, August, 2000

to the public and summarized in the consumer confidence reports issued by the water suppliers.

WELLHEAD PROTECTION PROGRAMS. Under a voluntary program, each state develops and implements a comprehensive program to protect the land areas around water supply wells from contaminants that may enter the groundwater and adversely affect human health. There are several steps involved in implementing wellhead programs:

- Delineating (determining) the land area that needs to be protected in order to protect the groundwater source

- Identifying the potential sources of contamination within the delineated area

- Developing and implementing a plan to adequately manage identified potential contaminant sources

- Establishing a plan to protect the groundwater source in case of an accidental spill of hazardous materials or some other emergency

The EPA approves state wellhead protection programs, and provides technical support to state and local governments to implement the program. In a report entitled *Summary of State Biennial Reports of Wellhead Protection Program Progress* (1999), the EPA reported that between 1990 and 1999 (the latest data available), 49 states and territories approved wellhead protection programs. (See Table 5.3.)

DRINKING WATER STATE REVOLVING FUND. This federal grant program provides money to the states, who in turn provide loans to water systems to upgrade their facilities and ensure compliance with drinking water standards. States must come up with a 20 percent match. The revenue can be used to make loans, purchase or finance government debt, buy local bond insurance to help cover the costs of constructing or repairing water treatment facilities, acquire land to buffer drinking water sources from contamination, or fund other water protection activities. To qualify for grants, states must have a drinking water state revolving fund in place. As loans are repaid, the state's funds are replenished, enabling them to make loans for other eligible drinking water projects. Table 5.4 shows the state and federal funds expended on implementing drinking water programs, 1997–99 (the latest data available), and shows the three-year average.

STATE CAPACITY DEVELOPMENT PROGRAM. As of October 2000 states were required to develop strategies to ensure that all water systems had the technical, financial, and managerial capability to provide safe drinking water to their customers. States were required to involve the public in strategy development and to make the final strategy available to the public.

OPERATOR CERTIFICATION PROGRAM. Operation of water treatment systems by trained staff is an important component of providing safe drinking water. Under this requirement, operators must complete a minimum of classroom training and experience. Certifications must be renewed at specified intervals and operators must have some continuing education in the intervals between renewals.

States with existing water system operator certification programs were required to revise their programs to meet new requirements and to submit their program changes to the EPA by February 2001. States with programs that met the new requirements had to submit their programs for the EPA review by August 2000. The EPA strongly recommended that states use advisory boards in implementing these guidelines.

PUBLIC NOTICE AND CONSUMER CONFIDENCE REPORTS. Public water suppliers must notify their customers through the media or posted signs when the water system violates a health-based drinking water standard. The notice must tell the customer which water quality standard has been violated, what actions the customer can take, and how soon the violation will be corrected.

Since 1999 water suppliers have been required to issue an annual report, and to provide access to the report for every customer served by the system. Generally, this is done through direct mailing with the water bill. The report provides information on the source of the water supply, the level of any regulated contaminants detected in the water supply, the health effects of contaminants detected above the safety limit, and the water system's compliance with other drinking water regulations.

HEALTH CARE PROVIDER OUTREACH AND EDUCATION. The very young, the elderly, the very sick, and immunocompromised individuals are more susceptible to microbial infection than healthy adults. Congress determined that it is important to educate health-care providers concerning health risks that may occur to this subpopulation from drinking water that would not adversely affect a normal, healthy person. The EPA and the CDC must jointly provide national health-care provider training and a public education campaign. The purpose of this effort is to increase the availability of information about waterborne disease and its symptoms to health-care providers and their patients.

STATE COMPLIANCE REPORT. By January of each year, each state is required to produce an annual report on whether water systems within the state are meeting drinking water standards. These reports must be made available to the public in each state. The EPA must summarize the information into an annual national report available to the public.

The information submitted annually by the states and the water suppliers is stored in the Safe Drinking Water Information System (SDWIS). The EPA uses this information to track the safety of the nation's drinking water, to track water system violations of the SDWA, and to prepare the national annual report. The public can access information about a particular water system through the SDWIS.

COMPANION LEGISLATION TO THE SAFE DRINKING WATER ACT

Water Efficiency Act of 1992

The Water Efficiency Act of 1992 established uniform national standards for manufacture of water-efficient plumbing fixtures, such as low-flow toilets and showers. The purpose was to promote water conservation by residential and commercial users.

Preliminary results from studies by the American Water Works Association and the EPA indicated that, by 2020, water consumption could be reduced by about 3 to 9 percent in the areas studied. Wastewater flows to sewage treatment plants could be reduced 13 percent by 2016. For 16 localities analyzed to date, the use of water-efficient plumbing fixtures would reduce the local water consumption enough to save local water utilities between $165 million and $231 million by 2020 because planned investments to expand drinking water treatment or storage capacity could be deferred or avoided.

Federal Water Pollution Control Act

The 1972 Federal Water Pollution Control Act (FWPCA) established the framework for regulating discharge of pollutants to waters of the United States. This framework was strengthened by the 1977 amendments (the Clean Water Act) and the 1987 amendments (Water Quality Control Act). The FWPCA is commonly known as the Clean Water Act.

The FWPCA and its amendments together established the National Pollution Discharge Elimination System (NPDES) to reduce discharge of pollutants to water, including drinking water sources. States may apply for and receive primacy for the NPDES program in a manner similar to SDWA primacy.

The FWPCA also requires the EPA and the states to identify water resources that need to be cleaned up to meet water quality standards and to establish stringent controls where needed to achieve the water quality standards. States are required to develop lists of contaminated waters, to identify the sources and amounts of pollutants causing water quality problems, and to develop individual control strategies for the sources of pollution.

Aggressive use of the FWPCA by the EPA and the states can reduce the contaminant loads reaching drinking water sources. Preventing contaminants from reaching drinking water sources protects public health and reduces the need for and cost of water treatment instead of passing the costs on to the water consumer.

FIGURE 5.9

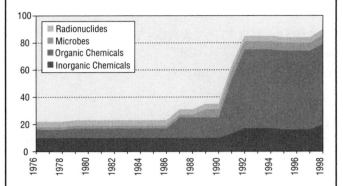

Number of contaminants regulated under the Safe Drinking Water Act, by contaminant type, 1976–98

SOURCE: "Figure 1. Number of contaminants regulated under the Safe Drinking Water Act, by contaminant type," in *Drinking Water: Past, Present, and Future,* U.S. Environmental Protection Agency, Washington, DC, February 2000

CLEAN DRINKING WATER IS COSTLY

Ensuring an adequate supply of safe drinking water requires investing not only in the physical infrastructure, such as water treatment and distribution systems, but also in essential oversight activities performed by the states, such as training water system operators and monitoring water systems' compliance with the drinking water standards...

— Peter F. Guerrero, *Drinking Water: Spending Constraints Could Affect States' Ability to Meet Increasing Program Requirements,* U.S. General Accounting Office, September 19, 2000

Supplying the public with safe drinking water is an expensive proposition. From 1976–1998 (the latest data available), the number of contaminants regulated under the SDWA roughly quadrupled (see Figure 5.9), and new treatment technologies have been required. This has significantly increased the cost of water treatment in many locations.

Public water supply systems must:

• Protect their water source

• Build, maintain, and repair the treatment plants and distribution systems

• Replace aging systems; recruit, pay, and train system operation staff

• Meet the expanding treatment requirements of the SDWA and its monitoring and reporting requirements

• Expand service areas

• Provide necessary administrative and support services to accomplish these tasks

The majority of money to support these services comes directly from users. Water rates are the primary mechanism by which customers are charged. The remainder of revenues comes from connection or inspection fees, fines, penalties, and other nonconsumption based charges, and local or state grants or loans.

Historically, drinking water has been underpriced. A gallon of bottled water typically sells for 240 to 10,000 times the price of a gallon of tap water. The rates most water systems have charged have not reflected the true cost of treating drinking water and making necessary infrastructure improvements. Systems serving fewer than 10,000 people have consistently charged higher residential rates than larger systems because they have fewer customers across which to spread costs. In 1999 (the latest data available), the EPA reported that the revenue earned from residential customers has generally increased since 1975 for all system sizes, and was rising at a faster pace than inflation.

In a May 9, 2003, address to the 15th Annual Federal Policy Conference sponsored by the Council of Infrastructure Financing Authorities, G. Tracy Meehan III, Assistant Administrator for Water, EPA, reported that the average household spends $474 per year on water and wastewater charges. According to the U.S. Bureau of Labor Statistics (*Consumer Expenditures in 2001,* April 2003), over the period 1999–2001 the national average household expenditure for all utilities, which includes water, electricity, natural gas, and public services, rose 16 percent. Total household expenditures over the same period rose just 7 percent.

Even people who rent are beginning to see the cost of water rise. In an article published by the *Washington Post* on April 19, 2003 ("The Cost of Water Is Tapping the Wallets of More Tenants"), author Denise Kersten explains that more and more renters are being asked by landlords to pay separately for their water utility service and often the cost is an add-on to existing leases. This is a relatively new practice. According to Marc Treitler, former chair of the National Submetering and Utility Allocation Association, in 2003 between 2 and 3 million apartment renters paid water bills and this figure is expected to grow at a rate of 25 percent annually into the foreseeable future. The article claims that this new practice is motivating officials at state and local levels to work towards establishing regulations over the practice.

The SDWA has also placed an additional financial burden on the states. States must find funding sources to help financially strapped water systems. In addition, the states are primarily responsible for implementing the programs to help ensure that the nation's thousands of drinking water systems have the financial, technical, and managerial ability to protect water sources from contamination and to comply with regulations. The states also must oversee the systems' compliance with complex new regulations addressing specific contaminants and continually encourage their upgrading as more requirements are imposed by the EPA.

FIGURE 5.10

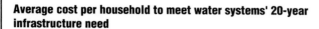

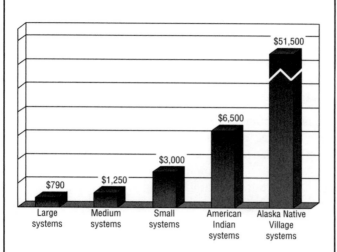

Average cost per household to meet water systems' 20-year infrastructure need

(Total needed in January 1999 dollars)

- $790 — Large systems
- $1,250 — Medium systems
- $3,000 — Small systems
- $6,500 — American Indian systems
- $51,500 — Alaska Native Village systems

Note: Does not include the costs associated with proposed or recently promulgated SDWA regulations.

SOURCE: "Exhibit ES-5: Average 20-Year Per-Household Need (in January 1999 dollars)," in *Drinking Water Infrastructure Needs Survey: Second Report to Congress,* U.S. Environmental Protection Agency, Office of Water, Office of Ground Water and Drinking Water, Washington, DC, February 2001

Recognizing the tremendous burden that the additional requirements of the SDWA imposed on the states and local water suppliers, Congress authorized additional funding to support drinking water programs, which is made available annually to the states through two programs. The Public Water System Supervision grants to the states are directed at implementation activities such as conducting inspections overseeing local systems' compliance with water treatment and testing requirements, and providing technical assistance to local water systems. The Drinking Water State Revolving Fund (DWSRF) creates a mechanism for providing low-cost financial aid to local water systems to build the treatment plants necessary to meet state and federal drinking water standards. Although states and water systems are taking advantage of the DWSRF to make infrastructure improvements, government funding will cover only part of the total needed investment.

The smallest water systems (3,300 or fewer people) are and will continue to be the hardest hit by the expanding SDWA requirements. More than 45,000 of these systems exist as of 2002. Besides having a smaller customer base to absorb costs, these systems are least able to get loans to finance needed infrastructure improvements. Large systems have a higher percentage of industrial, commercial, and agricultural customers. Smaller systems generally serve residential customers who, as a group, are less able to pay

for water. Small rural communities also usually have residents with lower incomes, higher unemployment rates, and a larger population of aging residents.

Recognizing the special needs of small systems, the SDWA requires the EPA, when setting new drinking water standards, to identify technologies that achieve compliance and are affordable for systems serving fewer than 10,000 people. When such technologies cannot be identified, the EPA must identify affordable technologies that maximize contaminant reduction and protect public health. The DWSRF emphasizes providing funding to small and disadvantaged communities, and to programs that encourage pollution prevention as a tool for ensuring safe drinking water.

In its *Drinking Water Infrastructure Needs Survey* (2001), the EPA estimated the projected 20-year costs (through 2018) small systems face to make infrastructure improvements to their facilities at $31.2 billion, about 20 percent of the national need ($150.9 billion). Figure 5.10 compares the projected average costs water systems will need to charge customers to meet treatment requirements. Although small systems generally have less total need than medium or larger systems, their customers face higher costs at $3,000 per household than do medium systems at $1,250 and large systems at $790 per household. Costs per household for drinking water infrastructure improvement needs are even higher for American Indian water systems, at $6,500 over the 20-year period. The highest need, however, is faced by Alaska Native Village systems, whose householders could pay $51,500 over the 20-year period to make improvements to drinking water infrastructure systems.

HOW CLEAN IS THE WATER?

Safe drinking water is a cornerstone of public health. Most importantly, the nation's drinking water is generally safe. The vast majority of U.S. residents receive water from systems that have no reported violations of MCLs or flaws in treatment techniques, monitoring, or reporting.

In 1994 in a 3,500-page report (Brian Cohen and Eric Olson, *Victorian Water Treatment Enters the 21st Century*), the Natural Resources Defense Council (NRDC), a private environmental group, documented some 250,000 violations of the SDWA in 1991 and 1992 alone. The council found that 43 percent of the water systems (serving about 120 million people) had committed violations.

Since that report, substantial progress has been made in reducing SDWA violations. The EPA reported in its 2002 *Factoid* report that a total of 61 million people were supplied with water from public services that registered one or more violations for health-based SDWA standards in 2002. This represented a drop of 11 percent from the number of

FIGURE 5.11

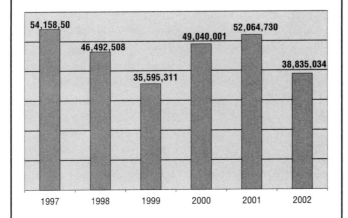

Population affected by community water systems registering violations of health-based standards, 1997–2002

54,158,50

46,492,508

35,595,311

49,040,001

52,064,730

38,835,034

1997   1998   1999   2000   2001   2002

SOURCE: Adapted from "CWS violations report by FY, Populations affected," in *Factoids: Drinking Water and Ground Water Statistics for 2002*, EPA-816-K-03-001, U.S. Environmental Protection Agency, Washington, DC, January 2003

people affected by systems registering violations in 2000 (68 million).

The report provides a breakdown of the violations by public water system type and size. The systems serving the largest part of the population are the community water systems. In 2002 a total of 38,835,034 people using water from community water systems were affected by violations of (1) maximum contaminant level, (2) treatment technique and/or (3) monitoring and reporting. (See Figure 5.11.) Although community water systems of all sizes have shown roughly the same decreasing trend in SDWA violations, very small water systems are 50 percent more likely to violate regulations than all other sizes. Because of their very small size, manpower and funding to maintain and upgrade equipment, and to meet monitoring and reporting requirements, is extremely limited.

National Public Water System Compliance Report

The SDWA requires public water systems to submit compliance reports about the quality of their drinking water. Using this information, the EPA prepares an annual national compliance report. The report provides a summary of violations of the SDWA at the nation's public water supplies. It also evaluates and summarizes the annual compliance reports prepared by the states.

The United States has the world's safest water supply. The EPA and its state partners are generally meeting the goal of ensuring that consumers receive safe drinking

water from public systems. According to the latest data available, in 1998, 80 percent of the public water supplies reported no SDWA violations. Nationwide, the vast majority of the violations reported were for monitoring and reporting requirements. These violations represent a lesser risk to the public than violations of health-based standards. For example, failure to collect one monitoring sample to be analyzed for 27 contaminants results in 27 violations, even though the water is safe to drink. The EPA found no information suggesting that failure to report or monitor resulted in adverse health effects.

Ninety-four percent of the nation's public water systems reported no violations of health-based standards in 1998 (the latest data available). Health-based standards are MCLs or TTs. Among the 6 percent with violations, the Total Coliform Rule (TCR), which must be met by all types and sizes of public water systems, was the most frequently violated (74 percent) of all the health-based standards. The TCR was also the most violated standard in 1996 and 1997. Coliform bacteria are generally no threat to humans, but their presence in drinking water can indicate a lapse in treatment, a break in the water line, and the possible presence of pathogens. Violations of the Surface Water Treatment Rule (SWTR) were responsible for 17 percent of the health-based violations.

Violations of health-based standards for chemicals (organic, inorganic, and radioactive contaminants) were less than 9 percent of the total health-based violations. Under the SDWA in 1998, states took a total of 1,468 enforcement actions against public water systems. During the same period, the EPA took 257 enforcement actions.

GAO Study of Private Wells

The U.S. General Accounting Office, in its 1997 *Drinking Water: Information on the Quality of Water Found at Community Water Systems and Private Wells* (the latest data available), reported the results of the CDC survey of the quality of water from 5,500 private wells in nine states. The survey measured coliform bacteria, *E. coli*, nitrates, and the herbicide atrazine. The wells studied ranged in age from 1 to 200 years and were of many different construction types. The CDC found that 41.3 percent of wells tested positive for coliform bacteria, 11.2 percent contained *E. coli,* and 13.4 percent contained nitrate levels above the EPA standards. In 4,847 wells in eight of the nine states, atrazine, an herbicide, was detected above the MCL in nine cases.

Several factors influenced the quality of drinking water from wells. The report found that source water quality was key. Community systems were much more likely to treat their water than were private well owners. Construction standards were much more stringent in community systems than in private wells. Only two of the nine states

TABLE 5.5

Waterborne-disease outbreaks associated with drinking water, by causative agent and type of water system, 1999–2000

Etiologic agent	Type of water system[1] Community Outbreaks	Community Cases	Noncommunity Outbreaks	Noncommunity Cases	Individual Outbreaks	Individual Cases	Total Outbreaks	Total Cases
AGI[2]	6[3]	57	3	164	8	195	17	416
Giardia intestinalis	0	0	2	39	4	13	6	52
Escherichia coli O157: H7	2	51	0	0	2	9	4	60
Norwalk-like viruses (NLV)	0	0	3	356	0	0	3	356
Salmonella species[4]	1	124	0	0	1	84	2	208
Campylobacter jejuni	0	0	1	15	1	102	2	117
Es. coli O157:H7/*Ca. jejuni*	0	0	1	781	0	0	1	781
Small round-structured virus	0	0	1	70	0	0	1	70
Cryptosporidium parvum	1	5	0	0	0	0	1	5
Sodium hydroxide	1	2	0	0	0	0	1	2
Nitrate	0	0	0	0	1	1	1	1
Total	**11**	**239**	**11**	**1,425**	**17**	**404**	**39**	**2,068**
Percentage	**28.2**	**11.6**	**28.2**	**68.9**	**43.6**	**19.5**	**100.0**	**100.0**

[1] Community and noncommunity water systems are public water systems that serve ≥15 service connections or an average of ≥25 residents for ≥60 days/year. A community water system serves year-round residents of a community, subdivision, or mobile home park with ≥15 service connections or an average of ≥25 residents. A noncommunity water system can be nontransient or transient. Nontransient systems serve ≥25 of the same persons for ≥6 months/year (e.g. factories or schools), whereas transient systems do not (e.g. restaurants, highway rest stations, or parks). Individual water systems are not owned or operated by a water utility and serve ≤15 connections or ≤25 persons. Outbreaks associated with water not intended for drinking (e.g. lakes, springs, and creeks used by campers and boaters; irrigation water; and other nonpotable sources with or without taps) are also classified as individual systems.

[2] Acute gastrointestinal illness of unknown etiology.

[3] One outbreak of four cases was caused by an unidentifed chemical.

[4] One outbreak was serotype Typhimurium, and one outbreak was serotype Bareilly.

SOURCE: "Table 4. Waterborne-disease outbreaks associated with drinking water, by etiologic agent and type of water system—United States, 1999–2000 (n=39)," in "Surveillance for Waterborne-Disease Outbreaks–United States, 1999–2000,"*Morbidity and Mortality Weekly Report, v*ol. 51, no. SS-8, Centers for Disease Control and Prevention, Atlanta, GA, November 22, 2002

surveyed (California and Illinois) required permits prior to construction. All the states required registration of new wells, although officials estimated that only 60 percent of wells are reported. Only two of the states tested water quality at new wells, and two states inspected new wells. Well contractors are licensed in some, but not all, states. In addition, problems are much more likely to occur in old wells.

Well owners remain responsible for continuing maintenance of private wells. Most states have ongoing programs, using various media, which make available to private well owners information about wells, how to protect their quality, and how to get the water tested.

Disease Caused by Contaminated Drinking Water

It is difficult to know the exact incidence of illness caused by contaminated drinking water. People may not know the source of their illnesses and may attribute them to food, chronic illness, or other infectious agents. Some researchers believe that the actual number of drinking water disease cases is higher than the reported number, but the diseases are not reported because victims believe them to be "stomach upsets" and treat themselves.

Since 1971 the CDC and the EPA have maintained a surveillance system for collecting and reporting data that relate to waterborne-disease outbreaks. The latest report,

Surveillance for Waterborne-Disease Outbreaks—United States, 1999–2000 (2002), includes data about outbreaks associated with water intended for drinking water and those associated with water used for recreation, such as beaches, Jacuzzis, and swimming pools.

During the period 1999–2000, 25 states reported a total of 39 outbreaks of disease associated with water intended for drinking. (One of the 39 reported outbreaks, a multistate outbreak of *Salmonella Bareilly,* spanned 10 states.) Those 39 outbreaks caused an estimated 2,068 people to become ill, 122 people to be hospitalized, and 2 people to die. (See Table 5.5.) The microbe or chemical that caused the outbreaks was identified in 22 of the outbreaks. Twenty of the 22 identified outbreaks were associated with pathogens, and 2 were associated with chemical poisoning.

Figure 5.12 shows that summer is the period when most outbreaks of waterborne diseases occur. The number of waterborne-illness outbreaks reported for the three-year period 1996 through 1998 was lower than for any three-year period since 1971. (See Figure 5.13.) This recent decrease in outbreak numbers may reflect the improved implementation of drinking water regulations, and increased efforts by water utilities and public health officials to improve drinking water quality. Some backsliding occurred in 1999 and 2000, however, as the number of outbreaks was up in

FIGURE 5.12

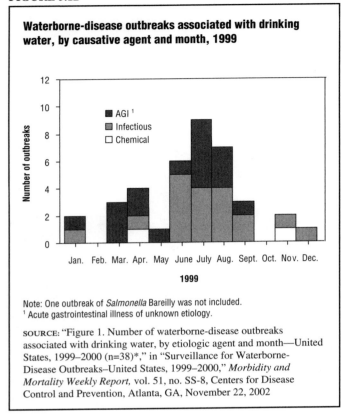

Waterborne-disease outbreaks associated with drinking water, by causative agent and month, 1999

Note: One outbreak of *Salmonella* Bareilly was not included.
[1] Acute gastrointestinal illness of unknown etiology.

SOURCE: "Figure 1. Number of waterborne-disease outbreaks associated with drinking water, by etiologic agent and month—United States, 1999–2000 (n=38)*," in "Surveillance for Waterborne-Disease Outbreaks–United States, 1999–2000," *Morbidity and Mortality Weekly Report,* vol. 51, no. SS-8, Centers for Disease Control and Prevention, Atlanta, GA, November 22, 2002

both of those years. In general the number of outbreaks is down over the period shown. Some fluctuation from year to year is to be expected.

Figure 5.14 shows the distribution of outbreaks during 1999 by disease-causing agents, water system, water source, and deficiency in water treatment. Bacteria and parasites were the two leading causes of most of the identified outbreaks. Most (28 of 39 outbreaks) were linked to groundwater sources; 18 of these were associated with private or non-community wells that were not regulated by the EPA. The proportion of outbreaks associated with groundwater sources during the 1999–2000 reporting period reflects an increase of 87 percent from the previous reporting period (1997–98). The reported outbreaks for the 1999–2000 period were primarily associated with untreated groundwater.

Two outbreaks of chemical poisoning were reported during the two-year period 1999–2000. Three people were affected by contamination of drinking water from nitrates and sodium hydroxide.

ARE AMERICANS CONCERNED ABOUT THEIR DRINKING WATER?

A 1998 Gallup Poll asked people if drinking water from the tap was safe to drink; 68 percent of respondents believed it was safe, while 30 percent did not. The 1998 poll indicated slightly higher consumer confidence than the 1985 poll where 60 percent thought the water was safe, and 34 percent did not. Seventy-nine percent of 1998 respondents reported they had never received a warning about safety problems with their drinking water supply.

AMERICA'S DRINKING HABITS

In 2000 Rockefeller University and the International Bottled Water Association commissioned the Yankelovich Partners to survey America's drinking habits. The survey of 2,818 Americans found that most Americans are aware of the importance of water consumption to their health. Ninety-one percent knew that water is the best choice to replace fluids after exercising, and that drinking enough water is important, particularly for pregnant and breast-feeding women. Furthermore, 88 percent knew that one should not wait until one is thirsty to drink, and 77 percent were aware that caffeine and alcohol can cause the body to lose water. Seventy-three percent knew that health and nutrition experts recommended drinking eight or more eight-ounce servings of water daily, but 51 percent drank less than this amount. Twenty-eight percent of those surveyed drank three or less servings per day, and 10 percent claimed to drink no water at all. Only 34 percent claimed that they drank the recommended eight or more servings of water per day.

BOTTLED WATER

Water is called "bottled water" only if it meets federal and state standards, is sealed in a sanitary container, and is sold for human consumption. The members of the International Bottled Water Association (IBWA) produce and distribute 85 percent of the bottled water sold in the United States.

Growing Market

According to "Bottled Water: Better Than the Tap?," an article published in the July/August 2002 issue of the U.S. Food and Drug Administration's *FDA Consumer* magazine, Americans are drinking bottled water in record numbers. The IBWA estimated that in 2001 Americans consumed about 5 billion gallons of bottled water. Experts in the bottled water industry expect bottled water to rank second to soda pop as the American beverage of choice in about 4 years. In 2002 consumption of bottled water ranked third in average daily consumption of beverages. Americans consumed 3.6 8-ounce servings of filtered or non-filtered tap water every day, 1.8 8-ounce servings of coffee, and 1.7 servings of bottled water.

Why Do Americans Like Bottled Water?

American consumers have given a variety of reasons for their preference for bottled water. Some say they dislike the smell or taste of water from the tap or drawn

FIGURE 5.13

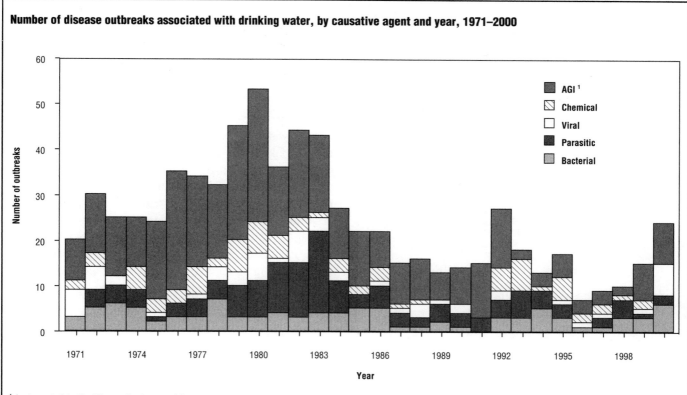

Number of disease outbreaks associated with drinking water, by causative agent and year, 1971–2000

[1] Acute gastrointestinal illness of unknown etiology.

SOURCE: "Figure 5. Number of waterborne-disease outbreaks associated with drinking water, by year and etiologic agent—United States, 1971–2000 (n=730)*," in "Surveillance for Waterborne-Disease Outbreaks–United States, 1999–2000," *Morbidity and Mortality Weekly Report,* vol. 51, no. SS-8, Centers for Disease Control and Prevention, Atlanta, GA, November 22, 2002

from wells. Others cite the convenience of bottled water. According to "Bottled Water: Better Than the Tap?," one mother of five children gives her children bottled water because she believes it is a healthier choice—bottled water typically contains no caffeine, no calories, and no sugar. She also mentioned the convenient packaging, making the bottles easier to carry from home to wherever the family goes.

In addition to convenience and taste, concerns over the safety of public water-supply systems since the September 11, 2001, terrorist attacks on the United States are prompting more Americans to rely on bottled water for their drinking water needs. According to "Take Me to the Water," an article published in the May 26, 2003, issue of *Supermarket News,* several retailers reported that concerns about terrorism have fueled a surge in the consumption of bottled water in the United States. The article states that between the years 1998 and 2003, sales of bottled water increased 150 percent.

Regulation of Bottled Water

Bottled water, like tap water, comes from one of two sources: groundwater or surface water. Depending on the source, it may be subjected to the same treatment as tap

water to remove contaminants and to make the taste more appealing.

In February 1999 the NRDC, a nonprofit environmental organization, announced results of its four-year study on the safety and benefits of bottled water. The study (*Bottled Water: Pure Drink or Pure Hype?*) included testing of more than 1,000 bottles of 103 brands of bottled water. In general, the study stated that while the market for bottled water is driven by an image of purity, that purity may be an illusion due to inadequate regulation of the product. The NRDC concluded, "Bottled water sold in the United States is not necessarily cleaner or safer than most tap water."

In July 1999 the Drinking Water Research Foundation (DWRF) issued a report that analyzed the findings of the NRDC report and the data supporting it. The report concluded that the data in the NRDC report did not support a finding that bottled water in the United States is an inadequately regulated product. The DWRF used both the NRDC's and WDRF testing to reach its conclusion. The DWRF also found that the U.S. Food and Drug Administration (FDA) regulatory system that governs bottled water was functional and provided a high level

FIGURE 5.14

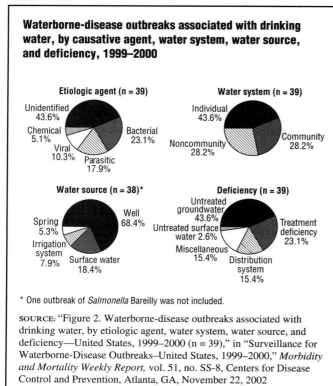

Waterborne-disease outbreaks associated with drinking water, by causative agent, water system, water source, and deficiency, 1999–2000

Etiologic agent (n = 39)

Unidentified 43.6%
Chemical 5.1%
Viral 10.3%
Parasitic 17.9%
Bacterial 23.1%

Water system (n = 39)

Individual 43.6%
Noncommunity 28.2%
Community 28.2%

Water source (n = 38)*

Spring 5.3%
Irrigation system 7.9%
Surface water 18.4%
Well 68.4%

Deficiency (n = 39)

Untreated groundwater 43.6%
Untreated surface water 2.6%
Miscellaneous 15.4%
Distribution system 15.4%
Treatment deficiency 23.1%

* One outbreak of *Salmonella* Bareilly was not included.

SOURCE: "Figure 2. Waterborne-disease outbreaks associated with drinking water, by etiologic agent, water system, water source, and deficiency—United States, 1999–2000 (n = 39)," in "Surveillance for Waterborne-Disease Outbreaks–United States, 1999–2000," *Morbidity and Mortality Weekly Report,* vol. 51, no. SS-8, Centers for Disease Control and Prevention, Atlanta, GA, November 22, 2002

of public health protection. When combined with the requirements of the "Model Code" (the sanitary production practices that IBWA members voluntarily accept as a condition of IBWA membership), the DWRF stated that there was an even better system to ensure that the public receives a safe and healthy product.

Bottled water is regulated as a "food" by the FDA, under the Federal Food, Drug and Cosmetic Act (FFDCA). Bottled water companies must also adhere to the FDA's *Good Manufacturing Practices,* and are subject to extensive general food safety and labeling requirements that are not applicable to tap water. Section 410 of the FFDCA requires that the FDA review all new EPA drinking water requirements for tap water and determine if they should be applied to bottled water. As a result, only very small discrepancies exist between the EPA's and FDA's contaminant limits. The primary difference is the emphasis of the bottled water industry on the secondary drinking water standards of taste, odor, and color.

The current relationship in required quality between bottled water and drinking water can best be summed up by the FDA's policy statement concerning bottled water (Drinking Water Research Foundation Analysis of the February 1999 Natural Resources Defense Council Report, July 1999):

> In general, adopting the EPA's standards for chemical contaminants as allowable levels in bottled water is appropriate because it will protect the public health,

maintain consistent standards for identical contaminants in bottled water and tap water, prevent duplication of efforts between the EPA and FDA in evaluation of the effects of contaminants in drinking water, prevent public confusion concerning the significance of different standards for bottled water and public drinking water, and not foster public perception that bottled water is required to be of better quality than tap water.

Many states have regulations that are binding on bottled water suppliers and more stringent than the FDA regulations. If the bottler is a member of the IBWA, the bottler is subject to IBWA's additional requirements over and above those required by the FDA and state or local jurisdictions. One of the more stringent IBWA requirements is an annual, unannounced plant inspection administered by an independent, internationally recognized third-party inspection organization to assure that members are implementing the agreed-to Model Code practices.

On March 3, 2003, the FDA amended its bottled water quality standard regulations by establishing an allowable level for the contaminant uranium. The final rule will take effect on December 8, 2003. It is expected to ensure that the minimum quality of bottled water, as affected by uranium, combined radium, gross alpha particle radioactivity, and beta particle and photon radioactivity will remain comparable with the quality of public drinking water that meets the EPA's standards. The new rule will mean that bottled water manufacturers will be required to monitor their finished bottled water products for uranium at least once each year under the Current Good Manufacturing Practice (CGMP) regulations for bottled water. Manufacturers also will be required to monitor their source water for uranium as frequently as is necessary, but must do so at least once every four years unless they meet the criteria for the source water monitoring exemptions under the CGMP regulations.

Despite stringent regulations imposed on bottled water manufacturing, bottled water was epidemiologically implicated in a ten-state outbreak of the disease in (2002). This was the first widespread outbreak implicating bottled water in the United States. The CDC also stated that prior to this outbreak bottled water had not been identified as a vehicle for transmission of infectious organisms in the United States. The CDC cautioned that because of the wide geographic distribution of bottled water products, an outbreak associated with the consumption of bottled water would be difficult to recognize and suggested that the CDC, EPA, FDA, and the bottled water industry work together to address concerns regarding consumption of bottled water and public health.

Imported European waters must meet the same federal and state standards. In addition, they must meet the strict standards set by the European Union. International bottler members who sell products in the United States must submit a certificate of inspection to the IBWA.

DRINKING WATER SOURCE PROTECTION AND CONSERVATION

Because good sources of drinking water are a limited resource, the cost of developing and treating new sources is expected to rise. In addition, existing water suppliers are faced with the need to provide water to expanding service areas. As a result, the water industry is looking for cost effective alternatives, and is evaluating water conservation and reuse practices, as well as removing salt from seawater (desalinization) to create drinking water. Water suppliers are offering customers rebates for using water efficient toilets and showers, and in some areas, limiting the amounts that can be used for lawn and landscape watering or car washing. In some locations, municipal and county water departments are promoting the reuse of treated wastewater for irrigation and lawn watering instead of precious drinking water.

FUTURE DRINKING WATER CHALLENGES

Tremendous progress has been made in the years since the adoption of the SDWA in the treatment, protection, and provision of safe drinking water to the public. This feat was accomplished primarily because of the efforts of drinking water and health professionals in the public and private sectors. Public health protection has been, and remains, the focus for providing safe drinking water. Nevertheless, as the American population has grown and its lifestyle has become more sophisticated, the problems of providing safe drinking water have become more technically complex.

The higher percentage of an elderly population, the increasing survival rate of cancer patients, and the growing HIV/AIDS population will make it increasingly critical that health information about drinking water and its potential contaminants be provided in a direct and easily understandable way to immunocompromised populations. In addition, the private and public sectors will have to work together effectively to increase our knowledge about the health effects of known contaminants and newly discovered microbes and chemicals on both healthy and immunocompromised populations. Efficient, sound scientific research will be needed to support this effort.

As population and development increase and urban and suburban areas expand, all communities, regardless of size, will have to embrace the practice of water conservation. Water source protection to reduce the negative effects that these trends can potentially have on the quality and availability of drinking water will require high priority and funding. Consumers will have to be educated to recognize that their actions affect the quality of drinking water sources, and the level of treatment that is required to provide safe drinking water. High-quality tap drinking water will cost more in the future, but will still cost significantly less than alternatives such as bottled water.

WATER IN THE THIRD WORLD, A DEADLY DRINK

Access to safe water and adequate sanitation is a fundamental need and a human right. It is vital for the dignity and health of all people.

— Kaj Bärlund, UN Economic Commission for Europe [Online] http://www.drytoilet.org/barlund.pdf [accessed October 23, 2003]

In general, water quality is improving in developed countries. While water quality varies greatly in developing nations, poverty often results in inadequate distribution of resources, including food and water, and sanitation practices are generally poor. In 2000, according to the World Health Organization (WHO), water supply availability ranged from 62 percent in Africa to 100 percent in North America. The percentage of people served with some form of improved water supply (water that has been treated) rose from 79 percent (4.1 billion) in 1990 to 82 percent (4.9 billion) in 2000. At the beginning of 2000, one-sixth (1.1 billion) of the world's population was without access to improved water supply. Although an enormous number of people (816 million) gained access to improved water supplies between 1990 and 2000, the percentage increases in coverage appear modest because of population growth during that time.

A March 5, 2003, article from the United States Department of State International Information Programs (*U.N. Report Warns of Worsening World Water Crisis*) summarized key findings of the United Nations (UN) publication *World Water Development Report*. According to the UN report, as many as 7 billion people in 60 countries could face water shortages by the year 2050. The report also suggests that pollution is a major problem, with 50 percent of the population in developing countries exposed to polluted water. A key goal, the UN report states, is to reduce by 50 percent the proportion of people who lack access to clean water by the year 2015.

Adequate quantities of safe water for drinking and for use in promoting personal hygiene are complementary measures for protecting public health. Lack of improved domestic water supply in the home leads to disease through two principal transmission routes. The fecal-oral transmission route is water contaminated with fecal material (sewage) and is of poor hygienic quality. When the sewage-contaminated water is drunk without being treated or boiled, the situation prevalent in developing countries, waterborne disease occurs. Diseases transmitted by the fecal-oral route include typhoid, cholera, diarrhea, viral hepatitis A, dysentery, and dracunculiasis (guinea worm disease).

Water-washed disease transmission, the second route, is caused by a lack of sufficient quantities of clean water for washing and personal hygiene. People cannot keep their hands, bodies and home environment clean and hygienic when there is not enough water. The quantity of water that people use depends on their access to it. When water is available through a hose or house connection, people will use large quantities for hygiene. When water has to be hauled for more than a few minutes from source to home, the use drops significantly. Without enough clean water for good personal hygiene, skin and eye infections are easily spread, as are the fecal-oral route diseases.

The impact of poor water supply on human lives in Third World countries is staggering. Diarrheal disease is one example. The WHO estimated that nearly 4 billion cases of diarrhea occur each year, and cause 2.2 million deaths, mostly among children five years of age or less. Diarrhea causes 15 percent of all child deaths under age five in developing countries, and leaves millions of people underweight, mentally and physically handicapped, and vulnerable to other diseases. Good drinking water, improved personal hygiene, and better sanitation practices have been shown to reduce diarrheal disease 25 to 30 percent.

CHAPTER 6
OCEANS AND ESTUARIES

OCEANS

A view of Earth from a satellite shows an azure planet composed almost entirely of water. The oceans that cover two-thirds of Earth's surface to an average depth of almost 2.5 miles contain 97 percent of its water and have a profound influence on its environment. If the ocean basins were shallower, the seas would spread across the continents, and the only dry land areas would consist of a few major high mountain ranges projecting above a continuous layer of water.

Only recently have scientists come to appreciate the important role that the oceans play in maintaining Earth's climate. The oceans determine Earth's weather and long-term climate changes. They can also cause widespread damage to human populations, destroying human lives and property. Scientists are also still discovering the incredible diversity of life forms within the ocean depths. The oceans are home to more than 80 percent of all the life forms found on Earth. The many levels in the oceans' complex food chain interact by producing food and structures as habitat for other species, as well as consuming organic material and wastes. Primary producers, such as phytoplankton, seaweed, and algae, are eaten by small animals and small fish, which in turn are eaten by larger fish. These in turn are eaten by birds, larger fish, and mammals such as seals and man. Surface currents and deep currents mix the waters and move nutrients about, replenishing the food source for all marine life living at various depths, providing a bounteous food supply for all.

Origin of the Oceans

The terms "ocean" and "sea" are sometimes used interchangeably. Earth's oceans are the North and South Pacific, North and South Atlantic, Indian, Arctic, and Antarctic waters. Generally, seas are a portion of a larger ocean, although they may be partially or completely enclosed by land, such as the Mediterranean Sea, the Red Sea, and the Black Sea. There are about 35 seas in the world.

Oceanographers (scientists who study the oceans) believe that the oceans are some 500 million years old. They also think that both the atmosphere on Earth and the oceans were formed through a process called "degassing" of Earth's deep interior. According to this theory, the ocean originated from the escape of water vapor from the melted rocks of the early Earth. The vapor rose to form clouds surrounding the cooling planet. After Earth's temperature had cooled to a point below the boiling point of water, rain began to fall, and then continued to fall for many centuries. As this water drained into the huge hollows of the planet's cracked surface, the early ocean was formed. The force of gravity kept this water on Earth.

Oceans as Controller of Earth's Climate

Oceans play a major role in Earth's weather and long-term climate change. The oceans have a huge capacity to store heat and can affect the concentration of atmospheric gases that control Earth's temperature. The top eight feet of the ocean holds as much heat as the entire atmosphere, making the oceans' ability to distribute heat a very important factor in climate changes. Changes such as unusually warm (El Niño) or cold currents (La Niña) in the eastern portion of the Pacific (the largest ocean) can disrupt global weather patterns.

The oceans play a crucial role in the cycle of carbon dioxide, a process affecting global warming. The world's oceans store some of the 22 billion tons of carbon dioxide added each year to the atmosphere by natural sources and the burning of fossil fuels. Some scientists believe that the oceans serve as a reservoir for about half of all the carbon dioxide emitted each year, while the other half accumulates in the atmosphere.

TABLE 6.1

The 10 deadliest tropical cyclones to strike the mainland, 1900–2000

Rank	Hurricane	Year	Category	Deaths
1	Unnamed (TX, Galveston)	1900	4	8,000[1]
2	Unnamed (FL, Lake Okeechobee)	1928	4	1,836
3	Unnamed (FL, Keys)	1919	4	600[2]
4	Unnamed (New England)	1938	3[3]	600
5	Unnamed (FL, Keys)	1935	5	408
6	Audrey (Southwest LA, inland TX)	1957	4	390
7	Unnamed (Northeast)	1944	3[3]	390[4]
8	Unnamed (LA, Grand Isle)	1909	4	350
9	Unnamed (LA, New Orleans)	1915	4	275
10	Unnamed (TX, Galveston)	1915	4	275

Note: Hurricanes, or tropical cyclones, were not named until the 1950s.
[1] This figure could be as high as 10,000 to 12,000.
[2] Over 500 lost on ships at sea, 600-900 estimated deaths.
[3] Moving more than 30 miles per hour.
[4] Of the total lost 344 were lost on ships at sea.

SOURCE: Adapted from Jerry D. Jarrell, et al. "Table 2. The thirty deadliest mainland United States tropical cyclones 1900–2000," in *The Deadliest, Costliest, and Most Intense United States Hurricanes from 1900 to 2000*, National Oceanic and Atmospheric Administration and the National Weather Service, Tropical Prediction Center, Miami, FL, October 2001 [Online] http://www.aoml.noaa.gov/hrd/Landsea/deadly/Table2.htm [accessed July 18, 2003]

When Oceans Become Deadly

COASTAL POPULATIONS GROW. In 2000 more than one-fifth of the world's population (over 1 billion people) lived in coastal areas. This living preference places huge segments of the world population at risk from coastal hazards (episodic or chronic destructive natural system events that affect coastal areas), and has increased pollution of both oceans and estuaries.

Coastal areas are particularly vulnerable to natural hazards such as hurricanes, tidal waves, and their associated flooding. They are also some of the fastest-growing areas in the United States. The National Oceanic and Atmospheric Administration (NOAA) reported that 54 percent of the U.S. population (occupying only 26 percent of the total land mass) lives in coastal counties. In the time period 1990–2000, 17 of the fastest-growing counties in the United States were located along the coast and 19 of the 20 most densely populated counties in the nation were coastal. The U.S. Census Bureau estimated that by 2010, 127 million people would live in coastal areas. According to *Coastal Areas and Marine Resources* (December 2001), a report from the National Coastal Assessment Group, over the next 25 years, the coastal states of Florida, California, Texas, and Washington alone are expected to gain approximately 18 million people.

According to "30 Years of Protecting Oceans and Coasts," a January 13, 2003, Environmental Protection Agency (EPA) press release, more than half of the United

TABLE 6.2

The 30 costliest tropical cyclones to strike the mainland, 1900–2000

Rank	Hurricane	Year	Category	Damage
1	Andrew (Southeast FL and LA)	1992	5[1]	$34,954,825,000
2	Hugo (SC)	1989	4	9,739,820,675
3	Agnes (FL, Northeast U.S.)	1972	1	8,602,500,000
4	Betsy (Southeast FL and LA)	1965	3	8,516,866,023
5	Camille (MS, Southeast LA, VA)	1969	5	6,992,441,549
6	Diane (Northeast U.S.)	1955	1	5,540,676,187
7	Frederic (AL, MS)	1979	3	4,965,327,332
8	Floyd (Mid Atlantic & Northeast U.S.)	1999	2	4,666,817,360
9	Unnamed (New England)	1938	3[2]	4,748,580,000
10	Fran (NC)	1996	3	3,670,400,000
11	Opal (Northwest FL, AL)	1995	3	3,520,596,085
12	Alicia (North TX)	1983	3	3,421,660,182
13	Carol (Northeast U.S.)	1954	3[2]	3,134,443,557
14	Carla (North & Central TX)	1961	4	2,550,580,095
15	Georges (FL Keys, MS, AL)	1998	2	2,494,800,000
16	Juan (LA)	1985	1	2,418,795,844
17	Donna (FL, Eastern U.S.)	1960	4	2,407,888,443
18	Celia (South TX)	1970	3	2,015,663,203
19	Elena (MS, AL, Northwest FL)	1985	3	2,015,663,203
20	Bob (NC, Northeast U.S.)	1991	2	2,004,635,258
21	Hazel (SC, NC)	1954	4[2]	1,910,582,732
22	Unnamed (FL, MS, AL)	1926	4	1,738,042,353
23	Unnamed (North TX)	1915	4	1,544,253,659
24	Dora (Northeast FL)	1964	2	1,540,946,262
25	Eloise (Northwest FL)	1975	3	1,489,250,000
26	Gloria (Eastern US)	1985	3[2]	1,451,277,506
27	Unnamed (Northeast U.S.)	1944	3[2]	1,221,342,593
28	Beulah (South TX)	1967	3	1,113,122,363
29	Unnamed (Southeast FL and LA, MS)	1947	4	930,099,359
30	Unnamed (Galveston, TX)	1900	4	928,160,793

[1] Reclassified as Category 5 in 2002.
[2] Moving more than 30 miles per hour.

SOURCE: Adapted from Jerry D. Jarrell, et al. "Table 3a: Costliest U.S. Hurricanes 1900–2000," in *The Deadliest, Costliest, and Most Intense United States Hurricanes from 1900 to 2000*, National Oceanic and Atmospheric Administration and the National Weather Service, Tropical Prediction Center, Miami, FL, October 2001 [Online] http://www.nhc.noaa.gov/pastcost2.shtml? [accessed July 18, 2003]

States population lives within 50 miles of the coasts. In addition, an estimated 180 million Americans visit United States coastal areas each year, spending more than $600 billion. One of every six jobs in the United States is marine-related, generating $54 billion in goods and services annually. Coastal waters provide diverse and biologically productive habitats, supporting 66 percent of all United States commercial and recreational fishing and 45 percent of all protected species.

DANGEROUS STORMS. The most common coastal hazard is the threat of the huge ocean storms that come ashore, generally during the warmer months of the year, and wreak devastating damage to property and human life. These storms go by different names in different parts of the world. They are called hurricanes or tropical storms in the North Atlantic, eastern North Pacific, and western South

FIGURE 6.1

Sources of salts in the ocean

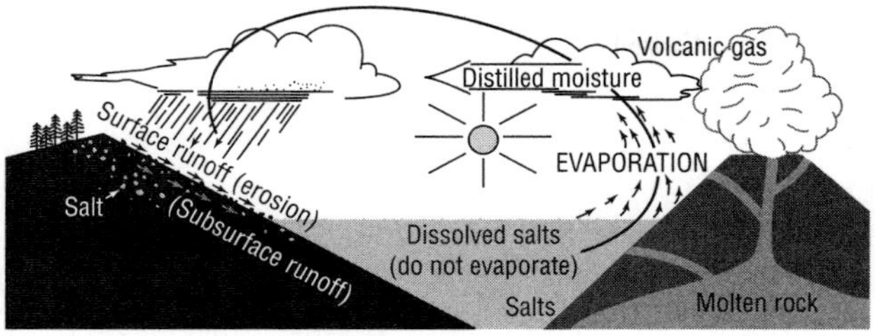

SOURCE: Herbert Swenson, "Sources of salts in the ocean," in *Why Is the Ocean Salty?*, U.S. Geological Survey, Denver, CO, 1993

TABLE 6.3

Principal constituents of seawater

Chemical constituent	Content (parts per thousand)
Calcium (Ca)	0.419
Magnesium (Mg)	1.304
Sodium (Na)	10.710
Potassium (K)	0.390
Bicarbonate (HCO$_3$)	0.146
Sulfate (SO$_4$)	2.690
Chloride (Cl)	19.350
Bromide (Br)	0.070
Total dissolved solids (salinity)	35.079

SOURCE: Herbert Swenson, "Principal constituents of seawater," in *Why Is the Ocean Salty?*, U.S. Geological Survey, Denver, CO, 1993

Pacific. "Typhoon" is the common term used for storms in the China Sea and western North Pacific, while "cyclone" is the word used for a storm in the Arabian Sea, the Bay of Bengal, and the South Indian Ocean.

Because of the spinning of planet Earth, a serious tropical storm's spiral is counterclockwise north of the equator and clockwise in the Southern Hemisphere. These tropical storms are the most dangerous weather phenomenon known, causing destruction through their very strong winds, torrential rains, and storm surges. By far, the greatest damage and the most deaths are caused by the storm surges, the elevated mounds of water pushed by the high winds. Surges can reach 20 feet or higher. In an ocean storm, a surge rolls over everything in its path, and combined with the violent waves and water currents, the surges cause not only death and destruction, but also immense erosion of land.

Coastal hazards such as hurricanes, tropical storms, and northeasters bring high winds, storm surges, flooding, and shoreline erosion, all of which are particularly damaging to coastal areas. They are not usually considered disastrous unless they involve damage to people and their property. Recent impacts have been increasingly devastating. Estimated disaster losses in the United States range from $10 billion to $50 billion annually; the average cost of a major disaster is $500 million. One of the primary factors contributing to the rise in disaster losses is the increasing population in high-risk coastal areas. Table 6.1 and Table 6.2 show the most deadly and the most costly tropical cyclones or hurricanes that have made landfall on the U.S. mainland during the 20th century.

The most costly tropical cyclone during this period was hurricane Andrew which devastated southeast Florida and southern Louisiana in 1992. The cost of damage done was in excess of $34 billion dollars and the storm left some 250,000 people homeless. The death toll was, thankfully, relatively low, claiming 35 lives. The cost of large hurricanes has been rising, but because of advances in storm prediction and preparation, the cost in lives has declined.

Table 6.1 lists the 10 most deadly storms in the 20th century and yet only one, an unnamed storm in New England in 1938, appears in the top 10 most costly storms listed in Table 6.2.

With populations growing in coastal areas, eliminating the destruction associated with tropical storms will be almost impossible. However, accurate forecasting and storm preparation are of ever greater importance in continuing to keep death tolls from such storms to a minimum.

TRYING TO GUESS THE FUTURE. Much research is targeted at understanding coastal storms and at being able to predict their occurrences and warn coastal residents. In addition to increasing the amount of property at risk, coastal population growth has created potentially life-threatening problems with storm warnings and evacuation. It has become increasingly difficult to ensure that the ever-rising numbers of residents and visitors can be evacuated and transported to adequate shelters during storm events. Sometimes, hurricane evacuation decisions must be made well in advance of issuing hurricane warnings in order to mobilize the appropriate manpower and resources needed for the evacuation. Also, when a significant percentage of the coastal population has not experienced an event such as a hurricane, people are less likely to prepare and respond properly before, during, and after the event.

Why Is the Ocean So Salty?

The salinity (saltiness) of the ocean is the result of several ongoing natural processes. Salts are the end products of the naturally occurring reactions between acids and metals and metal-like substances in the environment. Early in the life of the planet, the oceans probably contained very little salt. But since the first rains began descending on the young Earth many millions of years ago and ran over the land, breaking up rocks, absorbing and reacting with them to create dissolved solids (salts), and then transporting them to the oceans, the oceans have become progressively more salty. The activity of the hydrological cycle further

FIGURE 6.2

The amount of salt in the ocean

SALT

If all the salt in the sea could be removed and spread over the Earth's surface, it would cover approximately one-half of the Empire State Building.

SOURCE: Herbert Swenson, "If all the salt in the sea could be removed and spread over the Earth's surface . . . ," in *Why Is the Ocean Salty?*, U.S. Geological Survey, Denver, CO, 1993

concentrates the ocean salts. (See Figure 6.1.) The Sun's heat vaporizes almost pure, freshwater from the surface of the sea, leaving the salts behind. Table 6.3 shows the major types of salts found in ocean water.

The salinity of the ocean is currently about 35 pounds per 1,000 pounds of seawater, or parts per thousand (ppt). This is similar to having a teaspoon of salt added to a glass of drinking water. In contrast, freshwater has less than .5 ppt. Salinity in estuaries varies from slightly brackish (.5 to 5 ppt) at the freshwater end, to moderately brackish (5 to 18 ppt), to highly saline (25 to 30 ppt) near the ocean.

Scientists estimate that the rivers and streams flowing from the United States into the ocean discharge 225 million tons of dissolved solids (salts) and 513 million tons of suspended sediment into the ocean each year. Throughout the world, rivers annually transport about four billion tons of dissolved salts to the ocean. Nearly an equal amount of salt is deposited by the ocean as sediment on its floor.

If the salt in the ocean were taken out and spread evenly over Earth's entire land surface, it would form a layer more than 500 feet thick—about the height of a 40-story building. (See Figure 6.2.) Throughout the world the salinity of seawater is similar, although it is somewhat lower in the nearshore coastal waters, the polar seas, and near the mouths of large rivers.

USING SALINITY IN FORECASTING. According to a January 29, 2003 National Aeronautics and Space Administration (NASA) news release ("Ocean Surface Salinity Influences El Niño Forecasts"), NASA-sponsored scientists at the University of Maryland may have discovered how to improve the ability to predict El Niño events by knowing the salt content of the ocean's surface. Scientists have found that salinity and temperature combine to affect the density of the ocean. Greater salinity results in an increase in ocean density with a corresponding depression of the sea surface height. In warmer, fresher waters, the density is lower, causing an elevation of the sea surface.

The surface salinity in two regions contributes to El Niño events: an area of warmer temperatures and lower salinity in the western Pacific, and the higher salinity and cooler temperatures in the eastern Pacific. Differences in surface salinity are related to changes in temperature and upper ocean heat content, which are parts of the El Niño phenomenon. They have the potential to influence the Earth's climate through air-sea interaction at the ocean's surface.

According to the article, the study is among the first to look at ocean salinity in El Niño; Southern Oscillation predictions; and their relationship to tropical sea surface temperatures, sea level, winds, and fresh water from rain. Researchers studied data about sea surface temperatures, winds, rainfall, evaporation, sea surface height, and latent heat, for the period from 1980 through 1995. Using computer models, they performed a series of statistical predictions of the El Niño events for the period. They found that short-term predictions only require monitoring sea surface temperatures, while predictions over a season require the observation of sea level changes. They concluded that observations of salinity significantly improve predictions. When changes in salinity occur, they affect the El Niño event for the next six to 12 months. During this lag time, salinity changes have the potential to modify the layers of the ocean and affect the heat content of the western Pacific Ocean, the region where the unusual atmospheric and oceanic behavior associated with El Niño first develops.

Researchers believe that the study will be of great significance for the NASA Aquarius mission to monitor the surface salinity of the global ocean. According to data available on NASA's Aquarius mission Web site (http://aquarius.gsfc.nasa.gov/) in September 2003, this mission is scheduled for launch during 2008 and will have an operational life of three years. Aquarius will provide the first global maps of salt concentration on the oceans' surfaces. Salt concentration has been a key area of scientific uncertainty in the oceans' capacity to store and transport heat, which in turn affects Earth's climate and water cycle.

Coral Reefs—A Special Ocean Habitat

Coral reefs are among the richest marine ecosystems in terms of beauty, species, productivity, biomass, and structural complexity. They are dependent on intricate interactions between coral, which provides the structural framework, and the organisms that live among the coral. Corals thrive by acting at many levels in the food chain as producers of structures and food, and consumers of organic material. Coral reefs thrive in nutrient-poor habitats by containing many species that have complex food chains to recycle the essential nutrients with great efficiency, making the reefs particularly vulnerable to any event or process that disrupts the recycling.

Almost every group of marine organisms has its greatest number of individual kinds of organisms in coral reefs. For example, over 25 percent of all marine fish are found on the reefs. Estimates of fish productivity suggest that around 10 to 15 percent of the total worldwide catch comes from reefs. Since reefs occupy only about 600,000 square kilometers (less than .02 percent) of the ocean surface, their productivity and biodiversity are much greater than other marine ecosystems.

Most reefs form as long narrow ribbons along the edge between shallow and deep waters, and their assets are many. Fisheries for food, income from tourism and recreation, materials for new medicines, and shoreline protection from coastal storms are among the many economic benefits they provide.

CORAL REEF STRUCTURE. Corals are simple, bottom-dwelling organisms related to the sea anemone and jellyfish. The basic building block of coral is a polyp, a tiny animal that has a common opening used to take in food and excrete wastes, surrounding a ring of tentacles. The weak stinging cells of the tentacles are used to capture small animal plankton from the water for food. Each polyp sits in its own tiny bowl in a limestone skeleton, which the coral is constantly building as it grows up from the ocean floor. Reef-building corals live in large colonies formed by the repeated divisions of genetically identical polyps. The colonies can take a wide variety of shapes including branched, leafy, or massive forms, which may grow continuously for thousands of years.

The cells of coral contain symbiotic algae that make organic matter through photosynthesis and release it into the water to feed their coral hosts. Symbiosis is the living together of two dissimilar organisms in intimate association or even close union for mutual benefit. The algae remove carbon dioxide and excreted nutrients while supplying food and nutrients to the coral, and greatly enhance the rate at which the corals deposit their skeletons. The coral cells provide the algae with protective structure and access to light and nutrients. The vast majority of coral skeletons are white; their color comes from the pigmentation of the algae living among the polyps.

Because of their dependence on symbiotic algae, coral reefs can grow only under conditions favoring the algae. Coral reefs are confined to tropical waters because the algae require warm, shallow, well-lit waters that are free of turbidity and pollution. Corals act like plants, taking up dissolved and particulate material from the surrounding water and overgrowing one another in competition for light.

CORAL REEFS—ECOSYSTEMS AT RISK. The proximity of coral reefs to land makes them particularly vulnerable to human impacts. Because they depend on light, coral reefs can be severely damaged by silt smothering, nutrient enrichment leading to overgrowth by seaweed, and other factors that reduce water clarity and quality. Sport diving and overfishing for food and the aquarium trade can deplete species and damage coral, resulting in disruption to the intricate interactions among reef species, as well as coral decline. Introduction of exotic species through human activity can be devastating as the new predators consume the living reefs.

Coral "bleaching" is the unique response of corals to stress. The coral loses the microscopic algae that normally live within its cells and provide the coral with their color, their ability to rapidly grow skeleton, and much of their food. The bleached coral turns pale, transparent, or unusual colors, and then starves as it is unable to feed or reproduce. Increased bleaching is an early warning sign of deteriorating health, and can be caused by extremes of light, temperature, or salinity. In the 1980s coral bleaching began to spread dramatically. In October 1998 NOAA announced that it had recorded record-breaking coral bleaching in the tropics. Warm sea surface temperatures due to El Niño are believed to be the primary cause.

Little is known about most coral reefs and their inhabitants. Scientists have only recently begun the extensive and exhaustive studies necessary to determine if coral reefs are in decline and the causes of decline. Of prime concern is confirming the direct and indirect effects of human activities on coral reefs and their denizens.

CORAL REEFS IN THE UNITED STATES. Coral reefs are found only three places in the United States: Florida (primarily in the Florida Keys), throughout the Hawaiian archipelago, and in the offshore Flower Gardens of Texas. The Florida reef system is part of the Caribbean reef system, the third-largest barrier-reef ecosystem in the world. Five U.S. territories—American Samoa, Guam, the Northern Mariana Islands, Puerto Rico, and the U.S.

FIGURE 6.3

U.S. coral reef areas, 2000

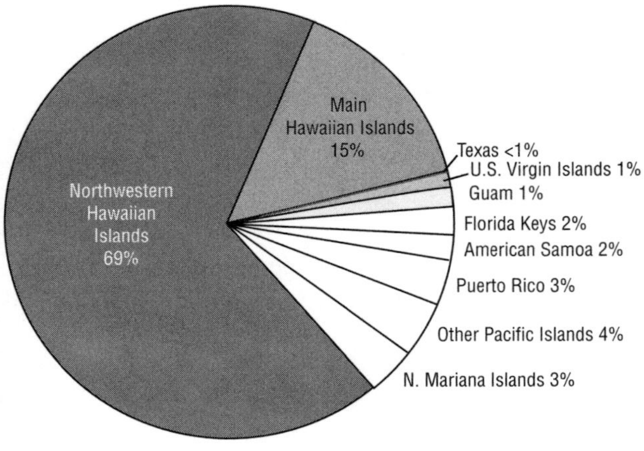

SOURCE: "U.S. Coral Reef Areas," in *National Water Quality Inventory: 1998 Report to Congress,* U.S. Environmental Protection Agency, Washington, DC, 2000

TABLE 6.4

Coral reef areas in the United States and the Freely Associated States, by population, tourism, and tourist expenditures, 2000

Coral reef area	Population (000)	Percent change in population (1990-2000)	Number of tourists (000)	Tourist expenditures (million $)
Florida (some counties)[1]	5,087	23.1	28,820	1,875
Puerto Rico	3,809	8.1	4,566	2,388
U.S. Virgin Islands	109	4.2	2,500	800
Flower Gardens	NA	NA	2	1
Hawaiian Islands	7,000	9.3	11,167	10,918
American Samoa	57	17.7	18	10
Guam	155	15.4	1,380	936
Northern Mariana Islands	69	57.2	737	587
Marshall Islands	51	9.9	5	3
Federal States of Micronesia	133	22.6	30	3
Palau	19	23.4	78	79

[1] Includes only Broward, Dade, Monroe, and Palm Beach Counties.
NA: not applicable
Note: The Flower Gardens are located in the Gulf of Mexico about 105 to 115 miles south of the Texas/Louisiana border. The area extends about 42 square nautical miles and was designated the Flower Garden Banks National Marine Sanctuary in January 1992.

SOURCE: Adapted from Turgeon, D.D., et al., "Table 1. Population and tourism statistics for the U.S. coral reef areas and the Freely Associated States," in *The State of Coral Reef Ecosystems of the United States and Pacific Freely Associated States: 2002,* U.S. Department of Commerce, National Oceanic and Atmospheric Administration, Washington, DC, 2002

Virgin Islands—also have lush reef areas. According to the *2000 Water Quality Inventory* published by the EPA, the northwestern Hawaiian Islands make up 69 percent of the country's coral reef areas, by far the largest percentage in the United States and its territories. (See Figure 6.3.)

To protect the U.S. coral reefs, many have been placed in marine sanctuaries with varying degrees of protection. The full extent and condition of most U.S. coral reefs is only beginning to be studied as a special area of focus.

On September 26, 2002, the NOAA released the first-ever national assessment of the condition of coral reefs in the United States. The report, *The State of Coral Reef Ecosystems of the United States and Pacific Freely Associated States,* was prepared under the auspices of the U.S. Coral Reef Task Force, and establishes a baseline that now will be used for biennial reports on the health of coral reefs in the United States. NOAA also released *A National Coral Reef Strategy,* a report to Congress outlining specific action to address 13 major goals, including the continuation of mapping and monitoring, to protect coral reefs.

According to *The State of Coral Reef Ecosystems of the United States and Pacific Freely Associated States,* there are an estimated 7,607 miles of United States reefs and a range of 4,479–31,470 miles of reefs off the Freely Associated States. An estimated 27 percent of the world's shallow water coral reefs may already be beyond recovery, and about 66 percent are severely degraded. The report also indicates that in all areas, some coral reefs in the United States were in good-to-excellent health. However, every reef system was suffering from both human and natural disturbances. These reefs suffer from the same problems as do reefs all over the world, especially those resulting from

rapidly growing coastal populations. The report states that 10.5 million people now live in U.S. coastal areas adjacent to shallow coral reefs, and every year about 45 million people visit the areas. Table 6.4 presents population and tourism data for the coral reefs located in the U.S. and in the Freely Associated States.

Among the major causes of damage to coral reefs, according to the report, are human-induced pressures such as coastal pollution, coastal development and runoff, and destructive fishing practices. Ship groundings, diseases, changing climate, trade in coral and live reef species, alien species, marine debris, harmful tourist activity, and tropical storms also contribute to the damage.

Florida and the U.S. Caribbean were considered to be in the most unfavorable condition, mainly because of nearby dense populations and the effects of hurricanes, disease, overfishing, and a proliferation of algae. Live coral cover in the Florida Keys had declined 37 percent over the last 5 years. During the past 20 years, white-band disease had killed nearly all the elkhorn and staghorn corals off the coasts of St. Croix (U.S. Virgin Islands), Puerto Rico, and southeast Florida.

Coral reefs are extremely important for a number of reasons. They are the Earth's largest biological structures. They are vital sources of food, jobs, chemicals, shoreline protection, and life-saving pharmaceuticals. Tourism in the United States and Freely Associated States coastal reef areas generated $17.6 billion in 2000. (See Table 6.4.) Commercial fishing generated an additional $246.9 million annually. In South Florida, reefs supported 44,500 jobs, providing a total annual income of $1.2 billion.

New and important discoveries about coral reefs continue. According to a June 11, 2003, report in the *Guardian* (David Fickling, "Huge New Coral Reef Discovered"), scientists from Geoscience Australia, the Australian national agency for geoscience research and geospatial information, discovered an uncharted coral reef in Queensland's Gulf of Carpentaria in mid-2003. The reef is about 120 square kilometers (46.3 square miles), making it larger than all of the reefs in Barbados combined. Most of it is 20 miles beneath the water surface. The article points out that the discovery of this reef is significant in part because of commonly held scientific beliefs that no reefs can exist in Australia's warm, muddy coastal waters.

Nearshore Waters

Nearshore waters occur in lakes, estuaries, and oceans, and reflect the conditions and activities within the watershed. A watershed is an area in which water, sediments and dissolved materials drain to a common outlet, such as a lake, river, estuary, or ocean. The nearshore is an indefinite zone extending outward from the shoreline, well beyond the shallow water (in oceans and estuaries, beyond the zone where the waves break). It defines the area where the current is caused primarily by wave action as opposed to current that is the result of water flow. Depending on the size of the water body, the nearshore waters may be minimal in size (a small lake) or very large (the coastal waters of the Atlantic Ocean).

Whether marine, estuarine, or fresh, nearshore waters serve a variety of functions. They are the prime recreational waters, providing opportunities for swimming, boating, diving, surfing, snorkeling, and fishing. Nearshore waters are intimately linked with wetlands and sea grasses, and provide a unique habitat for a variety of plants and animals. These waters are the source of food and shelter for many species of fish and shellfish, and provide habitat for 80 percent of the fish species in the United States. Nearshore waters also provide numerous opportunities for education and research for students, naturalists, the curious, and scientists.

Because of their proximity to the shoreline, nearshore waters are particularly vulnerable to pollution. As a result, water quality in most confined waters and some nearshore waters is deteriorating, which in turn affects the plant and animal life. In addition to pollution, nearshore waters are very vulnerable to the everyday (and to all appearances, harmless) activities of people. For example, swimming has been restricted in some shallow lagoons with coral reefs and beautiful beaches, because heavy swimmer use resulted in chemical concentrations of suntan oil and lotion in the water high enough to kill or impair the coral reefs. Wakes from recreational powerboats in high-use areas have been shown to increase wave action resulting in increased shoreline erosion. Increased pollutant levels from boat paints, spills during refueling, and leaks of gas and oil from recreational boat engines in areas of high recreational use affect both plants and animals. Private pier and boathouse construction result in shading of water, which contributes to seagrass decline. Balancing the need to accommodate the public's desire to enjoy water-related activities and ownership of waterfront property and the need to protect nearshore waters is a difficult management issue.

ESTUARIES

Estuaries are places of transition, where the rivers meet the sea. Salinity in estuaries varies from slightly brackish (.5 to 5 ppt) at the freshwater end to moderately brackish (5 to 18 ppt) to highly saline (25 to 30 ppt) near the ocean. An estuary is a partially enclosed body of water formed where freshwater from rivers flows into the ocean, mixing with the salty seawater. Although influenced by the tides, they are protected from the full force of ocean waves, winds, and storms by reefs, barrier islands, or fingers of land, mud, or sand that make up their seaward boundary. Estuaries come in all shapes and sizes. Examples include the Chesapeake Bay, Puget Sound, Boston Harbor, San Francisco Bay, and Tampa Bay. There are 130 estuaries in the United States.

The tidal sheltered waters of estuaries support unique communities of plants and animals, specially adapted for life under a wide range of conditions. Estuarine environments are incredibly productive, producing more organic matter annually than any equal-sized area of forest (including rain forests), grassland, or cropland. A wide range of habitats exists around and in estuaries, including shallow open water, tidal pools, sandy beaches, mud and sand flats, freshwater and salt marshes, rocky shores, oyster reefs, mangrove forests, river deltas, wooded swamps, and kelp and seagrass beds. Estuaries provide habitat for more than 75 percent of the U.S. commercial fish catch, and for 80 to 90 percent of the recreational fish catch.

Estuaries are very important to the economy of coastal communities and the United States. Nationwide, 28 million jobs in fields as diverse as shipbuilding, tourism, commercial and recreational fishing, real estate, and other coastal industries are dependent on estuaries. Nearly 70 percent of the nation's population (about 180 million people) visit the coasts annually generating $8 billion to $12 billion in revenue. These two examples provide insights into the billions of dollars in economic activity that are associated with estuaries each year.

National Estuary Program

The Water Quality Act of 1987 created the National Estuary Program (NEP) as an alternative to the traditional command-and-control regulatory approaches to water quality programs. Congress recognized that in order to achieve long-term protection of living resources and water quality (the basic "fishable/swimmable" goal of the Clean Water Act), the participation of those most affected by the environmental decisions was critical. Based on the highly successful Chesapeake Bay Program, with its collaborative approach to managing watersheds and estuaries, the NEP is a voluntary program.

To improve their estuary, the NEP brings together community members using a forum to establish working relationships and the trust necessary to find and implement solutions. Together, stakeholders define program goals and objectives, identify estuary problems, and design action plans to prevent or control pollution, while restoring habitats and living resources such as shellfish. This approach results in the adoption of a comprehensive conservation and management plan (CCMP) for implementation in each estuary. This integrated watershed-based, stakeholder-oriented, water resource management approach has led to some significant local environmental improvements since its founding. In 1987 the NEP consisted of six local estuary programs; as of 2003 it has grown to include 30 estuaries in 18 states and Puerto Rico.

Two examples of environmental improvement resulting from the NEP program can be found in the Leffis Key and Corpus Christi projects. The Leffis Key restoration project in Sarasota Bay, Florida, resulted in 30 acres of productive intertidal habitat being created and planted with more than 50,000 native plants and trees at a cost of $315,000. In Corpus Christi Bay, Texas, treated biosolids were applied to a 25-acre plot of aluminum mine tailings, resulting in plant growth promotion, wildlife habitat, and improved water quality. Biosolids are composed of sewage sludge that has been properly treated and processed to make a nutrient-rich material that can be safely recycled and applied as fertilizer.

Chesapeake Bay Program

The Chesapeake Bay ("the Bay") is the largest estuary in North America, and is one of the most productive estuaries in the world. It has a 64,000-square-mile watershed draining six states and the District of Columbia. Its watershed is home to 15.1 million people and 3,600 species of plants and animals. The Bay has 11,684 miles of shoreline and averages 21 feet deep with hundreds of thousands of acres of very shallow water. It is 200 miles long and 35 miles wide at its widest point.

The Bay is an incredibly complex ecosystem that includes many important habitats and food webs. A food web is a complex food chain where many different species of plants and animals interact by producing food, consuming organic material, and recycling wastes. Primary producers like phytoplankton, algae, and sea grasses are eaten by small animals and fish, which then become meals for larger fish and animals. These, in turn, are eaten by birds, larger fish, and mammals.

The Chesapeake Bay is a mixture of freshwater and saltwater from the Atlantic Ocean and is subject to seasonal weather. Plant and animal populations vary with changes in temperature, salinity, water clarity (light penetration), dissolved oxygen, and human impacts. Human impacts include activities such as overfishing, development, marina construction and operation, and farming. Excess nutrient, most of which comes from nonpoint sources (primarily agricultural activity and urban runoff) is the primary stressor in the Chesapeake Bay. A nonpoint source is a source that is widely spread and has no fixed location.

The first estuary in the United States to be targeted for restoration and protection, the Bay is protected under its own federally mandated program, separate from the NEP. The Bay Program began in 1983 with a meeting of the governors of Maryland, Pennsylvania, and Virginia; the mayor of the District of Columbia; and the EPA administrator. These individuals signed the Chesapeake Bay Agreement committing their states and the District of Columbia to prepare plans for protecting and improving water quality and living resources in the Chesapeake Bay. The Chesapeake Bay Program evolved as the institutional mechanism to restore the Bay and to meet the goals of the Chesapeake Bay Agreement. The program, which guides and coordinates multistate and multiagency activities, is the model for the NEP, and has resulted in a Chesapeake Bay that is cleaner than it was in 1983.

Two important habitat alterations in the Chesapeake Bay are the focus of intense restoration efforts. They are restoration of the once-extensive beds of submerged aquatic vegetation and oysters. Oyster reefs (oyster bars) play an important ecological role in the Chesapeake Bay. Oysters cluster together to grow upward and outward, creating a hard surface on the Bay's bottom and a three-dimensional structure used as habitat by many species. The hard oyster shell surfaces provide places of attachment for many sessile (not moving, permanently attached) species, including oyster larvae. They also provide habitat for worms, snails, and other invertebrates as well as food and protection for small fish and crabs. Many species of ducks find food on and around the oyster bars during the winter months.

Oysters have declined in the Bay because of introduced oyster diseases, harvest pressure and use of harvesting techniques that have flattened the large three-dimensional reefs, silting, and other pollution. Oyster populations are at or below the level of being naturally sustaining. The loss of oyster populations and their reef habitats has had important consequences for the oysters, as well as many other Bay species.

Both Maryland and Virginia have large-scale federally and state funded programs underway to artificially create reefs with oyster shell and other materials such as fly ash, rock, concrete, and other recycled materials. Oyster sanctuaries (areas off-limits to harvest) are being established as brood-stock areas to enhance the oysters' ability to maintain self-sustaining populations through natural recruitment (the ability of a population to reproduce and replace animals lost). In addition, private organizations such as the Oyster Recovery Partnership, the Chesapeake Bay Foundation, and the Tidewater Oyster Gardening Association are using volunteers to grow and plant millions of small oysters in the sanctuaries and other restored areas.

Submerged Aquatic Vegetation

Sea grasses—or submerged aquatic vegetation (SAV)—are very important in the productivity and habitat of estuaries. These grasses are vascular plants that grow completely underwater and have special adaptations to help them survive in the aquatic environment. A vascular plant is one that takes nutrients in through its roots and transports them through its roots and stems to all parts of the plant. SAV plays an important ecological role by:

- Providing food and habitat for waterfowl, fish, shellfish, crustaceans, and other invertebrates, as well as nursery habitat for the juveniles of many species, which hide from predators among the swaying fronds

- Producing oxygen in the water column through photosynthesis

- Filtering and trapping silt that can cloud the water and bury bottom-dwelling organisms such as oysters

- Protecting shorelines from erosion by retarding wave action

- Removing excess nutrients that could cause the growth of undesirable algae in the surrounding waters

The species of SAV in an estuary change in response to the salinity. Tidal fresh SAV species require a salinity of 0 to .5 ppt. Oligohaline (slightly brackish) species require .5 to 5 ppt. Mesohaline (moderately brackish) require 5 to 18 ppt, while polyhaline (high salinity) species require 18 to 30 ppt. Upstream activities, such as dam construction or water diversions, can radically alter freshwater flow into an estuary, changing the downstream salinity and thus the composition of SAV.

The health of SAV is a good indication of the health of an estuary. The single-most-important factor in SAV growth and survival is the amount of light that reaches the plants. When the amount of light is too low, the SAV can no longer photosynthesize and produce enough energy and food to grow. The amount of light reaching SAV is affected by turbidity, algae, epiphytes (microbes that attach to SAV leaf surface), and nutrients present in the water column. Significant reduction in SAV is a sign that the estuary is experiencing considerable stress. Reduction in SAV has been linked to decline in important fish, crab, shrimp, and waterfowl species.

The Chesapeake Bay has experienced significant SAV decline. According to the Chesapeake Bay Program, up to 200,000 acres of SAV may have grown in the area historically, but by 1984 that number had shrunk to 38,000 acres. In some areas, the grasses are returning naturally. In other areas, large-scale SAV monitoring and planting activities are being undertaken to try to reverse the decline. According to an article in the April 2003 issue of the EPA's *Coastlines* newsletter ("Submerged Aquatic Vegetation Being Restored in Chesapeake Bay"), in 1992 the Chesapeake Bay Program helped to develop an initial Bay-wide goal of having 114,000 acres of SAV, reflecting the total SAV area that existed between 1971 and 1990. Since annual Bay-wide surveys began in 1985, SAV has substantially increased in many areas. According to the report *2001 Distribution of Submerged Aquatic Vegetation in Chesapeake Bay and Coastal Bays* (Robert J. Orth and David J. Wilcox, Virginia Institute of Marine Science, Gloucester Point, VA, December 2002), in 2001 total SAV acreage in the Bay set a new record—77,855 acres.

Similarly, the Gulf of Mexico has experienced an SAV decline. The U.S. Geological Survey's (USGS) National Wetlands Research Center has documented significant decline in sea grasses in the northern Gulf of Mexico. Reduction in SAV acreage ranges from 12 to 66 percent in bays and estuaries of the northern Gulf of Mexico. In addition, the sea grasses are changing in species composition, densities, and distribution of their beds. Many scientists believe that Gulf of Mexico SAV decline is directly related to nutrient enrichment and hypoxia (lack of oxgen).

OCEAN AND ESTUARINE FISHERIES— A VALUABLE RESOURCE

Archaeological evidence from the western Pacific reveals that Homo erectus *began building boats as far back as 800,000 years ago, which suggests that people turned to the sea for food long before fields were plowed for planting.*

— Anne Platt McGinn, *Safeguarding the Health of Oceans,* Worldwatch Institute, Washington, D.C., March 1999

In many parts of the world, fish is the major source of protein in the diet. Humans on average worldwide obtain 16 percent of their animal protein from fish, and an estimated two billion people worldwide depend on fish for 40 percent of their protein supply. A staple in the diet of many cultures, fish are consumed in much greater quantities in countries other than the United States. The United States consumes only about 8 percent of the total world catch of fish and shellfish. This supply comes from U.S. commercial fishermen, aquaculture producers, and imports.

In the 1990s the United Nations Food and Agriculture Organization (FAO) reported record world marine harvests of over 100 million tons annually. Fisheries experts believed that the catch had peaked and that future harvests would begin to decline. The FAO supported this finding, claiming that most traditional marine fish stocks had reached full exploitation; therefore an intensified effort was unlikely to produce an increased catch, and any increase would produce a state of overfishing.

Eighty-two percent of the fish caught in 1996 came from oceans and estuaries. Growing fish, shrimp, and other aquatic species on coastal and freshwater farms ("aquaculture") increased greatly during the 1990s, accounting for 27 million tons in 1996, up from 7 million tons in 1984. According to the FAO, aquaculture in 1996 accounted for 26 percent of food fish. Fifty-nine percent of aquaculture fish were freshwater farmed while 41 percent were marine and estuarine farmed. Some scientists and fisheries experts predicted that aquaculture production would surpass the volume of harvest of wild fish in the first 25 years of the 21st century, but it is doubtful that aquaculture will ever be able to match the variety of species found in oceans and estuaries. According to *Fisheries of the United States 2001,* published in 2002 by the National Marine Fisheries Service, a part of the National Oceanic and Atmospheric Administration, total aquaculture production in the United States in 2000 was 823 million pounds.

For centuries, freedom of the seas was the reigning doctrine, and the waters beyond three nautical miles were open to all. Starting about 1945, after World War II, there was a boom in marine fishing, and fishermen began to engage in fierce competition over fishing grounds. In the 1970s, as conflict mounted, the world took a step toward curtailing fishing freedom on the high seas. As part of the Third United Nations Conference on the Law of the Sea, governments agreed to establish a zone no more than 200 nautical miles wide within which a coastal country has sole rights to natural resources. Known as an exclusive economic zone (EEZ), this area includes the most productive fishing grounds in the oceans. Outside the EEZ, however, freedom of the seas still largely stands.

Overfishing

Overfishing is the state created when fish catch exceeds the maximum sustainable yield (the amount of fish that can be harvested every year without depleting the natural breeding stock). When harvest exceeds recruitment

(the ability of a fishery to reproduce and replace animals lost to the fishery), both the fish population and the fish catch decline, causing both ecological and economic harm. Although fishing directly affects the abundance of adult and juvenile fish, the growth and survival of fish in their early life stages depends on the presence of necessary ocean, coastal, estuarine, and river habitats. Lack of abundant, high-quality habitat can be as devastating to fisheries as overfishing.

According to the National Fisheries Institute (the trade association for commercial fishermen and seafood suppliers), more than 170,000 people work in the United States as commercial fishermen. These fishermen operate many different types of vessels, ranging in size from small one-man boats to large purse seiners and trawlers. The vast majority of these vessels are independently owned and family operated, and harvest more than 300 species of seafood from U.S. waters. Seventy percent of the harvest is caught with purse seine and trawl nets. A purse seine is a net that is deployed with floats and traps the fish in a purse-like bag when pulled from the sea.

Fisheries of the United States 2001 reported that per capita consumption of fishery products in 2001 decreased to 14.8 pounds, down 0.4 pound from the per capita consumption of 15.2 pounds in 2000. U.S. commercial fish landings—the volume of fish brought to the dock by commercial fisheries—at ports in the 50 states amounted to 9.5 billion pounds and was valued at $3.2 billion in 2001.

NOAA described the general welfare of the U.S. living marine and estuarine resources as "guarded with vigilance needed." The decline in Northeast groundfish, the uncertain state of some West Coast salmon runs, and the reduced populations of sharks and other marine species are examples of areas that need special attention. Overfishing and habitat loss are causing many fisheries to fall below the levels required to produce long-term potential yield. The challenge is to maintain the long-term viability of the natural system, while at the same time addressing the social and economic needs of the fisheries.

In the United States, the EEZ is the responsibility of the federal government and regional fishery management councils. Nearshore fisheries, defined as those within zero to three miles of the coastline, are the responsibility of coastal states and interstate marine fishery commissions.

Shellfish Harvesting

He was a bold man that first eat an oyster.

— Jonathan Swift, *A Complete Collection of Genteel and Ingenious Conversation, According to the Most Polite Mode and Method Now Used at Court, and in the Best Companies of England,* B. Motte & C. Bathurst, London, 1738

Over 33,000 square miles (an area slightly larger than the state of Maine) of marine and estuarine water in the

FIGURE 6.4

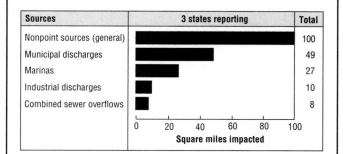

Sources associated with shellfish harvesting restrictions, 2000

Sources	3 states reporting	Total
Nonpoint sources (general)		100
Municipal discharges		49
Marinas		27
Industrial discharges		10
Combined sewer overflows		8

Square miles impacted

SOURCE: "Figure 7-3. Sources Associated with Shellfish Harvesting Restrictions," in *2000 National Water Quality Inventory*, EPA-841-R-02-001, U.S. Environmental Protection Agency, Office of Water, Washington, DC, August 2002

FIGURE 6.5

Summary of use support in assessed ocean shoreline waters, 2000

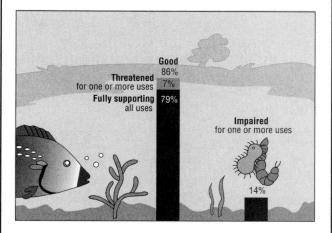

Note: Numbers may not add to 100% due to rounding.

SOURCE: "Figure 4-9. Summary of Use Support in Assessed Ocean Shoreline Waters," in *2000 National Water Quality Inventory*, EPA-841-R-02-001, U.S. Environmental Protection Agency, Office of Water, Washington, DC, August 2002

contiguous United States are classified as shellfish harvest waters under a program that is jointly administered by the coastal states and the National Shellfish Sanitation Program (NSSP). In this program shellfish are narrowly defined as "bivalves," that is, mollusks having two valves. Common bivalves are oysters, clams, and mussels. Once a common staple in the diet of people living near coastal waters, most bivalves are considered a delicacy today. The national commercial harvest of these mollusks is valued at more than $200 million when it is first put ashore.

Since the time of the Romans, bivalves have been identified as potential transmitters of infectious disease. The infectious, and sometimes dangerous, diseases that have been transmitted by bivalves range from typhoid and cholera to minor intestinal disorders. The disease agents may originate in the sewage of humans or other warm-blooded animals or may be naturally occurring in the environment. It is the unique biology of bivalves and the way in which people eat them that contribute to our vulnerability to disease.

Shellfish are filter feeders that tend to stay in one place and pump large amounts of water through their bodies. If pathogens (disease-causing bacteria and viruses) are present in the water, the bivalves may concentrate the pathogens in their tissues to levels that can cause disease in humans who eat the bivalves raw. The bivalves are not harmed by the microbes, and if exposed to clean water, will cleanse themselves. Crabs, shrimp, and other crustaceans do not concentrate the pathogens.

To protect the public that eats bivalves raw and to ensure a safe harvest, the coastal states carefully monitor the water and control commercial harvest under the NSSP guidelines. Special emphasis is given to identifying and eliminating the discharge of untreated or poorly treated

human and animal sewage in harvest areas. Harvesting is restricted in waters that do not meet NSSP guidelines. States determine if an area is safe for harvesting through monitoring the concentrations of the indicator bacteria, total coliform and fecal coliform. Indicator bacteria provide evidence of possible fecal contamination from human and domestic animal wastes. These wastes may contain pathogens that can be taken up and concentrated by the bivalves. Figure 6.4 shows the most common sources responsible for the presence of these indicator bacteria which led to shellfish harvest restrictions as reported by three states. The program has been very successful in preventing illness from contaminated bivalves, and outbreaks of illness rarely occur.

The filter feeding of bivalves also makes them vulnerable to the concentration of chemical contaminants that may be harmful to humans. Concentrations of chemicals in bivalves are directly related to the concentrations in the water column and the food that they consume. Because bivalves are low in body fat, they do not tend to bioaccumulate and retain chemicals to the extent that fish do.

NOAA has monitored chemical contaminants in mussels and oysters in its Mussel Watch Program since 1986. According to the latest report in 1998, while the levels of most chemical contaminants were decreasing, others remained the same. The best news, however, was that none of the chemicals monitored were increasing in concentration.

FIGURE 6.6

Leading pollutants in impaired ocean shoreline waters, 2000

Total ocean shoreline
58,618 miles

Assessed ocean shoreline
3,221 miles[1]

94% not assessed
6% assessed

2,755 miles
86% good

14% impaired 434 miles

Leading pollutants/stressors	Miles
Percent of impaired shoreline miles	
Pathogens (bacteria)	384
Oxygen-depleting substances	102
Turbidity	53
Suspended solids	50
Oil and grease	48
Metal	46
Nutrients	43

Percent of assessed shoreline miles

[1] Includes miles assessed as not attainable.

Note: Percentages do not add up to 100% because more than one pollutant or source may impair a segment of ocean shoreline.

SOURCE: "Figure 4-11. Leading Pollutants in Impaired Ocean Shoreline Waters," in *2000 National Water Quality Inventory*, EPA-841-R-02-001, U.S. Environmental Protection Agency, Office of Water, Washington, DC, August 2002

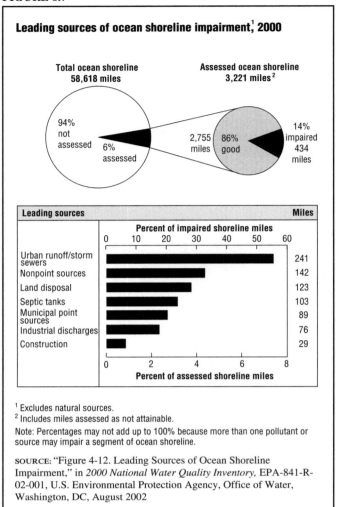

FIGURE 6.7

Leading sources of ocean shoreline impairment,[1] 2000

Total ocean shoreline
58,618 miles

Assessed ocean shoreline
3,221 miles[2]

94% not assessed
6% assessed

2,755 miles
86% good

14% impaired 434 miles

Leading sources	Miles
Percent of impaired shoreline miles	
Urban runoff/storm sewers	241
Nonpoint sources	142
Land disposal	123
Septic tanks	103
Municipal point sources	89
Industrial discharges	76
Construction	29

Percent of assessed shoreline miles

[1] Excludes natural sources.
[2] Includes miles assessed as not attainable.

Note: Percentages may not add up to 100% because more than one pollutant or source may impair a segment of ocean shoreline.

SOURCE: "Figure 4-12. Leading Sources of Ocean Shoreline Impairment," in *2000 National Water Quality Inventory*, EPA-841-R-02-001, U.S. Environmental Protection Agency, Office of Water, Washington, DC, August 2002

THE *2000 NATIONAL WATER QUALITY INVENTORY*

Oceans

In its *2000 National Water Quality Inventory* (2002), the EPA reported that 14 of the 27 coastal states and territories had rated the water quality of some of their coastal waters. The states had assessed 14 percent of the 22,618 miles of national coastline excluding Alaska, or 5.5 percent (3,221 miles) of ocean shoreline (including Alaska's 36,000 miles of coastline). Of the 14 percent of ocean waters assessed, 79 percent fully supported their designated uses, 14 percent were impaired, and 7 percent were supporting uses but threatened. (See Figure 6.5.) Designated uses are the beneficial water uses assigned to each water body by a state as part of its water quality standards. Examples of designated uses are fishing and drinking water supply.

In this 2000 EPA report, bacteria (pathogens) were identified by 10 states as the leading contaminants of ocean shoreline waters, followed by oxygen-depleting substances and turbidity (cloudiness). (See Figure 6.6.) Bacteria provide evidence of possible fecal contamination that may cause illness. States use bacterial indicators to determine if oceans are safe for swimming or secondary contact recreation, such as water skiing. Figure 1.7 in Chapter 1 shows the pathways of bacteria to surface waters. The most common sources of bacteria are urban runoff, inadequately treated human sewage, and runoff from pastures and feedlots, all of which were identified by 10 states as leading sources of ocean shoreline impairment (see Figure 6.7).

Turbidity is a chemical contaminant that is important in the control of pathogens. It is a measure of the relative clarity of water. Turbidity is caused by suspended matter or other impurities that make the water look cloudy. These impurities may include clay, silt, finely divided organic and inorganic matter, plankton, and other microscopic organisms. It interferes with the transmission of light to underwater grasses and other plant life in need of this light. If the transmission of light is reduced due to heavy silt in the water this can smother bottom-dwelling organisms such as oysters. Turbidity was responsible for more than 10

FIGURE 6.8

Individual use support in estuaries, 2000

Good water quality supports shellfishing in 75% of the waters assessed

Designated use	Square miles assessed	Percent	
		Good (fully supporting or threatened)	Impaired (partially supporting or not supporting)
Aquatic life support	22,047	48	52
Fish consumption	12,940	52	48
Shellfishing	20,967	75	25
Primary contact – swimming	21,169	85	15
Secondary contact	9,524	77	23

This figure presents a tally of the square miles of estuaries assessed by states for each category of designated use. For each category, the figure summarizes the proportion of the assessed waters rated according to quality.

SOURCE: "Figure 4-2. Individual Use Support in Estuaries," in *2000 National Water Quality Inventory,* EPA-841-R-02-001, U.S. Environmental Protection Agency, Office of Water, Washington, DC, August 2002

FIGURE 6.9

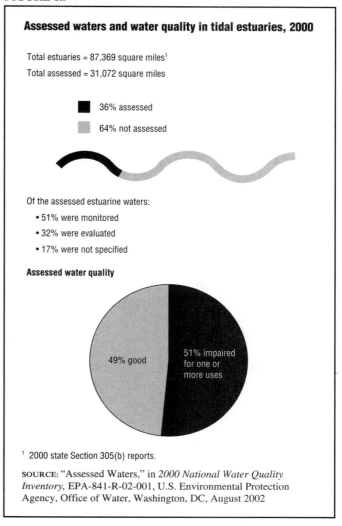

Assessed waters and water quality in tidal estuaries, 2000

Total estuaries = 87,369 square miles[1]

Total assessed = 31,072 square miles

- 36% assessed
- 64% not assessed

Of the assessed estuarine waters:
- 51% were monitored
- 32% were evaluated
- 17% were not specified

Assessed water quality

49% good

51% impaired for one or more uses

[1] 2000 state Section 305(b) reports.

SOURCE: "Assessed Waters," in *2000 National Water Quality Inventory,* EPA-841-R-02-001, U.S. Environmental Protection Agency, Office of Water, Washington, DC, August 2002

In general, most of the ocean waters assessed supported the five general-use categories shown for estuaries in Figure 6.8. The five general-use categories (aquatic life support, fish consumption, shellfishing, primary contact—swimming, and secondary contact) represent summaries of the designated uses and their achievement provided by the states to the EPA. Waters that either support their designated uses only part of the time, or do not support their uses at all, are considered impaired. Good water quality supports primary contact (swimming without risk to public health) in 85 percent of the assessed ocean waters (the same percentage for use support in estuaries), and fish consumption (fish are safe to eat) in 91 percent (compared to 52 percent of use support in estuaries).

In 94 percent of the waters assessed, the water was considered of good quality, capable of supporting aquatic life (suitable habitat for protection and propagation of desirable fish, shellfish, and other aquatic organisms). In the shellfish harvesting summary (water quality supports a population of bivalves free from toxicants and pathogens that could pose a health risk to people who eat them), 86

percent of the impaired ocean shoreline miles reported to the EPA in 2000. Three of the leading sources of ocean impairment are also contributors to turbidity. They are runoff from highly developed urban areas, agricultural activities, and construction projects (see Figure 6.7).

FIGURE 6.10

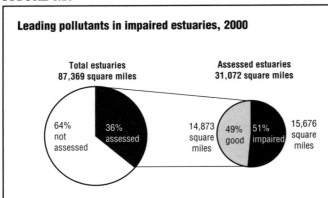

Leading pollutants in impaired estuaries, 2000

Total estuaries
87,369 square miles

64% not assessed

36% assessed

Assessed estuaries
31,072 square miles

14,873 square miles

49% good

51% impaired

15,676 square miles

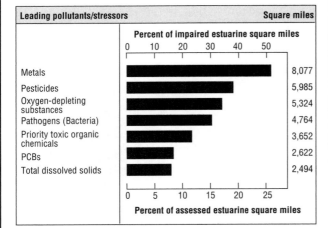

Leading pollutants/stressors	Square miles
Metals	8,077
Pesticides	5,985
Oxygen-depleting substances	5,324
Pathogens (Bacteria)	4,764
Priority toxic organic chemicals	3,652
PCBs	2,622
Total dissolved solids	2,494

Percent of impaired estuarine square miles
Percent of assessed estuarine square miles

Note: Percentages do not add up to 100% because more than one pollutant or source may impair an estuary. PCBs = polychlorinated biphenyls.

SOURCE: "Figure 4-3. Leading Pollutants in Impaired Estuaries," in *2000 National Water Quality Inventory,* EPA-841-R-02-001, U.S. Environmental Protection Agency, Office of Water, Washington, DC, August 2002

FIGURE 6.11

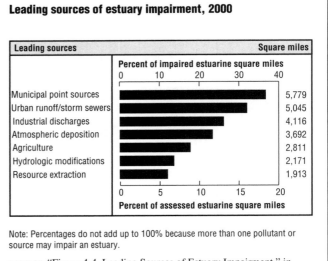

Leading sources of estuary impairment, 2000

Leading sources	Square miles
Municipal point sources	5,779
Urban runoff/storm sewers	5,045
Industrial discharges	4,116
Atmospheric deposition	3,692
Agriculture	2,811
Hydrologic modifications	2,171
Resource extraction	1,913

Percent of impaired estuarine square miles
Percent of assessed estuarine square miles

Note: Percentages do not add up to 100% because more than one pollutant or source may impair an estuary.

SOURCE: "Figure 4-4. Leading Sources of Estuary Impairment," in *2000 National Water Quality Inventory,* EPA-841-R-02-001, U.S. Environmental Protection Agency, Office of Water, Washington, DC, August 2002

percent of the ocean waters assessed had good water quality that supported this use. In addition, good water quality in 91 percent of the ocean waters assessed supported secondary contact recreation (people can perform water-based activities such as water skiing and boating without risk of adverse human health effects).

Estuaries

Twenty-three of the 27 coastal states provided data for use in the *2000 National Water Quality Inventory*. These 23 states assessed 36 percent of the nation's estuaries. (See Figure 6.9.) Of the 31,072 square miles assessed, 49 percent supported their uses and 51 percent were impaired. Figure 6.10 shows the major pollutants in U.S. estuaries. Metals were the most common pollutants, followed by pesticides and oxygen-depleting substances. This pollution came primarily from municipal point sources, urban runoff and storm sewers, and industrial discharges. (See Figure 6.11.)

As with the U.S. ocean shoreline, the five general use categories provide important details about the nature of

water quality problems in estuaries. (See Figure 6.9.) In general, most of the waters assessed supported the general use categories. The two use categories that showed the greatest impairment were aquatic life support (52 percent impairment), and fish consumption (48 percent impairment). Good water quality in 75 percent of the estuaries assessed supported use for shellfish harvesting, while 77 percent of the waters supported secondary contact recreation. Eighty-five percent of the estuarine waters assessed had good water quality for primary contact use. (See Figure 6.8.)

BEACH WATCH

Hundreds of times each year, beach closings take place to protect the public from possible exposure to pathogens (disease-causing organisms). The bacteria used to make this determination are generally harmless, but are present in large numbers in the sewage of humans and warm-blooded animals. Their presence indicates the possible presence of disease-causing organisms.

The most common problem caused by swimming in contaminated water is gastroenteritis, contracted by swallowing water while swimming and characterized by diarrhea, nausea, vomiting, and cramps. While gastroenteritis is generally not harmful to healthy adults, it can cause serious illness in children and immunocompromised individuals. Immunocompromised persons have weakened immune systems, and include infants, pregnant women, the elderly, HIV and AIDS patients, those receiving treatment for certain kinds of cancer, organ-transplant recipients, and people on drugs that suppress their immune system.

The major pollution sources responsible for the closings and advisories include runoff of storm water following rainfall, and sewage spills or sewage overflows. Some beaches are closed "just in case," or issue advisories against swimming when rainfall exceeds certain levels. Almost every coastal state reported having at least one beach where storm water drains onto or near bathing beaches.

The EPA established the BEACH program in 1997 to significantly reduce the risk of waterborne illness at the nation's beaches and recreational waters through improvements in recreational water protection programs and risk communication. Through the EPA's BEACH Watch Web site, the public can access detailed information on hundreds of individual coastal, Great Lakes, and freshwater beaches. Other information on local beach programs and health issues, and links to other relevant sites are provided. Users can also learn more about how to avoid unnecessary exposure to contaminated water while at the beach.

In the EPA's survey of the 2001 swimming season, 34 states and territories representing all coastal and Great Lakes states reported data on 2,445 beaches. Of this total, 1,403 were coastal beaches, 308 were Great Lakes beaches, and 734 were inland beaches. More than one quarter of these beaches (27 percent) was affected by at least one advisory or closing event during 2001.

A March 2003 fact sheet put out by the EPA ("EPA Makes Grants Available to States to Implement Water Quality Monitoring and Public Notification Programs at the Nation's Beaches") announced that the agency was making $9.93 million in grants available in 2003 to eligible states to protect public health at the nation's beaches. The EPA expected to award grants based on an allocation formula to all eligible states and territories that apply. The formula considers three factors: 1) length of beach season, 2) miles of beach, and 3) number of people who use the beach. If all eligible states and territories apply (the EPA believes that all will do so), the size of the grants will range from $149,025 to $544,552.

POLLUTANTS—SOURCES AND EFFECTS

Any number of manmade materials or excessive amounts of naturally occurring substances can adversely affect marine and estuarine waters and their inhabitants. Because water is such an effective solvent and dispersant, it is difficult to track and quantify many pollutants known to have been discharged into marine and estuarine waters, and in many cases, the source of pollution may be unknown. Some pollutants, such as oil spills, are easily detected the moment they enter the water. Others, such as toxic chemicals, are less obvious, and their presence may remain undetected until they have caused extensive damage.

Oil Spills

The volume of spills in U.S. waters has been on a steady downward trend since 1973.

— Captain Michael B. Karr, "A Letter from the Chief," *Pollution Incidents in and around U.S. Waters: A Spill/Release Compendium: 1969–2001*, U.S. Coast Guard Office of Investigations and Analysis, Washington, D.C., August 2003

The world runs on oil. Its uneven distribution on the planet, however, forces its transport over the high seas and through pipelines to distant lands. This inevitably results in accidents, some massive and some small, during drilling and transporting. In 1967 the 118,285-ton supertanker *Torrey Canyon,* carrying oil from Kuwait, caused the world's first massive marine oil spill off the coast of England.

Oil spills are a dramatic form of water pollution—visible, immediate, and sometimes severe. The sight of dead and dying otters and birds covered with black film arouses instant sympathy, and the bigger the spill, the more newsworthy. While it is true that oil can have a devastating effect on marine life, the size of the spill itself is often not the determining factor in the amount of damage it causes. Other factors include the amount and type of marine life in the area and weather conditions that would disperse the oil. Despite its drama, however, worldwide pollution from tanker spills is a relatively minor source of marine pollution. It represents a small fraction of the oil released to the environment worldwide when compared to industry sources, nontanker shipping releases, and oil seepage from natural sources.

When the *Exxon Valdez* ran into a reef in Prince William Sound, Alaska, in March 1989, 11 million gallons of oil spilled into one of the richest and most ecologically sensitive areas in North America. A slick the size of Rhode Island threatened fish and wildlife. Otters died by the thousands, despite efforts by trained environmentalists and local volunteers to save them. Oil-soaked birds lined the shores, only to be eaten by larger predator birds, which then succumbed to dehydration and starvation because the ingested oil destroyed their metabolic systems.

OCEAN POLLUTION ACT OF 1990. In response to the *Exxon Valdez* disaster, Congress passed the Oil Pollution Act of 1990 (OPA; Public Law 101-380). The majority of the OPA provisions were targeted at reducing the number of spills and reducing the quantity of oil spilled. Among its provisions were creation of a $1 billion cleanup-damage fund (the money comes from a tax on the petroleum industry), advance planning for controlling spills, stricter crew standards, and the requirement that new tankers have double hulls. When equipped with two hulls, if the tanker's exterior hull is punctured, the interior hull holding the oil may still remain intact. (The *Exxon Valdez* was not

FIGURE 6.12

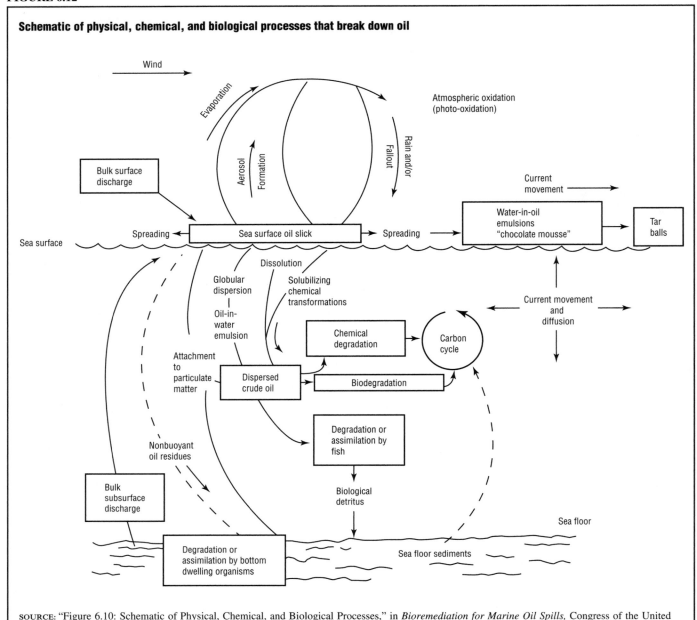

Schematic of physical, chemical, and biological processes that break down oil

SOURCE: "Figure 6.10: Schematic of Physical, Chemical, and Biological Processes," in *Bioremediation for Marine Oil Spills,* Congress of the United States, Office of Technology Assessment, Washington, DC, 1991

double-hulled.) The law requires older tankers to be fitted with double hulls by 2010. The OPA also:

- Compels the use of escort tugboats in certain harbors to assist tankers.

- Requires standards for tank levels and pressure-monitoring devices to detect leaks in cargo tanks.

- Requires the Coast Guard to establish minimum standards for overfill devices to prevent overfill oil spills. An overfill oil spill is the result of too much oil being pumped into a tanker during a transfer from a facility to a tanker or between two tankers. On occasion, overfill spills have involved large quantities of oil.

The issue of continuing danger from older, single-hulled oil tankers on the seas was highlighted in testimony before the United States Senate Committee on Commerce, Science and Transportation on January 3, 2003. Robert N. Cowen, Senior Vice President and Chief Operating Officer of Overseas Shipholding Group, Inc., spoke of the need for the United States to prevent these vessels from trading to the United States. Cowen described the November 19, 2002, sinking of the oil tanker *Prestige* (which was carrying 77,000 tons of heavy fuel oil) off the coast of Spain. He pointed out that cargo from the *Prestige* continues to wash up on the coastline of Galicia, Spain, where it pollutes sensitive fishing grounds. In addition, the cargo is washing ashore in the Landes region near Bordeaux, France. More-over, Cowen states that the governments of Spain, France, and Portugal have moved to ban substandard tonnage from their waters. According to Cowen, the United States continues to allow these older tankers to come into United States waters to trade. Cowen asked the Senate to ensure that restrictions are enacted to prevent older, single-hulled vessels from trading to the United States.

Between 1990 and 2000, the OPA resulted in 41 new rules that govern oil pollution prevention and response preparedness. The petroleum industry spent nearly $17 billion between 1990 and 2000 to comply with its requirements.

DECLINES IN OIL SPILLS. Declines in oil spills are being seen on a global scale. The International Tanker Owners Pollution Federation data show that between 1970 and 1979, the incident rate for large spills (more than 5,000 barrels) from the worldwide tanker industry was 24.2 spills per year. Between 1980 and 1989, that rate dropped to 8.9 spills per year. From 1990 to 1999, the global spill rate declined further, to 7.3 spills per year.

The decline in oil spills in the United States is even more dramatic. About 10 million barrels (420 million gallons) of oil per day are delivered into the United States by ship. According to the U.S. Coast Guard, the incident rate of large spills in the United States since 1991 has been .5 spills per year. There were no large spills in U.S. waters in the period 1991–2000 (the latest data available).

The Coast Guard data also show that the amount of oil spilled by tankers has decreased dramatically. The total amount of oil spilled by tankers in U.S. waters in 1990 was about 115,000 barrels; from 1991 to 2000, the total number of barrels of oil spilled by tankers was less than 8,000. In 1997 the number of barrels of oil spilled was the lowest ever since the Coast Guard began keeping its records in 1973. More than three-fourths of the 1997 spills were less than 10 gallons—less than a car's fuel tank holds.

Although oil tanker spills are highly visible cases of pollution entering the oceans, the EPA estimated that only about 5 percent of the oil entering marine waters originates from oil tanker spills. Coast Guard estimates conclude that water and sewage treatment plants in the United States discharge twice as much oil each year as oil tankers spill. Other sources of oil entering marine waters, other than through oil tanker spills, include the oil from street run-off, industrial liquid wastes, recreational boats, commercial fishing vessels, and intentional discharge from ships flushing their oil tanks.

CLEANING UP OIL SPILLS. Left alone, oil spills will eventually disappear as natural processes break down the oil. (See Figure 6.12.) If nothing is done, oil will "weather" naturally. Turbulent wave action and sunlight will break it down both chemically and physically. Within 24 to 48 hours, the most toxic portions of the oil will evaporate, posing less of a threat to wildlife. As the oil breaks up into smaller droplets, it is more easily attacked and digested by naturally occurring microbes, which will break the oil down into harmless substances. Human intervention to speed up this process can be more or less successful, depending on the spill size, its location, and the weather conditions. There are two basic approaches to cleaning up oil spills: use of dispersants and use of bioremediation agents. Two important differences exist in the way they work. One difference is the mechanism by which they clean up the oil. The other is where and how they are used. Recent research suggests that the best solution may be to use both techniques depending on the characteristics of the site.

Dispersants are products that are applied to the water surface to break up surface oil slicks and facilitate the movement of oil particles into the water column. Dispersants bind to oil on the water surface so that the oil can mix and disperse into the water, similar to the way grease and oil on dirty dishes bind to detergent so that the oil and grease can be washed away in rinse water. Scientific evidence suggests that dispersed oil is broken down more quickly than undispersed oil. This is believed to be caused by the increase in the total surface area of the oil in a slick due to dispersants breaking the slick up into small droplets and making it more vulnerable to breakdown by natural processes such as weathering and biodegradation (breakdown by microbes).

Bioremediation can be described as the process by which microbes eat oil molecules by breaking down their long hydrocarbon chains. Bioremediation agents are almost always applied to residual oil on shorelines for long-term cleanup situations. Usually, heavy oil is first removed before bioremediation is attempted. Bioremediation agents act to speed up the biodegradation of the petroleum molecules, a process that would occur naturally anyway.

The three types of bioremediation are nutrient enrichment, use of genetically engineered microorganisms designed to be especially effective at degrading oil, and techniques to make oxygen more available to native bacteria to speed up their breakdown of the oil. Table 6.5 provides details concerning various bioremediation approaches. Nutrient enrichment generally takes the form of fertilizer addition to accelerate the reproduction of the naturally occurring oil-eating bacteria. Seeding is an attempt to introduce large numbers of the naturally occurring oil-eating bacteria to an oil spill site to jump-start the biodegradation process. This process has not been clearly shown to be effective.

Although genetically engineered microbes have been successfully used under controlled conditions in groundwater and other land-based hazardous waste sites, there has been no scientifically validated demonstration of their

TABLE 6.5

TABLE 6.5

Principal features of alternative bioremediation approaches

Nutrient enrichment:
- Intended to overcome the chief limitation on the rate of the natural biodegradation of oil
- Most studied of the three approaches and currently seen as the most promising approach to most types of spills
- No indication that fertilizer use causes algal blooms or other significant adverse impacts
- In Alaska test, fertilizer use appeared to increase biodegradation rate by at least a factor of two

Seeding:
- Intended to take advantage of the properties of the most efficient species of oil-degrading microorganisms
- Results of field tests of seeding have thus far been inconclusive
- May not be necessary at most sites because there are few locales where oil-degrading microbes do not exist
- Requirements for successful seeding more demanding than those for nutrient enrichment
- In some cases, seeding may help biodegradation get started faster

Use of genetically engineered microorganisms:
- Probably not needed in most cases because of the wide availability of naturally occurring microbes
- Potential use for components of petroleum not degradable by naturally occurring microorganisms
- Development and use could face major regulatory hurdles

SOURCE: "Table 6.6: Principal Features of Alternative Bioremediation Approaches," in *Bioremediation for Marine Oil Spills,* Congress of the United States, Office of Technology Assessment, Washington, DC, 1991

TABLE 6.6

Bioremediation: Potential advantages and disadvantages

Advantages:
- Usually involves only minimal physical disruption of a site
- No significant adverse effects when used correctly
- May be helpful in removing some of the toxic components of oil
- Offers a simpler and more thorough solution than mechanical technologies
- Possibly less costly than other approaches

Disadvantages:
- Of undetermined effectiveness for many types of spills
- May not be appropriate at sea
- Takes time to work
- Approach must be specifically tailored for each polluted site
- Optimization requires substantial information about spill site and oil characteristics

SOURCE: "Table 6.7: Bioremediation: Potential Advantages and Disadvantages," in *Bioremediation for Marine Oil Spills,* Congress of the United States, Office of Technology Assessment, Washington, DC, 1991

successful use in oil spill cleanup. The reported success of this approach in the aftermath of the explosion of the tanker *Mega Borg* off the Texas coast in 1990 has not been scientifically substantiated. Many scientists believe that the fire associated with this tanker explosion was the primary factor in the rapid breakdown and disappearance of the spill.

A new bioremediation technique that is gaining credibility is increasing the availability of oxygen to the naturally occurring oil-eating microbes. Oxygen availability is increased through the addition of special chemicals or tilling the oiled substrate. Tilling breaks the oiled surface into smaller units and increases the exposure of these surfaces to the air (oxygen), making the oil more vulnerable to microbe attack. Table 6.6 shows the potential advantages and disadvantages of bioremediation.

Marine Debris

Marine debris is trash and garbage floating on the ocean or estuaries and washed up on beaches. Beaches and shorelines of U.S. estuaries and oceans are littered with debris carried to shore by the wind and tides. The effects of marine debris can be both costly to coastal communities and very dangerous to both humans and aquatic life.

According to NOAA's online *Ocean Report* (http://www.publicaffairs.noaa.gov/oceanreport/index.html [accessed June 12, 2003]), marine debris is a major problem on beaches and in coastal waters, estuaries,

and oceans. The report states that 80 percent of debris is washed, blown, or dumped from shore, while 20 percent is from recreational boats, ships, fishing vessels, and ocean platforms. The problem is exacerbated by the fact that most marine debris, such as cigarette butts, soda cans, plastic bags, and fishing gear is man-made and slow to degrade. Some studies have shown that marine debris threatens more than 265 different species of marine and coastal wildlife through entanglement, smothering, and interference with digestive systems.

GHOST FISHING. One important problem has been termed "ghost fishing." This is the entrapment of fish and marine mammals by lost or abandoned nets, pots, fishing line, bottles, and other discarded objects. When marine creatures are entangled in old six-pack beverage binders, or caught in abandoned fishing nets, they suffer and may die.

Certain types of marine debris, such as broken glass and medical waste wash-ups, can pose a serious threat to public health, causing beach closures and swimming advisories and robbing coastal communities of significant tourism dollars. The United States Army Corps of Engineers spends $9.4 million annually to remove drifting and floatable debris from the New York/New Jersey Harbor alone.

NOAA's *Ocean Report* cited these reasons for the persistence of marine debris:

- Implementation of effective marine debris control measures is currently hampered by a lack of consistent monitoring and identification of sources of debris.

- Implementation and enforcement of local antilitter regulations and management of debris entering and exiting sewer systems are inadequate to effectively address the marine debris problem.

- Marine debris can be the result of small-scale pollution by individuals who consider their discharges or littering to be of negligible impact compared with large-scale polluters. However, the cumulative impact of continuous, small-scale pollution can be dramatic.

- Plastic makes up about 60 percent of the debris found on beaches. The increase in the use of various kinds of plastic as durable, lightweight packaging has heightened the need for proper management and disposal.

MEDICAL WASTE. Trash washed up with the tide routinely litters beaches on both sides of the continent. In the summers of 1988 and 1989, medical refuse, such as syringes and blood vials, was found on ocean and estuarine beaches along many areas of the East Coast. Occurring about the same time as the growing public concern over AIDS and other needle-transmitted diseases, these occurrences provoked a public outcry for action. In response, Congress passed the 1988 Medical Waste Tracking Act (Public Law 92-532). The act holds producers of medical waste accountable for safe disposal of the waste, or they risk up to $1 million in fines and five years in prison.

In 1990 the Agency for Toxic Substances and Disease Registry (ATSDR), a division of the U.S. Department of Health and Human Services, concluded that medical waste presents little danger to the general public. According to Dr. Maureen Lichveld, senior medical officer at the agency and coordinator for the research project, hospital medical wastes disposed of in the oceans represented no particular risk. The most pressing concern for future medical waste disposal comes from in-home health-care products used by persons with chronic diseases, outpatient AIDS victims, and nursing homes. Subsequent studies by the Marine Conservancy, a private environmental group, indicated that medical waste accounts for only .01 percent of all waste washed up on the nation's beaches.

CRUISE SHIPS. In July 1999 Royal Caribbean, one of the world's largest cruise lines, pled guilty in federal court to dumping oil and hazardous chemicals in U.S. waters and lying about it to the Coast Guard. They agreed to pay a record $18 million fine, the largest ever paid (as of 2003) by a cruise line for polluting waters. This is in addition to the $9 million in criminal fines the company agreed to pay in a previous plea agreement. Six other cruise lines have pleaded guilty to illegal waste dumping since 1993 and have paid fines ranging up to $1 million. These cases have focused attention on the difficulties of regulating the fast-growing cruise-line industry, as most major ships sailing out of American ports are registered in foreign countries.

The luxurious lifestyle of cruise ships generates a lot of waste, much of which is reportedly disposed of through ocean dumping. In response to a petition from the Bluewater Network in 2000 on behalf of 53 organizations committed to protecting the oceans, the EPA is currently assessing cruise-ship discharges to U.S. waters. Among other things, the petition asks the EPA to:

- Quantify the volume of all waste streams such as sewage, garbage, fuel, and medical wastes from large passenger vessels and assess the adequacy of existing regulations to control the waste streams

- Provide scientific assessment of the impacts of the wastes on water quality, the marine environment, and human health

- Identify options for a comprehensive monitoring, record keeping, and reporting regulation for all pollutants discharged into U.S. waters and wastes offloaded at U.S. ports from large passenger vessels

- Evaluate the effect of repealing the National Pollutant Discharge Elimination System permit exemption for cruise ships and requiring them to have discharge permits

In March 2001 the Central Council of Tlingit and Haida Indian Tribes of Alaska passed the resolution Object to Cruise Ship Dumping of Pollutants in Southeast Alaska Waters. The resolution cited a contamination threat to subsistence foods from cruise-ship wastes. The petition asked the federal and state government to prohibit all discharges within 12 miles of the Alaska shore, require all cruise lines to have discharge monitoring devices, and to prohibit ships caught illegally discharging from entering southeast Alaskan waters.

The EPA has agreed to investigate cruise ships, their waste generation, and their waste disposal practices, and to publish an assessment report, which will be made available to the public. The assessment report will use data from literature searches of industry, academia, and government materials; information gathered through meetings with industry and government representatives; and the public hearings and solicitation of public comments. A series of meetings to solicit public comment was held in September 2000. The assessment report was scheduled for completion in 2001. As of February 2003 the report was being compiled.

PLASTICS. Plastics such as bags, containers, bottle caps, and beverage carriers are dumped daily from ocean-going vessels, commercial and recreational fishing boats, offshore oil and gas platforms, and military ships. Other types of plastic debris—factory wastes, sewer overflows, illegal garbage dumping, and human littering—come from land sources. An estimated two million sea birds and 100,000 marine animals die each year as a result of ingesting or becoming entangled in plastic.

Another concern is commercial fishing nets. Once made of natural materials, these nets are now made mainly of durable, nondegradable plastic. When they are lost or discarded in the water, they pose a floating hazard to seals, dolphins, whales, and diving birds, which can become entangled in the nets. In 1988, 31 nations ratified an agreement making it illegal for their ships to dump plastic debris, including fishing nets, into the ocean. As part of that agreement, the United States enacted the Marine Plastics Pollution Research and Control Act (PL 100-220), effective in 1989. Among other regulations, the act imposed a $25,000 fine for each violation.

Plastic pellets are the raw materials that are melted and molded to create plastic products. About 60 billion pounds of resin pellets are manufactured in the United States annually. The two primary ways that these pellets enter water are direct spills during cargo handling operations at ports or spills at sea, and storm-water discharges that carry the pellets from industrial sites. Plastic pellets may persist in the water environment for years, depending on the resin type, the amount and types of pellet additives, and how the pellets react to sunlight, wave action, and weathering. Although pellets have been found in the stomachs of wildlife, primarily seabirds and sea turtles, their impacts have not been clearly demonstrated to be harmful.

The Society of Plastics Industries, Inc. (SPI), the major national trade association for manufacturers who make about 75 percent of the plastic products in the United States, has been working with the EPA to identify and minimize the sources of plastic pellet entry into water. In July 1991 the SPI instituted Operation Clean Sweep, an industry wide education campaign to encourage members to adopt the SPI 1991 Pellet Retention Environmental Code and the 1992 Processor's Pledge aimed at committing the U.S. plastics industry to total pellet containment. The EPA planned to review the success of this program in the near future but as of the summer of 2003 it had not published the results of any follow-up review of the program. In the meantime, municipalities, state regulators, and the EPA will continue to use National Pollutant Discharge Elimination System guidelines to impose penalties on discharges of pellets into water.

Ocean Dumping

In 1972 Congress enacted the Marine Protection, Research, and Sanctuaries Act (MPRSA; Public Law 92-532) to prohibit the dumping into the ocean of material that would unreasonably degrade or endanger human health or the marine environment. The MPRSA applies to waters within 200 miles of the U.S. coast and was amended in 1988 to prohibit dumping industrial waste and sewage sludge into the ocean. As a result, ocean dumping today is confined to material dredged from the bottom of water bodies in order to maintain navigation channels and berthing areas. According to information available on the EPA Web site in 2003, several hundred million cubic yards of sediment are dredged from waterways, ports, and harbors

each year, and approximately 20 percent of this material is disposed of in the ocean. The remainder of the sediments are disposed of in inland waters, upland areas, or confined disposal areas adjacent to shorelines, or are used beneficially.

The act authorizes the EPA to assess civil penalties up to $50,000 for each violation, as well as criminal penalties (seizure and forfeiture of vessels). For dumping of medical wastes, the act authorizes civil penalties up to $125,000 and criminal penalties up to $250,000 and five years in prison, or both.

Dredging

Every year, millions of tons of materials are dredged from freshwater river channels and harbors, as well as estuarine channels and coastal harbors, to clear or enlarge navigational channels, to maintain ship-berthing areas, to facilitate recreational boating, or for development purposes. Dredged material (spoil) may be clean sand and sediment, or it may contain concentrations of pesticides, metals, and other toxic chemicals, depending on where the dredged material originated. During the dredging process or when the dredged spoil is placed overboard, some pollutants that have settled into the sediment may be released into the water at the disposal site. Dredged spoil disposal is closely regulated by both the U.S. Army Corps of Engineers and the EPA, who require testing of spoil for contaminants prior to disposal.

Disposal of dredged spoil is a difficult problem. Although many environmental groups prefer land-based disposal to overboard disposal (placement of dredged materials in the ocean or other water body at a distance from the dredging location), land-based disposal is frequently not an option. Land adjacent to waterways is usually the most expensive land in the area because of its desirability for development, or it may be wetland and cannot be disturbed or filled.

Land-based disposal sites require large tracts of land where bermed or leveed containment areas can be built to hold the dredged spoil. Berms and levees are raised earthen structures used to form holding areas for dredged spoil. Depending on the composition of the spoil, the dredged material may take 10 or more years to "dewater" (dry out) so that the berms can be dismantled and the land used for another purpose, or the containment pond converted to another use, such as fish ponds for aquaculture. Even if the land is available, many communities object to having the disposal area with its 8- to 20-foot levees, claiming it is unsightly and lowers property values. Transporting dredged spoil (a slurry mud that is about 98 percent water) any distance to a land-based site, unless it can be pumped to the location, is prohibitively expensive and may require additional dredging to obtain access for the transport barges.

In many cases, ocean and land-based disposal sites are not economically available to river and estuary sites that require dredging. Two techniques that are being used more often in these areas are containment islands and wetland construction or rehabilitation. Island construction is frequently used where shipping channels need to be maintained through repeated dredging at 5- to 10-year intervals, and the "island" site is used over a long time, or when the spoil is badly contaminated with toxic substances. In other cases, clean spoil is used to rebuild eroded islands. When filled and dewatered, island sites may become recreational areas or wildlife refuges, particularly nesting islands for birds. All island sites require extensive construction of costly bulkheads and other containment devices.

HARMFUL ALGAL BLOOMS

A lot of states never experienced a red tide before the last ten years. It's been a very alarming decade.

— Dr. Carmelo Tomas, "Toxic Tides: Planning Is Coastal Management's Best Prevention," *Coastal Services*, July/August 1999

Harmful algal blooms (HABs) are having significant impacts on coastal and estuarine areas of the United States and the rest of the world, affecting the health of both humans and aquatic organisms and the vitality of local and regional economies. The number and diversity of reported HAB events have increased since the 1970s.

Understanding the causes of HABs and mitigating and preventing their consequences are national concerns. As a result, Congress passed the Harmful Algal Bloom and Hypoxia Research Act of 1998. The act requires the formation of a federal multiagency task force to investigate the problem and report back to Congress with a plan and recommendations to address HAB and hypoxia. According to the NOAA Office of Legislative Affairs Web site (http://www.legislative.noaa.gov/), on June 12, 2003, the United States House of Representatives introduced amendments to that act. The House Science Committee, Subcommittee on Environment, Technology and Standards proposed that the amendment authorize the Coastal Ocean Science Program. The program is designed to focus on improving predictions of ecosystem trends, pollution, and coastal hazards. Congressman Brian Baird of Washington also introduced an amendment that requires the states and the president to develop and submit a plan "to protect the environment and public health from the impacts of harmful algal blooms" within one year of the date of enactment. If passed, the act will be known as the Harmful Algal Bloom and Hypoxia Research Amendments Act of 2003.

What Are Harmful Algal Blooms?

Algae are microscopic, single-celled plants that live in the sea. The vast majority of the thousands of algal species in U.S. coastal waters are not harmful and serve as the energy producers at the base of the food chain, without which higher life on Earth would not exist. Occasionally the algae grow very fast or "bloom," creating dense, visible patches near the water surface. "Red tide" is a common name for events where certain algae containing reddish pigments "bloom" so that the water appears to be red. Some HAB events are caused by algae that do not produce toxins, but instead consume all the oxygen in the water, resulting in hypoxia, which can have severe effects on local ecosystems. A small number of algal species produce potent neurotoxins that can be transferred through the food chain, where they affect and sometimes kill higher life forms such as shellfish, fish, birds, marine mammals, and humans that feed directly or indirectly on them.

Source of Harmful Algal Blooms

Most HABs are the result of the transport of offshore algal populations to inshore regions, that is, a naturally occurring physical relocation. For example, blooms of *Gymnodinium breve,* which causes neurotoxic shellfish poisoning, occur when algal cells from small offshore populations in the open Gulf of Mexico are blown into the west Florida shelf and into the coastal waters of other states bordering the Gulf of Mexico. This delivery of potentially harmful algal blooms from offshore into inshore regions in most areas of the world's coastal oceans occurs consistently but unpredictably. They occur even in areas that are unaffected by human activities. As a result, attempts to prevent HABs are somewhat impractical because people cannot control general oceanic circulation or even local coastal currents.

Effects on Human Health

The neurotoxins produced by some species of algae can be concentrated by bivalve mollusks (oysters, clams, and mussels) with no apparent ill effect to the bivalves. If bivalves with dangerous concentrations of neurotoxin are eaten by humans, severe illness or death can occur. In the U.S. areas where HAB events occur, the densities of harmful algal species are heavily monitored in the water column by the coastal states as part of the NSSP. When the algal density exceeds certain levels, the areas are closed to bivalve harvesting until both the water column and the bivalve meat show the absence of neurotoxin.

Other human health effects from the neurotoxins include skin irritation from water contact and respiratory irritation from aerosols. Neurotoxin aerosols from sea spray have caused watery and stinging eyes, as well as breathing difficulties because the tiny acid droplets penetrate into and irritate the nasal passages and throat.

Increases in Harmful Algal Blooms

Harmful algal blooms are increasing in frequency and severity worldwide. Whether the increase is a direct result of cyclic or long-term variations in climate, other natural factors, or human activities is unclear. The frequency,

FIGURE 6.13

Distribution of hypoxic water in the Gulf of Mexico from July 21–25, 1998

SOURCE: Adapted from "Distribution of water hypoxia from July 21-25, 1998," in *Restoring Life to the Dead Zone: Addressing Gulf Hypoxia, a National Problem*, USGS FS-016-00, U.S. Geological Survey, Washington, DC, June 2000

FIGURE 6.14

Interior watershed of the Mississippi River Basin

SOURCE: Adapted from "Interior watershed of the Mississippi Basin, the source of material causing the 6,000 to 7,000 square-mile "dead zone," or hypoxia in the Gulf of Mexico," in *Restoring Life to the Dead Zone: Addressing Gulf Hypoxia, a National Problem*, USGS FS-016-00, U.S. Geological Survey, Washington, DC, June 2000

duration, and intensity of algal blooms are related to a number of physical, biological, and chemical factors, the interaction of which is not clearly understood for many algal species.

Five possible reasons have been advanced for the increase in frequency and geographical extent of HAB events:

- Improved methods of detection and improved monitoring methods are detecting previously unreported blooms

- Introduction of new algal species into inshore areas through ship ballast water exchange or aquaculture

- Reduction in populations of grazers (microscopic animals that eat the algae) resulting in their failure to control the algal population

- Climate changes

- Human activities that cause increases in nutrient levels or increased river discharge. (These are believed to be species specific and not to apply to all HABs).

All of these reasons are possible explanations and it is likely that it is a combination of one or more of these factors that causes HAB.

What Is Hypoxia?

Hypoxia (lack of oxygen) occurs when the dissolved oxygen level in the water column is less than 2 parts per million (ppm). It kills most of the bottom-dwelling life forms such as oysters and clams, and mobile marine organisms such as fish and shrimp either flee the area or die. For this reason, areas where hypoxic conditions exist are frequently referred to as "dead zones." Excess nutrient is the most frequent cause. Hypoxia is a worldwide problem that often occurs where rivers carrying large amounts of agricultural runoff empty into lakes, estuaries, oceans, and seas.

One location in the United States where hypoxia occurs is the Gulf of Mexico, off the Louisiana coast. The Gulf's hypoxic zone is comparable to the largest hypoxic areas in the world such as those in the Black and Baltic Seas. The Gulf of Mexico hypoxic zone, shown in Figure 6.13, is approximately 6,000–7,000 square miles of water where the oxygen level is below 2 ppm. Under normal conditions, dissolved oxygen levels would be 5 to 6 ppm.

The zone is caused by harmful algal blooms that are believed to be the result of the discharge of increased nutrients from the Mississippi River watershed into the Gulf of Mexico. The nutrients (nitrogen and phosphorus) come from fertilizers, animal wastes, and domestic sewage. The nitrate-nitrogen level in the main stem of the Mississippi River, which drains 31 states, has doubled since the 1950s. Figure 6.14 shows the Mississippi Basin watershed and the states whose rivers drain into it.

Correcting the problem requires a coordinated multistate effort. The EPA, six other federal agencies, nine states, and two American Indian tribes have developed an action plan to reduce nutrient loads reaching the Gulf. The Action Plan for Reducing, Mitigating and Controlling Hypoxia in the Northern Gulf of Mexico (January 2000) was developed in response to the Congressional mandate in the Harmful Algal Bloom and Hypoxia Research Act of 1998. It has the goal of reducing the size of the hypoxic zone by 50 percent no later than 2015. The plan also called for implementation of nutrient management strategies to achieve a 30 percent reduction in the amount of nutrients reaching the Gulf of Mexico. Information generated through the research and monitoring portions of the plan will be used to modify future goals and actions as necessary.

The USGS has determined that about 25 percent of the nitrogen load in the Gulf comes from the Lower Mississippi River Valley, below the point where the Ohio River joins the Mississippi. In 2000 the USGS National Wetlands Center received funding to pursue the development of a strategy to use inland and coastal wetlands to reduce nutrients in this portion of the watershed.

What Are the Economic Consequences of Harmful Algal Blooms?

Direct and indirect losses to local economies from HAB events are enormous. The amount of irretrievable revenue due to lost fish and shellfish production, impairment and loss of important ecosystems such as coral reefs, human illness and medical treatment, increased insurance rates for fisheries activities, unemployment and bankruptcy of seafood and recreational related businesses, loss of tourist dollars, and loss of sales for all seafood is staggering. For example, the 1991 outbreak of domoic acid in the state of Washington had a negative impact on the entire community, from the tourism industry to unaffected fisheries, with losses estimated between $15 million and $20 million.

Even a nontoxic harmful algal bloom can have devastating consequences. In South Florida, blooms of macroalgae are overgrowing sections of coral reefs and seagrass beds. Coral reefs are a vital component of the Florida economy, attracting thousands of visitors each year. The seagrass beds are important to the survival of pink shrimp, spiney lobster, and finfish. Continued algae overgrowth could lead to severe economic losses for the local recreational, tourist, and seafood industries. In Washington (state), *Heterosigma akashiwo* blooms have caused losses of $4–$5 million per year to harvesters of wild and penned fish.

According to *Economic Statistics for NOAA* (March 2003), the economic impact of HABs in the United States averages $49 million per year. Individual outbreaks, however, can cause economic damage that exceeds the annual average. HAB outbreaks in the Chesapeake Bay in 1997

cost the Maryland seafood and recreational fishing industries almost $50 million in just a few months. The report states that total public health effects resulting from shellfish poisoning by HABs averaged $22 million over a six-year interval. HAB events have also affected commercial fisheries. Losses of wild harvest and aquaculture average $18 million per year.

Preventing Harmful Algal Blooms

The U.S. Department of Commerce released a report, *National Assessment of Harmful Algal Blooms in U.S. Waters* (February 2001), which presents the findings of the federal multiagency task force created to investigate the problem of HAB. Because management options are limited, the focus for now remains on minimizing the impacts of HAB events.

Recommendations from the report include:

- Continue and enhance the state programs that regularly sample shellfish and shellfish harvest waters for presence of HAB and their toxins and have been effective for many years in reducing human illness and deaths

- Develop communication programs that use educational and public health materials, electronic communication, and other techniques to educate and inform the public

- Improve communication and information exchange among scientists; agencies; and federal, state, and local governments to increase cooperation and avoid duplicative effort

- Improve sample collection techniques

- Improve the laboratory and field detection methods for HAB, including rapid method development. (Most of the standard laboratory tests take anywhere from four days to several weeks to provide a conclusive identification of the algae causing the bloom. A rapid method would be one that could identify the organism and its concentration in the water within 24 to 48 hours. The level of toxicity is determined by injecting mice in the laboratory to see if they die. A rapid method would eliminate the mice and provide a chemical or other reaction that would give a definitive answer concerning toxicity levels within a few hours. Field methods that can be done easily at the site of the bloom do not exist.)

- Establish long-term monitoring programs in areas currently affected by HAB and in areas that are likely to be affected in the future

- Develop forecasting capabilities for the occurrence and impacts of HAB

- Conduct basic research into the physiology, growth, and toxin production of HAB species; conditions that may stimulate blooms; and the toxin uptake, metabolism, and depuration in marine food webs, fisheries, and marine mammals

These tools will allow states and local jurisdictions to prepare for the bloom events and communicate with the public in a timely manner, as well as provide data that can eventually be used in predictive models.

Some states that have the potential for HAB events have already established long-term monitoring programs, or are in the process of doing so, to gather information in advance of bloom situations. In addition, some research is being directed toward finding naturally occurring bacterial and viral populations that might be used in the biological control of HAB events.

EXOTIC SPECIES

Exotic species are plants, animals, and microbes that have been carried from one geographic region to another, either intentionally or unintentionally. Unintentional introduction includes transport in ballast water of ships, or as pests on imported fruits, vegetables, and animals or animal products. Prior to modern times, movement from one geographical region to another was infrequent and slow, allowing time for the ecology to absorb and counterbalance the newcomers.

Today, because of rapid transport, organisms can move across continents in a matter of hours or days. Once removed from their natural ecological system, where eons of evolution have established predator-prey relationships, competitive species, and other devices to maintain balance, exotic species may reproduce unchecked in their new locations because they have no natural competitors or predators.

Both estuarine and ocean habitats have suffered from exotic species introduction. In the Chesapeake Bay, MSX (*Haplosporidium nelsoni*) and Dermo (*Perkinsus marinus*), two oyster diseases that have ravaged oyster populations, came to the Bay with oysters introduced from other regions. The coral reefs in the Northern Mariana Islands are being decimated by the introduction of the crown-of-thorns starfish. The green crab introduced from the Baltic Sea to the shores of New England occurs in such high numbers that the crab is believed to be eating young scallops and other valuable seafood.

Passage of the Nonindigenous Aquatic Nuisance Prevention and Control Act of 1990 was a first step in attempting to prevent species migration. This legislation authorized the U.S. Fish and Wildlife Service and NOAA to adopt regulations to prevent the unintentional introduction of aquatic nuisance species. In 1999 the Invasive Species Council was created by presidential executive order to oversee efforts to control unwanted exotic species. The council is chaired jointly by the secretaries of Interior, Agriculture, and Commerce. Council members include the secretaries of State, Treasury, and Transportation, and the administrator of the EPA. To date, however, no method has been found to stop the potential flood of exotic species to the U.S. shores.

On March 5, 2003, Senators Carl Levin of Michigan and Susan M. Collins of Maine introduced to Congress the National Aquatic Invasive Species Act of 2003 (NAISA). On the same day, Senator Levin stated in a press release that the proposed legislation will reauthorize and strengthen the National Invasive Species Act of 1996 so as to protect United States waters by preventing new introductions of aquatic invasive species.

In his statement before Congress, Senator Levin pointed out that the leading pathway for aquatic invaders is maritime commerce. Estimates of the annual economic damage caused nationwide by invasive species range as high as $137 billion. Because Great Lakes fisheries are valued at $4 billion annually, preventing invasions into them from ballast water, hulls, or the system of canals connecting the Great Lakes to the Mississippi River and Atlantic Ocean is critical.

The proposed NAISA of 2003 will prevent harmful invasive species from damaging the United States' aquatic ecosystems. This goal will be accomplished by:

- Reducing invasive species introductions from ships by establishing a mandatory ballast water management program for the entire United States

- Preventing invasive species introductions from other pathways

- Supporting development and implementation of State Aquatic Invasive Species Management Plans

- Conducting ecological surveys for early detection of invasive species and analysis of invasion rates and patterns

- Making $170 million in federal funds available for aquatic invasive species prevention, control, and research

- Preventing interbasin transfer of organisms by increasing funding and resources for dispersal barrier projects and research

- Making available federal funding and resources for rapid response to introductions of invasive species

- Establishing environmental soundness criteria to ensure all prevention and control measures enacted do not further harm the environment

- Creating education and outreach programs to inform the public on preventing transfers of invasive species by proper cleaning of recreational boats, and proper disposal of nonnative organisms for home aquariums

- Conducting research on high-risk invasion pathways and alternative prevention and control technologies

- Strengthening the Great Lakes program by improving the dispersal barrier in the Chicago Ship & Sanitary Canal, authorizing the International Joint Commission to analyze the prevention efforts in the Great Lakes, and requiring ships entering the system to comply with the mandatory water management programs

FUTURE OF OCEANS AND ESTUARIES

The environments of U.S. oceans and estuaries are flourishing at some locations, experiencing stress in others, and have been overwhelmed in a few localities. An increasing level of knowledge and awareness of environmental issues in the United States has led to more stringent regulatory protections for these ecosystems, and a slow but steady reversal of a downward trend. Private organizations are taking on the formidable task of monitoring the nations' extensive coastlines. They are also organizing so that they may exert social and political pressure for continued action and progress in restoring damaged coastal ecosystems. Corporations, agencies, and citizens are forging alliances and other partnerships to protect and repair these systems. Volunteers of all ages and from all walks of life are giving time, talent, and money to participate in ecological restoration. Much has been done, but much more remains to be accomplished.

CHAPTER 7
WETLANDS

WHAT ARE WETLANDS?

Wetlands are areas that are inundated or saturated by surface or groundwater at a frequency and duration sufficient to support, and that under normal circumstances do support, a prevalence of vegetation typically adapted for life in saturated soil conditions.

— Section 404 of the Clean Water Act, U.S. Army Corps of Engineers and the U.S. Environmental Protection Agency, 1994

Wetlands are transition zones between land and aquatic systems where the water table is usually near or at the surface, or the land is covered by shallow water. Wetlands can take many forms, some of which are immediately recognizable as "wet." Other wetlands appear more like dry land, and are wet during only certain seasons of the year, or at several year intervals. In fact, the U.S. Army Corps of Engineers reported that most wetlands lack surface water and waterlogged soils during at least part of each growing season.

Swamps are wetlands that are dominated by trees and shrubs. Swamp forests that are associated with rivers and streams in the Southeast are commonly known as bottomland hardwoods. Wetlands that consist of herbaceous plants, such as sedges, cattails, and bulrushes, are known as marshes. Marshes are highly variable and include fens, sloughs, potholes, and wet meadows. Bogs are generally dominated by sphagnum moss, which builds thick layers of peat as it dies. Other wetlands include seeps, vernal pools, pocosins, muskegs, and similar areas. Although many people do not think of them as such, the deep channels of rivers, streambeds, lake bottoms, and shallow tidal waters are also wetlands.

According to the EPA in its "Wetlands: Status and Trends" fact sheet (last updated in January 2003), as of 1997 there were an estimated 105.5 million acres of wetlands in the 48 conterminous states (does not include Alaska and Hawaii), which is about 5.5 percent of the total land area. Ninety-five percent of these wetlands were freshwater wetlands while 5 percent were estuarine (coastal saltwater wetlands). Wetlands range in size from less than one acre to thousands of acres. Table 7.1 shows the mean size and range of some representative types of freshwater wetlands. For example, the mean size for forested freshwater wetlands was 21 acres, with a range between 1 and 2,560 acres.

In "Wetlands: Status and Trends," the EPA reported that in the 1980s, an estimated 170-200 million acres of wetlands existed in Alaska—covering slightly more than half of the state—while Hawaii had 52,000 acres. After Alaska, Florida (11 million), Louisiana (8.8 million), Minnesota (8.7 million), and Texas (7.6 million) have the largest wetland acreage.

Indispensable Part of Life on Earth

Wetlands are distributed unevenly, but occur in every state and U.S. territory. (See Table 7.2.) They are found wherever climate and landscape cause groundwater to discharge to the land surface or prevent rapid drainage from

TABLE 7.1

Mean size and range of freshwater wetlands found in sample areas, 1997

Freshwater wetland category	Mean size (acres)	Range (acres)[1]
Freshwater forest	21	<1 to 2,560
Freshwater shrub	8	<1 to 2,416
Freshwater emergent	7	<1 to 2,560
Freshwater ponds	1–2	<1 to 1,000[2]
Other freshwater types	3–4	<1 to 700

[1] The upper limit is restricted by the sample plot size and cannot be determined.
[2] The upper limit reflects the area of ponds connected in series.

SOURCE: Thomas E. Dahl, "Table 5. Mean size and range of freshwater wetlands as they appeared within the sample units in 1997," in *Status and Trends of Wetlands in the Conterminous United States 1986 to 1997*, Department of Interior, Fish and Wildlife Service, Washington, DC, 2000

TABLE 7.2

Locations of various wetland types

Wetland type	Primary regions	States
Inland freshwater marsh	Dakota-Minnesota drift and lake bed; Upper Midwest; and Gulf Coastal Flats	North Dakota, South Dakota, Nebraska, Minnesota, Florida
Inland saline marshes	Intermontane; Pacific Mountains	Oregon, Nevada, Utah, California
Bogs	Upper Midwest; Gulf-Atlantic Rolling Plain; Gulf Coastal Flat; Atlantic Coastal Flats	Wisconsin, Minnesota, Michigan, Maine, Florida, North Carolina
Tundra	Central Highland and Basin; Arctic Lowland; and Pacific Mountains	Alaska
Shrub swamps	Upper Midwest; Gulf Coastal Flats	Minnesota, Wisconsin, Michigan, Florida, Georgia, South Carolina, North Carolina, Louisiana
Wooded swamps	Upper Midwest; Gulf Coastal Flats; Atlantic Coastal Flats; and Lower Mississippi Alluvial Plain	Minnesota, Wisconsin, Michigan, Florida, Georgia, South Georgia, South Carolina, North Carolina, Louisiana
Bottom land hardwood	Lower Mississippi Alluvial Plain; Atlantic Coastal Flats; Gulf-Atlantic Rolling Plain; and Gulf Coastal Flats	Louisiana, Mississippi, Arkansas, Missouri, Tennessee, Alabama, Florida, Georgia, South Carolina, North Carolina, Texas
Coastal salt marshes	Atlantic Coastal Zone; Gulf Coastal Zone; Eastern Highlands; Pacific Moutains	All Coastal States, but particularly the Mid- and South Atlantic and Gulf Coast States
Mangrove swamps	Gulf Coastal Zone	Florida and Louisiana
Tidal freshwater wetlands	Atlantic Coastal Zone and Flats; Gulf Coastal Zone and Flats	Louisiana, Texas, North Carolina, Virginia, Maryland, Delaware, New Jersey, Georgia, South Carolina

SOURCE: "Table 3.—Locations of Various Wetland Types in the United States," in *Wetlands: Their Use and Regulation*, OTA-O-206, U.S. Congress, Office of Technology Assessment, Washington, DC, March 1984

the land surface so that soils are saturated for some time. All wetlands have one common trait: hydric (oxygen-poor) soils. Wetlands are covered by shallow water or have water just below the ground surface long enough to create water-logged soils for long periods during the growing season. These conditions cause hydric soils.

Almost all plants and animals use oxygen to convert sugar and other organic molecules into the energy that they need to grow and survive. When soil microbes decompose dead plants and animals, they use oxygen that is trapped in the soil. Normally that oxygen is replaced from the air.

In wetlands, when the hydric soil is flooded or satu-rated, the oxygen used by the microbes is not replaced fast enough. This is because oxygen moves through water about 10,000 times slower than air. As a result, wetland plants are specially adapted to temporarily survive without oxygen in their roots or to transfer oxygen from the leaves or stem to the roots. This anaerobic (without oxygen) con-dition also causes the soils to have the sulfurous odor of rotten eggs.

Local hydrology (the pattern of water flow through an area) is the primary determinant of wetlands. Wetlands can receive groundwater in-flow, recharge groundwater, or experience both inflow and outflow at different locations. Figure 7.1 illustrates water movement in several different wetland situations. Wetlands do not always occupy low

points and depressions in the landscape. They can occur at the soil interface with complex underground water sys-tems. (See Figure 7.1, Part A.) Fens are examples of wet-lands that occur on slopes at groundwater seepage faces, and are subject to a continuous supply of the chemicals that are dissolved in the groundwater. (See Figure 7.1, Part B.) Locations that are down gradient of a break in the slope of the water table, such as along streams or rivers, receive a continuous water supply and are ideal for wetland growth. They also, however, may receive some groundwa-ter discharge. (See Figure 7.1, Part C.) Bogs are wetlands normally found on uplands or extensive flatlands. Most of their water and chemistry comes from precipitation. (See Figure 7.1, Part D.)

Riverine (areas along streams, rivers, and irrigation canals) and coastal area wetlands are highly subject to periodic water level changes. Coastal area wetlands, for example, are affected by predictable tidal cycles. Other coastal and riverine wetlands are highly dependent on flooding and seasonal water level changes. An example is the floodplains of the Illinois and Missouri Rivers.

TYPES OF WETLANDS

A wide variety of wetlands exist across the United States because of regional and local differences in hydrol-ogy, water chemistry, vegetation, soils, topography, and

FIGURE 7.1

Examples of water sources for wetlands

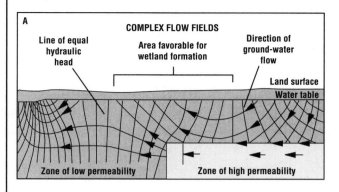

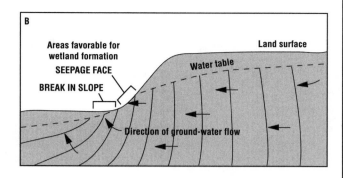

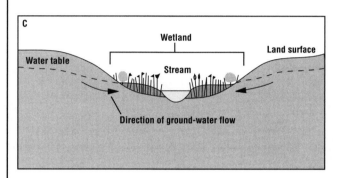

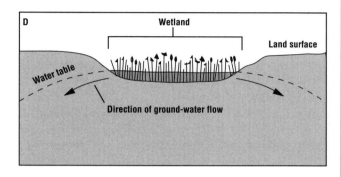

The source of water to wetlands can be from ground-water discharge where the land surface is underlain by complex ground-water flow fields (A), from ground-water discharge at seepage faces and at breaks in slope of the water table (B), from streams (C), and from precipitation in cases where wetlands have no stream inflow and ground-water gradients slope away from the wetland (D).

SOURCE: Thomas C. Winter, Judson W. Harvey, O. Lehn Franke, and William M. Alley, "Figure 17," in *Ground Waters and Surface Waters—A Single Resource,* USGS Circular 1139, U.S. Geological Survey, Denver, CO, 1998

other factors. There are two large groups of wetlands: estuarine (coastal) and palustrine (inland). Estuarine wetlands are linked to estuaries and oceans, and comprise 5 percent of the wetlands in the 48 conterminous states. Estuaries are places where fresh and salt water mix, such as a bay or where a river enters the ocean. In estuaries, the environment is one of ever changing salinity and temperature. The water level fluctuates in response to wind and tide. Examples of estuarine wetlands are saltwater marshes and mangrove swamps.

Palustrine wetlands comprise the other 95 percent of wetlands. The most common location of palustrine wetlands is the floodplains of rivers and streams, the margins of lakes and ponds, and isolated depressions surrounded by dry land. Some examples of inland wetlands are the Florida Everglades, wet meadows, swamps, fens, bogs, prairie potholes, playa lakes, and wet tundra.

Wetlands are further divided by their vegetation. Emergent wetlands (marshes and wet meadows) are dominated by grasses, sedges, and other herbaceous (nonwoody) plants. Emergent wetlands are the most common types

of estuarine wetlands, accounting for 74 percent, while representing only 25 percent of palustrine wetlands. Shrub wetlands (including shrub swamps and bogs), characterized by low-to-medium-height woody plants, make up 13 percent of estuarine wetlands and account for 18 percent of freshwater wetlands. Forested wetlands, mostly wooded swamps and bottomland hardwood forests, are dominated by trees, and account for 51 percent of freshwater wetlands. (See Figure 7.2.)

The U.S. Fish and Wildlife Service (FWS) is the agency charged with conducting wetland status and trend studies of the nation's wetlands at 10-year intervals. To accurately report wetland status, the FWS has further subdivided estuarine and palustrine wetlands into numerous habitat categories. The categories and their common descriptions are shown in Table 7.3.

Geographically isolated wetlands are another type of important wetland in the United States. The U.S. Fish and Wildlife Service defines them as "wetlands with no apparent surface water connection to perennial rivers and streams, estuaries, or the ocean." They have no surface

FIGURE 7.2

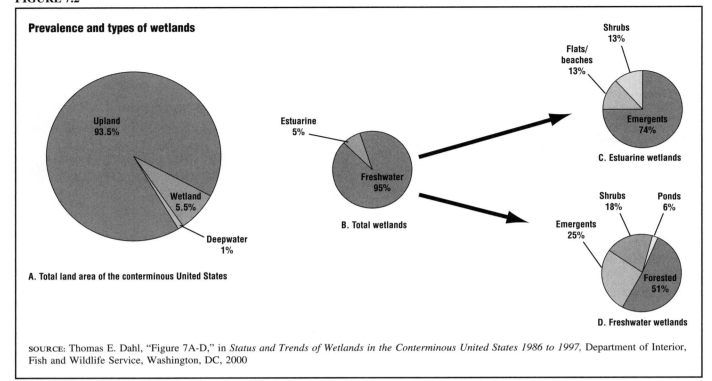

Prevalence and types of wetlands

Upland
93.5%

Wetland
5.5%

Deepwater
1%

A. Total land area of the conterminous United States

Estuarine
5%

Freshwater
95%

B. Total wetlands

Shrubs
13%

Flats/
beaches
13%

Emergents
74%

C. Estuarine wetlands

Shrubs
18%

Ponds
6%

Emergents
25%

Forested
51%

D. Freshwater wetlands

SOURCE: Thomas E. Dahl, "Figure 7A-D," in *Status and Trends of Wetlands in the Conterminous United States 1986 to 1997,* Department of Interior, Fish and Wildlife Service, Washington, DC, 2000

water outlet, and therefore are vulnerable to changes in surrounding land use practices. According to Steve Williams, Director of the U.S. Fish and Wildlife Service, in a June 11, 2002 news release, "In desert areas, isolated wetlands provide vital fresh water oases for wildlife and function as stepping stones for migrating birds. Their isolation has promoted the evolution of unique plant and animal life that is specially adapted to these habitats." Williams also pointed out in the FWS news release that isolated wetlands are important to human beings because many of the wetlands contribute important subsurface water flows to other wetlands and streams. In areas such as the Prairie Pothole Region, isolated wetlands store rainwater, which reduces flooding and recharges groundwater supplies, in addition to providing habitat for wildlife. On June 11, 2002, the U.S. Fish and Wildlife Service released a report (*Geographically Isolated Wetlands: A Preliminary Assessment of their Characteristics and Status in Selected Areas of the United States*) that describes 19 types of isolated wetlands in 72 study areas and provides ecological profiles of their fish and wildlife conservation values.

MANY ROLES OF WETLANDS

Wetlands provide essential ecological functions that benefit people and the ecological systems surrounding the wetlands, as well as the wetland itself. The plants, microbes, and animals in wetlands are part of the global cycles for water, nitrogen, and sulfur. Some scientists also suggest that an unrecognized benefit of wetlands is atmospheric maintenance. Wetlands store carbon in their plant communities and soils instead of releasing it to the air as carbon dioxide, making them part of the global cycle for carbon.

Wetland functions fit into several broad categories (see Figure 7.3 and discussion below):

- High plant productivity
- Temporary water storage
- Trapping of nutrients and sediments
- Soil anchoring

Not all wetlands perform all functions, nor do they perform all functions equally. The location of the wetland in the watershed and its size determine its functions. A watershed is the land area that drains to a stream, river, or lake. Other factors that will affect wetland functions and their performance are weather conditions, quality and quantity of water entering the wetland, and human alteration of the wetland or the land surrounding it. The values of wetland functions to human communities depend on the complex relationship between the wetland and the other ecosystems in the watershed. An ecosystem consists of all the organisms in a particular area or region and the environment in which they live. The elements of an ecosystem interact with each other in some way and depend on each other either directly or indirectly.

TABLE 7.3

Categories of wetland, deep water, and dry land

Category	Common description
Salt water habitats	
Marine Subtidal*	Open ocean
Marine Intertidal	Near shore
Estuarine Subtidal*	Open water/bay bottoms
Estuarine Intertidal Emergents	Salt marsh
Estuarine Intertidal Forested/Shrub	Mangroves or other estuarine shrubs
Estuarine Intertidal Unconsolidated Shore	Beaches/bars
Estuarine Aquatic Bed	Submerged or floating estuarine vegetation
Riverine* (may be tidal or non-tidal)	River systems
Freshwater habitats	
Palustrine Forested	Forested swamps
Palustrine Shrub	Shrub wetlands
Palustrine Emergents	Inland marshes/wet meadows
Palustrine Unconsolidated Shore	Shore beaches/bars
Palustrine Unconsolidated Bottom	Open water ponds
Palustrine Aquatic Bed	Floating aquatic/submerged vegetation
Lacustrine*	Lakes and reservoirs
Uplands	
Agriculture	Cropland, pasture, managed rangeland
Urban	Cities and incorporated developments
Forested Plantations	Planted or intensively managed forests; silviculture
Rural Development	Non-urban developed areas and infrastructure
Other Uplands	Rural uplands not in any other category; barren lands

*Constitutes deepwater habitat.

SOURCE: Thomas E. Dahl, "Table 1: Wetland, deepwater, and upland categories used in this study," in *Status and Trends of Wetlands in the Conterminous United States 1986 to 1997*, Department of Interior, Fish and Wildlife Service, Washington, DC, 2000

Wetlands—Nursery, Pantry, and Way Station

Wetlands are diverse and rich ecosystems, which provide food and shelter to many different plants and animals. The combination of shallow water, high nutrient levels, and primary productivity (plant growth and reproduction) is perfect for the development of organisms that form the base of the food chain. The water, dense plants, their root mats, and decaying vegetation are food and shelter for the eggs, larvae, and juveniles of many species. Smaller animals avoid predators by hiding among the vegetation while they wait to prey on still smaller life forms. Fish of all sizes seek the warmer, shallow waters to mate and spawn, leaving their young to grow on the rich diet provided by wetlands. Food and organic material that is flushed out of wetlands and into streams and rivers during periods of high flow feed downstream aquatic systems, including commercial and sport fisheries.

Estuarine marshes, for example, are among the most productive natural ecosystems in the world. They produce huge amounts of plant leaves and stems that make up the base of the food chain. When the plants die, they break down in the water and form detritus. Algae that grow on plants and detritus are the principal foods for shellfish such as oysters and clams, crustaceans such as crabs and shrimp, and small fish. Small fish are the food for larger commercial species such as striped bass and bluefish. (See Figure 7.4.) According to the EPA's *Functions and Values of Wetlands* (March 2002), 75 percent of commercially harvested fish are wetland-dependent. When shellfish species are factored in, the number increases to 95 percent.

Both estuarine and palustrine wetlands also serve as way stations for migrating birds. The 30,000-acre Central Flyway extending from south-central Canada through north-central United States and into Mexico, for example, provides resting places and nourishment for over 400 of some 800 species of protected migratory birds (which individually number in the millions) during the migration season. Without this stopover area, the flight to their Arctic breeding grounds would be impossible. The Chesapeake Bay with its extensive tidal and freshwater marshes on the East Coast Atlantic Flyway gives winter refuge to thousands of ducks and geese.

Wetland Biodiversity

Wetlands are the source of a wealth of natural products, including furs, fish and shellfish, timber, wildlife, and wild rice. A wide variety of species of microbes, plants, insects, amphibians, reptiles, fish, birds, and other animals make their homes in or around wetlands because of the availability of water. For others, wetlands provide important temporary seasonal habitats. Physical and chemical features such as landscape shape (topology), climates, and abundance of water help determine what species live in what wetland.

According to the EPA's *Wetlands and People* (last updated January 17, 2003), more than one-third of the United States' threatened and endangered species live only in wetlands, and nearly half use wetlands at some point in their lives. When wetlands are removed from a watershed or damaged by human activity, the biological health of the watershed declines. Many species of plants and animals are lost to the watershed or decline in number. The EPA estimated that approximately two-thirds of freshwater mussels (67 percent) and crayfish (65 percent) were rare or imperiled and more than one-third of freshwater fish (37 percent) and amphibians (35 percent) dependent on aquatic and wetland habitats were at risk. Nearly one-fifth (18 percent) of dragonflies and plants were at risk. (See Figure 7.5.) Forty-six percent of the threatened and endangered species listed by the FWS rely directly or indirectly on wetlands for survival. All (100 percent) amphibians, fish, clams, and crustaceans listed as threatened or endangered

FIGURE 7.3

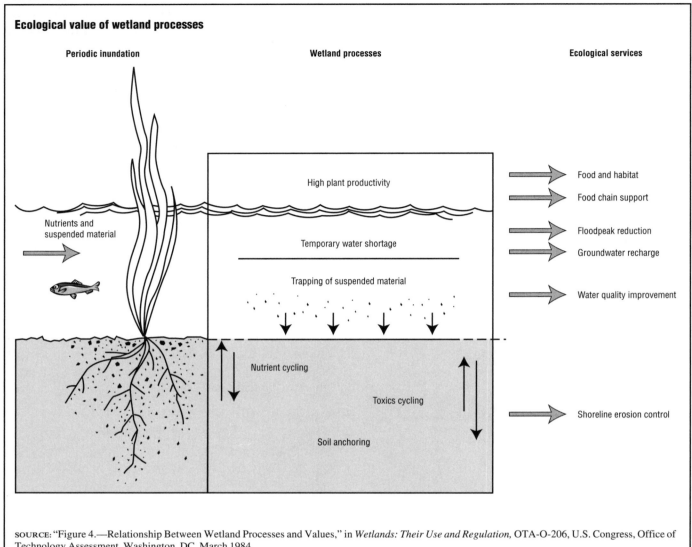

Ecological value of wetland processes

Periodic inundation

Wetland processes

Ecological services

Nutrients and suspended material

High plant productivity

Temporary water shortage

Trapping of suspended material

Nutrient cycling

Toxics cycling

Soil anchoring

Food and habitat

Food chain support

Floodpeak reduction

Groundwater recharge

Water quality improvement

Shoreline erosion control

SOURCE: "Figure 4.—Relationship Between Wetland Processes and Values," in *Wetlands: Their Use and Regulation,* OTA-O-206, U.S. Congress, Office of Technology Assessment, Washington, DC, March 1984

rely directly or indirectly on wetlands for their survival. (See Table 7.4.)

According to the Division of Bird Habitat Conservation of the United States Fish and Wildlife Service, waterfowl remain the most prominent and economically important group of migratory birds of the North American continent. By 1985 (when waterfowl populations had decreased to record lows) approximately 3.2 million people were spending nearly $1 billion annually to hunt waterfowl. Interest in waterfowl and other migratory birds also had expanded in other areas. About 18.6 million people observed, photographed, and otherwise appreciated waterfowl and spent $2 billion on waterfowl-related activities.

When expanding the focus from waterfowl-related activities to all wildlife watching activities the number of interested people grows. According to the *2001 National Survey of Fishing, Hunting, and Wildlife-Associated Recreation,* in 2001 some 66 million residents spent $38.4 billion on all wildlife-watching activities.

The well-being of waterfowl populations is tied directly to the status and abundance of wetland habitats. Populations of ducks in North America dropped from 1955 through 1993, primarily because of declining wetland acreage. New wetland protection measures, however, are beginning to help reverse the trend. Under the Conservation Reserve Program (CRP) during the period 1986–90, farmers enrolled 8.2 million acres of cropland within the Prairie Pothole Region, a vast glaciated area of the north-central United States and Canada from which almost 70 percent of North America's ducks originate. Nearly 13,000 square miles (an area larger than the state of Maryland) was converted to dense nesting cover under the CRP.

In the early 1990s, when the prolonged drought in the northern Great Plains was over, prairie potholes that had

FIGURE 7.4

Coastal wetlands produce detritus that support fish and shellfish

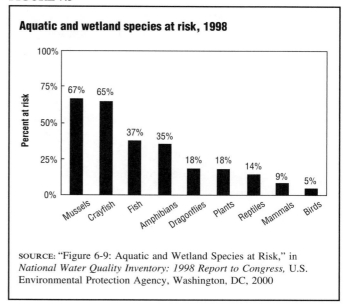

SOURCE: "Figure 6-8: Coastal Wetlands Produce Detritus that Support Fish and Shellfish," in *National Water Quality Inventory: 1998 Report to Congress*, U.S. Environmental Protection Agency, Washington, DC, 2000

FIGURE 7.5

Aquatic and wetland species at risk, 1998

SOURCE: "Figure 6-9: Aquatic and Wetland Species at Risk," in *National Water Quality Inventory: 1998 Report to Congress*, U.S. Environmental Protection Agency, Washington, DC, 2000

TABLE 7.4

Summary of wetland-associated species that are threatened and endangered, as of May 31, 1997

Category	Number of wetland-associated endangered and threatened species	Total number of endangered and threatened species	Percent of total
Mammals	42	63	66.7
Birds	72	89	80.9
Reptiles	21	33	63.6
Amphibians	15	15	100.0
Fishes	107	107	100.0
Snails	10	22	45.5
Clams	62	62	100.0
Crustaceans	18	18	100.0
Insects	9	33	27.3
Arachnids	0	5	0.0
Plants	143	635	22.5
Totals	**499**	**1,082**	**46.1**

SOURCE: "Table 6-1. Summary of Threatened and Endangered Species That Are 'Wetland-Associated'," in *National Water Quality Inventory: 1998 Report to Congress*, U.S. Environmental Protection Agency, Washington, DC, 2000

been dry for more than 10 years filled with water. The prairie came to life and great numbers of waterfowl occupied the potholes. Surrounded by the CRP grass, nesting ducks were no longer easy targets for predators. Prior to the CRP, nest success of only 10 percent was common, that is, the rate of successful breeding was exceeded by the waterfowl mortality rate. With abundant grass and wetlands, spring survey numbers of ducks began to climb. In 1993, 26.3 million ducks were reported in the area, 32.5 million in 1994 and 36.9 million in 1995. Studies by the FWS and Ducks, Unlimited, Inc., a hunting and conservation group dedicated to protecting ducks and their habitat, showed

that the CRP has tripled nest success throughout the Prairie Pothole Region.

Additional measures to preserve and protect the waterfowl population include the North American Waterfowl Management Plan. A joint strategy adopted by the governments of the United States, Canada, and Mexico, the Plan established an international committee with six representatives from each of the three countries. Its purpose is to provide a forum for discussion of major, long-term international waterfowl issues and to make recommendations to directors of the three countries' national wildlife agencies. It approves the formation of Joint Venture partnerships and reviews and approves Joint Venture implementation and evaluation plans. The Committee is responsible for updating the Plan, considering new scientific information and national and international policy developments, and for identifying the need to expand or diminish activities carried out on behalf of the Plan. According to the Division of Bird Habitat Conservation of the United States Fish and Wildlife Service, as of 2001 Plan partners had invested more than $1.7 billion to protect, restore, and/or enhance more than 5 million acres of habitat.

Water Storage

Wetlands function like sponges, absorbing water. By temporarily storing runoff and flood waters, wetlands help protect adjacent and downstream property owners from flood damage. Wetland plants slow the flow of water, which contributes to the wetland's ability to store it. The combined effects of storing and conveying (in this case, to carry and slow the flow) permit water to percolate through the soil into groundwater recharging aquifers, and to move through the watershed with less speed and force.

Wetlands are particularly valuable in urban areas because the paved and other impermeable surfaces shed water, increasing the rate, velocity, and volume of runoff so that the risk of flood damage increases. Loss or degradation of wetlands indirectly intensifies the flooding by eliminating their ability to absorb the peak flows and gradually release floodwaters, thereby helping to maintain stream flow, particularly at times of runoff or low flow.

Nutrient and Sediment Control

Wetlands are natural filters that cleanse water. When water is stored or slowed down in a wetland by wetland plants and root masses, sediment settles out and remains in the wetland so that the water leaving the wetland is much less cloudy than the water that entered. The loss of cloudiness or turbidity has important consequences for both human health and the ecological health of the watershed. Turbidity has been implicated in disease outbreaks in drinking water. Turbid water bearing silt has been responsible for smothering plants and animals in rivers, streams, estuaries, and lakes.

Wetlands can also trap nutrients (phosphorous and nitrogen) that are dissolved in the water or attached to the sediment. Nutrients are either stored in the wetland soil or used by the plants to enhance growth. Studies in the Chesapeake Bay watershed, for example, have shown that some forested streamside wetlands are capable of removing 80 percent of the phosphorous and 90 percent of the nitrogen from water.

Too much nutrient, such as silt, reaching rivers, streams, lakes, and reservoirs can affect both human health and ecological health. Too much nitrogen in drinking water can cause "blue baby syndrome" in infants and young livestock. Too much nutrient can cause eutrophication (depletion of dissolved oxygen by aquatic plant growth) in estuaries, lakes, rivers, and streams.

Soil Anchoring

Increase in water volume and velocity result in damage to stream and river banks, causing severe erosion and changing the contours of channels, making them deeper and flatter. As a result, aquatic communities at the erosion location are disrupted or eliminated, and downstream aquatic systems are damaged by silt.

Marsh plant fringes in lakes, estuaries, and oceans protect shorelines from erosion. The plants reduce soil erosion by binding the soil in their root masses as a function of anchoring the marsh. At the same time, the plants and root masses break up the force of wave action, retarding scouring of shorelines.

ECONOMIC BENEFITS OF WETLANDS

Appreciation of the economic value of wetlands has undergone a dramatic change since the 1970s. Prior to that time, wetlands were considered useless, good only for taking up space and breeding mosquitoes. The emphasis was on filling and draining wetlands to turn them into productive land for development and agriculture. In the mid-1970s the growing environmental movement with its emphasis on clean water caused a closer examination of wetlands and their role in watersheds and the global ecosystem. Wetlands are now valued not only for their ecological role but also for their contribution to the economy. Some examples are presented below.

Recreation

Some of the most popular recreational activities, including fishing, hunting, and canoeing, occur in and are dependent on healthy wetlands. According to the Environmental Protection Agency (EPA) Web site on wetlands (last updated January 17, 2003) more than half of all U.S. adults (98 million people) hunt, fish, bird-watch, or photograph wildlife. Spending on these activities amounts to $59.5 billion annually. Individual states gain additional economic benefits from the spin-offs (boat rentals, bait, film, ammunition, and other gear) as well as tourist dollars. Wetland areas also provide more areas of open space.

An example of the value of these wetland-related recreational activities can be found in the *National Survey of Fishing, Hunting and Wild-Life Associated Recreation* conducted every five years by the FWS. The most recent survey (2001) reported that in that year 34.1 million people aged 16 years and older went fishing and spent an average of $1,046 each; 28.4 million anglers went freshwater fishing while 9.1 million went saltwater fishing. Overall, anglers alone spent $35.6 billion in 2001 on fishing trips, $4.6 billion on equipment, $14.7 billion on travel-related costs, $6 billion on food and lodging, and $3.5 billion on transportation. They spent nearly $5.3 billion on land use fees, guide fees, equipment rental, boating expenses, and bait. Camping equipment, binoculars, and special fishing clothing accounted for $721 million in expenditures. Equipment such as boats, vans, and cabins cost $11.6 billion. Anglers spent $3.2 billion on land leasing and ownership, and $860 million on magazines, books, membership dues and contributions, licenses, stamps, tags, and permits.

Commercial Fisheries

According to *Fisheries of the United States 2001,* a publication of the National Marine Fisheries Service, the value of the U.S. commercial fish landings in 2001 was about $3.2 billion. Eighty-seven percent of the value of U.S. finfish landings was from species that are dependent on near-coastal waters and their wetlands for breeding and spawning. The EPA's *National Coastal Condition Report*

(September 2001) estimated that about 95 percent of commercial fish and 85 percent of sport fish spent a portion of their life cycles in coastal wetland and estuarine habitats. Adult stocks of commercially harvested shrimp, blue crabs, oysters, and other species throughout the United States were directly related to wetland quality and quantity.

Flood Control

In its 1998 *National Water Quality Inventory—1998 Report to Congress* the Environmental Protection Agency (EPA) cited the following two examples of the economic benefits of flood control associated with wetlands.

In Massachusetts, the Army Corps of Engineers estimated that annual flood damage costing more than $17 million would occur from the destruction of 8,422 acres of wetland in the Charles River watershed. For this reason, the corps decided to preserve wetlands rather than construct extensive flood-control facilities along a stretch of the Charles River near Boston. This preservation project has resulted in annual benefits of about $2.1 million per year and costs an average $617,000 annually.

In determining the value of wetlands, the Minnesota Department of Natural Resources estimated that it cost the public about $300 to replace the water storage capacity lost by one acre of wetland that holds 12 inches of water. Using this estimate, the cost of replacing 5,000 acres of wetland would be $1.5 million, more than the state's annual appropriation for flood control.

HISTORY OF WETLANDS USE

What is better, the reclamation of a fertile and productive country or the protection of a shallow mosquito breeding swamp which harbors mainly worthless inedible birds?

— Chief Justice of the Wisconsin Supreme Court, 1911

Until well into the twentieth century, wetlands were considered nature's failure, a waste in nature's economy. For this reason, people sought to increase the usefulness of wetlands. In the agricultural economy of that time, land unable to produce crops or timber was considered worthless. Many Americans began to think of draining these lands, an undertaking needing government funds and resources.

In the nineteenth century, state after state passed laws to facilitate drainage of wetlands by the formation of drainage-districts and statutes. When a number of landowners in an area petitioned for a drainage project, a hearing was held. A district encompassing the area affected could be created with the power to issue bonds, drain the area, and bill the landholders—petitioners and opponents alike. Coupled with an agricultural boom and technological improvements, reclamation projects multiplied in the late nineteenth and early twentieth centuries. The farmland under drainage doubled between 1905 and 1910 and again between 1910 and 1920. By 1920 state drainage districts in the United States encompassed an area larger than Missouri.

Early Conservationists

The earliest effective resistance came from hunters, sportsmen, and naturalist lobbies. Organizations such as the Izaak Walton League, the Audubon Society, and the American Game Protective Association deplored the destruction by drainage of wildlife habitats, and began to press for protection of wetlands. These early conservation efforts met chilly receptions both from the public and the courts. A growing number of Americans, however, were beginning to sympathize with conservationists. Drainage projects were often disappointing—soils had proven to be poorer than expected, and the costs were generally greater than expected.

Reclamation's Failures

Lower Klamath Lake, in Northern California, became a striking example of reclamation's potential for creating wastelands far more desolate than those they replaced. The lake, a shallow sheet of water fringed by marshes, had been set aside by Theodore Roosevelt in 1908 as a waterfowl sanctuary. In 1917 the water inflow was cut off. The lakebed dried up and became prey to dust storms. The peat in the marsh bottom caught fire. The transformed area became less a reclaimed area of extraordinary fertility and more an ecological travesty. Time helped to reverse the damage, but as of 2002 less than 25 percent of the historic wetland basin remained. In spite of this, the basin continues to support tremendous bird life on a smaller scale.

Efforts to reclaim the Klamath Basin continue. According to a January 30, 2003, news release from the U.S. Department of Agriculture (USDA) (*President Bush to Propose Record-Level $3.9 Billion for Conservation Programs*) in the fiscal year budget for 2004, President George W. Bush proposed $8 million for water conservation and water quality enhancements in the Klamath Basin.

Similarly, Florida had long sought to drain the Everglades. Efforts there resulted in lands prone to flooding and peat fires. Peat fires are particularly dangerous because they burn underground and can flare up without warning long distances from where they were originally ignited. Costs escalated, and the drainage district went broke. Across the nation, the gap between the cost and the value of reclaimed land widened even more. The agricultural depression beginning in the 1920s increased the growing skepticism as to the value of reclamation.

Nonetheless, during the Great Depression (1929–41), programs such as the Works Progress Administration and the Reconstruction Finance Corporation encouraged wetland conversion as a way to provide work for many unemployed people. By the end of World War II (1945), the total area of drained farmland had increased sharply.

Tide Turns for Wetlands

Since the early 1970s, conservationists have turned to the courts to challenge wetland reclamation and protect wetlands. If drainage once seemed to improve the look of the land, today it is more likely to be seen as degrading it. Wetlands turned out to be not wastelands, but systems efficient in harnessing the sun's rays to feed the food chain, and important in the global cycle of water, nitrogen, carbon, and sulfur. A number of studies have shown that the value of wetlands for flood protection is far greater than their potential value for agriculture.

No Net Loss

As the drainage movement once found support in state laws and federal policies, so did the preservation movement. In 1977 President Jimmy Carter issued an executive order instructing federal agencies to minimize damage to wetlands. In 1989 the EPA adopted a goal of "no net loss" of wetlands, meaning that where a wetland is developed for other uses, the developer must create a wetland elsewhere to maintain an overall constant amount of wetland acreage.

COMPENSATORY MITIGATION. A major part of the no net loss policy is the practice of compensatory mitigation. Mitigation requires that a party who alters or destroys a wetland area must offset that loss by restoring, creating, or enhancing wetlands elsewhere. For example, a builder can be permitted to build a highway that will disrupt a wetland if the builder will construct or restore a wetland elsewhere. The premise of mitigation is the same amount or more wetlands will be created or restored without unnecessarily retarding economic growth.

The Army Corps of Engineers determines the number of credits required to obtain the permit needed. The ratio the corps seeks is usually 1 to 1.5 acres—this means that for every wetland acre the person is destroying or harming, the person must assume the cost of restoring 1.5 acres of wetlands.

Mitigation banking, a variation of compensatory mitigation, allows people who build on wetlands to pay to a "bank" to enhance another wetland area. This is particularly advantageous to the small property owner who seeks to build only one or two structures. The person purchases "credits" in the bank and transfers full responsibility to an agency or environmental organization that runs the bank. Environmental professionals design, construct, and maintain a specific natural area using these funds. Several states use mitigation banking.

Critics contend that new or improved wetlands may not provide the same value over the same span of time and dislike mitigation because it presumes that wetlands destruction at certain sites is acceptable. Many mitigation projects have not worked well because mitigators often have not kept their agreements, it is difficult to mimic natural systems, and even where it is done properly, a wetland can take as much as 30 years to mature. In the intervening years, however, since the mitigation policy went into effect, the science of wetland creation and restoration has made significant advances, so that the number of sites with successful wetland mitigation is growing.

CONCERN OVER PROPERTY RIGHTS

No person shall ... be deprived of ... property without due process of law, nor shall private property be taken for public use, without just compensation.

— Fifth Amendment to the Constitution of the United States of America

The dispute over wetlands regulation reflects the nation's ambivalence when private property and public rights intersect, especially since three-fourths of the nation's wetlands are owned by private citizens. In recent years, many landowners have complained that wetland regulation devalued their property by blocking its development. They have argued that efforts to preserve the wetlands have gone too far, citing instances where a small wetland precludes the use of large tracts of land. Many people believe that this constitutes taking without just compensation.

The federal government has no right to take property without compensation, and then only in limited circumstances. The "takings" clause of the Constitution provides that when private property is taken for public use, just compensation must be paid to the owner. Wetland owners claim that when the government, through its laws, eliminates some uses for their land, the value is decreased, and they believe that they should be paid for the loss.

While some people believe that wetland protection should take priority over property concerns, a significant part of the public is troubled over what it sees as growing government infringement on the rights of property owners. They believe that just as landowners must be compensated for property seized by eminent domain (the authority of the government to take private property for public use, with compensation to the owner), so should the losses (devaluation of wetland acreage) be compensated, even though no physical taking of property occurs.

State Must Reimburse an Owner for Loss

In the 1970s and 1980s, state courts and the lower federal courts frequently handed down contradictory rulings on the issue of compensation for wetland-related takings. In 1992 the U.S. Supreme Court, in the case of *Lucas v.*

FIGURE 7.6

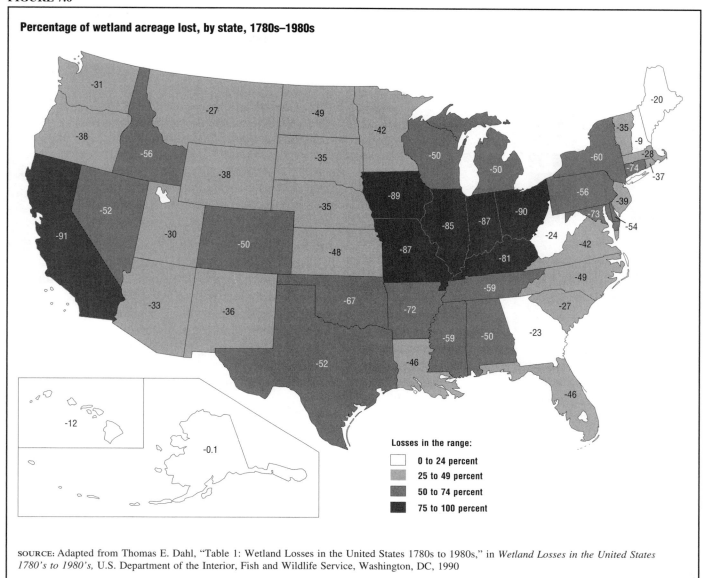

Percentage of wetland acreage lost, by state, 1780s–1980s

Losses in the range:
- 0 to 24 percent
- 25 to 49 percent
- 50 to 74 percent
- 75 to 100 percent

SOURCE: Adapted from Thomas E. Dahl, "Table 1: Wetland Losses in the United States 1780s to 1980s," in *Wetland Losses in the United States 1780's to 1980's,* U.S. Department of the Interior, Fish and Wildlife Service, Washington, DC, 1990

South Carolina Coastal Council (60 LW 4842), resolved the issue of compensation when land taken for an accepted public good loses significant value.

David Lucas, a homebuilder, bought two residential lots on a South Carolina barrier island in 1986. He planned to build and sell two single-family houses similar to those on nearby lots. At the time he purchased the land, state law allowed house construction on the lots. In 1988 South Carolina passed the Beachfront Management Act to protect the state's beaches from erosion. Lucas's land fell within the area considered in danger of erosion; as a result, Lucas could no longer build the houses.

Lucas went to court, claiming that the Beachfront Management Act had taken his property without just compensation because it no longer had any value if he could not build there. Lucas did not question the right of the

State of South Carolina to take his property for the common good. Rather, he claimed the state had to compensate him for the financial loss that resulted from the devaluing of the property.

On June 29, 1992, the U.S. Supreme Court, in a 7–2 decision, agreed:

> There are good reasons for our frequently expressed belief that when the owner of real property has been called upon to sacrifice all economically beneficial uses in the name of the common good, that is, to leave his property economically idle, he has suffered a taking.... When ... a regulation ... declares "off-limits" all economically productive or beneficial use of land ... compensation must be paid.

The Supreme Court said that a state could stop a landowner from building on his property only if he was using it for a "harmful or noxious" purpose—for example, building

FIGURE 7.7

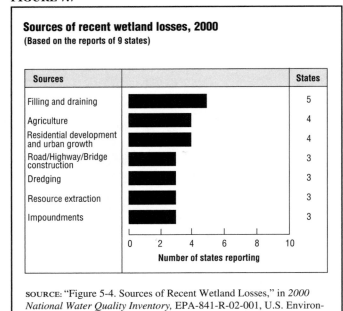

Sources of recent wetland losses, 2000
(Based on the reports of 9 states)

Sources		States
Filling and draining		5
Agriculture		4
Residential development and urban growth		4
Road/Highway/Bridge construction		3
Dredging		3
Resource extraction		3
Impoundments		3

Number of states reporting

SOURCE: "Figure 5-4. Sources of Recent Wetland Losses," in *2000 National Water Quality Inventory,* EPA-841-R-02-001, U.S. Environmental Protection Agency, Office of Water, Washington, DC, August 2002

a brickyard or a brewery in a residential area. This was not the case. Lucas had planned to build homes, a legitimate purpose that was neither harmful nor noxious. Although it was possible to define the planned buildings as harmful to South Carolina's ecological resources, this would not be consistent with earlier Court interpretations of "harmful." Only by showing that Lucas had intended to do something "harmful or noxious" with the land could the state take his land without compensation. This they did not do, and, therefore, they owed him the money.

LOSS IN WETLAND ACREAGE

Since the first European settlers came to North America, we've lost more than 50 percent of our wetlands.

— World Wildlife Fund

When the first Europeans arrived in America, there were an estimated 215 million acres of wetlands in the mainland 48 states; today there are approximately 105.5 million acres. In the intervening years, over 50 percent of the wetlands in the lower 48 states have been lost. Wetlands have been drained, dredged, filled, leveled, and flooded to meet human needs. Although natural forces such as erosion, sedimentation, and rise or drop in sea level may erase wetlands over time, 95 percent of the wetland losses since 1780 are believed to have been caused by man. Many of the nation's older cities, such as New York City, Baltimore, Philadelphia, New Orleans, and Charleston, are built on filled wetlands.

The FWS has been tracking wetland losses. In *Wetland Losses in the United States 1780s to 1980s* (1990), the

FWS reported that 22 states had lost more than 50 percent of their wetlands, an area equal to the size of California. (See Figure 7.6.) Seven states (California, Indiana, Illinois, Iowa, Missouri, Kentucky, and Ohio) had lost more than 80 percent of their wetlands. According to the report, for the first time in United States history, there are fewer than 50 million acres of forested wetlands in the conterminous United States.

In its first wetlands status and trends report in 1983, the FWS estimated the wetland loss between the mid-1950s and the mid-1970s (the years prior to wetland protection) at 458,000 acres per year. In 1991 the FWS reported that estimated wetland loss in the mid-1970s to mid-1980s had declined to 290,000 acres per year. In its *Wetlands Overview* (March 2002), the loss rate reported by the EPA was 60,000 acres annually, an almost 87 percent reduction from the mid-1970s level. The decline in wetland loss was attributed to "increased public awareness of the functions and value of wetlands and the need to protect them, the implementation and enforcement of wetland protective measures, elimination of incentives to drain wetlands, private land initiatives, coastal monitoring and protection programs, and wetland restoration and creation actions."

FWS findings are supported by the December 2000 *Summary Report—1997 National Resources Inventory,* released by the U.S. Department of Agriculture (USDA). The USDA reported a significant decline in wetland loss from the levels reported in its 1992 report. The USDA has a different mandate than the FWS, which affects the way in which the USDA collects its data. The USDA has a slightly different methodology for identifying and classifying wetlands and the causes of wetland loss. Because of these differences, FWS data and USDA data are not comparable or interchangeable. An interagency task force was working to resolve this dilemma. Nonetheless, both studies agreed that the annual rate of wetland loss has declined significantly.

In its 2000 report concerning wetland status and trends, the FWS stated that 98 percent of wetland losses occurred in freshwater wetlands. Freshwater emergent wetlands experienced the most substantial loss while the rate of loss of wooded wetlands declined from 6.2 percent reported in 1991 to 2.9 percent. Shrub wetlands were the only freshwater wetland type that experienced substantive gains.

Urban and suburban development accounted for 30 percent of wetland losses in the FWS 2000 report while agriculture was blamed for 26 percent, forestry for 23 percent, and rural development for the remaining 21 percent. The USDA 1997 natural resources inventory reported that development was responsible for 49 percent of the wetland losses and agriculture for 26 percent. Miscellaneous sources accounted for the remainder.

FIGURE 7.8

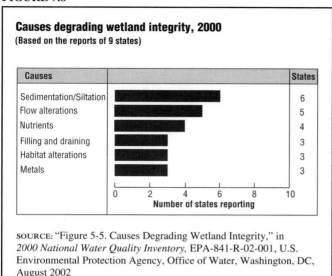

Causes degrading wetland integrity, 2000
(Based on the reports of 9 states)

Causes		States
Sedimentation/Siltation		6
Flow alterations		5
Nutrients		4
Filling and draining		3
Habitat alterations		3
Metals		3

Number of states reporting

SOURCE: "Figure 5-5. Causes Degrading Wetland Integrity," in *2000 National Water Quality Inventory,* EPA-841-R-02-001, U.S. Environmental Protection Agency, Office of Water, Washington, DC, August 2002

FIGURE 7.9

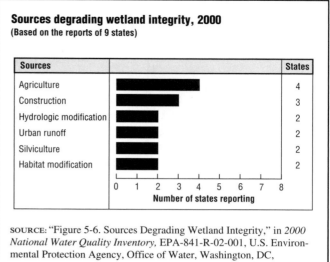

Sources degrading wetland integrity, 2000
(Based on the reports of 9 states)

Sources		States
Agriculture		4
Construction		3
Hydrologic modification		2
Urban runoff		2
Silviculture		2
Habitat modification		2

Number of states reporting

SOURCE: "Figure 5-6. Sources Degrading Wetland Integrity," in *2000 National Water Quality Inventory,* EPA-841-R-02-001, U.S. Environmental Protection Agency, Office of Water, Washington, DC, August 2002

FIGURE 7.10

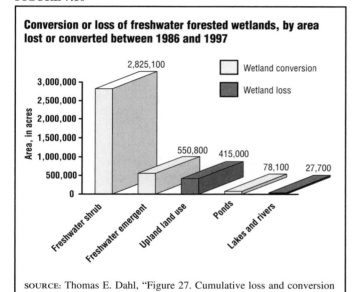

Conversion or loss of freshwater forested wetlands, by area lost or converted between 1986 and 1997

Wetland conversion
Wetland loss

Area, in acres

Freshwater shrub — 2,825,100
Freshwater emergent — 550,800
Upland land use — 415,000
Ponds — 78,100
Lakes and rivers — 27,700

SOURCE: Thomas E. Dahl, "Figure 27. Cumulative loss and conversion of freshwater forested wetlands 1986 to 1997," in *Status and Trends of Wetlands in the Conterminous United States 1986 to 1997,* Department of Interior, Fish and Wildlife Service, Washington, DC, 2000

In their 305(b) filings with the EPA, nine states reported wetland losses. Figure 7.7 shows the sources contributing to these losses. Filling and draining were cited by five states as sources of wetland loss. Agriculture, residential development, and urban growth were cited among other causes.

The states also identified the leading causes of the loss of wetland integrity, that is, the impairment of wetland functions. Six of the nine reporting states identified sedimentation or siltation as the leading cause. Flow alterations, nutrients, filling and draining, habitat alterations, and metals also were cited as causes of loss of wetland integrity. (See Figure 7.8.) The primary sources identified as causing integrity loss were agriculture, construction, and hydrologic modification. (See Figure 7.9.)

Not all wetland losses result in the total obliteration of a wetland. The conversion of a wetland from one type to another may be considered a "loss" because the wetland has changed in one or more functions, particularly if the change results in a wetland perceived as less valuable.

For example, the FWS reported that between 1986 and 1997 (the latest data available) four million acres of forested wetland were removed. The removal was the result of timbering and other practices that removed the tree canopy but left the wetland character, that is, did not drain or fill the wetland. Loss of forest canopy can radically change the hydrology and wildlife habitat value of a wetland. Most of the forested wetlands were converted to freshwater shrub (2.8 million acres) or emergent wetlands (.5 million acres). Other conversions include upland land use, ponds, and lakes and rivers. (See Figure 7.10.)

INVASIVE SPECIES

People are not the only ones who can dramatically alter wetlands. Nonnative—also called exotic—species can be as devastating to wetlands as humans by changing the nature of the ecosystem, thereby interfering with its function and the survival of native plants and animals. Plants and animals introduced accidentally, or deliberately, can cause unexpected harm by displacing native species from their habitat or by placing stress, such as disease or predation, on a native species.

In 1899 the nutria or coypu (*Myocastor coypus*) was introduced into California for the fur-farming trade. This introduction was originally viewed as a way to provide economic benefit. Subsequently, state and federal agencies as well as private interests were responsible for introducing nutria into the wild in 15 states to provide a new fur resource. In coastal states such as Maryland and Louisiana, the results have been disastrous.

Nutria are large (about 15 pounds), semi-aquatic rodents that live in fresh, intermediate, and brackish marshes and wetlands, and feed on the vegetation. They eat all vegetation in an area, changing a marsh to a barren mudflat. Nutria feed on the base of plant stems and dig for roots and rhizomes in the winter. Their grazing strips large patches of marsh and their digging turns over the upper peat layer. This conversion of marsh to open water destroys valuable habitat for muskrat, wading birds, amphibians, reptiles, ducks, fish, crabs, and a host of other species, as well as causing erosion and siltation. According to the U.S. Geological Survey, nutria currently affect 100,000 acres of coastal wetland in Louisiana alone. To date, the best control method is trapping and harvest for meat and fur.

Plant species can be as harmful as animals. Eurasian watermilfoil, phragmites (common reed grass), hydrilla, and purple loosestrife are introduced species that have disrupted wetland systems. Purple loosestrife (*Lythrum salicaria*) is a good example. It is a perennial herb with reddish-purple flowers that may reach six feet in height under the right conditions. It was an important medicinal herb and ornamental as early as 200 years ago on the East Coast and was probably introduced for this reason. It has no known North American predators and has high reproductive capacity—up to 300,000 seeds per stalk. Because it can outcompete most native wetland plants, it can change the character and ecological function of a marsh. This is a serious threat since many wetland and other wildlife species are adapted to and depend on specific plants.

GOVERNMENT WETLAND PROGRAMS

The protection of America's vanishing wetlands is a vital step toward ensuring cleaner water for everyone. In addition to serving as habitat for wildlife, wetlands help filter and protect our country's water supply.

— Christine Todd Whitman, Administrator, Environmental Protection Agency, April 2001

Clean Water Act

The goal of the Clean Water Act is to "restore and maintain the chemical, physical, and biological integrity of the nation's water." Wetlands are considered part of the nation's water and are covered by the act.

SECTION 404. Section 404 of the Federal Water Pollution Control Act of 1972 (Public Law 92-500), commonly called the Clean Water Act, authorizes the Army Corps of Engineers to issue permits for "discharge" into the nation's waters and is the primary federal authority for the protection of wetlands. "Discharge" is defined as the addition of dredged or fill materials to U.S. waters. These discharges include material removed from one portion of a water body (dredging) for placement in another portion of the same water body or another water body (overboard disposal, or placement of dredged material on wetlands adjacent to the area of dredging), and materials brought from other sources to be used as fill. "Fill" is defined as any material used for the primary purpose of replacing an aquatic area with dry land or changing the bottom elevation of a water body. Examples are soil and debris used to fill in wetlands, and rubble placed overboard to create fishing reefs. Under section 404, the corps does not regulate dredging (removal of materials from water), but only addition of materials to water.

Section 404 jurisdiction encompasses all navigable waters of the United States plus their tributaries and adjacent wetlands, and includes ocean waters within three nautical miles of the coastline and isolated waters where the use, degradation, or destruction of these waters could affect interstate commerce or foreign commerce. The Corps evaluates the impact of proposed projects that involve wetlands, considering comments from the EPA, the FWS, the National Marine Fisheries Service, and the affected states. Regulations established under section 404 require that any project affecting more than one-third of an acre of wetlands or 500 linear feet of streams must be approved by the Corps.

Section 404 Jurisdiction Questioned

Between 2000 and 2002, legal challenges arose over the extent of the Army Corps of Engineers' (the Corps) authority under section 404 of the Clean Water Act (CWA) and the meaning of certain terms used in the Act (e.g., "waters of the United States" and "navigable waters.") In its Clean Water Act Information Brief, (*The Supreme Court's SWANCC Decision,* December 2002), the United States Department of Energy detailed one such challenge.

According to the brief, the Solid Waste Agency of Northern Cook County (SWANCC) wanted to develop a nonhazardous solid waste disposal facility on a site that contained isolated ponds and wetlands. The Corps denied the Agency a section 404 permit to fill those wetlands because they were used by migratory birds. Lower courts found in favor of the Corps, and SWANCC appealed the finding to the United States Supreme Court.

On January 9, 2001, the United States Supreme Court issued its decision [*Solid Waste Agency of Northern Cook County v. United States Army Corps of Engineers* (the SWANCC decision), 531 U.S. 159 (2001)]. The Court determined that the Corps' authority under the Clean Water Act did not extend to isolated wetlands if they were not "adjacent" to navigable waters. It held that the Corps exceeded its statutory authority by asserting CWA jurisdiction over the ponds that SWANCC wanted to fill based solely on the use of those "non-navigable, isolated, intrastate" waters by migratory birds.

Other legal challenges detailed in the Department of Energy's information brief include *Idaho Rural Council v. Bosma* [143 F. Supp. 2d 1169, 1179 (D. Id. 2001)]. In this case, the court found that springs connected to nonnavigable streams and groundwater connected to surface water were both waters of the United States. In *United States v. Buday* [138 F. Supp. 2d 1282 (D. Mont. 2002)] the court found that the United States had jurisdiction to regulate a discharge to a tributary of a navigable water.

The implications of the Supreme Court's decision in SWANCC have prompted a move to restore protection to America's wetlands. On February 27, 2003, Congressmen John D. Dingell of Michigan and James Oberstar of Minnesota introduced the Clean Water Authority Restoration Act of 2003 to the United States House of Representatives. According to a news release from Congressman Dingell's office on February 27, 2003, wetlands are in jeopardy because of the Supreme Court's decision in SWANCC and Bush administration regulatory actions. The Clean Water Authority Restoration Act is intended to restore the original intent of the Clean Water Act and to re-establish protections for "isolated" wetlands throughout the United States. According to Congressman Dingell's news release, the Clean Water Authority Restoration Act includes a set of findings that explain the factual basis for Congress to assert its constitutional authority over waters and wetlands. It also reaffirms the original intent of the Congress by creating a statutory definition of "waters of the United States" based on longstanding definitions in the Army Corps of Engineers regulations. The legislation also deletes the term "navigable" from the Act to reinforce that the original concern of the Congress in the 1972 Act related to pollution rather than navigability.

The EPA and the U.S. Army Corps of Engineers remain committed to helping Americans comply with the Clean Water Act's requirements for protection of the nation's wetlands. According to a January 10, 2003 EPA news release, the EPA and the Army issued clarifying guidance for the federal government's rules used to protect wetlands that are regulated under the Clean Water Act. At the same time, the EPA announced its intention to publish an Advance Notice of Proposed Rule Making (ANPRM) to solicit from the public data and information to clarify the extent of Clean Water Act coverage in light of the Supreme Court's decision in SWANCC.

TULLOCH RULE. Another highly litigated regulation adopted under section 404 is the Tulloch rule. This regulation was adopted as the result of a successful challenge brought against the Army Corps of Engineers by several environmental interest groups to stop the draining of wetlands in North Carolina. The corps district engineer named in the lawsuit was Colonel Tulloch. The rule provides that any "incidental fallback" constitutes a discharge that requires a permit if the deposit is part of an activity that destroys or degrades a wetland. Incidental fallback is soil or other materials that drop from the dredges, backhoes, shovels, or other excavating devices into virtually the same place from which they were removed. This expansion of the definition of "discharge" brought all wetland ditching and excavation under 404 jurisdiction, including activities such as sand and gravel mining, which were previously not within corps jurisdiction. The new rule effectively stopped almost all draining and dredging of wetlands.

In 1998 the Tulloch rule was overturned by the D.C. Circuit Court on the grounds that the Corps had exceeded its authority in adopting the Tulloch rule. The court stated that section 404 was clearly intended to regulate the addition of dredged or fill materials, and not their removal. The Corps and several environmental groups appealed the ruling, but the decision of the lower court was upheld in 1998 twice by federal appeals court decisions. The appeals court further admonished the Corps and the EPA that if they believed that they needed to regulate the removal of materials in wetlands, the appropriate remedy was congressional action, not arbitrary regulation. The Corps and the EPA declined to pursue the issue with the Supreme Court.

In 2000 the Corps and the EPA issued a new rule that narrowly defines incidental discharge, and establishes the presumption that because of the nature of the equipment and activities, mechanized land clearing, ditching, channelization, in-stream mining, or other mechanized excavation activities produce more than incidental fallback and therefore are subject to section 404 regulation. The new rule, which appears to ignore the appeals court admonition about arbitrary regulation, was published January 1, 2001, with an effective date of April 1, 2001. The National Stone Manufacturers Association entered suit over the revised Tulloch rule in February 2001.

SECTION 401. Section 401 of the Clean Water Act empowers the states to approve, condition, or deny a permit or activity approved by the Army Corps of Engineers by refusing to issue "401 certification," that is, the state's concurrence with the project. Congress granted the states this authority because of state complaints that their objections to massive Corps and other federal projects were not considered, and that these federally approved projects were often not in the best interests of the state.

No 404 permit may be issued by the corps without 401 certification or waiver of the certification by the state. The 401 certification applies not only to section 404 permits issued by the corps, but also to any application for a federal license or permit that might result in discharge of any type

FIGURE 7.11

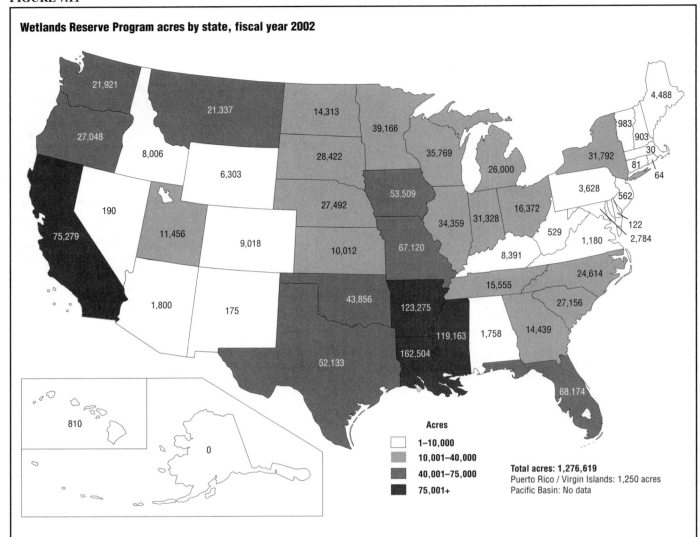

Wetlands Reserve Program acres by state, fiscal year 2002

Acres

1–10,000
10,001–40,000
40,001–75,000
75,001+

Total acres: 1,276,619
Puerto Rico / Virgin Islands: 1,250 acres
Pacific Basin: No data

SOURCE: "WRP Acres by State FY2002," in *Wetlands Reserve Program Maps and Statistics,* U.S. Department of Agriculture, Natural Resources Conservation Service, Washington, DC, November 2002 [Online] http://www.nrcs.usda.gov/programs/wrp/State_Maps_Stats/National_Maps/7047.jpg [accessed June 24, 2003]

to navigable waters. In some states, section 401 authority forms the basis for all state activities to protect wetlands.

Swampbuster Program

The Swampbuster provision of the 1985 Food Security Act (Public Law 99-198), as amended by the Food, Agriculture, Conservation, and Trade Act of 1990 withholds federal farm program benefits, such as price supports, special loans, disaster relief, crop insurance, and conservation easements, from any person who:

- Plants an agricultural commodity on a converted wetland that was converted by drainage, dredging, leveling, or any other means after December 23, 1985

- Converts a wetland for the purpose of or to make agricultural commodity production possible after November 28, 1990

Farmers are asked to report on whether they plan to or have altered any "wet area" when they apply for their farm benefits. The Natural Resources Conservation Service assists farmers in making wetland determinations with regard to the Swampbuster program.

The 1996 Farm Bill

The current conservation provisions Congress is looking at have created more wildlife habitat than any other federal program.

— Scott Sutherland, Ducks Unlimited, Inc., testimony before Congress, June 6, 2001

The 1996 Farm Bill (Public Law 104-105) reauthorized one program, the Conservation Reserve Program, and created a new program, the Wetlands Reserve Program. The two programs are designed to protect and restore wetlands.

CONSERVATION RESERVE PROGRAM. The CRP was originally authorized in the 1985 Farm Bill as a soil conservation strategy that included paying farmers to retire marginal cropland from production for 10 years. Its political support came from its potential to reduce expensive crop surpluses. Farmers who may not want to completely retire their land from production, as required under the Wetland Reserve Program, can retire it in 10-year intervals under the CRP. As a wetland protection and restoration strategy, the program has been successful beyond anyone's expectations

The CRP was reauthorized in the 2002 Farm Act, extending the program through 2007. According to the *Fiscal Year Summary 2002* of the Conservation Reserve Program, as of 2002, 33.9 million acres have been enrolled in the program. A coalition made up of a broad spectrum of 40 environmental, hunting, fishing, and shooting sports organizations with more than 10 million members has endorsed reauthorization of this program in 2002. The coalition includes groups as diverse as the Bass Anglers Sportsman's Society, Ducks Unlimited, Izaak Walton League of America, Nature Conservancy, and the National Rifle Association.

WETLANDS RESERVE PROGRAM. The Wetlands Reserve Program (WRP) is a voluntary USDA program created by the 1996 Farm Bill and has been implemented in 49 states. The program provides farmers with financial incentives, such as fair market price for land, to retire marginal farmland, and in many cases, restore and protect wetlands. The program had enrolled a total of 1,276,619 acres as of fiscal year 2002. (See Figure 7.11.) Retiring cropland through the WRP has benefited the recovery of threatened or endangered species, as well as protected wetlands. The WRP was reauthorized under the Farm Bill of 2002 and is to extend through 2007. The same 40-group coalition supporting the reauthorization of the CRP is supporting reauthorization of the WRP.

State Programs

Many states have enacted their own state laws to protect wetlands. These laws may complement or be more stringent than federal regulations. For example, the state of Maryland has had state laws to protect tidal wetlands since the early 1970s. In 1989 Maryland adopted its Non-tidal Wetland Act to provide the same protections to freshwater wetlands.

In addition to using their section 401 authority, states have included wetland protection in their state water quality standards, passed laws protecting ecologically important wetlands such as the Dismal Swamp in Virginia and North Carolina, established mitigation banking, and created public education programs to increase public awareness of the value of wetlands. Several states have set up special funds to buy important wetlands.

WETLAND GAINS

Not all wetlands are being destroyed or threatened. Numerous efforts are ongoing at the private, local, state, and federal level to protect existing wetlands and to create new ones. Wetland losses can be offset by restoring, creating (mitigating), enhancing, reallocating, or replacing wetlands:

- Wetland restoration—the return of a wetland to a close approximation of its condition prior to disturbance, including reestablishment of its predisturbance aquatic functions and related physical, chemical, and biological characteristics

- Creation—the construction of a wetland in an area that was not a wetland within the past 100 to 200 years and is isolated from other wetlands

- Enhancement—the modification of one or more structural features of an existing wetland to increase one or more functions based on management objectives. Enhancement, while causing a positive gain in one function, frequently results in a reduction in another function

- Replacement or reallocation—activities in which most or all of an existing wetland is converted to a different type of wetland, and has the same drawback as enhancement

Each of these approaches has benefits and drawbacks.

Private Initiatives

More than 75 percent of the wetlands in the United States are privately owned. Therefore, the protection and restoration or enhancement of most wetlands will be done on private property. A number of government programs, both regulatory and voluntary, exist to foster wetland protection, and some exist to foster wetland restoration and enhancement. Many have been successful, but government cannot do it all. Some of the most successful wetland programs and projects are the result of private initiatives. Frequently, private organizations form partnerships with landowners to buy, lease, or create easements paid for with private, or a mix of private and public, funds.

Organizations such as the Nature Conservancy, Ducks Unlimited, the Audubon Society, the Chesapeake Bay Foundation, and hundreds of others are working with private landowners, corporations, local communities, volunteers of all ages, and federal and state agencies in innovative projects to protect and restore wetlands. For example, the Nature Conservancy has two wetland restoration projects on the Illinois River, Spunky Bottoms and Emiquon, that aim to return more than 8,500 acres of farmed land to their original, wetland state.

FIGURE 7.12

A constructed wetland

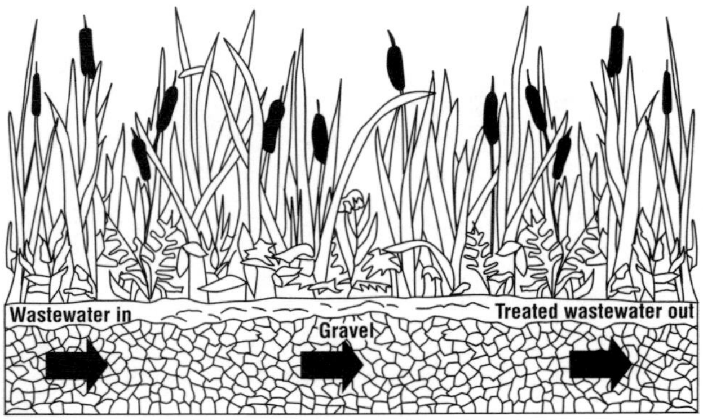

Wastewater in → Gravel → Treated wastewater out

Notes:
Marsh plants (cattails, reeds, etc.) are grown in beds of soil or gravel through which wastewater flows.
Wetlands are useful to further treat wastewater from a lagoon.
This is a low-cost system that needs minimal attention from an operator.
Periodically, plants need to be checked and sometimes harvested at the end of the growing season.
The system requires relatively less land than many land treatment systems.
The system may be operated year-round in most climates.

SOURCE: "A Constructed Wetland," in *Water Pollution: Information on the Use of Alternative Wastewater Treatment Systems,* U.S. General Accounting Office, Washington, DC, 1994

In another example, Ducks Unlimited is working with the National Resource Conservation Service to implement the Wetland Reserve Program in the Mississippi Alluvial Valley, which historically comprised 24 million acres of hardwood bottom stretching from southern Illinois to Louisiana. Since the partnership formed, 8.7 million hardwood seedlings have been planted on 29,000 acres in Arkansas, Louisiana, and Mississippi.

Constructed Wetlands

One growing source of constructed wetlands is wastewater treatment. Constructed wetland treatment systems are designed and constructed to use the natural processes involving wetland soils, vegetation, and their associated microbes to assist with the treatment of wastewater. They are designed to take advantage of many of the same processes that occur in wetlands but in a more controlled manner. While some of these systems are operated solely to treat wastewater, others were designed with the multiple objectives of using treated wastewater effluent as a source of water for the creation or restoration of wetland habitat for wildlife and environmental enhancement. The cost is often competitive with traditional wastewater treatment alternatives. The primary drawback is that they are land intensive; large land tracts are not always available at affordable prices.

There are two general types of constructed wetland treatments: subsurface flow systems and free water surface systems. Both types are usually constructed in basins or channels with a natural or constructed subsurface barrier to limit seepage. The subsurface flow systems create subsurface flow through a permeable medium (soil, sand, gravel, or crushed rock), keeping the water below the surface to minimize odors and other nuisance problems. (See Figure 7.12.) These are also known as rock-reed filters, vegetated submerged bed systems, and root-zone systems. Free water surface systems are designed to simulate natural wetlands, with the water flowing over the soil surface at shallow depths.

Wetlands constructed for wastewater treatment can be found throughout the United States. Alabama, Arizona, California, Colorado, Florida, Illinois, Maryland, Michigan, Mississippi, Nevada, Oregon, and South Carolina are some of the states using constructed wetlands for this purpose.

Marsh construction and wetland rehabilitation as a method of disposing of dredged spoil materials are another growing source of wetland construction. The Army Corps of Engineers has been using dredged material to restore or construct marshes since 1969. Dredged material is placed on shallow bay bottoms to build up elevations to an intertidal level, usually by pumping hydraulically dredged material to the marsh construction site. If the site is exposed to high wind or wave action, protective structures such as rip-rap breakwaters are built to protect the site. Vegetation can be actively planted or the site may rely on natural recruitment. Generally within two to three years, these sites are indistinguishable from natural wetlands in appearance.

Restoration of the Florida Everglades

Here is a land tranquil in its quiet beauty, serving not as the source of water, but as the last receiver of it. To its natural abundance we owe the spectacular plant and animal life that distinguishes this place from all others in the country.

— President Harry S. Truman, December 1947

The Everglades is America's premier wetland. It has been designated an International Biosphere Reserve, a World Heritage Site, and a Wetland of International Importance. According to the World Heritage Committee in its May 15, 2000 report, it is one of two U.S. sites (Yellowstone National Park is the other) on the List of World Heritage in Danger. Figure 7.13 shows how agricultural and industrial activities and urbanization have reduced the Everglades to about half its former size.

The Everglades is part of the South Florida Ecosystem, an 11,000-square-mile region extending from the Kissimmee River near Orlando to the Florida Keys. Originally, a wide expanse of wetland, pine forests, mangroves, coastal islands, and coral reefs, today it is one of the nation's most highly populated and manipulated regions. Its freshwater supply comes from rainfall (40–65 inches per year) in the

FIGURE 7.13

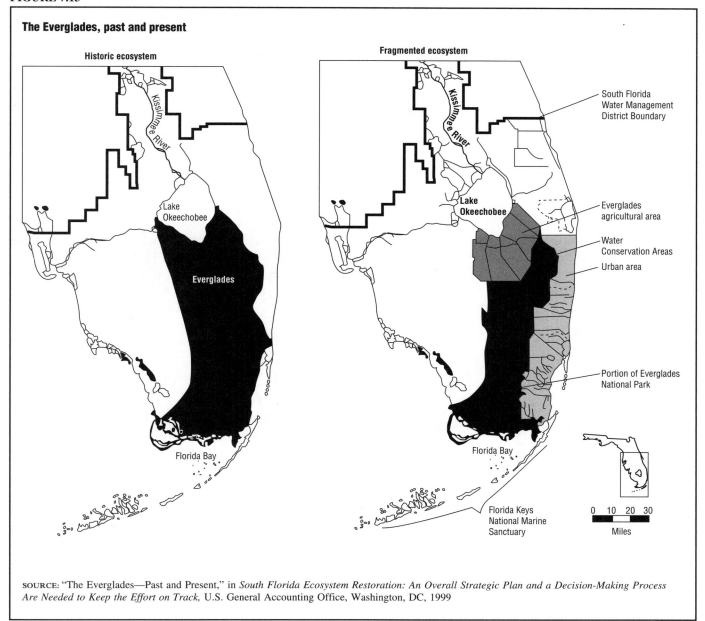

The Everglades, past and present

Historic ecosystem

Fragmented ecosystem

South Florida Water Management District Boundary

Kissimmee River

Lake Okeechobee

Everglades

Everglades agricultural area

Water Conservation Areas

Urban area

Florida Bay

Portion of Everglades National Park

Florida Keys National Marine Sanctuary

0 10 20 30

Miles

SOURCE: "The Everglades—Past and Present," in *South Florida Ecosystem Restoration: An Overall Strategic Plan and a Decision-Making Process Are Needed to Keep the Effort on Track*, U.S. General Accounting Office, Washington, DC, 1999

Kissimmee River Basin and southward, mostly in May through October.

Slow and rain driven, the natural cycle of freshwater circulation feeding the Everglades historically built up in shallow Lake Okeechobee, which averages 12 feet deep and covers about 730 square miles. Thus began the flow of the wide, shallow "river of grass," as it was called by the American Indians. Fifty miles wide in places, one to three feet deep in the slough's center and only six inches deep elsewhere, it flowed south at a rate of about 100 feet per day across the sawgrass of the Everglades to the mangrove estuaries on the Gulf of Mexico. A six-month dry season followed this flow. During the dry season, water levels gradually drop. The plants and animals of the Everglades are adapted to the alternating wet and dry seasons.

During the past one hundred years, an elaborate system of dikes, canals, levees, floodgates, and pumps have been built to move water to agricultural fields, urban areas, and finally, to the Everglades National Park. Water runoff from agriculture and urban development have brought excess nutrients into the Everglades, reducing production of beneficial algae and promoting unnatural growth of other vegetation. Ill-timed human manipulation of the water supply has interfered with the natural water cycle, ruining critical spawning, feeding, and nesting conditions for many species.

The Florida Legislature has enacted a number of laws to combat the growing water shortage in Florida, including the Everglades. The 1981 Save Our Rivers Act and the 1990 Preservation 2000 Fund authorize the water management districts to buy property to protect water sources, groundwater recharge, and other natural resources. The South Florida Water Management District (SFWMD), the agency that oversees flood protection and water supply, began buying out landowners in the east Everglades area in hopes of retaking more than 200,000 acres of agricultural and residential property at an estimated cost of $2.2 billion. The action is aimed at restoring water flow to the Everglades National Park. (For updated status reports on land acquisition efforts, see http://www.evergladesplan.org/pm/progr_land_aquisition.cfm [accessed September 16, 2003]).

In 1998 the Army Corps of Engineers and the SFWMD released their plan for improving Florida's ecological and economic health. This plan covers the entire region and its water problems, and focuses on recovering the major characteristics that defined the "river of grass." Specifically, the plan calls for:

- Reducing the freshwater flows into the Caloosahatchee River and St. Lucie Canal, restoring to the Everglades water now lost to the tide

- Returning the water flow in the Kissimmee River to its former floodplain to achieve a more meandering river system

- Restoring 40,000 acres of marshes for water storage and filtration to remove nutrients prior to water entering the Everglades

- Modifying water deliveries through improved timing and distribution to mimic historic water conditions

- Reestablishing historic flows and water levels to sloughs feeding into Florida Bay to restore natural estuarine salinity

In 2000 Congress passed the Comprehensive Everglades Restoration Plan, the largest environmental restoration project ever attempted anywhere in the world. Over its 30-year life, the project will implement the corps and SFWMD plan. The project will restore critical water flows to the Everglades and ensure adequate water supplies for south Florida cities, communities, and farmers well into the future. The cost of the project will be shared equally between Florida and the federal government.

Funding for Wetlands Conservation

As part of its efforts to conserve, restore, and protect coastal wetlands, the U.S. Fish and Wildlife Service expected to award more than $15.7 million in grants to 15 states during fiscal year 2003. Alabama, Alaska, California, Connecticut, Florida, Hawaii, Maryland, Massachusetts, New Jersey, New York, Ohio, Oregon, Texas, Virginia, and Washington State will receive the grants, which will help fund 21 projects. The grant awards will be supplemented by $33 million from state and private partners.

According to its November 18, 2002 news release (*U.S. Fish and Wildlife Service Grants Fund Wetland Conservation Projects in 15 States*) when the 2003 grants projects are complete, they will have protected and/or restored more than 17,000 acres. Overall, 150,000 acres will have been protected or restored since the wetlands grants program began in 1990.

CHAPTER 8
THE ARID WEST—WHERE WATER IS SCARCE

WATER IN THE WEST—LIQUID GOLD

The United States is a nation relatively rich in water resources. According to the U.S. Geological Survey publication *Estimated Water Use in the United States 1995* (the latest data available) in the lower 48 states, the total renewable supply of water is about 1,400 billion gallons per day—more than 14 times the nation's daily water consumption. Nevertheless, while the nation as a whole is water-rich, this abundance is not spread evenly over the country. Some areas have more water than others, while some have a higher need than others. Those with the greatest need do not always have adequate water resources, a situation that can lead to serious problems and conflicts.

The American West is arid (characterized by desert land) and semiarid (prairie land), with limited and inconsistent supplies of water. From the Rocky Mountains, which form the Continental Divide, to the shores of California, lie the dry basins and deserts of the vast western region of the country. Some sources consider the threshold of the "Great American Desert" roughly at the hundredth meridian, where the landscape turns from green to brown. (A meridian is an imaginary line drawn from the North to the South Pole and numbered according to the degrees of longitude. In this case, the hundredth meridian runs approximately from the central Dakotas through Abilene, Texas.)

Of the 1.9 billion acres of land in the lower 48 states, almost half are in the semiarid and arid regions, which receive less than 20 inches of precipitation per year. The small amount of rain and snow that falls is unevenly distributed. For example, Flagstaff, Arizona, receives over 20 inches a year, but in Phoenix and Tucson, where most of the people live and most of the agriculture is located, the yearly rainfall averages barely nine inches. The reason for this is the Pacific high, a bewildering and persistent meteorological phenomenon, a huge immobile zone of high pressure that shoves virtually all precipitation toward the north.

No resource is as vital to the West's urban centers, agriculture, industry, recreation, scenic beauty, and environmental preservation as its "liquid gold"—water. Throughout the history of the West, especially in California, battles have raged over who gets how much of the precious resource. The fundamental controversy is one of distribution, combined with conflicts between competing interests over the use of available supplies.

SOURCES OF WESTERN WATER SUPPLIES
Surface Water and Runoff

Precipitation (rain, snow, and sleet) is the main source of essentially all freshwater supplies. The amount of precipitation largely controls the availability of surface water and groundwater. In the arid areas of the West, much of the available precipitation evaporates shortly after rains. Tucson, Arizona, for example, receives most of its annual rainfall from heavy thunderstorms during the hottest months of the year—between July and September—when much of the rainfall is lost through evaporation.

Runoff refers to water that is not immediately absorbed into the ground during a rain and runs off into lower-lying areas or surrounding lakes and streams. Runoff is the primary measure of a region's renewable water supply. In addition to rain, a large share of the West's runoff comes from the melting of mountain snowpacks, which are essentially huge reservoirs of frozen water that slowly release their supplies during the spring and summer. Much of western agriculture depends on this meltwater becoming available during the growing season.

Changes in climate can adversely affect this important water source. The U.S. Global Change Research Program (USGCRP) projected that snowpack was very likely to decrease as the climate continued to warm despite a projected

FIGURE 8.1

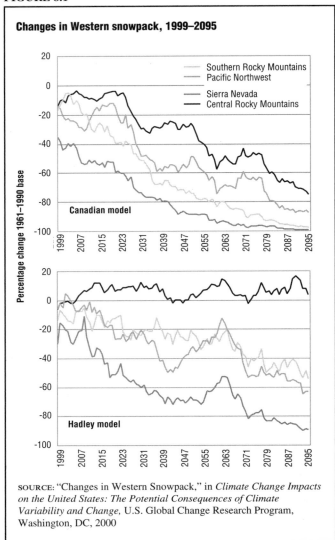

Changes in Western snowpack, 1999–2095

SOURCE: "Changes in Western Snowpack," in *Climate Change Impacts on the United States: The Potential Consequences of Climate Variability and Change,* U.S. Global Change Research Program, Washington, DC, 2000

increase in precipitation. (See Figure 8.1.) Their research suggested that in the coming years more precipitation would fall as rain (rather than as snow) and that snowpack would develop later and melt earlier. As a result, peak streamflows would very likely come earlier in the spring, and summer flows would be reduced. The change in the timing of runoff from snowmelt is likely to have implications for water management, flood protection, irrigation, and planning.

Groundwater

The other source of water in the West is groundwater, or subterranean supplies. Most groundwater is found in aquifers, underground saturated zones full of water (all the spaces between soil and rocks, and the rocks themselves, contain water). These saturated zones are recharged (replenished) primarily from rainfall percolating through the soils. Water from streams, lakes, wetlands, and other water bodies may also seep into the saturated zones. In the saturated zone, water is under pressure that is higher than

atmospheric pressure. When a well is dug into the saturated zone, water flows from the area of higher pressure (in the ground) to the area of lower pressure (in the hollow well), and the well fills with water to the level of the existing groundwater. If the pressure is strong enough, the water will flow freely to the surface; otherwise the water must be pumped.

An example of an aquifer is the Ogallala or High Plains aquifer, one of the world's largest aquifers. Located in the United States, it covers 156,000 square miles stretching from southern South Dakota to the Texas panhandle and is the largest single source of underground water in the United States. The Environmental Protection Agency (EPA) has designated the Ogallala aquifer a sole source aquifer, meaning that at least 50 percent of the population in the area depend on it for its water supply. The Ogallala aquifer provides water to portions of eight western states—Colorado, Kansas, Nebraska, New Mexico, Oklahoma, South Dakota, Texas, and Wyoming. Like many aquifers in the West, this once plentiful source of underground water is rapidly being depleted because its water supply is being extracted by thousands of wells at a faster rate than can be replenished through annual rainfall. Falling water tables invariably signal that withdrawal of groundwater is exceeding the rate of replacement and that, eventually, the source of water could disappear.

In July 2002, concerns about excessive pumping of the Ogallala Aquifer prompted Senators Sam Brownback of Kansas and Jeff Bingaman of New Mexico to introduce to Congress the Ogallala Aquifer Bill. Officially named the High Plains Aquifer Hydrogeologic Characterization, Mapping and Modeling Act, the bill would establish a program within the Department of the Interior to map and study the aquifer. The United States Geological Survey (USGS) would coordinate the program and would provide grants and technical assistance to those eight states (or local agencies and education institutions) for projects that address groundwater issues. According to a March 18, 2003 Congressional Budget Office (CBO) report, for fiscal years 2003 through 2011 the bill would authorize the appropriation of whatever amounts are necessary for federal projects, technical assistance, and state grants. The CBO estimates that implementation of the bill would cost about $1 million in fiscal year 2003 and $44 million over the 2003–08 period. For the 2003–13 period the CBO estimates the cost at $90 million.

Because of the arid and semiarid climate found in much of the West, the natural replenishment of aquifer water is slow, and the consequences of the large-scale removal of groundwater are becoming more evident. These consequences include land subsidence; loss of springs, streams, wetlands and their associated habitat; and degradation of water quality. Land subsidence is the sinking of the land

FIGURE 8.2

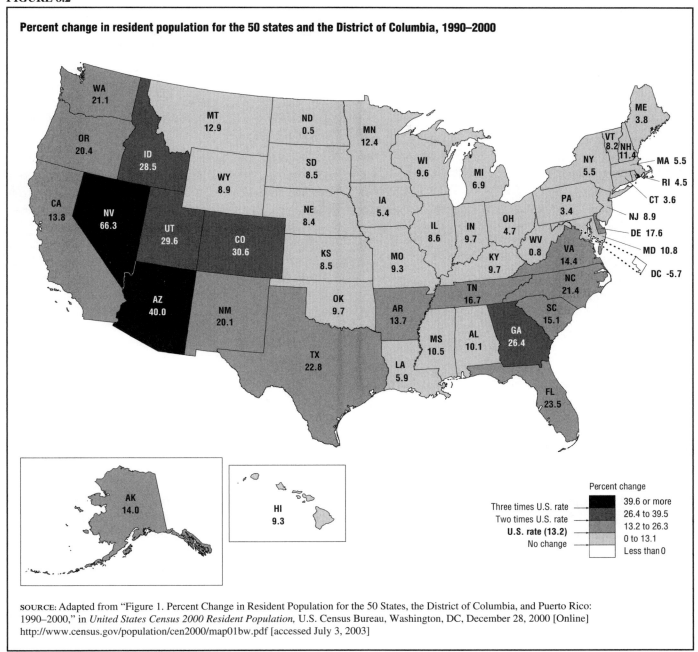

Percent change in resident population for the 50 states and the District of Columbia, 1990–2000

SOURCE: Adapted from "Figure 1. Percent Change in Resident Population for the 50 States, the District of Columbia, and Puerto Rico: 1990–2000," in *United States Census 2000 Resident Population,* U.S. Census Bureau, Washington, DC, December 28, 2000 [Online] http://www.census.gov/population/cen2000/map01bw.pdf [accessed July 3, 2003]

surface, and can be caused by the slow drainage of water from the clay and silt sediments in and next to aquifers. As water levels in aquifers decline and the water is drained from the silt and clay soils, they compact, causing the land surface to drop. Uneven land subsidence can cause large cracks and holes in the ground, causing damage to roads, pipelines, buildings, canals and drainage ditches, railroads, and other structures. Significant land subsidence ranging from six to 29 feet in depth has already occurred near Mendota and Lancaster, California; Las Vegas, Nevada; and Eloy and Phoenix, Arizona.

California has a vast network of underground water reserves. This groundwater resource is especially valuable when surface water is in short supply, as in a drought. In 1991 alone (during a seven-year drought), farmers withdrew a record 4.9 trillion gallons more than was put back in—an amount that could support every Californian at that time for almost three years. As long as the amount of groundwater extraction continues to increase, as is expected with the growing population, and recharge (the process by which water is added back to the reserves) remains below normal, the levels of available groundwater will continue to decline.

As water levels go down, a water supplier can deepen a well. The amount of energy, however, necessary to lift the remaining water to the surface increases, adding to the farmer's or water utility's cost of producing a crop or providing water supplies for cities. These additional energy costs are ultimately passed along to the water's users. Alternatively, a farmer may switch to a higher-value crop or let the land lie fallow (unplanted). Ultimately, if the groundwater is depleted, the well will go dry.

DESERT BOOM

The population growth in Arizona, Nevada, Utah, and New Mexico is a testament to the drawing power of the American desert. The creation of new jobs and the influx of more people continue. The growth of the job market there since 1980 has exceeded that of the United States as a whole, and population increase has mirrored the job opportunities. Some new residents, drawn by the natural beauty of the West, "telecommute" to offices in faraway cities.

According to data from the United States Bureau of the Census, population growth exploded in the West between 1990 and 2000. (See Figure 8.2.) Nevada, where the population increased by 66 percent during those years, and Arizona, with an increase in population of 40 percent, lead the nation.

The Bureau of the Census projected continued significant population growth in the West through the year 2025. In its report *Population Projections for States by Age, Sex, Race, and Hispanic Origin: 1995 to 2025* the Bureau projected that population in the West would increase at a rate of nearly twice the national average from 1995 through 2025. California, which contained 12 percent of the population in 1995, was projected to contain 15 percent of the population by the year 2025, adding about 17.7 million people during the 30-year period.

In its November 23, 1998 seminar (updated May 22, 2003), the United States Global Change Research Program (USGCRP) discussed how population increases have affected use of water from the Colorado River Basin. According to the seminar, four of the top five fastest-growing states in the United States are in the Colorado River Basin. In addition, populations in the northern Mexico states of Sonora and Baja are also increasing significantly at 5 percent per year, a rate of growth expected to continue.

The accompanying increase in water demand has been very rapid. In 1988, Nevada used less than 130,000 acre-feet of its 300,000 acre-foot Colorado River entitlement. By 1995, however, its use of the water grew to 225,000 acre-feet per year. The state is expected to use its full entitlement before 2025. Moreover, the population of Las Vegas grew by more than 26 percent between 1990 and 1994, and the total population of southern Nevada in 1990 (800,000) is expected to more than double by the year 2020. Populations in the state of Arizona and in the northwestern region of Mexico are both expected to grow by 90 percent over the same period.

Growth has another price. Water is the ultimate source of growth and political power in the arid West. Often, water has to be brought to western cities from distant sources. Although most of the West's cities sprang up alongside rivers, their increasing needs for water long ago outstripped the local supplies. Nationwide, southwestern states are more dependent on public and private community water systems than are other states where use of individual wells is more prevalent.

Drilling a well in the desert is unlikely to produce an adequate supply of water. Hence, even the smallest communities now depend increasingly on water imported from other states. In 1990, for the first time, states in the lower Colorado River Basin (Arizona, California, and Nevada) used their full 7.5-million acre-foot allotment. The unprecedented growth of Phoenix, Arizona, and Las Vegas, Nevada, has resulted in warnings to California from those states that they will likely cut their annual allotments of water to California, perhaps by as much as 50 percent.

Changes Coming to California

A crucial question is how California is preparing itself for times of greater stringency.

— U.S. Secretary of the Interior Bruce Babbitt, in an address to the Colorado River Water Users Association, 1996

Southern California relies on the Colorado River for 70 percent of its water. For years, California has been able to take more than its lawful portion of Colorado River water because the other six states dependent on the river—Arizona, Nevada, Colorado, Utah, Wyoming, and New Mexico—did not need their allotted share. But that situation is changing as the population of the West surges, and the other states are pushing the government to curtail California's use of water. California is currently exceeding its allotment by at least one-fifth. According to an article in the May 22, 2003, *Sacramento Bee* ("Officials Turn Up Water Pressure"), California missed a December 31, 2002 deadline (issued by the U.S. Department of the Interior) to come up with a plan to voluntarily reduce its overuse of the Colorado River. The state was allotted 4.4 million acre-feet per year under the 1922 Colorado River Pact, but had been using 5.2 million acre-feet per year. California's failure to come up with a strategy for reducing its overuse of Colorado River water resulted in the shutoff of eight massive water transfer pumps on January 1, 2003, according to a PBS Web Feature (*Who Owns the Sea?* [Online] [accessed June 30, 2003]).

Additional measures to curb California's overuse of the Colorado River included a decision by the state's Department of Water Resources (DWR) to withhold money from the Metropolitan Water District of Southern California (MWD). According to an article in the *Sacramento Bee* ("Officials Turn Up Water Pressure") in March

2003, the administration of California Governor Gray Davis brokered a water-sharing deal between the MWD and other major water agencies of Southern California. The agreement, in which Imperial Valley farmers would sell a portion of their water to the San Diego County Water Authority, would have given California about 15 years in which to decrease its use of the Colorado River (a time-table ordered by the U.S. Department of the Interior). The MWD objected to the agreement when it learned that Davis wanted to spend $200 million to clean up environmental damage in the Imperial Valley that would result from the water transfer. The MWD fears that spending on the Imperial Valley might divert money that would otherwise be spent on water projects in MWD's territory. According to the article, the state DWR has withheld less than $1 million from the MWD, but it could withhold up to $30 million unless the MWD agrees to sign the deal concerning use of the Colorado River.

According to the USGCRP in *Environmental Water Security* (November 1998), one of the issues compounding the Colorado River Basin problem is the fact that when the Colorado River Pact was signed in 1922, it was assumed by those signing it that the long-term average flow of the river was close to the 18 million acre-feet per year measured at Lee's Ferry. In 2003, the Bureau of Reclamation estimated the average flow at Lee's Ferry to be approximately 15 million acre-feet per year. Despite its error, subsequent laws and decrees have been based upon this original estimate.

THE WEST'S FRAGILE ECOSYSTEM

The natural environmental systems of the West are very fragile. Because much of the West is arid or semiarid in climate, the ecosystems are in precarious balance. Alteration of the life-sustaining water supply can dramatically affect habitat and the plant and animal species that reside there. Under natural conditions, most of the surface water and groundwater recharge occurs at higher elevations, resulting in flow toward the center of the basins. Many of the discharge points are wetlands, springs, and streams fed by groundwater. These oases are water-dependent habitats in an otherwise harsh, dry environment and are necessary to the continued survival of plant and animal populations.

When groundwater is continually withdrawn, particularly in excess of replenishment, the effects spread outward from the area of withdrawal, decreasing the amount of water in the aquifer. Entire natural ecosystems can be affected. For example, in 1942 a mesquite woodland was present along the Santa Cruz River near Tucson, Arizona. It was a thriving habitat valued for its wild bird population. By 1989 the mesquite woodland was gone. Groundwater levels in the area had declined by more than 100 feet, depriving the plants of their water supply.

In another example, the Cienega de Santa Clara, the largest remaining bird habitat in the Colorado River delta, is now sustained mostly by the agricultural drainage water from the Wellton-Mohawk Irrigation District, a very saline water supply. The salinity of this supply has increased the salinity of the Colorado River water entering Mexico, resulting in a dispute over water quality. The problem is so severe that Congress enacted the Colorado River Basin Salinity Control Act of 1974 to deal with the problem. Because so much of the water's flow has been captured and used long before the river reaches the sea, the Colorado River delta continues to shrink and dry out, cutting off delivery of nutrients to the sea and reducing critical habitat for fisheries. This has had a detrimental effect not only on the environment but also on the economics and society of local communities.

Under Title II of the Colorado River Basin Salinity Control Act of 1974 the U.S. Department of Agriculture (USDA) and the U.S. Department of the Interior (USDOI) manage the river's salinity, including salinity contributed from public lands. According to the Natural Resources Conservation Service (NRCS), salts dissolved in the Colorado River cause more than $300 million in damages each year.

UNREASONABLE EXPECTATIONS

The American pioneers who settled the West knew how precious water was. They had to dig their own wells and haul the water. They watched crops dry up and turn to dust and cattle die from lack of this precious commodity. Today, most people in the United States take a plentiful supply of water for granted because of our many very efficient water supply systems. But as populations grow, particularly in the arid and semiarid West, where the availability of water has been an issue since the earliest settlement days, water supplies are becoming more limited and increasingly vulnerable to drought.

Estimating the Water Supply

There were dry years too and they put terror in the valley. The water came in a thirty year cycle. And it never failed that during the dry years the people forgot about the rich years, and during the wet years they lost memory of the dry years. It was always that way.

— John Steinbeck, *East of Eden*, 1952

Many people base their expectations of "normal" on their experiences when they were younger or what conditions have been like for the past few years. Because of limited human lifetimes, very few people, including water planners, are conscious of the fluctuations in climate across decades or centuries. Some scientists argue that the only real climatic constant is change and that people have invented the idea of "normal weather" for their peace of mind.

Comparison of a region's worst recorded drought (the drought of record) against expectations of water supply can provide a harsh reality check. Urban and agricultural planning would undergo dramatic changes if city, state, and regional planners, managers, and officials operated as if the drought of record would be the next drought. According to the National Drought Mitigation Center (NDMC), droughts of record typically last three to seven years. For most of the country, the drought of record occurred between the 1930s and 1960s. While the same weather conditions could recur, the effects would almost certainly be different because water-use patterns and population concentrations have shifted substantially since then. These effects can be simulated using economic input/output computer models to determine the effects on society.

Planning for drought has its limitations. One limitation is that there is no way of knowing if the next drought will be worse than the drought of record. Another is that our climate records do not go back more than 100 to 120 years, while some drought cycles can span several decades or centuries. Scientific research into tree rings (dendochronology) is providing information as to how limited our knowledge really is. For example, the work of Charles Stockton and David D. Meko at the University of Arizona's Laboratory of Tree-Ring Research tells a compelling story about climate history. In January 1983 they reported their findings in the *Journal of Climate and Applied Meteorology*. Although 1934, 1936, and 1939 were very dry years in the Great Plains, the drought of the 1930s paled in comparison to the droughts of 1860 and 1757 when they averaged conditions over 3 to 10 years.

A good portion of California's water supply depends on runoff from precipitation (rain and snow) in the Sierra Nevada Mountains. Scott Stine, a geographer at California State University at Hayward used carbon dating to study trees growing in lakes, rivers, and swamps. In June 1994 he reported in *Nature* evidence that for spans of more than a century at a time, the climate was so dry that there was little or no runoff from the Sierra Nevada Mountains. Stine was able to document that past dry spells lasted from 892 to 1112 (220 years) and from 1209 to 1350 (141 years). Stine also found that despite two droughts, the twentieth century was among the wettest in four thousand years.

What Records to Use?

Deciding which of the historic records to use in planning always involves some arbitrary judgments. The effects of these judgments can have far-reaching consequences. A good example is the basis for the 1922 Colorado River Compact, which determines how the river's water is allocated. In 1988 Barbara Brown of the National Center for Atmospheric Research investigated the data used by the U.S. Bureau of Reclamation to establish the allocations and reported her findings in *Societal Responses to*

Regional Climatic Change: Forecasting by Analogy (Michael H. Glantz, editor, Westview Press, 1988). She reported that the bureau used roughly calculated data gathered between 1899 and 1920 to arrive at an estimated average annual flow of 16.4 million acre-feet at Lee's Ferry, a point on the river. An acre-foot (43,560 cubic feet) is a unit of measure that is equivalent to the volume of water it takes to cover an acre to a depth of one foot.

Subsequent climatic record information now shows that the period from 1899 to 1920 was an unusually wet period in the Colorado Basin. Colorado River flows calculated from tree-ring records for the period reveal that they were the wettest 20 years in the past 450 years. Tree-ring records also show that the flow in the river has been as low as 4.7 million acre-feet per year. The 10-year annual average has been estimated to be 9.7 million acre-feet. Since the 1922 compact, flows in the river have been as low as 6.6 million acre-feet in 1934, with a 10-year annual average low of 12.5 million acre-feet a year from 1931 to 1940.

The planners and engineers at the Bureau of Reclamation did not have the climate records and sophisticated technology available to us today. Despite our greater knowledge, drought management continues to be that of response to crisis instead of thoughtful advanced planning. Cities, states, and regions are reluctant to take actions that will anger citizens by restricting growth and access to water use and to raise taxes and increase expenditures to conserve water when the need for the water may not occur for many years. People are naturally optimistic and, even under drought conditions, frequently will not accept the fact that they are in a drought. They continue to reassure themselves that it will rain tomorrow, or that the next year will be a good year, despite the climatic data that show that droughts of record typically occur for two or more years in a row, or that new technology will find a way to solve the problem.

SPECTER OF INEVITABLE DROUGHT

Drought is a recurring and inevitable phenomenon. In arid and semiarid regions where water is particularly scarce, the effects of drought may be more immediately felt, but it happens everywhere in the world at some time and all climates are susceptible. For example, an analysis of climate data for river basins in the United States from 1896 to 1995, based on National Oceanic and Atmospheric Administration data, shows that some part of the nation experienced an extreme or severe drought in every year in that period, and that in 72 of those years, these conditions affected more than 10 percent of the United States. During that same period, the Pacific Northwest river basins experienced extreme or severe drought 86 times, while California river basins had these conditions only 53 times.

The Tennessee River Basin had the lowest number (31) of these drought events.

There is no such thing as "normal weather." The idea of normal or average weather is a mathematical construction used by the media to describe weather in terms of deviation from a mathematical norm. Close examination of climate records demonstrates that variation is normal in weather. Weather changes day to day, week to week, and one year to the next. Some weather patterns may last for years with some decades being cool and wet while others are hot and dry. Drought is a naturally occurring part of the climate cycle.

The misconception that weather is normal and drought is an unusual circumstance is a very serious problem. Weather, in one form or another, is the source of all water for drinking, irrigation, power supply, industry, wildlife habitat, and other uses. When planners, managers, and citizens fail to recognize drought and its converse, flooding, as inevitable parts of the normal weather range, their plans fall short in anticipating water and societal needs.

A 2000 report from the U.S. Global Change Research Program (USGCRP) stressed the importance of factoring in potential effects of climate variability when developing water conservation and supply strategies. The report, *Climate Change Impacts on the United States,* described various scenarios that would result from changes in climate in the United States. In addition, scientists and other researchers offered suggestions for water planners and managers to aid in efficient and effective water-supply strategies. Using historical climatic data, climate models, and sensitivity analyses (which ask how, and how much, the climate would have to change to cause major impacts on particular regions or sectors of the country) scientists suggested that in the coming years there will be more precipitation in the United States, with more of it coming in heavy downpours. In spite of this, however, scientists believe that some areas are likely to become drier as increased evaporation due to higher temperatures outpaces increased precipitation. They also suggested that droughts and flash floods are likely to become more frequent and more intense.

What Is Drought?

Drought can be defined simply as a deficiency of precipitation over an extended period, usually a season or more. This deficiency results in a water shortage for some group, activity, or part of the environment. Drought should be judged relative to some long-term average condition of balance between precipitation and evapotranspiration in a particular area. Drought is also related to the timing and the effectiveness of the precipitation. Timing refers to factors such as the period when drought is most likely to occur, delays in the start of the rainy season, and the occurrence of

rain in relation to principal crop growth. Precipitation effectiveness refers to the duration, intensity, and frequency of rains or other precipitation events. In many regions of the United States and the world, high temperature, high winds, and low relative humidity are also associated with drought, increasing its severity. In normally arid and semi-arid regions, the precipitation deficiency is over and above the more typical dry season.

The interaction between drought, a natural event, and the demand that people place on water supply affects society. Human activity often worsens the drought's impact. Changes in land use, land degradation, and the construction of dams all affect the hydrological characteristics of a water basin (the land area drained by a particular river and its tributaries). For example, changes in land use upstream may alter hydrologic characteristics such as water infiltration and runoff rates, causing more variable stream flow and a higher frequency of water shortage downstream.

Predicting Drought

Anyone can predict with absolute certainty that drought will occur because inevitably it will. It is the how, when, where, and for what duration that is difficult. Drought is never the result of a single cause, but comes from the interaction, and sometimes compounding, of the effects of many causes. On the largest scale, global weather systems (teleconnections) play an important part in explaining global and regional weather patterns. These patterns occur with enough frequency and similar characteristics over a sufficient length of time to provide opportunities to strengthen our ability to predict long-range climate, particularly in the tropics. An example of these global systems is the El Niño/Southern Oscillation.

On a lesser scale, high-pressure systems inhibit cloud formation and result in lower relative humidity and less precipitation. Regions that are under the influence of high-pressure systems most of the year are generally deserts such as the Sahara and Kalahari Deserts in Africa. Most climatic regions experience high-pressure systems at some time, often depending on the season. Prolonged drought occurs when the large-scale deviations in atmospheric circulation patterns persist for months, seasons, or years. The extreme drought in 1988 that affected the United States and Canada was caused by the persistence of large-scale deviations in atmospheric circulation patterns, and is estimated to have cost the United States $40 billion.

There are too many variables for climatologists to accurately predict drought. Prediction depends on our ability to forecast two fundamental factors, precipitation and temperature. Scientists know that climate is inherently variable and that deviations of precipitation and temperature may last from several months to several decades. Other factors affecting their duration are air-sea interactions, soil

TABLE 8.1

State-by-state list of EQIP funding for ground and surface water conservation, 2003

(EQIP stands for Environmental Quality Incentive Program)

State	Allocation
Arizona	$ 2,014,800
California	11,626,500
Colorado	4,361,600
Idaho	4,459,100
Kansas	4,132,300
Montana	2,400,600
Nebraska	5,613,100
Nevada	771,900
New Mexico	1,324,700
North Dakota	107,100
Oklahoma	962,600
Oregon	2,143,700
South Dakota	504,000
Texas	7,075,700
Utah	1,236,400
Washington	2,090,700
Wyoming	2,175,600
Total	**53,000,400**

SOURCE: "State-by-State List of EQIP Ground and Surface Water Conservation 2003 Funding," in *USDA News Release: USDA Provides $53 Million to Farmers and Ranchers in 17 States to Help With Drought Recovery*, U.S. Department of Agriculture, Washington, DC, May 2003

moisture, topography, and the accumulated influence of dynamically unstable weather systems at the global scale. Until we can describe, interpret, and predict the interplay among all these factors, we cannot predict weather, including drought, with any real accuracy.

The USGCRP is actively working to promote understanding of climate change and the implications it has for the United States. According to their report *Climate Change Impacts on the United States,* advances in climate science are paving the way for scientists to project climate changes at the regional scale, allowing them to identify regional vulnerabilities and to assess potential regional effects. For example, the report suggested that the Earth's climate has changed in the past and that even greater climate change is very likely to occur during the 21st century. It also suggested that reduced summer runoff, increased winter runoff, and increased demands are likely to compound current stresses on water supplies and flood management, particularly in the western United States. Understanding of the implications of these changes may help Americans adapt to an uncertain and continuously changing climate.

An emerging area of science that may help with drought prediction is the extraction of information from tree rings, the Arctic and Antarctic ice caps, prehistoric sites, and other naturally occurring "records." This information is being used to calculate the frequency of droughts in a region's history and to identify the normal precipitation in a given period. Using this information,

climatologists may not be able to predict a drought, but can calculate the probability of a drought occurring in a specific region under a particular group of climatic conditions.

DROUGHT MANAGEMENT: TOO LITTLE, TOO LATE

Hydro-Illogical Cycle

The National Drought Mitigation Center (NDMC) has characterized drought management in the United States as the hydro-illogical cycle. The public in the West and elsewhere tends to assume that abundant water supplies are normal, when in fact, occasional droughts of moderate duration and intensity are unavoidable. When rainfall is plentiful, the public is apathetic about the need to conserve water and to plan for severe drought conditions. Once drought begins, and signs such as failing crops and restrictions on water use begin to penetrate the public awareness, the public becomes uneasy.

The longer the drought continues, the more concern, until panic sets in, particularly as socioeconomic effects such as a decline in crops, loss of water-related recreational opportunities and the income they generate, and stringent water rationing become evident. Calls go out for the federal, state, and local governments to "do something," resulting in crisis management. Response to immediate needs, conflicting government activities and initiatives (almost always at higher costs than under noncrisis circumstances), and the need to balance competing interests in an emotionally charged atmosphere is neither good public policy nor good resource management.

Some federal government efforts are underway toward assisting farmers and ranchers to implement technologies and practices to conserve water and to mitigate the long-term effects of drought. In a June 5, 2003, news release ("Initiative Will Help Agriculture Producers, Communities Hit by Severe Water Shortage"), the USDA announced that it was making $53 million in Ground and Surface Water Conservation funding available to promote water conservation efforts and to ameliorate conditions caused by a multi-year drought that has left several critical reservoirs at historic lows and led to water shortages across the West. Seventeen states will share the funding. (See Table 8.1.)

California and the Drought Years

Drought plagued California from 1986 until 1993, the longest dry period in nearly one hundred years of record keeping. California was not alone in experiencing the drought. In many ways, the water conflicts and issues it experienced were similar to, although more severe than, those found in many western states. In recent years, however, the rising population and the increased demand for water for wildlife, recreation, and scenic enjoyment

FIGURE 8.3

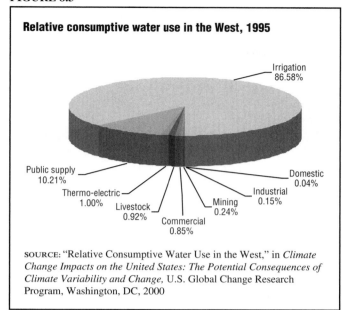

Relative consumptive water use in the West, 1995

Irrigation 86.58%

Public supply 10.21%

Thermo-electric 1.00%

Livestock 0.92%

Commercial 0.85%

Mining 0.24%

Industrial 0.15%

Domestic 0.04%

SOURCE: "Relative Consumptive Water Use in the West," in *Climate Change Impacts on the United States: The Potential Consequences of Climate Variability and Change,* U.S. Global Change Research Program, Washington, DC, 2000

taxed water supplies. The seven-year drought illustrated to California and the nation its vulnerability to financial and ecological ruin and inconvenience and prompted residents to consider new technologies.

California's elaborate system of dams, reservoirs, aqueducts, and canals permits residents to ignore the fact that they live in a naturally semiarid climate. California is located in a climatic high-pressure zone that hovers off its coast, causing rainfall to be diverted northward. The state normally receives less than half (44 percent) as much precipitation as does the southeastern portion of the United States, the nation's wettest region. The rain that does fall in California is not evenly distributed; two-thirds of the state receives fewer than 20 inches of rain a year, and significant swings in annual rainfall occur regularly. Although Northern California provides two-thirds of the state's water supply, two-thirds of the state's population lives in Southern California, which has little water of its own.

The early settlers knew this harshness in its natural state and warned about it. Nonetheless, the rugged individualists who migrated to California developed a powerful myth about their state—that in this potential Eden, everything was possible. California's development of its most precious resource, water, has been a major factor in making the myth a reality.

Throughout the preceding century, Californians had worked to develop a state of unparalleled abundance. More than 350 canals were dug to convert the arid soil into lush fields and orchards, and 1,200 dams and reservoirs helped to alter the state's natural cycles from drought to flood and back again. The attitude that has typified the history of modern California is a confidence in the human ability to conquer the forces of nature and a contempt for the

dry environment from which their state, despite the odds, has flourished. For a century, Californians have managed to fulfill their water-dependent images of what their state should be: an agricultural empire, an industrial giant, and a green paradise for the 34.5 million residents there as of 2001.

California's agricultural survival, and that of the other Western states, has been possible only because of extensive irrigation. (See Figure 8.3.) Although only approximately 15 percent of the country's harvested acres are irrigated, most of the irrigation takes place in those states that are west of the Mississippi (except Florida), particularly in the Southwest. In California, Nevada, Arizona, and New Mexico, 75 to 100 percent of the acreage is irrigated. As a result, much of that acreage is affected by the pollutants and salinity that accompany irrigation. For example, approximately 94 percent of California's estuaries have been affected by agricultural practices, including irrigation.

PENDULUM SWINGS. Public attitude is changing about what constitutes the best use of water. State, local, and federal officials say the tug-of-war over water is a reminder of the political complexity of water, an issue that historically pitted farmers and cities against conservationists, but in which farmers now stand largely alone. Farmers concede their power is eroding. Although some crops still thrive, watered by sprinklers with snowmelt from the mountains, thousands of acres that once produced crops have reverted to sagebrush and tumbleweed. As Californians have concentrated in cities, they have come to care more about urban issues. While urban interests once joined with farmers to build more dams, urban dwellers now usually align with conservationists.

Attitudes are also changing about the "right" to water-extravagant life styles in an arid climate. Northern Californians are increasingly resentful of what they see as water waste in Southern California, a land of swimming pools, golf courses, and car washes. Southern Californians answer that they live in an area of perpetual drought and have invested hundreds of millions of dollars over the years to ensure their water supplies; they deserve to use them as they see fit.

Reality of Drought

A drought occurs when the water supply is reduced to a level that cannot support existing demands. A recent California drought lasted more than seven years, the fiercest drought since the Dust Bowl in the 1930s, when California had 7 million people instead of the 34.5 million who officially lived there as of 2001. Beginning in 1986, water supplies dwindled to a point where reservoir storage was only 54 percent of normal. Thirty-nine of the state's 58 counties rationed water, and many asked the governor to proclaim a state of emergency. In 1990 the State Water Project (SWP) was forced to reduce water deliveries to agricultural customers by 50 percent. The severity of the continuing drought was worsened by the steadily increasing demands created by industrial growth and a population increase of nearly 750,000 additional people per year.

In the San Joaquin Valley, an area the size of Connecticut, the earth dropped more than a foot, damaging roads and buildings. Water resource authorities suspended the agricultural deliveries of water. More than 2.1 million acres of crops such as grapevines and fruit trees failed due to insufficient water. Farmers who planted thirsty crops such as cotton, alfalfa, and rice were the hardest hit. Grocery shoppers in every part of the country paid higher prices for some fruits and vegetables since California is the nation's largest agricultural producer, growing more than 50 percent of the nation's fresh produce.

Throughout the drought, many cities and towns in California instituted severe penalties for excessive water use. Rationing, cutbacks, and conservation were required. The average mandatory reduction was 50 percent. The first steps by urban residents to save water were to buy low-flow showerheads, install ultralow-volume toilets, avoid washing cars, stop filling swimming pools (every fifteenth home in California has a swimming pool) and hot tubs, use dishwashers less frequently, and let lawns become brown. City dwellers were then forced to adopt more severe measures to save their meager allotments of water.

Water was categorized either as "clear" (direct from the tap), "gray" (recycled water from showers, bathtubs, sinks, and washing machines), or "black" (toilet wastewater). The "gray" water was reused to water vegetable gardens or plants. Some Californians switched to paper plates to avoid using dishwashers. Others never allowed the tap water to run while brushing teeth or did not wait for hot water when taking showers. As water rationing became increasingly serious, code enforcers watched for violators and issued citations with fines.

The area's wildlife may require years to recover from the effects of the drought. The drought years also had a significant impact on trees. Insects, which can survive adverse conditions more easily than many other forms of life, killed enough trees to equal 12 billion board feet of lumber. Because of the dryness, fire officials continually battled forest fires. In 1990 wildfires forced the closing of Yosemite National Park for the first time in history. Many expensive homes burned to the ground as wildfires roared down the canyons. With water from rivers and reservoirs severely limited, helicopters were fitted with large buckets to allow them to scoop water from swimming pools, if necessary. These events could be relived any time the rain does not come.

WATER POLICIES—STATES LEAD THE WAY

Water shortfalls are first and foremost a local and regional problem. Because of the lack of a cohesive federal water policy, states have become important innovators in devising ways to reduce long-term vulnerability to drought. In 1976–77, during the widespread U.S. drought, no state had a drought plan. In 1982 only three states had drought plans. According to the National Drought Mitigation Center (NDMC) as of April 2003, 35 states had drought plans, 4 states had plans in development, 2 states delegated drought planning to local authorities in lieu of a state plan, and 9 states remained without plans.

Most, but not all, of the more drought-prone states are committed to drought planning, as are many states in the East. The drought occurrence since 1996 has led to a rapid increase in drought planning in the southwest, south-central, and southeast states. The 2001 report of the National Drought Policy Commission to Congress emphasized the need for drought planning at the local, state, tribal, and federal levels of government.

Most state plans do not meet all the goals of the NDMC recommended planning process. Most of the plans address the response component of drought planning, defining the basic linkages between local, state, and federal entities for coordinated planning and response efforts.

Western Water Policy Review Act of 1992

At the recommendation of the Western Governors' Association, Congress adopted the Western Water Policy Review Act of 1992 (Public Law 102-575, Title XXX), which directed then-President George H. W. Bush to undertake a comprehensive review of federal activities affecting the allocation and use of water in 19 western states. The Western Water Policy Review Advisory Commission was appointed and chartered in 1995.

The commission released its findings and recommendations in 1997. In the arid West, providing adequate water supplies to meet future demands remained a top priority. Deep concern exists about the ramifications of the claims being advanced by American Indian tribes to water resources and the impacts of those claims on existing rights in non-Indian communities. Better cooperative efforts among the states, tribes, and federal agencies are needed.

In addition to the need for additional supplies to meet growing water demands, the commission recognized that a need exists to overhaul existing water infrastructure (irrigation canals and ditches, water piping, and water storage devices). There is a significant challenge in addressing these needs while meeting the expanding demands to sustain in-stream flow and water quality for environmental maintenance and enhancement. Overlaying all of these challenges are legal and institutional conflicts that need to be addressed at the federal-state level, between states, and among various water users. The commission recommended the development and implementation of an integrated, coordinated federal policy for federal activities affecting the allocation and use of water in 19 western states. The policy was to be developed with the full involvement of the affected states.

National Drought Policy Act of 1998

The United States is poorly prepared to deal with serious drought emergencies ... although the federal government has numerous drought related programs on the books, we have no integrated, coordinated system of implementing these programs.

— Senator Pete Domenici, Senate sponsor of the National Drought Policy Act, June 1998

As a result of the devastating $6 billion drought in 1996 in the West and the recommendation of the Western Governors' Association in *Status of Drought Report Recommendations* (Response Working Group, March 1998) "to develop a national framework that integrates actions and responsibilities among all levels of government (federal, state, regional, local, and tribal)," Congress passed the National Drought Policy Act of 1998 (Public Law 105-199). The new law established a National Drought Policy Commission to make recommendations concerning the creation and development of an integrated, coordinated federal drought policy. The commission was to seek public input on recommendations for legislative and administrative actions to help prepare for and alleviate drought's adverse economic, social, health, and environmental effects.

In June 2001 the commission released its report, *Preparing for Drought in the 21st Century—Report of the National Drought Policy Commission* (the latest data available). The commission recommended the following national policy basis:

National Drought policy should use the resources of the federal government to support but not supplant nor interfere with state, regional, local, tribal and personal efforts to reduce drought impacts. The guiding principles of national drought policy should be:

1. Favor preparedness over insurance, insurance over relief, and incentives over regulation.

2. Set research priorities based on the potential of the research results to reduce drought impacts.

3. Coordinate the delivery of federal services through cooperation and collaboration with non-federal entities.

The policy is a marked shift from emphasis on drought relief, and encourages the adoption of a forward-looking stance to reduce the nation's vulnerability to drought impacts. The commission summarized its findings by stating that preparedness was the key to successful drought management; that information and research are needed to support and achieve preparedness; that insurance against

drought impacts needs to be reevaluated and revamped to accommodate some new subscribers and eliminate some historic subscribers; and that a safety net is needed for the period of transition from relief-oriented drought programs to drought preparedness.

The commission recommended that the United States, through its federal government, take up a national drought policy with preparedness at its core. Federal resources should be dedicated to assisting nonfederal interests and the public-at-large to prepare for drought. The commission provided specific recommendations as to how this should be done and urged Congress to pass a National Drought Preparedness Act to achieve the implementation of the recommended policy.

WATER RIGHTS, WATER FIGHTS
This Land Is My Land; This Land Is Not Your Land

The early history of the migration of people to the American West in the latter part of the nineteenth century has been told in innumerable histories, films, and stories. Two important events in the process of settling the West led to laws for the allocation of the scarce water supplies in the extremely arid environment—the discovery of gold and silver in the western mountain regions and the widespread use of irrigation for crop production.

Miners searching for gold and silver diverted stream water into pipes. As a result, an informal code of water regulations started in the mining camps. The first person to file a claim to a gold or silver mine was allowed priority in getting water over any later claims. To remain the owner of a mining claim, the individual had to mark it off, take possession of it, and "work" the claim productively. This informal water law, conceived over one hundred years ago, was called the "prior appropriation doctrine."

A few years later, this legal practice was adopted by farmers, whose absolute needs for water for irrigating the parched desert were similar to those of the miners. The "first in time, first in right" priority system gave the first farmers guaranteed water supplies in times of drought, which were frequent. This right to use water by both the miners and the farmers, who were the first nonnative settlers of the West, was exclusive and absolute. Where water was concerned, the early pioneers envisioned a dreamland with hundred-mile-long canals, emerald-green farms, and bustling cities. The prior appropriation and first in time, first in right practices conflict with the more traditional riparian rights (the right to use water, such as a stream or lake, that abuts one's property) used in the East. Riparian rights cannot be sold or transferred.

As the population of the West expanded and states began to write down their laws, the rules for water rights and use changed. The prior appropriation doctrine was

FIGURE 8.4

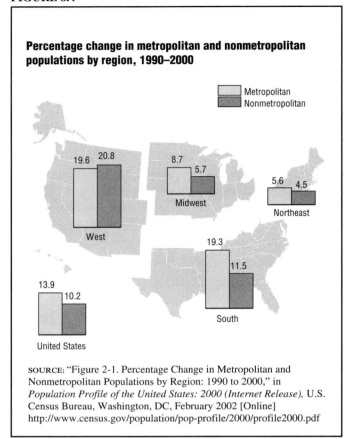

Percentage change in metropolitan and nonmetropolitan populations by region, 1990–2000

Metropolitan
Nonmetropolitan

West 19.6 20.8
Midwest 8.7 5.7
Northeast 5.6 4.5
South 19.3 11.5
United States 13.9 10.2

SOURCE: "Figure 2-1. Percentage Change in Metropolitan and Nonmetropolitan Populations by Region: 1990 to 2000," in *Population Profile of the United States: 2000 (Internet Release),* U.S. Census Bureau, Washington, DC, February 2002 [Online] http://www.census.gov/population/pop-profile/2000/profile2000.pdf

the priority date. There also may be constraints against changes or transfers involving these priority uses.

Water Projects

The federal government played a major role in encouraging the economic growth and settlement of the West. The Reclamation Act of 1902 (PL 57-161) began many years of federal involvement in constructing and subsidizing water projects in the West. The Reclamation Act was designed to provide subsidized water for small farmers who worked up to 320 acres. Over the years, however, farmers and corporations have used subsidized water to farm thousands of acres by entering into arrangements in which they lease (but do not own) farms.

Based on the existence of irrigated farmland guaranteed by federal subsidies, the West grew rapidly. Cities sprang up in the deserts, attracting a large array of support industries as people from the eastern and midwestern United States moved to the Southwest to enjoy the warm, dry climate, stark beauty, and sunshine.

Although some continue to argue that the American West is still a frontier—the total land area is sparsely populated, with an average of 29.4 people per square mile in New Mexico, Colorado, Utah, Nevada, and Arizona combined—the low average population density is deceptive. According to the Bureau of the Census (*All Across the U.S.A.: Population Distribution and Composition, 2000*), population growth in metropolitan areas in the West increased almost 20 percent between the years 1990 and 2000, while the population in nonmetropolitan areas in the West increased by almost 21 percent. (See Figure 8.4.) In fact, the West has become the most urban region of the country, and this urban growth continues.

UNANTICIPATED CONSEQUENCES OF IRRIGATION. In much of the West, millions of acres of profitable irrigated land overlie a shallow and impermeable clay layer, the residual bottom of an ancient sea, that is sometimes only a few feet below the surface. Significant changes in the land can be caused by the interaction of irrigation water and this ancient seabed. During the irrigation season, temperatures in much of the desert fluctuate between 90 and 110 degrees, and much water is lost because of evaporation and plant transpiration. The water lost in evapotranspiration is relatively pure because chemicals are left behind to precipitate as salts and to accumulate in the soil. Evapotranspiration is the combined effect of evaporation of moisture from water bodies and land surfaces and the transpiration of plants.

Water retained in the soil seeps downward, carrying the salts with it, until it hits the impermeable clay layer. Because the water has nowhere to go, it rises back up into the plant root zone, increasing the salt content. The excessive salts can interfere with crop growth. Generally,

modified. "Beneficial use" became the basis for a landowner's rights to water. Beneficial use has two components: the nature or purpose of the use and the efficient or nonwasteful use of water. State constitutions, statutes, or case law may define the beneficial uses of water. The uses may be different in each state, and the definitions of what uses are beneficial may change over time. The right to use water established under state law may be lost if the beneficial use is discontinued for a prescribed period, frequently summarized as "use it or lose it." Abandonment requires intent to permanently give up the right. Forfeiture results from the failure to use the water in the manner described in state statutes. Either requires a finding by the state resource agency that a water right has been abandoned or forfeited.

Priority determines the order of rank of the rights to use the water in a system, that is, the person first using the water for a beneficial purpose has a right superior to those who begin to use the water at a later date. Priority becomes important when the quantity of available water is insufficient to meet the needs of all those having rights to use water from a common source. Under a priority system, water shortages are not shared as they are under a riparian water rights system. Some western state statutes contain priority or preference categories of water use, under which higher-priority uses (such as domestic water supply) have first right to water in times of shortage, regardless of high salt concentrations obstruct germination and impede the absorption of nutrients by plants, and in some cases, have rendered the soils unable to grow crops. The salts (dissolved solids) continue to accumulate as irrigation continues. A few thousand acres have already gone out of production because the soil is too salty; salt is actually visible on the ground.

To stop excessive buildup of the salts in the soil, extra irrigation water is required to flush out the salts, generally into surface drainage or groundwater. In locations where these dissolved solids reach high concentrations, the artificial recharge from irrigation return flow can result in degradation of the quality of groundwater and the surface water to which the groundwater discharges. In severe cases, the increased salinity renders the water useless for irrigation or drinking and contributes to degraded aquatic habitats.

Buying and Selling Water Rights

Prior to the mid-1980s, the preferred method of getting water was to develop a new supply. As new supplies became less accessible and environmental regulations made supply development more difficult and expensive, creating mechanisms for voluntary water reallocation as a component of managing the demand for water has become more important. Water marketing and demand management promote efficiency and allow a considerable amount of flexibility in water resource management.

In 1986 Aurora, Colorado, a growing suburb of Denver, went shopping for water to meet its ever-increasing needs. For $50 million, the city bought the water rights from 300 financially strained farmers in the Arkansas River valley and thus increased Aurora's water supply by 30 percent. At one time, this sale of water rights by farmers was considered unthinkable, but the growing water demands by the West are now forcing such sales to increase. While demand for water for growing cities is far outpacing the available supplies, federal money to finance huge water projects has all but dried up. Realizing that water scarcity will inhibit future growth, western cities and industries are looking to the agricultural community for water.

Agriculture has traditionally claimed the lion's share of the West's water supplies, accounting for 80 to 90 percent of consumption in most states. If farmers or ranchers, however, can earn more money selling water to a nearby city than spraying it on their crops or watering their stock, shifting the water from farm to city is in their economic best interest. If the city is saved from damming a local river to increase supplies or depleting an aquifer, it may also benefit the environment.

The value of water rights has varied enormously. Advocates of the sale of water rights maintain that a free market will allow for more efficient distribution of a source that is often subsidized and just as often squandered. Conservative politicians favor it because it reduces the federal government's role in developing new water supplies. Liberal politicians also like it because more efficient use of water could lessen the need for dams, which are often environmentally harmful, and benefit the environment. Since 1981 and continuing into the twenty-first century, western state legislatures have been slowly changing the old laws dealing with water rights to make water right transfers more flexible.

Opponents, including some of the farmers who agreed to sell, claim that the sales are draining the life from small, rural communities and can cause irreparable damage to the environment in the long run as the now waterless land is left to crack, bake, and turn into dust. The farmers and ranchers who have refused to sell their water rights are concerned about not only their own water supplies but also the surrounding weeds, dust, and barren land. Once water rights are sold, the use of the land for farming is over. But in hard financial times, many landowners take whatever price they can get.

Whether water marketing continues or not, agriculture water rights will probably erode over time wherever water demands exceed the water supply because the value of crops is normally far less than the value of drinking water or industrial water supply. Urban dwellers do not identify with the needs or problems of agriculture in maintaining the food supply. Worldwatch Institute, a private environmental group, estimated that a given amount of water used in industry generates more than 60 times the economic value of the same amount used to produce food. This trend, however, could have consequences in the future as a growing national and world population has increased need for food.

Water Banks

Not all water right transfers require that water be shifted permanently away from agriculture. Voluntary market transactions can reallocate water on a temporary, long-term, or permanent basis. A water bank (a clearinghouse between the buyers and sellers of water), acting as a water broker and usually subsidized by the state, can be authorized to spend money to buy water from farmers or other sellers who are willing to temporarily reduce their own use. The bank then resells the water to drinking water suppliers, farmers, ranchers, and industries that need the water. California, Idaho, Montana, and Texas are among the states that operate water banks.

Water Ranching

In Arizona, where state law prohibits buying the rights to water without also buying the land, a more drastic measure for obtaining water has evolved. Growing cities such as Tucson and Phoenix have purchased 575,000 acres of farmland to be used as "water ranches." Some of the land will be farmed until the cities actually need the water, but if rapid growth continues, as is expected, all of it will eventually be removed from farming. In Pima County, where Tucson is located, irrigated agriculture is expected to disappear by the year 2020 as the city expands and continues to buy even more land for its water needs.

Water Conservation and Transfers in the West

Under the doctrines of prior appropriation and beneficial use, water that is not put to beneficial use will be appropriated by those next in line. If less water is needed due to a change in crops or more efficient water use, the holder risks losing the full amount of the original right. There is little incentive to conserve water unless that water can be used to irrigate additional acreage on the same property or be transferred to another user for a price. Most experts believed that legislation was necessary to encourage conservation and permit the transfer of water to other uses. California, Montana, Oregon, Texas, and Washington have enacted legislation to accomplish this.

California, the first state to pass such legislation (1982), allows conserved water to be sold, leased, or exchanged. Under the statute, a person who conserves water does not risk loss of water if it is not put to immediate use, since conservation is now defined as beneficial use. Oregon (1987) also protects the holder's allocation, although the statute allocates 25 percent of the conserved water to the state to maintain or enhance flows for fish and wildlife protection. Washington (1990), however, also provides financial assistance to encourage conservation efforts. Water transferred to the state is placed in a trust program to enhance stream flows, irrigation, or municipal water supplies.

Montana (1991) authorizes holders who conserve water to retain that water right and transfer the water to another user, with approval of the state government. To encourage water conservation, Texas (1993) allows appropriated water saved through a documented conservation plan to be sold or leased without fear that the right will be lost or amended under the use it or lose it rule. Despite the legislation, it is difficult to attribute actual water savings to these laws. The states continue to study the practices and will likely pass further legislation.

DESALINATION—A GROWING WATER SUPPLY SOURCE

According to the American Water Works Association (AWWA), as of 2003 there were more than 12,500 desalination plants operating in 120 countries. These plants convert seawater, brackish water, and wastewater to freshwater suitable for a variety of purposes. According to an article on MSNBC.com ("Turning Salt Water into

Gold," October 10, 1999 [Online] www.msnbc.com/news/319483.asp?cp1=1 [accessed July 1, 2003]), 60 percent of desalination plants are located in the Middle East. As of August 2002, Saudi Arabia had 27 plants desalinating 30 percent of the world's drinking water. Its largest plant produces about 128 million gallons per day (mgd) of desalted water. Only 12 percent of the world's desalination capacity is located in the Americas, with most of the plants in the Caribbean and Florida.

In the past few years, desalination has become a rapidly growing alternative to water scarcity. With population growth and the threat of drought throughout the United States—particularly in the 19 western states and Florida—desalination, once considered too expensive, is looking more attractive. Hundreds of desalination plants of all sizes are operating throughout the United States, and more are coming online everyday.

The growth in the use of desalination was fueled by the adoption of the Reclamation Wastewater and Groundwater Study and Facilities Act of 1992 (Public Law 102-575, Title XVI). The act directed the Secretary of the Interior to undertake a program to investigate and identify opportunities for water reclamation and reuse and authorized participation in five water-recycling projects. In 1996 Congress reauthorized the act, expanding it to include another 18 projects, 8 of which are in Southern California, an area in desperate need of water. At the same time, Congress enacted the Water Desalination Act of 1996. The act is based on the fundamental need to find additional sources of potable water. Its primary goal is development of more cost-effective and technologically efficient means to desalinate water.

What Is Desalination?

Desalination is the removal of dissolved minerals (including, but not limited to, salts) from seawater, brackish water, or treated wastewater. A number of technologies have been developed for desalination. In the United States, desalination research is directed by the Bureau of Reclamation, which is a bureau of the Department of the Interior.

There are several desalination processes:

- Reverse osmosis—filtered water is pumped at high pressure through permeable membranes, separating the salts from the water

- Distillation—water is heated and then evaporated to separate out the dissolved minerals. The most common methods of distillation are:

  1. multistage flash distillation, where the water is heated and the pressure lowered so that the water "flashes" into vapor that is drawn off and cooled to provide desalted water

2. multiple effect distillation, where the water passes through a number of evaporators in series with the vapor from one series being used to evaporate the water in the next series

3. vapor compression, where the water is evaporated and the vapor compressed; the heated compressed vapor is used to evaporate additional water

- Electrodialysis—electric current is applied to brackish water, causing positive and negative ions of dissolved salt to split apart

The two most common desalination processes worldwide are multistage flash distillation and reverse osmosis. Although water of different quality, including seawater, brackish water, or impure industrial wastewater, can be desalinated, seawater and brackish water are the most common water sources.

Desalination Plants

In 1962 Buckeye, Arizona, became the first town in the United States to have all its water supplied by its own electrodialysis-desalting plant. The plant provides about 650,000 gallons of water daily at a cost of about $1 per 1,670 gallons. In 1967 Key West, Florida, opened a flash-evaporation plant and became the first city in the United States to draw its freshwater from the sea.

The Yuma desalting plant in Arizona is the second-largest reverse osmosis desalting plant in the world, producing about 95 mgd. The plant was built as a result of a dispute with Mexico over the salinity of drainage water from the Wellton-Mohawk Irrigation District in Arizona. The salinity of this irrigation return flow has caused marked deterioration in Colorado River water quality in Mexico. The problem was so severe that Congress enacted the Colorado River Basin Salinity Control Act to fund the plant's construction.

The saline drainage water from farmlands east of Yuma flows in a concrete drainage canal to the desalting plant. The drainage water enters the plant intake system where screens remove algae and large debris such as tree limbs. As the drainage water flows into the plant, it is treated with chlorine to kill organisms and stop the growth of algae, which would damage or plug the filters and membranes.

Before being desalted, the water passes through several pretreatment steps to remove all solids that would interfere with the membrane performance. Pretreatment extends the life of the reverse osmosis membranes three to five years. Without pretreatment, the membranes would last about one hour. It takes about 4.5 hours for a unit of water to travel through the plant, from where it enters as untreated drainage water, is pretreated and subjected to reverse osmosis and then discharged to a small canal that empties into the Colorado River.

LIMITATIONS OF SEAWATER DESALINATION. One major limitation of desalination projects is their cost. The cost to produce water through desalination depends on the technology used, the plant capacity, and other factors. Price estimates for water produced by desalination plants in California ranged from $1,000 to $4,000 per acre-foot. In comparison, traditional water source costs range from $27 to $269 per acre-foot. For new supplies that are developed, costs are about $600 to $700 per acre-foot. During the 1988 drought, however, Santa Barbara, California, paid $2,300 per acre-foot, while permanently tying into the California Water Project would cost about $1,300 per acre-foot. Given the cost of new supplies, the cost of desalting water becomes more competitive.

Desalination requires relatively large parcels of land, preferably near the coast. Pumping seawater and brine over long distances to avoid the need for a coastal location would add to desalination's already considerable expense. Nevertheless, the demand for water by a growing population, the effects of drought on the cost and availability of water, and the technical improvements in the desalination process have led city planners to consider the expensive alternative. As other sources of water become more expensive or less available, desalination becomes more attractive. Advocates of desalting plants claim that the price of water in the West will inevitably rise as demand outpaces supply, while the cost of desalting will fall as technology improves.

On February 12, 2003, the U.S. Bureau of Reclamation and the U.S. Department of Energy's Sandia National Laboratories announced the release of a "research road map" designed to guide future investments necessary to reduce the cost of desalination. The report, *Desalination and Water Purification Technology Roadmap: A Report of the Executive Committee,* also described related advanced water treatment technologies and enhanced uses of desalination.

While recognizing the high cost of desalination technologies—$1 to $3 per thousand gallons of desalinated water compared to prices as low as pennies per thousand gallons—researchers believe that by 2020 desalination and water purification technologies can contribute significantly to ensuring a safe, sustainable, affordable, and adequate water supply for the United States. In fact, the report stressed the increasing strain on water supplies in the United States and the possibility that desalination technologies will have to be used to keep up with demand.

Researchers suggested that while the desalination cost of $3 per thousand gallons of water might appear to be expensive, consumers have shown a willingness to pay the equivalent of $7,945 per thousand gallons for "designer" bottled water (based on a shelf price of $.99 per half-liter

TABLE 8.2

Water supply costs, 2002
(Per 1,000 gallons)

Water supply type	Cost
Treatment cost for fresh water from a conventional water treatment plant	$0.30–0.40
Reclaimed water for industry in Southern California	$2.22
Treatment cost for desalinated brackish water for residential use	$1.00–3.00
Treatment cost desalinated seawater	
Santa Barbara, CA (1992)	$5.50
Cyprus-2 (1999)	$3.00
Tampa Bay (2001)	$2.08

SOURCE: "Figure A6. Water Supply Costs – Today," in *Desalination and Water Purification Technology Roadmap: A Report of the Executive Committee,* Sandia National Laboratories and U.S. Department of the Interior, Bureau of Reclamation, Denver, CO, January 2003

bottle). Table 8.2 shows a comparison of water supply costs for various types of treated water.

Desalination is becoming increasingly important in this age of severe water shortages. On March 12, 2003, five major municipal water agencies in California joined together to form the United States Desalination Coalition. According to information on their Web site (www.usdesal.org/news.htm), the coalition's mission is to encourage the development of seawater and brackish groundwater desalination projects and to promote their visibility to Congress as a viable and important alternative to meeting the future demand for reliable and clean water. The Coalition plans to ask Congress to approve legislation designed to provide financial incentives and grants for desalination projects.

WATER REUSE

Wastewater from sewage treatment plants is one of the largest potential sources of freshwater where freshwater supplies are limited. About 60 to 90 percent of the potable (drinkable) water delivered to urban residents in the United States is discharged into sewage collection systems. After it has been treated to kill pathogens and remove contaminants, it can be reused for irrigation, and industrial use, and to maintain stream flow.

Indirect reuse of treated municipal wastewater is becoming increasingly attractive to many municipalities, especially in the West. The Orange County (California) Water District injects treated wastewater from a sewage treatment plant into its water supply aquifer to prevent the intrusion of salt water. Throughout California, construction is already under way on a number of reclamation facilities to provide reclaimed water for irrigation, and landscape and lawn watering. When completed, the program will serve an area of more than 700 square miles, providing 50,000 acre-feet of reclaimed water annually to local water supplies. Facilities will include up to 11 new or expanded water reclamation plants, state-of-the-art water purification plants, and hundreds of miles of reclaimed water delivery pipelines.

WATER 2025

Problems in the West, including explosive population growth, existing water shortages, conflicts over water, aging water facilities, and ineffective crisis management have led to a U.S. Department of the Interior proposal designed to assist communities in addressing these needs. A May 2, 2003, Department of the Interior press release, *Water 2025: Preventing Crises and Conflict in the West,* calls for concentrating existing federal financial and technical resources in key western watersheds and in critical research and development, such as water conservation and desalinization, that will help to predict, prevent, and alleviate water supply conflicts. The president's budget for fiscal year 2004 calls for an initial investment of $11 million dollars to aid in these efforts.

The proposal emphasizes the need for states, tribes, local governments, and the public to decide how best to resolve the water supply crisis in the West. As part of this plan, the Bureau of Reclamation prepared an analysis of potential water supply crises and conflicts that may occur by the year 2025. The Bureau of Reclamation intends to seek extensive input from states, tribes, and the public on the prepared analysis and will revise and improve the analysis as needed.

Water 2025 is a departure from previous plans in that its focus is on strategies and measures that can be put in place before events such as drought bring further divisiveness to communities in the West. The Bureau of Reclamation believes that conflict can be minimized or avoided when potential water supply crises are addressed in advance by local and regional communities. Its water-crisis prevention efforts will focus on four key tools:

- Water conservation, water-use efficiency, and markets
- Collaboration
- Improved technology
- Removal of institutional barriers and increasing interagency coordination

WATER CONSERVATION, WATER-USE EFFICIENCY, AND MARKETS. The Bureau of Reclamation has identified Supervisory Control and Data Acquisition (SCADA) systems as one area in which water conservation efforts can be improved in the management of rivers. These systems allow river managers to remotely monitor and operate key river and canal facilities on a real-time basis. The Bureau recommends that individual stations be set to monitor river levels or flow rates continuously. This will help the Department of the Interior and water district managers to respond to daily water management needs and emergencies in a timely fashion by controlling pump and canal facilities remotely. According to the Bureau of Reclamation, although the cost of this high-tech equipment has become more affordable over time, less than 20 percent of irrigation water delivery systems use this technology.

Research indicates that for every dollar spent on canal modernization (such as rehabilitating canal gates), an expected return of three to five dollars in conserved water can be achieved. In addition, for every dollar spent on maintaining an existing canal lining, a return of up to $10 in conserved water can be achieved. Canal-lining technologies have reduced seepage losses in central Oregon by as much as 50 percent.

Additional measures recommended by the Department of the Interior's Bureau of Reclamation include improvement in design and construction of new measuring devices for irrigation water delivery systems, continued support for water banks and water markets, and interagency efforts to coordinate existing and new water conservation programs.

COLLABORATION. The Bureau of Reclamation points to litigation over competing water rights as one of the problems affecting water supply and conservation efforts in the West. Water managers sometimes must wait years or even decades until adjudication is completed. In the meantime, they do not know how to allocate water in times of scarcity. The Department of the Interior intends to work with states, tribes, and other interested stakeholders to find ways in which to accelerate court proceedings in order to protect existing federal and nonfederal rights.

An example of successful facilitation efforts occurred in California. According to the Bureau of Reclamation, for more than two decades, the East Bay Municipal Utility District and several localities struggled over the management of the Sacramento River, resulting in the disruption of the efficient use of water. Facilitation sponsored by the Bureau of Reclamation led to a sustainable and locally developed agreement among the interested parties.

IMPROVED TECHNOLOGY. Recognizing that wastewater, salty water, and other impaired water can be purified to increase their usefulness, the Department of the Interior will facilitate research to reduce the high costs that impede adoption of new water purification technologies. The Department of the Interior recommends that the United States Geological Survey (USGS) make a comprehensive study of untapped but impaired water supplies with a focus on locations with a high probability of water demands exceeding supplies by 2025.

Another recommendation by the Bureau of Reclamation is the reduction of the high costs of water desalination. The Department of the Interior intends to facilitate the implementation of desalination and advanced water treatment through improved interagency coordination of research and focused investments to areas most in need of planning support.

REMOVAL OF INSTITUTIONAL BARRIERS AND INTERAGENCY COOPERATION. According to the Department of the Interior, in some areas of the West, federal facilities have excess capacity during certain times of the year that could be used to satisfy unmet demands elsewhere. Sometimes this excess capacity is not available because of policy or legal constraints. The Department of the Interior believes that in some cases, this additional capacity can be made available with appropriate changes in Department of the Interior policies.

The Department of the Interior will cooperate with other federal agencies to more effectively focus federal dollars on critical water shortage areas. Through active support of the National Drought Monitoring Network the Department will help accelerate the development of strategies for drought preparedness.

Additional measures under consideration include the formation of Drought Action Teams to focus scarce resources quickly when and where they are needed, and the creation by the USGS and other agencies of a monthly Water Resources Assessment. The assessment will be available online so that decision makers can better understand the water supply component of drought conditions.

Disputes over water and its use will continue to be a major issue in the West well into the twenty-first century. Recommendations suggested in *Water 2025,* the full development and implementation of the National Drought Policy, and the National Desalination Act among other strategies demonstrate both recognition of the problems and willingness to tackle them. At the same time, numerous partnerships are being formed among private, public, and government agencies to address these issues at all levels of government.

CHAPTER 9
ACID RAIN

WHAT IS ACID RAIN?

Sulfur dioxide and nitrogen oxides are gases that occur naturally in Earth's atmosphere. These gases react with water, oxygen, and other chemicals in the atmosphere to form various acidic compounds, including mild sulfuric acid and nitric acid. In nature, the combination of rain and these oxides is part of a natural balance that nourishes plants and aquatic life. When human activity increases the amount of acid forming chemicals in the air, the results can be harmful to humans and the environment.

Acid rain is the common name applied to any form of precipitation that contains a greater than normal amount of acid. It would be more accurate to call it "acid deposition." It occurs in two ways: wet and dry. Acidic fog, hail, rain, sleet, and dew are wet deposition. Dry deposition consists of acidic aerosols, particles, and gases. About half of the acid in the atmosphere falls to Earth as dry deposition.

Dry deposition introduces acidic particles and gases into water in two ways: direct deposition onto the water body surface and through indirect deposition. One example of indirect deposition is snowpack melt. In cold parts of the country, pollutants are concentrated in the upper layers of the snowpack because of wet deposition during snowfall, and dry deposition during periods of clear weather. During the spring snowmelt, runoff containing large amounts of acidic particles accumulated over the winter can flow into a lake or river, causing acid shock to its aquatic inhabitants.

Origin of the Term "Acid Rain"

The concept of acid rain originated in 1872 when the term was first used by Robert Angus Smith, an English chemist, to describe acidic precipitation in and around the city of Manchester, England. Subsequent scientific research on acid rain was sporadic and largely focused on local problems until the late 1960s, when Scandinavian scientists began more systematic studies. Acid precipitation was not identified in North America until 1972, when scientists found that precipitation was acidic in eastern North America, especially in the northeastern United States and eastern Canada. The 1975 First International Symposium on Acid Precipitation and the Forest Ecosystem (in Columbus, Ohio) helped scientists define the acid rain problem and initiated further research.

Formation of Acid Rain

One of the main components of acid rain is sulfur dioxide. When sulfur dioxide reaches the atmosphere, it oxidizes to first form a sulfate ion. It becomes sulfuric acid when it joins with hydrogen atoms in the air, and falls back to Earth. The most oxidation occurs in clouds, especially in heavily polluted air where other compounds such as ammonia and ozone help catalyze (accelerate) the reaction, converting more sulfur dioxide to sulfuric acid. Not all of the sulfur dioxide, however, is converted. In fact, a substantial amount of sulfur dioxide can float up into the atmosphere, be transported to another location, and return to Earth unconverted.

Nitric oxide and nitric dioxide are the other major components of acid rain. Like sulfur dioxide, these nitrogen oxides rise into the atmosphere and are oxidized in clouds to form nitric acid. These reactions are also catalyzed in heavily polluted clouds where iron, manganese, ammonia, and hydrogen peroxide are present.

Figure 9.1 illustrates how sulfur and nitrogen oxides, as well as hydrocarbons, are carried into the air to become acid deposition. Gases and particulate matter are carried into the atmosphere where they mix with moisture and other pollutants to form dry and wet acid deposition. Wet deposition returns to Earth as precipitation, which either enters the water body directly, percolates through the soil, or becomes runoff to nearby water bodies. Dry deposition builds up over time on all dry surfaces to be transported to

FIGURE 9.1

Transported air pollutants: emissions to effects

Transported pollutants result from emissions of three pollutants: sulfur dioxide, nitrogen oxides, and hydrocarbons. As these pollutants are carried away from their sources, they form a complex "pollutant mix" leading to acid deposition, ozone, and airborne fine particles. These transported air pollutants pose risks to surface waters, forests, crops, materials, visibility, and human health.

The pollutant mix:
Acid deposition (wet and dry), ozone, airborne fine particles

Transport and transformation:
Prevailing winds, complex chemistry

At risk:
Lakes and streams, forests, crops, materials, visibility, human health

Emissions:
Sulfur dioxide, nitrogen oxides, hydrocarbons

SOURCE: *Acid Rain and Transported Air Pollutants: Implications for Public Policy,* U.S. Congress, Office of Technology Assessment, 1984

water bodies in runoff during periods of precipitation, or falls directly onto a water surface.

Measuring Acid Rain

The acidity of any solution is measured on a pH (potential hydrogen) scale, numbered from 0 to 14, with a pH value of 7 considered neutral. Values higher than 7 are considered more alkaline or basic (the pH of baking soda, a mild alkali, is 8); values that are lower than 7 are considered acidic (the pH of lemon juice, an acid, is 2). Pure, distilled water has a pH level of 7. The pH scale is a logarithmic measure. This means that every pH drop of 1 is a tenfold increase in acid content. Therefore, a decrease from pH 6 to pH 5 is a tenfold increase in acidity; a drop from pH 6 to pH 4 is a hundredfold increase in acidity; and a drop from pH 6 to pH 3 is a thousandfold increase. (See Figure 9.2.)

Normal rainfall has a pH value of 5.65. It is not pure because it accumulates naturally occurring sulfur oxides and nitrogen oxides as it passes through the atmosphere. In comparison, acid rain has a pH of about 4. "Normal" pH for freshwater streams and lakes in the United States is about 6. Introduction over time of large volumes of acid deposition into unbuffered water bodies (mostly freshwater systems) can increase natural acidity as much as a hundredfold. Buffers are substances in the soils or water that offer resistance to changes in pH. When levels of alkaline chemicals that neutralize the acid rain are low in the soil or water, acid deposition directly affects the surface water pH.

FACTORS AFFECTING ACID DEPOSITION

The interplay between soil, water, climate, and winds can have a profound impact on the effects of acid deposition. The effects of acid rain can be greatly reduced by the presence of alkali (basic) substances. Sodium, potassium, magnesium, calcium, and bicarbonate are examples of chemicals with buffering (neutralizing) capacity. In areas where soils contain limestone (calcium carbonate) or other minerals with high buffering capacities, acidity is reduced as runoff runs over soil, mixes with dust, and percolates through soil. Brackish and salt water are more resistant to pH change from acid deposition than freshwater because they contain many substances with good buffering capacity.

Areas most sensitive to acid deposition have hard, crystalline bedrock and very thin surface soils. When no buffering particles are in the soil, acid rainfall and runoff

FIGURE 9.2

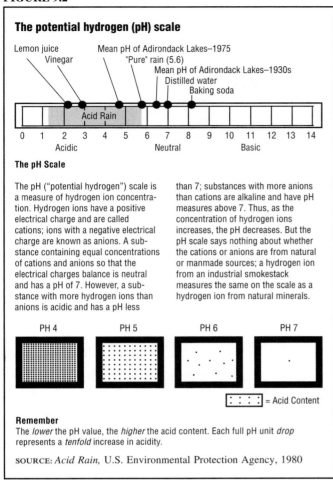

The potential hydrogen (pH) scale

The pH Scale

The pH ("potential hydrogen") scale is a measure of hydrogen ion concentration. Hydrogen ions have a positive electrical charge and are called cations; ions with a negative electrical charge are known as anions. A substance containing equal concentrations of cations and anions so that the electrical charges balance is neutral and has a pH of 7. However, a substance with more hydrogen ions than anions is acidic and has a pH less than 7; substances with more anions than cations are alkaline and have pH measures above 7. Thus, as the concentration of hydrogen ions increases, the pH decreases. But the pH scale says nothing about whether the cations or anions are from natural or manmade sources; a hydrogen ion from an industrial smokestack measures the same on the scale as a hydrogen ion from natural minerals.

Remember
The *lower* the pH value, the *higher* the acid content. Each full pH unit *drop* represents a *tenfold* increase in acidity.

SOURCE: *Acid Rain,* U.S. Environmental Protection Agency, 1980

---

directly affect surface waters, such as mountain streams. In contrast, a thick soil covering or soil with a high buffering capacity neutralizes acid rain better. Generally, lakes tend to be most susceptible to acid rain because of low alkaline content in lakebeds, the water, and the watershed soils, and the longer residence time of water in lakes.

Like lakes, freshwater streams flowing over streambeds and draining watersheds with low buffering capacity can also be susceptible to acid deposition. For example, 580 freshwater streams in the Mid-Atlantic Coastal Plain have been identified as acidic because of acid deposition.

In drier climates, such as the western United States, windblown alkaline dust blows freely and tends to help neutralize atmospheric acidity. On the other hand, on the eastern seaboard where dust is more acidic, the dust contributes to atmospheric acidity.

Sometimes the acid deposition events are more severe than others. Episodic acidification refers to brief periods during which pH levels drop because of runoff from the influx of large amounts of water, such as heavy downpours and snowmelt. An example would be heavy rainfall following a long dry period. The runoff would be very acidic because of the combination of the acidic rain and the dry acid deposition washed from all surfaces.

Freshwater lakes and streams in many areas of the United States are susceptible to episodic acidification, that is, they become temporarily acidic during and immediately after storms and snowmelt. Effects may last for several hours or days, depending on the water flow, as opposed to waters that are acidic year-round. For example, during rainstorms and snowmelts, mountain streams in New York, North Carolina, Pennsylvania, Tennessee, and Arkansas have shown increased acidity between 3 to 20 times the level occurring the rest of the year. If episodic acidification occurs during periods when fish are spawning or seed is germinating, the results can be devastating. In severe cases, it has caused fish kills.

The prevailing winds in an area are determinants in the transport systems that distribute acid pollutants in definite patterns across the planet. The movement of air masses transports air pollutants many miles, during which time these pollutants are transformed into sulfuric and nitric acid by mixing with other pollutants, clouds, and water. This process is known as "transport and transformation." For example, a typical European transport pattern carries pollutants from the smokestacks of the United Kingdom over Sweden. In southwestern Germany, many trees of the famed Black Forest (mostly coniferous) are dying from the effects of acid rain transported from industrial sites to the region by wind.

Northeastern United States Hit Hardest

The areas of greatest acidity (lowest pH values) occur in the northeastern United States. This high acidity is caused by the large number of cities, dense populations, and the concentration of power and industrial plants in the Northeast. Because the area is characterized by generally acidic soils and copious freshwater lakes and streams with low buffering capacity, it is very vulnerable to effects of acid deposition.

The prevailing wind direction in the Northeast also brings storms and air pollutants from the Ohio River Valley, an area rich in coal-fired utilities. A typical transport pattern brings pollutants from the Ohio River Valley to the northeastern United States on prevailing winds that tend to move from west to east and from south to north. As the Attorney General for the State of Maine, Steven Rowe, so graphically put it in a January 1, 2003, article, the Clean Air Act benefits Maine people most because the state is at the end of the country's "air pollution tailpipe"(*Northeast States Sue Over Relaxed Clean Air Rules,* [Online] http://www.MaineToday.com [accessed June 19, 2003]). About one-third of the total sulfur compounds deposited over the eastern United States originate from sources in the Midwest, more than 300 miles away. In addition to the

FIGURE 9.3

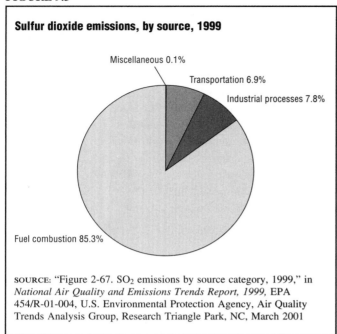

Sulfur dioxide emissions, by source, 1999

Miscellaneous 0.1%

Transportation 6.9%

Industrial processes 7.8%

Fuel combustion 85.3%

SOURCE: "Figure 2-67. SO₂ emissions by source category, 1999," in *National Air Quality and Emissions Trends Report, 1999*, EPA 454/R-01-004, U.S. Environmental Protection Agency, Air Quality Trends Analysis Group, Research Triangle Park, NC, March 2001

FIGURE 9.4

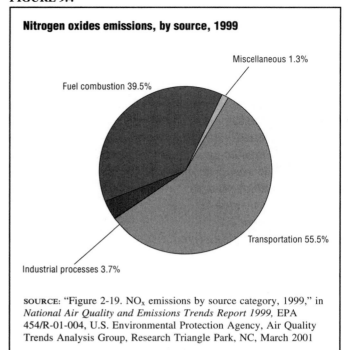

Nitrogen oxides emissions, by source, 1999

Miscellaneous 1.3%

Fuel combustion 39.5%

Transportation 55.5%

Industrial processes 3.7%

SOURCE: "Figure 2-19. NOₓ emissions by source category, 1999," in *National Air Quality and Emissions Trends Report 1999*, EPA 454/R-01-004, U.S. Environmental Protection Agency, Air Quality Trends Analysis Group, Research Triangle Park, NC, March 2001

problems in the northeastern United States, eastern areas of Canada have also been affected by pollutants from the Ohio River Valley.

SOURCES OF SULFATE AND NITRATE IN THE ATMOSPHERE

Natural Causes

Natural causes of sulfate (sulfur oxides) in the atmosphere include ocean spray, volcanic emissions, and readily oxidized hydrogen sulfide released from the decomposition of organic matter found on land and in water. Natural sources of nitrogen or nitrates include nitrogen oxides produced by microorganisms in soils, by lightning during thunderstorms, and by forest fires. Scientists believe that one-third of the sulfur and nitrogen emissions in the United States comes from these natural sources.

The island of Hawaii provides a good example of the natural occurrence of acid rain. Sulfur dioxide gas and other pollutants emitted from Kilauea Volcano on the island of Hawaii combine and interact chemically in the atmosphere with water, oxygen, dust, and sunlight to produce "vog" (volcanic smog) and acid rain. Vog is a visible haze consisting of gas and aerosols (a suspended mix of very tiny liquid and solid particles) that can be a health hazard because it aggravates preexisting respiratory ailments. When rain falls in areas that have vog, crops and local water supplies can be damaged by the resulting acid rain.

Many residents and visitors on the island of Hawaii report physical symptoms associated with vog. These include headache, breathing difficulties, greater susceptibility to respiratory ailments, general lack of energy, sore

throat, watery eyes, and other flu-like symptoms. Although the amount of particulate material in the air does not routinely exceed the federal standards, sulfur dioxide concentrations do. Sulfur dioxide emission rates from Kilauea Volcano were first measured in 1975 and have been measured on a regular basis since 1979. Periodic reporting of these sulfuric dioxide emission rates is done by the U.S. Geological Survey.

The tiny sulfuric acid droplets in vog have the corrosive properties of diluted battery acid. When these droplets combine with moisture in the air to form acid rain, plant damage and acceleration of the rusting of metal objects such as vehicles and machinery occurs. Crop damage is another frequent occurrence, even in greenhouses, because the vog enters through vents and mixes with the moisture on plant leaves.

The combination of vog and acid rain created an unusual water supply problem on the Island of Hawaii. Many homes relied on rooftop rainwater catchment basins for drinking water. In 1988 the drinking water in more than 40 percent of the homes was found to contain elevated lead levels. Upon further study it was determined that the process of acid-induced leaching from lead roofing and plumbing materials was the cause of the elevated lead levels. Tests confirmed elevated lead levels in the blood of residents. This finding led to a major island-wide effort to remove lead materials from rainwater catchment systems.

Manmade Causes

Most man–made emissions of sulfur dioxide and nitrogen oxides are the result of burning fossil fuels (coal,

FIGURE 9.5

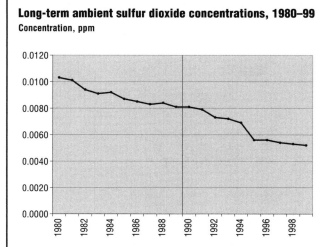

Long-term ambient sulfur dioxide concentrations, 1980–99
Concentration, ppm

Note: There were 438 sulfur dioxide monitoring sites for the period 1980–1989 and 480 sites during the period 1990–99.

SOURCE: Adapted from "Table A-11. National Long-Term Air Quality Trends, 1980–1999," in *National Air Quality and Emissions Trends Report, 1999,* EPA 454/R-01-004, Environmental Protection Agency, Air Quality Trends Analysis Group, Research Triangle Park, NC, March 2001

FIGURE 9.6

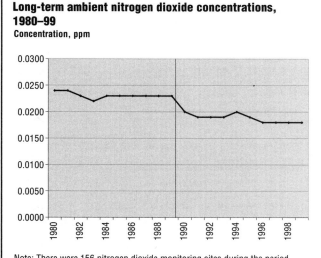

Long-term ambient nitrogen dioxide concentrations, 1980–99
Concentration, ppm

Note: There were 156 nitrogen dioxide monitoring sites during the period 1980–1989 and 230 sites during the period 1990–99.

SOURCE: Adapted from "Table A-11. National Long-Term Air Quality Trends, 1980–1999," in *National Air Quality and Emissions Trends Report, 1999,* EPA 454/R-01-004, Environmental Protection Agency, Air Quality Trends Analysis Group, Research Triangle Park, NC, March 2001

oil, and gas) for energy. This includes fossil-fueled electric utilities and industrial plants, motor vehicles using gasoline or diesel fuel, and commercial or residential heating. Nonenergy sources of emission include metal smelters that emit sulfur compounds and nitrogen compounds from agricultural fertilizers that are carried by the wind to other areas.

Levels of pollutants are measured in two ways: emissions and concentrations. Emissions are those pollutants expelled into the air by a source, whereas concentrations are the total saturation of a contaminant over time. Figure 9.3 shows sulfur dioxide emission sources in 1999, while Figure 9.4 shows the sources of nitrogen oxides. Fuel combustion from fossil-fueled utilities accounted for 85.3 percent of the manmade sulfur dioxide emissions, but only 39.5 percent of the nitrogen oxides. The primary source of manmade nitrogen oxides was transportation (car, truck, bus, and other vehicle emissions), which accounted for 55.5 percent of manmade nitrogen oxides emissions. The category transportation, however, made up only 6.9 percent of the sulfur dioxide emissions.

There has been great progress in reducing sulfur dioxide concentration. Between 1980 and 1999 the average annual mean concentration of sulfur dioxide dropped by half. (See Figure 9.5.) Annual mean nitrogen oxides concentrations declined in the early 1980s, were relatively stable during the mid-to-late 1980s, and resumed their decline in the 1990s. Concentrations of nitrogen oxides declined 25 percent between 1980 and 1999. (See Figure 9.6.)

EFFECTS OF ACID DEPOSITION ON LIVING ORGANISMS

An ecosystem is a particular environment and the biological organisms that live there. The scale may be as large as global or as small as a terrarium (a glass enclosure containing plants or small animals, such as turtles). The plants and animals living within the ecosystem are very interdependent. For example, frogs eat water insects. If the insects disappear because of acid deposition effects, the frogs may not thrive because part of their food supply has disappeared. Because of the many and varied interconnections among the plants, animals, and microorganisms living in an ecosystem, changes in pH may change the ecosystem's biodiversity or overall health.

The duration of the effects of acid rain on living organisms can vary from a few hours to many years. Table 9.1 lists the estimated time periods needed for a selected ecosystem to respond to decreases in emissions and acid deposition. For example, soils that are depleted of essential nutrients may take decades to centuries to recover. Once acid rain is reduced to normal levels, the slow process of nutrient buildup in the soil is dependent on the gradual succession over time of plant life. Plants that are tolerant of depleted soils will restore nutrients over time as they grow, die, and decompose, putting essential nutrients in the soils. In the natural order, these plants will be followed by plants that require more nutrient-rich soil, and as they grow, die, and decompose they will return more nutrients to the soil. Animals attracted to each stage of plant succession will

TABLE 9.1

Time periods needed for recovery of selected ecosystems

Ecosystem	Time period for recovery
Acute human health effects	Hours to weeks
Episodic effects on aquatic resources	Days to months
Chronic effects on aquatic resources	Years to decades
Soil nutrient reserves	Decades to centuries

SOURCE: "Table 3: Time Period Needed for Recovery of Selected Ecosystems," in *Acid Rain: Emissions Trends and Effects in the Eastern United States*, GAO/RCED-00-47, U.S. General Accounting Office, Washington, DC, March 2000

also add their wastes to the process, bringing in additional nutrients. This process will continue through time until a healthy balanced population appropriate to the ecosystem is restored.

Aquatic Systems

The effects of acid rain on aquatic systems are varied and many. They include great harm or death to fish, reduction in fish population numbers, loss of a species in a particular water body, and reduction in biodiversity. As acid rain moves through soils in a watershed, aluminum is released from soils into the lakes and streams. As pH goes lower in a waterbody, the aluminum level climbs. Both low pH and elevated aluminum levels are toxic to fish (aluminum burns the gills of fish and accumulates in organs, causing organ damage). They can also cause chronic stress, which does not immediately kill an individual fish, but impairs its ability to take in the oxygen, salts, and nutrients needed to stay alive.

Freshwater fish need to maintain their osmoregulation to stay alive. Osmoregulation is the process of maintaining the delicate balance of salts and minerals in their tissues. Acid molecules stimulate the formation of mucus in the gills, which interferes with their ability to absorb oxygen. If mucus buildup continues, the fish suffocates. In addition, a low pH disrupts the balance of salts in fish and other aquatic life, interfering with reproduction and maintenance of bones or exoskeleton.

Some aquatic plants and animals are able to tolerate more acidic waters. For example, frogs can tolerate lower pH than trout, crayfish, or clams. Acid-sensitive species, however, are lost as pH declines. It is usually the young of most species that are the most sensitive to environmental conditions. Some of the documented effects of acid deposition on aquatic systems are shown in Table 9.2. For example, at less than pH 5, trout and salmon eggs cannot hatch. At lower pH levels (pH 4 to 4.9), some adult fish die. Some extremely hardy fish such as the roach (a type of carp) can survive at a pH as low as 3.5 if the change is gradual and they have time to adjust.

TABLE 9.2

Generalized short-term effects of acidity on fish

pH range	Effect
6.5-9	No effect
6.0-6.4	Unlikely to be harmful except when carbon dioxide levels are very high
5.0-5.9	Not especially harmful except when carbon dioxide levels are high or ferric ions are present
4.5-4.9	Harmful to the eggs of salmon and trout species (salmonids) and to adult fish when levels of Ca^{2+}, Na^+ and Cl^- are low
4.0-4.4	Harmful to adult fish of many types which have not been progressively acclimated to low pH
3.5-3.9	Lethal to salmonids, although acclimated roach can survive for longer
3.0-3.4	Most fish are killed within hours at these levels

SOURCE: Adapted from "Generalized short-term effects of acidity on fish," in *National Water Quality Inventory: 1996 Report to Congress*, U.S. Environmental Protection Agency, Washington, DC, 1998

Other effects include:

- Sudden, short-term shifts in pH levels, resulting in acid shock to freshwater ecosystems

- Gradual declines in fish populations and numbers of adult and juvenile fish over time as pH decreases

- Unsuccessful reproduction by many aquatic species including poor egg production, abnormal eggs, and poor juvenile survival

- Physical impairment in juveniles of some species

- Loss of the ability in salmon to find home streams because of impaired smell

- Loss of important components of the food web leading to poor nutrition or starvation in species dependent on those components

- Changes in the plant and animal species within an ecosystem

Nitrogen has been shown to play an important role in both episodic and long-term acidification. It is also an important nutrient, but excess nitrogen can cause water quality degradation. Of the nitrogen released to the atmosphere through human activities, 10 to 45 percent of the nitrogen is transported to U.S. oceans and estuaries through air deposition. In the Chesapeake Bay, for example, 30 percent of the nitrogen contributed from manmade sources is atmospheric deposition.

Another area in which excess nitrogen from acid deposition, among other sources, is being watched very carefully is along the coastline. Studies of a phenomenon nicknamed *dead zones* have been underway for many years. The term *dead zone* actually refers to a state of hypoxia. A water body that is hypoxic—suffering from hypoxia—is one in which excess nitrogen has caused the dissolved oxygen in the water to deplete to the point where the water can no longer support life, both fish and higher forms of life. The three sources of nitrogen known to be causing large dead zones to appear every summer in the Gulf of Mexico are agricultural run-off, industrial waste, and acid deposition.

Forest Systems

Acid deposition can have serious impacts on trees and soils, causing slower growth, injury, or death of forests. Acid deposition has been implicated in forest and soil degradation in the eastern United States Forest Systems. USGS research has identified a new mechanism by which acid rain decreases the availability of calcium in the soil.

— Dr. Gregory Lawrence, USGS, March 1999

Acid deposition can have serious impacts on trees and soils, causing slower growth, injury, or death of forests. Acid deposition has been implicated in forest and soil degradation in the Eastern United States, particularly in the high elevations of the Appalachian Mountains from Georgia to Maine, an area including the Shenandoah and Great Smoky Mountain National Parks.

When rain falls to the forest floor, the buffering capacity of the soil may neutralize some or all of the rain's acidity. The differences in soil-buffering capacity is the reason that some areas that receive a lot of acid rain show little damage, while other areas receiving the same amount of acid rain show a lot of damage. The ability of forest soil to resist becoming acidified depends on the thickness of the soil and the type of bedrock below the soil.

When the soils cannot buffer the acid rain, vital nutrients present in the soil, such as calcium and magnesium, are stripped away by the acid-driven reactions. Aluminum, a toxic element present in all soils, is made more available to the trees and taken up by their roots. The combination of toxic aluminum and poor nutrition retard growth, make the trees more vulnerable to infection, and can eventually kill the trees.

In March 1999 the U.S. Geological Survey (USGS), in *Soil Calcium Depletion Linked to Acid Rain and Forest Growth in the Eastern United States,* reported that calcium levels in forest soils had declined at locations in 10 states in the eastern United States. Calcium is necessary to neutralize acid rain and is an essential nutrient for tree growth. Sugar maple and red spruce trees, in particular, showed reduced resistance to stresses such as insect defoliation and low winter temperatures. Although the specific relationships among calcium availability, acid rain, and forest growth are uncertain, Dr. Gregory Lawrence, scientist and coauthor of the report, speculated:

Acid rain releases aluminum from the underlying mineral soil layer, which is followed by the upward transport of the aluminum into the forest floor (the nutrient-rich organic soil layer where root activity is greatest) by root

uptake and water movement. The result is that aluminum replaces calcium, and the trees have a harder time trying to get the needed calcium from the soil layer.

Acid deposition can affect trees in other ways. Sulfur dioxide that has not been converted to sulfuric acid has been shown to clog up the leaf stomata (tiny openings in leaves where gases diffuse in and out), impairing plant respiration and photosynthesis. Nitric acid and nitrogen oxide have been shown to stimulate tree growth outside the growing season, leaving trees vulnerable to winterkill. Forests in high mountain regions often are surrounded by acidic clouds and fog that are more acidic than rainfall. Scientists believe that when the tree leaves and needles are frequently wetted in this acid fog, essential nutrients are stripped away. Loss of nutrients in the foliage makes the trees more vulnerable to other environmental threats, particularly winterkill. Winterkill resulting in damage or death is the result of naturally occurring stress caused by cold, wind, ice, and dehydration on trees and other woody plants that have been weakened by insect damage, nutrient deficiency, or drought.

Plants that are found in locations that are susceptible to high acid deposition experience the same fate as trees. The processes causing growth retardation and ultimately death are believed to be the same.

Human Health

Walking in acid rain is no more dangerous than swimming in clean rain. It feels, tastes, and looks just like clean rain. Sulfur dioxide and nitric oxides, the pollutants that cause acid rain, however, can damage human health. These gases interact with particulate in the atmosphere to form aerosols (a mixture of very tiny liquid and solid particles) that can travel long distances transported by winds. When inhaled, aerosols penetrate deep into the lungs, and are readily retained. Because of their very fine size, they can also penetrate indoors through ventilation systems.

Air pollution studies have indicated that elevated levels of acidic particles can cause asthma attacks, particularly in adolescents, and can also impair the ability of the upper respiratory track to remove other potentially harmful particles. Some scientific studies have also established a relationship between elevated levels of fine particles and increased deaths from heart and lung disorders, such as bronchitis and asthma. Other scientists believe that these pollutants may increase the health risks to those over age 65; those with asthma, chronic bronchitis, and emphysema; pregnant women; and those with histories of heart disease.

In a report entitled *Effects of Acid Rain: Human Health* (U.S. Environmental Protection Agency [Online] http://www.epa.gov/airmarkets/acidrain/effects/health.html [accessed July 12, 2003]), sulfate aerosols are reported

FIGURE 9.7

Effects of acid rain on statues and monuments

1. Acid rain, or dry deposition falls

2. Crust forms

3. Crust washes off

4. Layer of stone is removed

SOURCE: *Acid Rain and Transported Air Pollutants: Implications for Public Policy,* U.S. Congress, Office of Technology Assessment, Washington, DC, 1984

to make up about 25 percent of fine particles in the air in the eastern United States. The lowering of levels of fine sulfate and nitrate particles in the air by lowering their emission from power plants should eventually reduce the incidence and severity of the health problems believed related to these pollutants. The Environmental Protection Agency (EPA) estimated that when fully implemented in 2010, the public health benefits of the Acid Rain Program (created by Congress under Title IV of the 1990 Clean Air Act Amendments) would be about $50 billion annually in reduced health costs because of decreases in emergency room visits, hospital emissions, and number of deaths.

Decreased nitric acid emissions are expected to lower the amount of ozone formed. Ozone is believed to increase the risk of illness or death from lung inflammation, including asthma and emphysema.

An indirect effect of acid deposition on human health is the increased reactivity in acid water of toxic metals and other chemicals. Increased reactivity means that the chemicals and toxic metals in the water are more likely to be taken up in fruits, vegetables, and animal tissue. Air deposition is believed to be the leading source of mercury bioaccumulation in fish. This sort of bioaccumulation has lead to advisories against eating fish. In 2000, 48 states reported 2,822 fish and wildlife consumption advisories. A map of the United States with the number of advisories per state appears in Chapter 3, Figure 3.19.

The principal pollutants generated by coal combustion that can cause health problems are particulate, sulfur and nitrogen oxides, trace elements (such as arsenic, fluorine, selenium, and the radionuclides, uranium and thorium) and organic compounds as a result of incomplete coal combustion. Some of these trace elements have been shown to cause severe health effects in other countries, such as China, Romania, and Bulgaria.

The EPA conducted a detailed study of possible health effects from the exposure to emissions of about 20 potentially toxic substances from coal-burning electric utilities. In this study, the EPA used USGS information on U.S. coal quality to assess the potential health impact of 14 potentially toxic trace elements that may be mobilized by coal burning. The USGS fact sheet *Health Impacts of Coal Combustion* (July 2000) reported that, with the possible exception of mercury, there is no compelling evidence to indicate that emissions from U.S. coal-burning electric utilities cause human health problems. The absence of detectable health problems was credited in part to the use in the United States of coals that contain low to modest amounts of sulfur and other potentially toxic trace elements. Another reason for the absence of detectable health problems was the common use of sophisticated pollution control systems by coal-burning utilities. These systems are specifically designed to reduce the emission of hazardous elements.

OTHER EFFECTS OF ACID RAIN

Reduction in Visibility

Sulfates and nitrates in the air contribute to reduced visibility, which means that people cannot see clearly or as far through the air. The air looks "hazy." Sulfate particles account for 50 to 70 percent of the visibility reduction in the eastern United States. Visibility in the East was expected to improve by 30 percent by 2010 because of acid rain program controls. The EPA has projected that this improvement will be worth over $1 billion per year to the tourist industry in and around the eastern national parks.

In the western states, sulfates, nitrates, and carbon all play roles in reduced visibility. Sulfates have been shown to be important contributors to reduced visibility in many of the national parks found on the Colorado Plateau. These include Bryce Canyon, Grand Canyon, and Canyonlands. On the other hand, increased particulate in the air contributes to the spectacular sunrises and sunsets in the Red Rock country.

Manmade Objects

Limestone and marble turn to gypsum, a crumbling substance, when exposed to acid. Many of the world's most beautiful buildings, monuments, and statuary are composed of these materials. Throughout the world,

important art treasures and cultural and historic sites, such as the Taj Mahal in India; the Colosseum in Rome, Italy; and the Lincoln Memorial in Washington, D.C., are at risk. (See Figure 9.7.)

Investigations into the effects of acid rain on manmade objects in the United States, such as buildings, statues, metals, and paints, began only in the 1990s. A joint study conducted by the EPA, the Brookhaven National Laboratory, and the Army Corps of Engineers in 1993 found that acid rain caused $5 billion worth of damage annually in a 17-state region. Two-thirds of the damage was created by pollution whose source was less than 30 miles away.

New kinds of protective chemicals called consolidants, which adhere to limestone and marble, are being used to save some of the world's decomposing monuments from acid rain and other pollutants. Consolidants were developed in the 1960s in response to widespread water damage to stone buildings in Venice. Experts reported, however, that these chemicals have many limitations. They are toxic and difficult to apply. Their effects are only temporary, yet they permanently alter the nature of the stone. Most important, their long-term effects are uncertain. For those reasons, their use was banned on the Acropolis in Athens, Greece.

Automotive Coatings

Between 1990 and 1999, reports of damage to automotive textured roofs and paints increased. The damage generally occurs on flat, horizontal surfaces and appears as permanently etched, irregularly shaped areas. The damage is most easily observed on dark-hued vehicles, and can be detected with the aid of fluorescent lights on many vehicles that show no signs visible to the naked eye. Usually the damage is permanent.

The general consensus within the automobile industry is that the damage is caused by some form of environmental fallout. In the auto industry, the term "environmental fallout" refers to a wide variety of happenings including bird droppings, decaying insects, acid rain, and tree sap. Chemical analysis of the damaged areas of some car finishes, however, has shown elevated levels of sulfate, implicating acid rain.

Quantifying the contribution of acid rain to paint finish damage relative to other forms of environmental fallout, deficient paint formulas, or improper paint application has been difficult. The best way to determine the exact cause of the damage is chemical testing, an expensive proposition.

The auto industry is actively pursuing the development of coatings that are more resistant to acid rain and other environmental fallout. Until acid rain is controlled or until a universal protective technology is developed, the best protection for a vehicle is to keep it covered during precipitation events, and wash it frequently, followed by hand drying.

POLITICS OF ACID RAIN

The early acid rain debate centered almost exclusively in the eastern portion of the United States and Canada. The controversy was often defined as a problem of property rights. The highly valued production of electricity in coal-fired utilities in the Ohio River Valley caused acid rain to fall on land in the Northeast and Canada. An important part of the acid rain controversy in the 1980s was the adversarial relationship between U.S. and Canadian federal governments over emission controls of sulfur dioxide and nitrogen oxides. More of these pollutants crossed the border into Canada than the reverse. Canadian officials very quickly came to a consensus over the need for more stringent controls, while this consensus was lacking in the United States.

Throughout the 1980s, the major lawsuits involving acid rain all came from eastern states. States that passed their own acid rain legislation were also from the eastern part of the United States. There has been a clear difference in the intensity of interest between the eastern and western states regarding acid rain.

Legislative History

The U.S. Congress passed the first federal legislation aimed at reducing air pollution in 1967 (Air Quality Act of 1967). In 1970 the Environmental Protection Agency was founded and the Clean Air Act was passed. This law mandated the EPA to identify and set standards for pollutants identified as harmful to human health. The six pollutants identified and labeled "criteria" pollutants were:

- Sulfur dioxide

- Nitrogen dioxide

- Carbon monoxide

- Particulate matter less than or equal in size to 10 micrometers

- Lead

- Ozone

The first two pollutants on this list are the biggest contributors in the production of acid deposition.

In 1975 the First International Symposium on Acid Precipitation and the Forest Ecosystem convened in Columbus, Ohio, to define the acid rain problem. The scientists used the meeting to propose a precipitation monitoring network in the United States to cooperate with the European and Scandinavian networks and to set up protocols for collecting and testing precipitation.

In 1977 President Jimmy Carter's Council of Environmental Quality was asked to develop a national acid rain research program. Several scientists drafted a report that eventually became the basis for the National Acid Precipitation Assessment Program (NAPAP). Carter's initiative eventually translated into legislative action with the passage of the Energy Security Act (Public Law 96-264) in June 1980. Title VII of the Act (the Acid Precipitation Act of 1980) created the NAPAP and authorized federally financed support.

The Clean Air Act was amended in 1977. New legislation was added to address the problem of older fossil-fuel electric power producers that were not covered in the original law. The new program was called the New Source Review (NSR) under which these older plants would be required to undergo an EPA assessment if they chose to make changes to their operations. The EPA review would determine whether the planned changes would result in significantly higher emissions rates and if so these plants would be required to install pollution control technologies that brought them up to the new standards.

The first international treaty aimed at limiting air pollution was the United Nations Economic Commission for Europe (UNECE) Convention on Long-Range Trans-boundary Air Pollution, which went into effect in 1983. It was ratified by 38 of the 54 UNECE member states, which included not only European countries but also Canada and the United States. The treaty targeted sulfur emissions, requiring that the parties reduce emissions 30 percent from 1980 levels, the so-called 30 percent club.

In 1990 the Clean Air Act was amended for a second time and provisions designed specifically for reducing acid deposition were a significant part of the amendments passed.

Acid Rain Program—1990 Clean Air Act Amendments, Title IV

Title IV of the 1990 Clean Air Act Amendments (Public Law 101-549) set as its objective achieving a 10-million-ton annual reduction in emissions from 1980 levels by the year 2010. Traditionally, environmental regulation has been achieved by the "command and control" approach, in which the regulator specifies how to reduce pollution, by what amounts, and what technology to use. Title IV, however, gave utilities flexibility in choosing how to achieve these reductions. For example, utilities may reduce emissions by switching to low-sulfur coal, installing pollution control devices called scrubbers, or shutting down plants.

SULFUR DIOXIDE EMISSIONS. Title IV introduced a new regulatory approach to reduce acid rain—allowing electric utilities to trade allowances to emit sulfur dioxide. Utilities that reduce their emissions below the required levels can sell their extra allowances to other utilities to help them

FIGURE 9.8

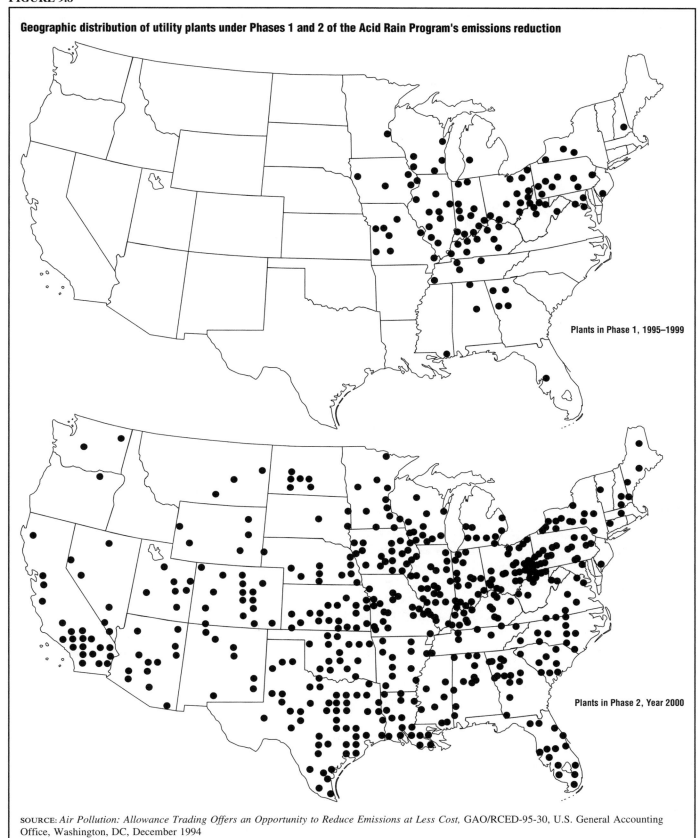

Geographic distribution of utility plants under Phases 1 and 2 of the Acid Rain Program's emissions reduction

Plants in Phase 1, 1995–1999

Plants in Phase 2, Year 2000

SOURCE: *Air Pollution: Allowance Trading Offers an Opportunity to Reduce Emissions at Less Cost,* GAO/RCED-95-30, U.S. General Accounting Office, Washington, DC, December 1994

FIGURE 9.9

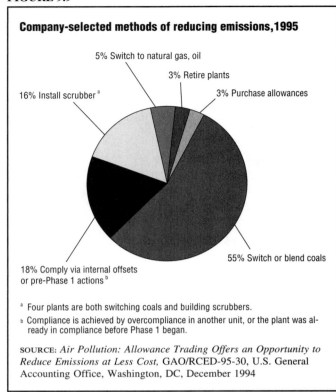

Company-selected methods of reducing emissions, 1995

5% Switch to natural gas, oil

3% Retire plants

16% Install scrubber [a]

3% Purchase allowances

18% Comply via internal offsets or pre-Phase 1 actions [b]

55% Switch or blend coals

[a] Four plants are both switching coals and building scrubbers.

[b] Compliance is achieved by overcompliance in another unit, or the plant was already in compliance before Phase 1 began.

SOURCE: *Air Pollution: Allowance Trading Offers an Opportunity to Reduce Emissions at Less Cost,* GAO/RCED-95-30, U.S. General Accounting Office, Washington, DC, December 1994

meet their requirements. Because in 1990 electric utilities were the source of 70 percent of sulfur dioxide emissions and 30 percent of nitrogen oxide emissions, the act targeted emissions from electric utilities. Of the desired 10-million-ton reduction in sulfur dioxide, 8.5 million tons is to come from the nation's major source, electric utilities.

The emissions reduction was implemented in two phases. In Phase I, the 263 units at 110 utility plants in 21 states with the highest levels of emissions were mandated to reduce their annual emissions by 3.5 million tons beginning January 1995. An additional 182 units joined Phase I voluntarily, bringing the total of Phase I units to 445. Phase II, which began January 1, 2000, affected 2,000 more units in all 48 contiguous states and the District of Columbia. Figure 9.8 shows the location of the highest-emitting plants in Phase I and the approximately 2,000 cleaner and smaller units throughout the nation that became involved in Phase II.

ALLOWANCE TRADING FOR SULFUR DIOXIDE. Title IV allows companies to buy, sell, trade, and bank sulfur dioxide pollution rights. Utility units are allocated allowances based on their historic fuel consumption and a specific emissions rate. Each allowance permits a unit to emit one ton of sulfur dioxide during or after a specific year. For each ton of sulfur dioxide discharged in a given year, one allowance is retired and can no longer be used. Companies that pollute less than the set standards will have allowances left over (banked allowances). They can then sell

the difference to companies that pollute more than they are allowed, bringing them into compliance with overall standards. Companies that can clean up their pollution less expensively by changing fuel or persuading their customers to conserve energy would recover some of their costs by selling their pollution rights to other companies. The EPA holds an allowance auction each year. The sale offers allowances at a fixed price. This use of market-based incentives by Title IV is regarded by many as a major new method for controlling pollution.

Utilities also took advantage of their flexibility under Title IV to choose less costly ways to reduce emissions, such as switching from high- to low-sulfur coal, and are achieving sizable reductions in their sulfur dioxide emissions. As shown in Figure 9.9, 55 percent of Phase I plants opted to switch to low-sulfur coal, and 16 percent chose to install scrubbers. Air scrubbers are treatment devices placed on the exhaust or smoke stack and used to reduce the particulate matter and other contaminants in plant emissions. Only 3 percent of plants initially planned to purchase allowances. Not surprisingly, the market for low-sulfur coal is growing as a result of Title IV and the market for high-sulfur coal decreasing.

From 1995 to 1998, however, there was considerable buying and selling of allowances among utilities. Because the utilities that participated in Phase I reduced their sulfur emissions more than the minimum required, they did not use as many allowances as they were allocated for the first four years of the program. Those unused allowances could be used to offset sulfur dioxide emissions in future years. According to figures published by the EPA in the *Acid Rain Program, 2001 Progress Report* (November 2002) a total of 9.55 million allowances were granted nationally. To this was added the large stockpile of banked allowances carried over from prior years. The total allowance stockpile in early 2001 was 19.93 million tons.

In 2001 utility sources emitted 10.63 million tons of sulfur dioxide, 1.08 million tons more than the allowances granted in 2001 but far fewer than were in the pool of allowances available since that pool includes all the stockpiled allowances from prior years. The balance of banked allowances at the end of 2001 equaled 19.12 million, slightly lower than the 19.93 million that existed at the beginning of the year. Over time the bank of allowances is expected to be depleted further as plants use stockpiled allowances to comply with the more stringent emissions requirement of Phase II.

NITROGEN OXIDE EMISSIONS. Title IV of the Clean Air Act Amendments (Public Law 101-549) maintained the traditional environmental "command and control by regulation" approach for nitrogen oxides. Under this approach, the EPA specifies how the pollution will be reduced, by what amounts, and what technology to use. The nitrogen

FIGURE 9.10

Average emissions of sulfur dioxide from power plants by state, 1990 and 2000–01
(Does not include Alaska and Hawaii)

1990

2000–01

Power plant SO$_2$ emissions
(thousand tons)

	0 - 150		1,150 - 1,650
	150 - 650		> 1,650
	650 - 1,150		

SOURCE: Adapted from "Figure 15. Geographic Distribution of Average SO$_2$ Emissions from Acid Rain Sources by States, 1990-2001," in *EPA Acid Rain Program, 2001 Progress Report,* EPA-430-R-02-009, U.S. Environmental Protection Agency, Washington, DC, November 2002

FIGURE 9.11

Average emissions of nitrogen oxides from power plants by state, 1990 and 2000–01
(Does not include Alaska and Hawaii)

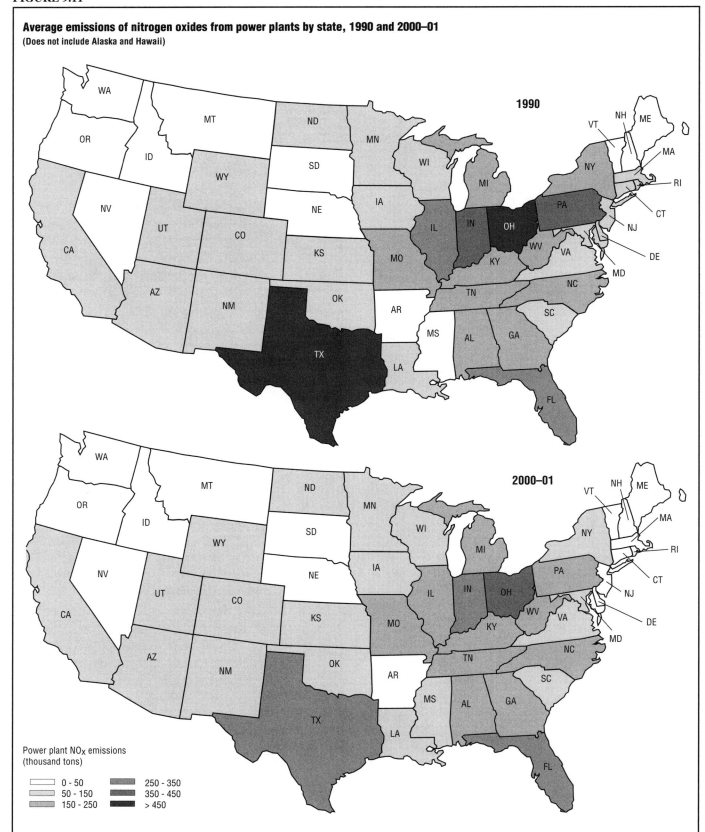

Power plant NO$_X$ emissions
(thousand tons)

0 - 50
50 - 150
150 - 250
250 - 350
350 - 450
> 450

SOURCE: Adapted from "Figure 15. Geographic Distribution of Average NO$_X$ Emissions from Acid Rain Sources by States, 1990-2001," in *EPA Acid Rain Program, 2001 Progress Report,* EPA-430-R-02-009, U.S. Environmental Protection Agency, Washington, DC, November 2002

FIGURE 9.12

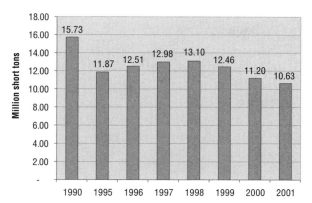

Sulfur dioxide emissions from power plants, selected years, 1990–2001

SOURCE: Adapted from "Figure 3. SO₂ Emissions from Acid Rain Sources, 1980-2001," in *EPA Acid Rain Program, 2001 Progress Report,* EPA-430-R-02-009, U.S. Environmental Protection Agency, Washington, DC, November 2002

FIGURE 9.13

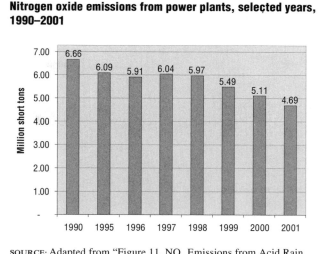

Nitrogen oxide emissions from power plants, selected years, 1990–2001

SOURCE: Adapted from "Figure 11. NOₓ Emissions from Acid Rain Sources, 1990-2001," in *EPA Acid Rain Program, 2001 Progress Report,* EPA-430-R-02-009, U.S. Environmental Protection Agency, Washington, DC, November 2002

oxides program establishes standard emissions limitations (the amount that can be discharged) for the affected units.

To encourage industry to reduce nitrogen oxides emissions before the required January 2000 date, the EPA adopted regulations in April 1995 that provided an incentive. The EPA allowed Phase II, Group I nitrogen oxides affected units, which would not have been subject to nitrogen oxide emission limits until January 2000, to use an "early election" compliance option. Under this provision, these Phase II, Group I units can demonstrate compliance with the higher Phase I limits for their boiler type from 1997 through 2007, and postpone having to meet the more stringent Phase II limits until 2008. There is one catch, however. If the utility fails to meet the annual Phase I limit for the boiler in any year, the unit is subject to the more stringent Phase II limit for Group I boilers beginning in 2000, or the year following the exceedance, whichever is later.

Clear Skies Act of 2003

On February 27, 2003, new legislation was introduced to the U.S. House of Representatives (HR 999) and the U.S. Senate (S 485) entitled Clear Skies Act of 2003. This legislation would build on the Clean Air Act and create a mandatory program that would reduce power plant emissions of sulfur dioxide, nitrogen oxides, and mercury by setting national caps on each pollutant. The stated pollution caps are as follows:

• Cut emissions of sulfur dioxide by 73 percent, reducing the emissions experienced in 2000 (11 million tons) to a cap of 3 million tons in 2018

• Reduce nitrogen oxide emissions by 67 percent, reducing the 2000 emissions of 5 million tons to a cap of 1.7 million tons in 2018

• Cut mercury emissions by 69 percent, reducing the 48 tons emitted in 1999 to a cap of 15 tons in 2018

ARE EFFORTS TO REDUCE ACID RAIN WORKING?

The Good News

During the first 11 years since the enactment of the Acid Rain Program much progress has been made in reducing power plant emissions across the nation and most particularly in the Ohio Valley and the Northeast where they have been historically highest. Figure 9.10 shows the average sulfur dioxide emissions from power plants by state for the year 1990 and for the two–year period 2000–01. The first period shown presents a picture of the emissions situation that exited before the Acid Rain Program was underway and the later period shows the situation that existed 11 years into the program.

Figure 9.11 presents average power plant emissions of nitrogen oxide for the same time periods. Here one sees that the areas showing most improvement are the Ohio Valley, and the state of Texas.

According to the EPA in its *Acid Rain Program, 2001 Progress Report* great progress has been made in reducing the pollutants that cause acid deposition. Sulfur dioxide emissions from power plants have been reduced 39 percent between 1980 and 2001 and by 33 percent during the period 1990–2001. (See Figure 9.12.) The reduction in power plant emissions of nitrogen oxides over the period

FIGURE 9.14

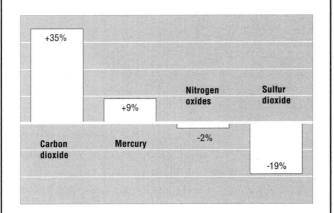

Projected percentage change in emissions by electric utilities, by pollutant, 2000–2020

+35%

+9%

Nitrogen oxides

Sulfur dioxide

Carbon dioxide

Mercury

-2%

-19%

SOURCE: Adapted from "Figure 7: Percent Change in Emissions under Three Scenarios, 2000-2020," in *Air Pollution, Meeting Future Electricity Demand Will Increase Emissions of Some Harmful Substances,* GAO-03-49, U.S. General Accounting Office, Washington, DC, October 2002

1990–2001 was 30 percent, from 6.66 million tons to 4.69 million tons. (See Figure 9.13.)

In 2001, the second year of the Acid Rain Program's Phase II implementation, all 2,792 Phase II affected utility units except for two complied with the requirements to hold sufficient allowances to cover their sulfur dioxide emissions. For all 2,792 affected power plants nitrogen oxide emissions in 2001 were 1.97 million tons lower than emissions in 1990.

These reductions are even more encouraging when taken in the light of increased economic activity. The reduced sulfur and nitrogen oxide rates were achieved during a period of economic growth in which the amount of fuel burned to produce electricity increased by 28 percent. Without the Acid Rain Program's mandated reductions in emission rates both sulfur dioxide and nitrogen oxide emissions from power plants would have been expected to rise in most parts of the nation as fossil fuel use rose. The fact that utility plant emissions of these pollutants have declined in the face of rising electrical production is very encouraging.

This encouraging news is offset somewhat by the contents of a report recently published by the U.S. General Accounting Office (GAO), *Air Pollution, Meeting the Future Electricity Demand Will Increase Emissions of Some Harmful Substances,* (October 2002). The report presents a forecast of energy requirements that was prepared by the Energy Information Administration. By the year 2020 electricity generation is expected to have risen by 42 percent. Emissions of pollutants by electric utilities

are also expected to rise over this period. The good news in the report was that acid deposition producing pollutants were not expected to rise despite a significant increase in the production of electricity. Figure 9.14 presents pollution emissions by type that were projected to accompany the rise in electricity generation.

Another positive piece of information reported in the EPA's *Acid Rain Program, 2001 Progress Report* stated that improvements in the acid neutralizing capacity of some Northeast streams, including the hard hit Adirondack region, have been recorded. The increased acid neutralizing capacity of a body of water is an indicator that recovery from acidification is beginning. Nitrate deposition has not, however, decreased regionally as a result of the Acid Rain Program. This, the report explains, is because the nitrogen oxide reductions experienced over the period 1990–2001 were smaller than the sulfur dioxide reductions. Fewer of the nitrogen oxide emissions sources were covered by the Acid Rain Program than was the case for sulfur dioxide sources. In 2001 approximately 65 percent of total sulfur dioxide emissions nationwide were the byproduct of producing electricity and were, therefore, covered under the Acid Rain Program. In the case of nitrogen oxides, emissions from electric utilities account for only 20 percent of all emissions.

The Bad News

Important reductions in the emissions of acid rain producing pollutants have been documented. The ground level data being collected on actual acid deposition has provided a somewhat less optimistic assessment. The Clean Air Status and Trends Network (CASTNET) is a scientific monitoring network established by the EPA under a mandate set forth in the 1990 Clean Air Act Amendments. The network is operated jointly by the EPA and the National Park Service (NPS).

In its most recent report, *Clean Air Status and Trends Network 2001 Annual Report* (November 2002), CASTNET presents data on the concentrations of sulfate and nitrogen particulates in the precipitation that has fallen on eastern states over the period 1990–2001. These data differ from the emissions data seen earlier. The power plant emissions of these two chemicals are down over the period in question. Their concentrations in precipitation are also down, but only very slightly.

Figure 9.15 presents the sulfur particulate concentrations in precipitation collected by CASTNET in their eastern collection sites. The bars on the graphic represent the sulfate concentrations and the line represents the total rain and snow that fell in these areas for each year. Sulfate concentrations are down, but by less than are sulfate dioxide emissions over the same period (21 percent versus 33 percent).

FIGURE 9.15

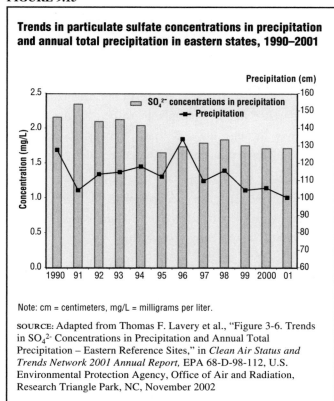

Trends in particulate sulfate concentrations in precipitation and annual total precipitation in eastern states, 1990–2001

Note: cm = centimeters, mg/L = milligrams per liter.

SOURCE: Adapted from Thomas F. Lavery et al., "Figure 3-6. Trends in SO₄²⁻ Concentrations in Precipitation and Annual Total Precipitation – Eastern Reference Sites," in *Clean Air Status and Trends Network 2001 Annual Report,* EPA 68-D-98-112, U.S. Environmental Protection Agency, Office of Air and Radiation, Research Triangle Park, NC, November 2002

FIGURE 9.16

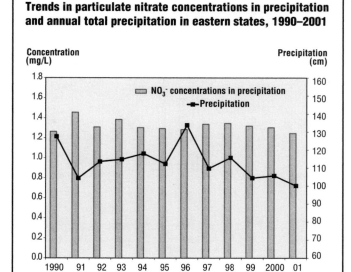

Trends in particulate nitrate concentrations in precipitation and annual total precipitation in eastern states, 1990–2001

Note: cm = centimeters, mg/L = milligrams per liter.

SOURCE: Adapted from Thomas F. Lavery et al., "Figure 3-15. Trends in NO₃⁻ and NH₄⁺ Concentrations in Precipitation and Annual Total Precipitation – Eastern Reference Sites," in *Clean Air Status and Trends Network 2001 Annual Report,* EPA 68-D-98-112, U.S. Environmental Protection Agency, Office of Air and Radiation, Research Triangle Park, NC, November 2002

Nitrate concentrations presented for the same geographical area and time frame showed a more discouraging result. Figure 9.16 shows that nitrate concentrations in the eastern states have shown no real decline over the period 1990–2001 despite declining utility plant emissions of nitrogen oxides over the period. Here again, the fact that nitrogen oxide emissions are down from sources participating in the Acid Rain Program does not mean that all man-made emissions are down.

Rising Nitrogen Oxide Emissions

A detailed analysis of the nitrogen oxide emissions data presented for all sources of emissions in the EPA's report *National Air Quality and Emissions Trends Report 1999* (March 2001) shows clearly that total nitrogen oxide emissions were higher in 1999 than they had been in 1970, 1980, and 1990. (See Figure 9.17.) National emissions of sulfur dioxide fell steadily over the period 1970–99.

Nitrogen oxide emissions from transportation sources were responsible for the greatest portion of the increase between 1970 and 1999, rising from 9.3 million short tons to 14.1, an increase of 51 percent. The transportation category is divided into two sections, on-road vehicles and non-road engines and vehicles. The on-road portion rose but at a much slower pace than the non-road portion. On-road vehicle emissions, which include all automobiles and trucks, rose from 7.4 million short tons in 1970 to 8.6 million short tons in 1999, an increase of 16 percent. The

non-road engine and vehicle category includes recreational vehicles, construction machinery, lawn and garden equipment, airplanes, railroad machinery, and marine vessels. This category rose from 1.9 million short tons in 1970 to 5.5 million in 1999, an increase of 186 percent. Nitrogen oxide emissions from fuel combustion sources, the second largest category in 1999, remained statistically unchanged over the period.

The Acid Rain Program had greater success in stemming sulfur dioxide emissions than it had, as of 1999, in stemming nitrogen oxide emissions.

A 1999 Assessment

In April 1999 the National Acid Precipitation Assessment Program released findings from its latest study, *National Acid Precipitation Assessment Program Biennial Report to Congress: An Integrated Assessment.* The study warned that, despite important strides in reducing air pollution, acid deposition remains a serious problem in sensitive areas and provided more evidence that acid deposition is more "complex and intractable than was believed 10 years ago." Among the findings were:

- New York's Adirondack Mountain waterways suffer from serious levels of acid. Even though sulfur levels are declining, nitrogen levels are still climbing. The agency predicted that by 2040, about half the

FIGURE 9.17

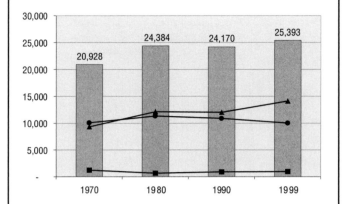

National nitrogen oxide emissions by source category and total emissions, selected years 1970–1999
(Thousand short tons)

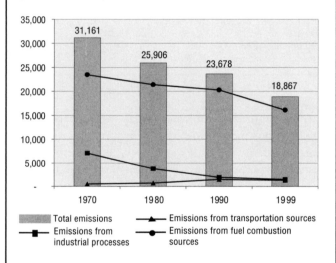

National sulfur dioxide emissions by source category and total emissions, selected years 1970–1999
(Thousand short tons)

SOURCE: Created by Information Plus from "Table A-4. National Nitrogen Oxides Emissions Estimates, 1970, 1975, 1980, 1985, 1989–1999," and "Table A-8. National Sulfur Dioxide Emissions Estimates, 1970, 1975, 1980, 1985, 1989–1999," in *National Air Quality and Emissions Trends Report, 1999*, EPA 454/R-01-004, U.S. Environmental Protection Agency, Air Quality Trends Analysis Group, Research Triangle Park, NC, March 2001

region's 2,800 lakes and ponds would be too acidic to sustain life.

- The Chesapeake Bay is suffering from excess nitrogen, which is causing algae blooms that can suffocate other life forms.

- High elevation forests in Colorado, West Virginia, Tennessee, and Southern California are nearly saturated with nitrogen, a key ingredient in acid deposition. (Nitrogen saturation is a condition where the nitrogen levels in the soil exceed the plant needs with the result that excess nitrogen is flushed into streams where it can cause undesirable plant growth. As the nitrogen moves through the soil it strips away chemicals essential for forest fertility, increasing lake and stream acidity).

- High elevation lakes and streams in the Sierra Nevada, the Cascades, and the Rocky Mountains may be on the verge of "chronically high acidity."

In conclusion, the report recognized the important strides made in reducing sulfur dioxide emissions since passage of the 1990 Clean Air Act Amendments. However, the slow recovery that was being recorded in lakes, streams, and forests indicated that further reductions in sulfur and nitrogen were necessary.

Anticipated Benefits of Further Abatement

The anticipated benefits of recovering from the effects of acid rain are varied and many. Table 9.3 summarizes some of them. The benefits to human health are believed to be reduced illness and death from lung disorders and heart disease, resulting in decreased need for medical services and medical treatment. Aquatic systems and forests are expected to experience less stress, thereby preserving vital habitat and resources important to the nation's economy. In some locations, the return of badly damaged ecosystems to healthy, thriving ecosystems is another anticipated benefit.

Reduced destruction of man-made objects is also a potential benefit of further abatement of acid deposition. The reduced deterioration of vehicles, buildings, monuments, and other structures should reduce the costs that society has to pay to repair and correct destruction of this kind. And a reduction in damage and loss of cultural objects preserves our heritage for future generations.

Taken together, the overall benefits of further reducing acid deposition should be a healthier, more environmentally sound habitat for man and all living organisms.

TABLE 9.3

Effect of acid rain on human health and selected ecosystems and anticipated recovery benefits

Human health and ecosystem	Effects	Recovery benefits
Human health	In the atmosphere, sulfur dioxide and nitrogen oxides become sulfate and nitrate aerosols, which increase morbidity and mortality from lung disorders, such as asthma and bronchitis, and impacts to the cardiovascular system.	Decrease emergency room visits, hospital admissions, and deaths.
Surface waters	Acidic surface waters decrease the survivability of animal life in lakes and streams and in the more severe instances eliminate some or all types of fish and other organisms.	Reduce the acidic levels of surface waters and restore animal life to the more severely damaged lakes and streams.
Forests	Acid deposition contributes to forest degradation by impairing trees' growth and increasing their susceptibility to winter injury, insect infestation, and drought. It also causes leaching and depletion of natural nutrients in forest soil.	Reduce stress on trees, thereby reducing the effects of winter injury, insect infestation, and drought, and reduce the leaching of soil nutrients, thereby improving overall forest health.
Materials	Acid deposition contributes to the corrosion and deterioration of buildings, cultural objects, and cars, which decreases their value and increases costs of correcting and repairing damage.	Reduce the damage to buildings, cultural objects, and cars, and reduce the costs of correcting and repairing future damage.
Visibility	In the atmosphere, sulfur dioxide and nitrogen oxides form sulfate and nitrate particles, which impair visibility and affect the enjoyment of national parks and other scenic views.	Extend the distance and increase the clarity at which scenery can be viewed, thus reducing limited and hazy scenes and increasing the enjoyment of national parks and other vistas.

SOURCE: Adapted from "Appendix I, Effect of Acid Rain on Human Health and Selected Ecosystems and Anticipated Recovery Benefits," in *Acid Rain: Emissions Trends and Effects in the Eastern United States*, GAO/RCED-00-47, U.S. General Accounting Office, Washington, DC, March 2000

IMPORTANT NAMES AND ADDRESSES

American Ground Water Trust
16 Centre Street
Concord, NH 03301
(603) 228-5444
FAX: (603) 228-6557
URL: http://www.agwt.org

American Petroleum Institute
1220 L Street NW
Washington, DC 20005-4070
(202) 682-8000
FAX: (202) 682-8099
URL: http://www.api.org

American Waterworks Association
6666 W. Quincy Avenue
Denver, CO 80235
(303) 704-7711
(800)
926-7337
FAX: (303) 347-0804
URL: http://www.awwa.org

Association of State Drinking Water Administrators
1025 Connecticut Avenue NW, Suite 903
Washington, DC 20036
(202) 293-7655
FAX: (202) 293-7656
URL: http://www.asdwa.org

Bureau of Land Management
U.S. Department of Interior
1849 C Street NW, Room 406-LS
Washington, DC 20240
(202) 452-5125
FAX:(202) 542-5124
URL: http://www.blm.gov

Centers for Disease Control and Prevention
U.S. Department of Health and Human Services
1600 Clifton Road NE

Atlanta, GA 30333
(800) 311-3435
URL: http://www.cdc.gov

Chesapeake Bay Program
410 Severn Avenue, Suite 109
Annapolis, MD 21403
FAX: (410) 267-5777
(800) YOUR BAY
URL: http://www.chesapeakebay.net

Ducks Unlimited, Inc.
One Waterfowl Way
Memphis, TN 38120
FAX: (901) 758-3850
(800) 453-8257
URL: http://www.ducks.org

Environmental Protection Agency
Ariel Rios Building
1200 Pennsylvania Avenue NW
Washington DC 20460
(202) 272-0167
FAX: (202) 501-1450
URL: http://www.epa.gov

General Accounting Office
441 G Street NW
Room 7149 Washington, DC 20548
(202) 512-4800
FAX: (202) 512-8546
URL: http://www.gao.gov

International Bottled Water Association
1700 Diagonal Road, Suite 650
Alexandria, VA 22314
(703) 683-5213
FAX: (703) 683-4074
URL: http://www.bottledwater.org

National Drought Mitigation Center
239 L. W. Chase Hall
P.O. Box 830749
University of Nebraska—Lincoln

Lincoln, NE 68583-0749
(402) 472-6707
FAX: (402) 472-6614
URL: http://www.drought.unl.edu/

National Oceanic and Atmospheric Administration
U.S. Department of Commerce
14th Street and Constitution Avenue NW,
Room 603
Washington, DC 20230
(202) 482-6090
FAX: (202) 482-3154
URL: http://www.noaa.gov

National Wildlife Federation
11100 Wildlife Center Drive
Reston, VA 20190
FAX: (703) 438-6000
(800) 822-9919
URL: http://www.nwf.org

Natural Resources Conservation Service
U.S. Department of Agriculture
PO Box 2890
Washington, DC 20013
(202) 690-4811
URL: http://www.nrcs.usda.gov

The Nature Conservancy
4245 North Fairfax Dr., Suite 100
Arlington, VA 22203-1606
(703) 841-5300
FAX: (703) 841-1283
URL: http://www.nature.org

Soil and Water Conservation Society
7515 NE Ankeny Road
Ankeny, IA 50021
(515) 289-2331
FAX: (515) 289-1227
URL: http://www.swcs.org

U.S. Fish and Wildlife Service
Department of Interior
Main Interior Building
1849 C Street NW (M.S. 3012)
Washington, DC 20240
(202) 208-4717
FAX: (202) 208-5634
URL: http://www.fws.gov

U.S. Geological Survey
U.S. Department of the Interior
12201 Sunrise Valley Drive
Reston, VA 20192
(703) 648-4000
FAX: (703) 648-5548
URL: http://www.usgs.gov

U.S. Water News
230 Main Street
Halstead, KS 67056
(316) 835-2222
FAX: (316) 835-2223
URL: http://www.uswaternews.com

Water Environment Federation
601 Wythe Street
Alexandria, VA 22314-1994
(800) 666-0206
(703) 684-2400
FAX: (703) 684-2492
URL: http://www.wef.org

Water Wiser
6666 W. Quincy Avenue
Denver, CO 80235
FAX: (303) 794-6303
(800) 559-9855
URL: http://www.waterwiser.org

Western Water Policy Review Advisory Commission
P.O. Box 25007, D-5010
Denver, CO 80225-0007
(303) 236-6211
FAX: (303) 445-6693
URL: http://www.den.doi.gov

RESOURCES

Responsibility for the protection, management, and use of water is spread across many federal agencies. The U.S. Geological Survey (USGS), a branch of the U.S. Department of Interior, has the principal responsibility within the federal government for appraising the nation's resources and providing hydrological information. Among the USGS publications used in this book are several USGS Fact Sheets including *Health Impacts of Coal Combustion* (2000), *Volcanic Air Pollution—A Hazard in Hawaii* (1997), *Desert Basins of the Southwest* (2000), *Land-Subsidence and Ground Water Storage Monitoring in the Tucson Active Management Area, Arizona* (2000), *Investigation of the Geology and Hydrology of the Mogollan Highlands of Central Arizona: A Project of the Arizona Rural Watershed Initiative* (2000), *U.S. Geological Survey Ground-Water Resources Program* (2000), *Arsenic in Ground-Water Resources of the United States* (2000), *Seagrasses in the Northern Gulf of Mexico: An Ecosystem in Trouble* (2000), *Restoring Life to the Dead Zone: Addressing Gulf Hypoxia, a National Problem* (2000), and *Nutria, Eating Louisiana's Coast* (2000).

Other USGS publications used included *Methods to Identify Areas Susceptible to Irrigation-Induced Selenium Contamination in the Western United States* (1997), *Soil Calcium Depletion Linked to Acid Rain and Forest Growth in the Eastern United States* (1999), *Natural Processes of Ground-Water and Surface-Water Interaction* (1998), *Natural Processes for Managing Nitrate in Ground Water Discharged to Chesapeake Bay and Other Surface Waters: More Than Forest Buffers* (1997), *Ground Waters and Surface Waters—A Single Resource* (1998), *Water-Level Changes, 1980 to 1997, and Saturated Thickness, 1996-97, in the High Plains Aquifer* (1999), *Ground Water Atlas of the United States—Oklahoma, Texas* (1996), and *Retrospective Analysis on the Occurrence of Arsenic in Ground Water Resources of the United States and Limitations in Drinking Water Characterization* (2000).

The Environmental Protection Agency (EPA) is the federal regulatory agency charged with, among other things, protection of surface and ground water quality, the development of water quality standards, and the enforcement of laws addressing water quality. Its *Liquid Assets 2000: America's Water Resources at a Turning Point* (2000), *The Quality of Our Nation's Waters—A Summary of the National Water Quality Inventory: 1998 Report to Congress* (2000), and *National Water Quality Inventory—1998 Report to Congress* (2000) report data collected from every state concerning their water quality and provide the most current information concerning water quality nationwide. The EPA documents *State of the Great Lakes 1999* (1999), *Great Lakes 2001—a Plan for the New Millennium: A Strategic Plan for the Great Lakes—Our Environmental Goals and How We Plan to Achieve Them* (2001), and *Final Regulation to Ban Mixing Zones in the Great Lakes* (2000) were very useful in addressing Great Lakes water quality issues. Additional EPA documents used were *Class V Injection Wells—EPA Announces New Regulatory Requirements for Certain Class V Injection Wells* (1999), *Coastlines, Issue No. 2—Pinpointing the Source of Oil Spills* (2000), *Nearshore Waters and Your Coastal Watershed* (1998), *BEACH Watch—EPA's BEACH Watch Program: 2000 Update* (2000), *Plastic Pellets in the Aquatic Environment* (1993), *1999 Acid Rain Compliance Report* (2000), *National Air Quality and Emissions Trends Report 1998* (2000), and *Constructed Wetlands for Wastewater Treatment and Wildlife Habitat* (2001).

The EPA also oversees the states' management of drinking water protection programs. EPA documents useful in providing information concerning this program were *Water Facts* (1999), *25 Years of the Safe Drinking Water Act: History and Trends* (1999), *Providing Safe Drinking Water in America—1998 National Public Water Systems Compliance Report* (2000), *National Primary Drinking Water Regulations: Interim Enhanced Surface Water*

Treatment (1998), *National Primary Drinking Water Regulations: Disinfectants and Disinfection Byproducts* (1998), *Lead in Your Drinking Water* (1993), *Community Involvement in Drinking Water Source Assessments* (2000), *It's Your Drinking Water: Get to Know It and Protect It!* (2000), *Public Drinking Water Systems: Facts and Figures* (2001), *Drinking Water Treatment* (1999), *Drinking Water Standards & Health Effects* (1999), *Drinking Water: Past, Present, and Future* (2000), *Protecting Drinking Water Sources* (1999), *25 Years of the Safe Drinking Water Act: Protecting Our Health from Source to Tap* (2000), *Guidance For People With Severely Weakened Immune Systems* (1999), and *Safe Drinking Water Act, Section 1429– Ground Water Report to Congress* (1999).

The General Accounting Office, the investigative arm of Congress, has published numerous reports on a variety of water issues. Publications reviewed for information for this book include *Acid Rain: Emission Trends and Effects in the Eastern United States* (March 2000), *Water-Efficient Plumbing Fixtures Reduce Water Consumption and Wastewater Flows* (2000), *Drinking Water: Spending Constraints Could Affect States' Ability to Implement Increasing Program Requirements* (2000), *Oregon Watersheds—Many Activities Contribute to Increased Turbidity During Large Storms* (1998), *An Assessment of the Draft Environmental Impact Statement of the Lower Snake River Dams* (2000), *Identification and Remediation of Polluted Waters Impeded by Data Gaps* (2000), *Corps of Engineers' Actions to Assist Salmon in the Columbia River Basin* (1998), and *Improved Inspections and Enforcement Would Better Ensure the Safety of Underground Storage Tanks* (2001).

The National Oceanic and Atmospheric Administration (NOAA), a branch of the Department of Commerce, has the principal responsibility within the federal government for appraising and protecting the nation's aquatic resources, managing its fisheries, and predicting weather and climate. NOAA publications used for this book include *Alien Ocean—Understanding Species Invasions* (2001), *National Assessment of Harmful Algal Blooms* (1999), *NOAA's State of the Coast Report* (1998), *State of the Coast Report* (1999), *Chemical Contaminants in Oysters and Mussels* (1998), *The Extent and Condition of US Coastal Reefs* (1998), *Populations of Harvested Fishes and Invertebrates* (1998), *Classified Shellfish Growing Waters* (1998), and *Populations at Risk from Natural Hazards* (1998). The U.S. Fish and Wildlife Service (USFWS), a branch of the Department of Interior, is charged with protection of living resources. USFWS documents used for this report include *National Survey of Fishing, Hunting, and Wildlife-Associated Recreation* (1996) and *Status and Trends of Wetlands in the Conterminous United States 1986 to 1997* (2000).

The U.S. Department of Agriculture documents *USDA Farm Bill Conservation Provisions—Protection of Wetlands* (1997) and *Summary Report—1997 National Resources Inventory* (2000) were consulted to explain the role this agency plays in wetland conservation. The U.S. Army Corps of Engineers is the federal agency with primary jurisdiction in wetland and dredging issues. This report consulted its publications *Recognizing Wetlands* (1998) and *Dredged Material Marshes: Summary of Three Research Projects* (2000).

The Public Health Service (PHS) and U.S. Centers for Disease Control and Prevention (CDC) are branches of the U.S. Department of Health and Human Services. The PHS Agency for Toxic Substances and Disease Registry (ATSDR) document, *ATSDR TOX FAQs—Arsenic* (1993) provided background information on arsenic toxicity. CDC documents used in this book include *Surveillance for Waterborne-Disease Outbreaks—United States, 1997–1998* (2000), *Blood Lead Levels in Young Children—United States and Selected States, 1996–1999* (2000), *CDC's Lead Poisoning Prevention Program* (1998), and *CDC Surveillance Summaries* (2000).

Other important publications include the United Nations Children's Fund (UNICEF) report *Global Water Supply and Sanitation Assessment 2000 Report* (2000), and *Cadillac Desert* (Marc Reisner, Penguin Books, New York, 1986, updated 1993), a discussion of water resources and use in the western U.S. Water reuse information from "Safeguarding Our Water—How We Can Do It" in *Scientific American* (2001) and wetland restoration information from "Add Water and Stir" in *Nature Conservancy* (2001) were valuable. *Harmful Algal Blooms in Coastal Waters: Options for Prevention, Control and Mitigation* (Chesapeake Research Consortium, Solomons, Maryland, 1997) was useful in identifying the current state of knowledge. "Coral Reefs," in *The Encyclopedia of the Environment* (Houghton Mifflin Co., Boston, 1997), was also helpful.

Additional important publications about water use in the western United States include "Climate Variability and the Colorado Compact" in *Societal Responses to Regional Climatic Change: Forecasting by Analogy* (Westview Press, Boulder CO, 1988), "Drought Recurrence in the Great Plains as Reconstructed from Long-Term Tree-Ring Records" in *Journal of Climate and Applied Meteorology* (1983), "Reallocating Texas Water; Slicing up the Leftover Pie" in *Texas Water Resources* (1993), *Water in the West Today: A States' Perspective—Report to the Western Water Policy Review Commission* (1997), and "Changing Water Use and Demand in the Southwest" in *Impact of Climate Change and Land Use in the Southern United States* (1997).

Many organizations devote their time and resources to the protection of water to meet human and ecological needs. In so doing they also produce useful reference materials. The Gallup Organization provided public opinion polls and the League of Women Voters provided *Groundwater: A Citizen's Guide* (1986). The Nature Conservancy supplied information concerning endangered and threatened species and Ducks Unlimited discussed wetlands restoration. The American Dental Association's publications entitled *American Dental Association Statement on Water Fluoridation Efficacy and Safety* (2000) and *Story of Fluoridation* (2000) provided useful material as did the American Waterworks Association Research Foundation's *Research Applications: Research in Use—How Utilities Are Building Watershed Partnerships* (1999) and the Association of State Drinking Water Administrators' *ASDWA Comments on EPA Proposed Arsenic Rule.* The American Petroleum Institute's information concerning oil spills and the International Bottled Water Association's survey *America's Drinking Habits* (2000) were also helpful.

INDEX

Kuwait, 33

L

La Niña, 7, 103, *See also* El Niño
Lake Baikal (Russia), 36
Lake death, *See* Eutrophication
Lake Erie, 49, *See also* Great Lakes
Lake Okeechobee, 147
Lake Ontario, 49, *See also* Great Lakes
Lake Superior, 36, *See also* Great Lakes
Lakes and ponds
    acid rain, 169
    characteristics of, 36
    deaths of, 36
    excessive nutrients effects on, 49f
    freshwater, 36
    metals, 47
    nutrients, 47
    pollutants, 47
    pollution control, 37
    pollution sources, 47-48
    saltwater, 36
    sources of impairment, 48f
    summary use support, 47f
    water quality, 39, 47
Landfills, 71-72
Lead, 82, 83f
Lebanon, 33
Leffis Key restoration project, 110
Legislation
    Air Quality Act of 1967, 176
    Alternative Water Sources Act of
      2000, 21
    Appropriation Doctrine, 24
    Clean Water Act, 7, 9, 22, 77t, 143
    Clean Water Authority Restoration
      Act, 143
    Clear Skies Act of 2003, 181
    Colorado River Basin Salinity Control
      Act of 1974, 153
    Endangered Species Act, 46
    Farm Bill (1996), 145
    Federal Insecticide, Fungicide, and
      Rodenticide Act, 77t
    Federal Land Policy and Management
      Act (1976), 24
    Federal Water Pollution Control Act
      1972, 93
    Food Security Act 1985, 144
    Food, Agriculture, Conservation, and
      Trade Act of 1990, 144
    Great Lakes Water Quality
      Agreement, 49
    Harmful Algal Bloom and Hypoxia
      Research Act of 1998, 123
    High Plains Hydrogeologic
      Characterization, Mapping and
      Modeling Act, 60, 150

Marine Protection, Research and
    Sanctuaries Act, 122
Medical Waste Tracking Act (1988), 121
Multiple Use and Sustained Yield Act
    (1960), 24
National Aquatic Invasive Species Act of
    2003, 126
National Drought Policy Act of
    1998, 159
National Forest Management Act
    (1976), 24
National Invasive Species Act of
    1986, 126
Non-tidal Wetland Act, 145
Nonindigenous Aquatic Nuisance
    Prevention and Control Act of
    1990, 126
Ocean Pollution Act of 1990, 117
Organic Administration Act (1897), 24
Public Health Security and Bioterrorism
    Act of 2002, 33
Reclamation Act of 1902, 160
Resource Conservation and Recovery
    Act (RCRA), 77t
Safe Drinking Water Act, 75-76, 77t, 89
Save Our Rivers Act 1981, 147
State Water Sovereignty Protection
    Act, 26
Superfund Act, 76-77
Water Efficiency Act, 17, 93
Water Quality Act of 1987, 110
Western Water Policy Review Act of
    1992, 158
Liquid water, 1-2
Little Rabbit River Watershed (Michigan),
    38-39
Livestock and water use, 19
Low-flow showerheads, 31
Low-flow toilets, 31
Lower Granite Dam, Idaho, 46f
*Lucas v. South Carolina Coastal
    Council*, 139

M

Maps
    aquifers, 59f
    distribution of utility plants, 177f
    fish advisories by state, 54f
    freshwater usage by state, 18f, 20f, 22f
    groundwater contributions, 63f
    groundwater usage by state, 63f
    irrigation water usage by state, 23f
    nitrogen oxide concentrations, 180f
    population changes by region
      (1990 to 2000), 160f
    population changes by state
      (1990 to 2000), 144f
    population relying on groundwater, 62f

    projected population changes by
      state, 32f
    projected water supply, 160f
    sulfur dioxide concentrations, 179f
    thermoelectric usage by region, 26f
    underground storage tanks, 71f-73f
    water usage by region, 15f
    wetlands, 139f, 144f
Marine debris, 120
Marine Protection, Research and
    Sanctuaries Act, 122
Marshes, 146
Maximum containment levels (MCL),
    81-84, 90
MCL, *See* Maximum containment levels
Medical waste, 121
Medical Waste Tracking Act (1988), 121
Mega Borg, 120
Methyl Tertiary Butyl Ether (MTBE), 69-70
Metropolitan Water District of Southern
    California, 152
Michigan, 38-39
Microorganisms, *See* Pathogens
Middle East
    conflicts over water, 33
Milwaukee, WI, 86
Mining, 20
Minnesota Department of National
    Resources, 137
Mississippi, 19
Mississippi-Missouri River system, 36, 124
Mississippi River, *See* Mississippi-Missouri
    River system
Missouri River, *See* Mississippi-Missouri
    River system
Mitigation banking, 138
Mixing zones, 52
Model Code, 100
Mollusks, *See* Shellfish
Montana, 162
MSX (oyster disease), 126
MTBE, *See* Methyl Tertiary Butyl Ether
Multiple Use and Sustained Yield Act, 24
Muskegs, *See* Wetlands
Mussels, 133, *See also* Shellfish
Myocastor coypus, 141

N

NAISA, *See* National Aquatic Invasive
    Species Act of 2003
National Acid Precipitation Assessment
    Program, 176, 183
National Aquatic Invasive Species Act of
    2003, 126
*National Assessment of Harmful Algal
    Blooms*, 125
National Coastal Condition Report, 136
National Drought Mitigation Center, 154

coral reefs, location, 108f

coral reefs, tourism industry effects on, 108t

drinking water, 62f, 92t

drinking water, diseases associated with, 99f

emissions by electric utilities, 182f

endangered species, 135t

EQIP funding, 156

erosion, 38f

estuaries, 116f

fish and wildlife advisories, 55f

freshwater usage, 18f, 20f

Great Lakes, individual use support, 51f

Great Lakes, phosphorous trends, 51f

Great Lakes, summary of use support, 50f

Great Lakes, water quality, 52f

groundwater, 63f-64f

groundwater, contamination, 66f, 69f

groundwater, uses, 61f

hydroelectric power, 27(t2.5)

industrial water usage, 25t

irrigation, 24t

lakes and ponds, sources of impairment, 48f

largest rivers, 36t

lead levels in children's blood, 83f

MCL violations, 84f

nearshore waters, water pollution, 114f

nitrates, monitoring results, 68t

oceans, designated use support, 113f

off-stream water use, 14t

population, 151f

population, changes, 160f

population, fastest-growing states, 32f

Safe Water Drinking Act, 94f

Shellfish harvesting, 113f

snowpack changes, 150f

Superfund sites, 75t

thermoelectric power usage, 26f

underground storage tanks, 71f-73f

wastewater treatment, 27(t2.5)

water quality assessment, 39f

water supply costs, 164t

water systems, 80t, 96f

water systems, cost of infrastructure, 95f

waterbourne diseases, 97t

Western United States, water use, 157f

wetland species at risk, 135f

wetlands, causes of degraded integrity, 141f

wetlands, lost acreage, 141f

wetlands, sources of losses, 140f

wetlands, types, 132f

Statues and effects of acid rain, 174f

Status of Drought Report Recommendations, 159

Storms, 104

Streams, *See* Rivers and streams

Submerged aquatic vegetation, 111-112

Subsurface flow systems, *See* Wetlands

Sulfates, 175

concentration in precipitation, 183f

Sulfur dioxide, *See* Sulfuric oxides

Sulfur oxide, *See* Sulfuric oxides

Sulfuric oxides, 170f

allowance trading, 178

concentrations, 171, 171f

emissions, 171

power plant emissions, 179f, 181f

Summary of State Biennial Reports of Wellhead Protection Program Progress, 92

Superfund Act, 75t, 76-77

Surface impoundments and groundwater contamination, 72

Surface water, 23f, 35-55, 91

Surface Water Treatment Rule (SWTR), 91

Surveillance for Waterbourne-Disease Outbreaks–United States (1999-2000), 97

Swampbuster provision, 144

Swamps, 129

Swimmable waters, *See* Swimming

Swimming

gastroenteritis, 116

swimmable waters, 117

Swimming advisories, 54-55

SWTR, *See* Surface Water Treatment Rule

T

Tampa, FL, 32

Tankers, *See* Oil tankers

TCR violations, *See* Coliform bacteria

Tertiary sewage treatment, 44,
    See also sewage

Texas, 65, 162

Texas Critical Management Plan, 65

Thermoelectric power, 20-21, 26f

Threatened species, 135t, 135f,
    See also Endangered species

Tidewater Oyster Gardening Association, 111

Title IV of the Clean Air Act,
    See Clean Air Act

Tlingit Indian tribes, 121

TMDL, *See* Total Maximum Daily Load

Toilets, low-flow, 31

Tooth decay prevention, 89

Torrey Canyon oil spill, 117

Total Coliform Rule, 96

Total Maximum Daily Load (TMDL), 41

Total trihalomethanes (TTHMs), 88, 89f

Tourism in the coral reef, 109

Toxicity, 125

Transpiration, 4

Treatment trains, 88

Trophic status of lakes and ponds, 50t

Tropical storms, 105

Trout Unlimited v. United States Department of Agriculture, 24

TTHMs, *See* Total trihalomethanes

Tulloch rule, 143

Turbidity, 6, 85, 85f, 114

Typhoons, 105

U

Unconfined aquifers, 58, *See also* Aquifers

Underground Interjection Control Program, 90

Underground storage tanks, 70f-73f

United Nations Conference on the Law of the Seas, 112

United Nations Economic Commission for Europe Convention, 176

U.S. Army Corps of Engineers, 45, 137, 143

U.S. Coast Guard, 119

U.S. Coral Reef Task Force, 108

U.S. Fish and Wildlife Service, 28, 126, 140

U.S. Forest Service, 24, 31

U.S. Geological Survey (USGS), 13, 15, 60-61, 63

United States Global Change Research Program, 149, 152

United States v Buday, 143

Unsaturated zones (groundwater), 57

USFWS, *See* U.S. Fish and Wildlife Service

V

Vernal pools, *See* wetlands

Vog, 170

W

Waste disposal, 8

Water, 1-9

conflicts over shortages, 10

See also Drinking water; Estuaries; Groundwater; Ice; Liquid water; Oceans; Surface water; Water pollution; Water quality; Water supply; Water usage

Water banks, 161

Water-borne diseases, *See* Pathogens

Water conservation, 31, 164

California, 158

low-flow toilets, 31

See also water reclamation

Water cycle, 3f

Water distribution on earth, 2f

Water Efficiency Act, 17, 93

Water hardness, *See* hard water

Water molecule, 1f

Water pollution, 7-8, 37, 41, 82